Financial Management

Pankaj K Agarwal
B.Sc (Maths), MBA (Finance), CFA (ICFAI), CAIIB (Gold Medalist)
Dean
Jhunjhunwala Business School, Faizabad

Neeraj Agarwal
M.Com, ACA
Senior Manager (Finance)
Rohit Surfactants Pvt. Ltd., Kanpur

Published by

Khushnuma Complex Basement
7, Meerabai Marg (Behind Jawahar Bhawan)
Lucknow 226 001 U.P. (INDIA)
Tel. : 91-522-2209542, 2209543, 2209544, 2209545
Fax : 0522-4045308
E-Mail : word-press@hotmail.com

First Edition 2011

Price: ₹ 295/-

ISBN 978-93-80257-08-2

Composed & Designed at :
Panacea Computers
3rd Floor, Agrawal Sabha Bhawan
Subhash Mohal, Sadar Cantt. Lucknow-226 002
Tel. : 0522-2483312, 9335927082, 9452295008
E-mail : prasgupt@rediffmail.com

Printed at:
Salasar Imaging Systems
C-7/5, Lawrence Road Industrial Area
Delhi - 110 035
Tel. : 011-27185653, 9810064311

To our parents
(Mr Govind Prasad Agarwal and Mrs Uma Agarwal)
– Pankaj K Agarwal and Neeraj Agarwal

To my son Ayush
– Pankaj K Agarwal

Preface

There is no dearth of good books on financial management. When the idea of writing this book was still an idea, we wondered whether there existed a gap, which a new book could fill. Though we have the highest regards for some of the wonderful texts available on this subject, we still felt that those books served to a different audience. This humble effort distinguishes itself on many grounds.

1. Most of the existing texts have been written around the time when management courses were accessible to a privileged few. Only the best and the brightest were chosen to study in very few B-Schools that existed.

   Therefore, the texts were written for a readership that was perhaps in a different trajectory. The treatment of the subject matter, though, was very rigorous and comprehensive, appealed to a select few.

   With the "democratization" of business education, a large number of students entered the scene. They had a different level of aptitude and required a thorough, yet more lucid discussion on the subject matter of financial management. This is where this text comes into picture. This book has been penned in a very simple and lucid ***conversational*** style. The treatment of concepts has been done not to intimidate or exhibit the scholarship of the authors, but to encourage and sustain the interest of the students, in a language that is easily comprehensible. The authors have utilized their experience and insights developed by years of teaching and interaction with students, thereby not losing sight of linguistic limitations of students.

2. However, sometimes it is felt that price of simplicity is quality. Here again, though the treatment is most lucid, the book is almost up to the minute. We have made our earnest endeavor to present the most recent body of knowledge so that the students can face the challenges of the real world with confidence.

3. As the rigor of the subject matter increases, often texts tend to become more scholarly and less practice oriented. However, this book has been conceptualized with the practicing manager in mind. An exclusive feature **"managerial tool kit"** has been included in the book to facilitate application of theory in the real world. In addition, all the chapters contain numerous numerical problems to help students develop "skill" as much as "knowledge".

4. Most of the finance texts pre-suppose a certain level of familiarity with accounting, business law etc. However, this book does not presuppose prior knowledge of these subjects. All background knowledge necessary for learning

the subject matter has been readily provided right within the main body of chapters for a seamless, uninterrupted learning experience.

5. To aid the respected colleagues in academia, chapter summaries have been provided at the end of each chapter to enable them to effectively use these in PowerPoint. This will also help the student in quick revision and reference.
6. Students have also been encouraged to use MS Excel frequently, again with the objective of skill building.

Having said that, we hope that the book will be found useful by students of MBA, PGDM, BBA and other such professional courses. The proof of the pudding lies in the eating. The readers are the real judge of this effort and if they feel that the complex concepts of finance have been presented in simple conversational style without losing comprehensiveness, we would feel that our efforts have met success.

We would be grateful if esteemed readers could provide their valuable feedback/ suggestions for further improvement of this book. We may also add that we remain responsible for any inadvertent errors or omissions which might have skipped our attention.

Pankaj K Agarwal
pankajsbi@yahoo.com
Neeraj Agarwal
neeraj2807@gmail.com

Acknowledgement

First of all we wish to thank the divine grace of ***Mahaprabhu Shri Hanuman Ji*** who gave us the strength to accomplish this effort. Secondly, we wish to thank our parents who nurtured us to be able to do justice to this challenging task. We also wish to express our gratitude towards our teachers especially Prof. Savyasachi Sengupta, Professor of Finance, XLRI Jamshedpur, who inspired us to go deeper into the wonderful world of finance. It was Prof. Sengupta who taught us that the acid test of conceptual clarity lied in ability to explain most complicated theories even to a 4 year child!

We also place on record our sincere appreciation and gratefulness to numerous authors and scholars whose works we have liberally drawn from to synthesize the contents of this book. We have taken utmost care to identify and quote the sources correctly. However, any omissions may please be considered inadvertent and condoned.

This book has evolved out of many years of our collective experience in teaching and industry. We wish to thank all students, colleagues and seniors who have offered feedback and valuable suggestions on the initial drafts of the book. We also thank all our friends who encouraged us and often offered valuable suggestions and modifications.

A few people whose names deserve a special mention are:

(Acknowledge by Prof. Pankaj K Agarwal)

1. Sri L K Jhunjhunwala, Chairman, Sri Lakshmi Public Charitable Trust
2. My mentor Mr Sanjay Jhunjhunwala, Vice Chairman, Sri Lakshmi Public Charitable Trust
3. Sri Ashvini Kumar Tiwari, DGM (Cash Management), State Bank of India
4. Dr. R.N. Rai, HOD, Department of Business Management, Dr. RML Awadh University, Faizabad
5. Ms Deepshikha Gupta, Manager, State Bank of India
6. Mr Abhijit Srivastava, AGM, IDBI Bank

(Acknowledge by CA Neeraj Agarwal)

1. My elder brother Prof. Pankaj Agarwal who encouraged me to contribute to this book

2. My family, colleagues, friends and my corporate guru Dr. Inish Roy, Vice President (Systems & Finance, Ghari Group), who has always supported me in every walk of life

3. Dr. Prem Mohan Srivastava, Reader, Commerce Deptt., KNIPSS, Sultanpur.

We are also grateful to the wonderful team at the Word-Press, under the able leadership of my friend Mr. Suneel Gomber and Mr. Sushant Gomber. I thank Mr. Sushant Gomber especially for his demanding standards and almost saint-like patience with our deadline breaches! The entire team in editing, composing, designing has contributed enormously in making the book what it is in the hands of the reader.

In this journey, many of our friends, students, and teachers helped and motivated us whose names may not find mention here, but we remain grateful to them nonetheless.

Authors

List of Formulae Used

Chapter 2

- ***Future value of a single flow***

  $FV=PV(1+r)^n$

  Where PV = Present Value

  FV = Future Value

  n= number of time periods of compounding

  r = interest rate or required rate of return per time period.

  FV=PV FVIF(r, n)

  $FVIF(r, n) = (1+r)^n$

  Where FVIF(r,n) is future value interest factor for r and n.

- ***For infinite compounding the formula is***

  $FV = PV e^{rn}$, **where e = 2.71828.**

- ***Number of time periods of compounding*** = time period given x frequency of compounding

  Required rate of interest per time period = rate given/ frequency of compounding

- ***Present Value of a Single Flow***

  $PV = FV(1+r)^{-n}$

  $PVIF(r, n) = (1+r)^{-n}$

  PV = FV x PVIF(r, n)

  Where PVIF (r,n) = Present Value interest factor

- ***Effective Rate of Interest vs. Quoted Rate of Interest***

  $$(1+r_e) = \left(1+\frac{r}{m}\right)^m$$

  Where r_e = Effective rate of interest

  r = nominal or quoted rate of interest per annum

  m= number of compounding periods in a year

- ***Future Value of a series of Equal Cash flows (Annuities):***

  $$FVA = A\left[\frac{(1+r)^n - 1}{r}\right]$$

  Where FVA = Future value of an ordinary annuity

  A = Equal annual payments

  r = interest rate per time period

  n =number of time periods

  FVA=A x FVIA(r, n)

$$FVIA(r,n)=\left[\frac{(1+r)^n-1}{r}\right]$$

Where FVIF (r,n) is future value interest factor.

- ***Future value of annuity due is:***

$$FVA_{due} = A\,x\,FVIA(r,n)\,x(1+r)$$

- ***Future Value of a growing annuity:.***

$$FVA_{Growing} = A_1\left[1-\left(\frac{1+g}{1+r}\right)^n\right]$$

Where g = growth rate in annual payments per period
A_1 = First annual payment

- ***Sinking Fund Factor***

$$A = FVA * \frac{r}{(1+r)^n-1}$$

Here, the expression $\frac{r}{(1+r)^n-1}$ is called sinking fund factor.

We can also express sinking fund factor in a different way:
*A = FVA * Sinking Fund Factor (r, n)*

$$Sinking\ fund\ factor = \frac{1}{FVIA(r,n)}$$

- ***Present Value of a series of Equal Cash flows (Annuities):***

$$PVA = A\left[\frac{(1+r)^n-1}{r(1+r)^n}\right]$$

Where PVA = Present value of an ordinary annuity
A = Equal annual payments
r = interest rate per time period
n =number of time periods

$$PVA = A\,x\,PVIA(r,n)$$

Where $PVIA(r,n)=\frac{(1+r)^n-1}{r(1+r)^n}$

PVIA(r,n) is called present value interest factor for annuity.

- ***In case of annuity due, the present value formula becomes:***

$$PVA\,due = A\,x\,PVIA(r,n)\,x\,(1+r)$$

- ***Present value of growing annuity becomes:***

$$PVA_{Growing} = \frac{A}{r-g}\left[1-\left(\frac{1+g}{1+r}\right)^{n}\right]$$

Where g = growth rate in annual payments per period
A = First annual payment

- ***Capital Recovery Factor***

$$A = PVA * \frac{1}{PVIA(r,n)} = PVA * \text{Capital Recovery Factor}$$

$$\text{Capital Recovery Factor} = \frac{1}{PVIA(r,n)}$$

$$\text{Where } PVIA(r,n) = \frac{(1+r)^{n}-1}{r(1+r)^{n}}$$

$$\text{Capital recovery Factor} = \frac{r(1+r)^{n}}{(1+r)^{n}-1}$$

- ***Present Value of A Perpetuity***

$$\text{Present Value of Perpetuity} = \lim_{n\to\infty} A\left[\frac{(1+r)^{n}-1}{r(1+r)^{n}}\right]$$

$$PVA_{Perpetuity} = \frac{A}{r}$$

$$\text{Present Value of a growing perpetuity} = \frac{A}{r-g}$$

Chapter 3

- *Total Rupee Return from an Asset = Cash Income from asset + Capital Gain / Loss*
- *%return from an asset = (Total Rupee Return x100) / Initial investment*
- % returns can also be divided into two components.

$$\%\text{ Return from an asset} = \frac{(\text{Cash income} + \text{Capital Gain/Loss})\,x\,100}{\text{Initial Investment}}$$

%Return from an asset = (Cash income x100) / (Initial investment) + (Capital gain OR losses x100) / Initial investment

% Return from an asset = income yield+Capital Gain / Loss Yield

- $Average\ Annual\ return = \frac{1}{n}\sum_{i=1}^{n} R_i$
- $Compounded\ annual\ return = \sqrt[n]{(1+r_1)(1+r_2)(1+r_3)\ldots\ldots\ldots(1+r_n)} - 1$
- Range = Highest R – Lowest R
- *Variance*

  $$\sigma^2 = \frac{1}{n-1}\sum_{1}^{n}\left(\overline{R} - R_i\right)^2$$

  Where $\overline{R}$ is the average or mean return.
- *Standard Deviation*

  $$Standard\ deviation(\sigma) = \sqrt{Variance(\sigma^2)}$$

  $$\sigma = \sqrt{\frac{1}{n-1}\sum_{1}^{n}\left(\overline{R} - R_i\right)^2}$$

- $Expected\ Return\ E(R) = \sum_{1}^{n} P_i R_i$
- $Variance\ \sigma^2 = \sum_{1}^{n} P_i\{E(R) - R_i\}^2$
- $Standard\ Deviation(\sigma) = \sqrt{Variance(\sigma^2)}$

  Here R_i represents returns, E(R) is the expected return and P_i represent the probability of obtaining a particular return R_i.
- If a portfolio has n assets, each having an expected return $E(R_1), E(R_2), E(R_3)\ldots\ldots\ldots E(R_n)$, the expected return of the portfolio, $E(R_p)$, can be found by the formula:

  $$E(R_P) = \sum_{i=1}^{n} w_i E(R_i), \qquad Where \sum_{i}^{n} w_i = 1$$

  Where, w_i = weights of security i

  $$w_i = \frac{Amount\ invested\ in\ security\ i}{Total\ portfolio\ value}$$

  Alternatively:

  $$E(R_p) = w_1 E(R_1) + w_2 E(R_2) + w_3 E(R_3)\ldots\ldots\ldots w_n E(R_n)$$

➢ ***Portfolio Risk***

$$\sigma_p^2 = \sum_{1}^{n} w_1^2 \sigma_1^2 + 2\sum_{i=1}^{n}\sum_{i=1}^{n} w_i w_j \operatorname{cov}_{ij}$$

Where "cov_{ij}" represents covariance of returns between two assets, i and j.
Covariance is calculated by the formula:

$$Cov_{ij} = \rho_{ij}\sigma_i\sigma_j$$

Where ρ_{ij} = correlation coefficient between security i and j.

➢ $$\sigma_p^2 = \sum_{1}^{n} w_i^2 \sigma_1^2 + 2\sum_{i=1}^{n}\sum_{j=1}^{n} w_i w_j \rho_{ij}\sigma_i\sigma_j$$

➢ In case of a portfolio consisting of two securities, we can write the formula for expected return and variance with the help of equation above.

Expected return of two security portfolio $E(R_P) = w_1 E(R_1) + w_2 E(R_2)$,

Variance of two security portfolio:

$$\sigma_p^2 = w_2^1 \sigma_1^2 + w_2^2 \sigma_2^2 + 2w_1 w_2 \rho_{12}\sigma_1\sigma_2$$

➢ Total Risk = systematic risk +Unsystematic Risk

➢ ***Measures of Systematic and Unsystematic Risk***

Total risk of security i=σ_i^2

Systematic risk of security=β^2_{im}

Where, β_{im} is called beta of security. It is given by the formula

$$\beta_{im} = \frac{Cov_{im}}{\sigma_m^2}$$

and σ_m^2 is known as variance of the market portfolio.

Another formula for beta is; $\beta_{im} = \dfrac{\rho_{im}\sigma_i\sigma_m}{\sigma_m^2} = \dfrac{\rho_{im}\sigma_i}{\sigma_m}$

➢ ***Portfolio beta***

$$\beta\, portfolio = \sum_{i=0}^{n} w_i \beta_{im}$$

$$Systematic\ risk\ of\ portfolio = \beta^2_{portfolio}\sigma_m^2$$

Also:

$$Systematic\ risk\ of\ portfolio = \left(\sum_{i=0}^{n} w_i \beta_{im}\right)^2 \sigma_m^2$$

➢ ***Interpretation of beta***

$\%\, change\ in\ security\ returns = \beta\ x\, \%\, change\ in\ market\ returns$

➢ ***Relationship between Risk and Return***

❖ **Risk Premium =Expected Return from a risky investment – Expected return from risk free security.**

❖ Expected premium on **risky asset = beta** x expected risk premium on market protfolio.

❖ **CAPM**

$r = r_f + \beta\ (r_m - r_f)$

where, r = expected return from a security

r_f = risk free rate

r_m = return on market portfolio

Chapter 4

The procedure of obtaining cash flows can be summarized as follows:

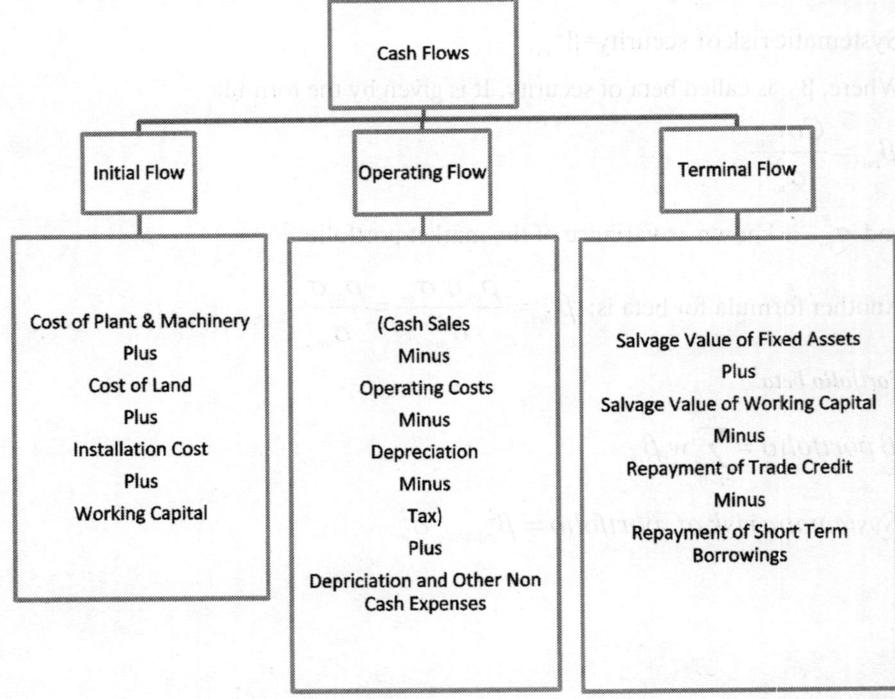

Once we have correctly estimated these cash flows, step 1 of financial appraisal is complete. The next step is to apply a suitable appraisal criterion on these cash flows.

Appraisal Criteria

There are a number of criteria that can be employed to study the financial desirability of a project. Broadly they can be divided into two categories: Non-Discounting Criteria and Discounting Criteria.

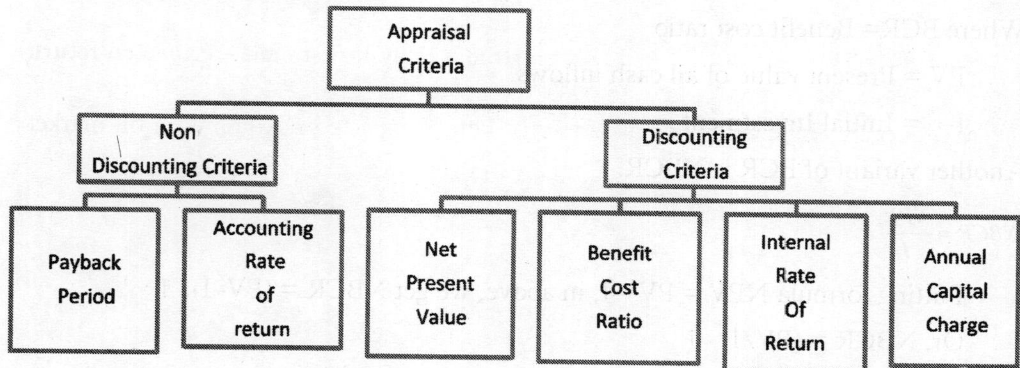

- $Payback\ Period = \dfrac{Initial\ investment}{Constant\ annual\ cash\ flow}$

Discounted payback period

$A * PVIFA\ (k, n) = I,$

Where,A = constant cash flow generated by the project every year

I = Initial Investment

k = discount rate

n = discounted payback period

Accounting Rate of Return (ARR)

ARR = Average profit it after tax / average book vlue of investments

Net Present Value (NPV):

$$NPV = \sum_{t=1}^{n} \frac{CF_t}{(1+k)^t} + \frac{S_n + W_n}{(1+k)^n} - I$$

Here, CF_t = cash inflow at the end of year t.

S_n = salvage value of fixed assets

W_n = salvage value of working capital in the nth year

I= Initial Investment

Benefit Cost Ratio

This technique is a variant of NPV technique. It is also known as profitability index. It is defined as follows:

$$BCR = \frac{PV}{I}$$

Where BCR= Benefit cost ratio

PV = Present value of all cash inflows

I = Initial Investment

Another variant of BCR is NBCR.

$$NBCR = \frac{NPV}{I}$$

Putting formula NPV = PV – I, in above, we get NBCR = (PV- I)/ I

Or, NBCR = (PV/I) - 1

NBCR = BCR – 1

Internal Rate of Return (IRR)

We may write the formula for IRR, by putting NPV = 0.

$$NPV = \sum_{t=1}^{n} \frac{CF_t}{(1+k)^t} + \frac{S_n + W_n}{(1+k)^n} - I = 0$$

$$I = \sum_{t=1}^{n} \frac{CF_t}{(1+r)^t} + \frac{S_n + W_n}{(1+r)^n}$$

Therefore, r is the IRR in the above equation.

Chapter 5

- ***Standard Deviation (Absolute Measure of Risk)***

$$Expected\ cash\ flow\ \overline{CF} = \sum_{1}^{n} P_i CF_i$$

Where CF_1, CF_2, CF_3 ....CF_n are cash flows.

P_1, P_2, P_3 ....P_n are probability of cash flows.

$\overline{CF}$ = mean or expected cash flow

$$\text{Variance } \sigma^2 = \sum_{1}^{n} Pi\{CF_i - \overline{CF}\}^2$$

$$\text{Standard Deviation}(\sigma) = \sqrt{Variance\,(\sigma^2)}$$

➢ ***Coefficient of Variation (Relative Measure of Risk)***

$$\text{Co-efficient of Variation} = \frac{\text{standard deviation}}{\overline{CF}}$$

Sometimes coefficient of variation may also be expressed as a percentage. In this case the formula becomes:

$$\text{Co-efficient of Variation (\%)} = \frac{\text{standard deviation}}{\overline{CF}} \times 100$$

➢ ***Risk Adjusted Discount Rate***

$k = k_f + k_r$

Where, k_f is risk free rate and k_r is the risk premium.

➢ ***Certainty Equivalent***

We may write the formula for NPV with certainty equivalent method as:

$$NPV = \sum_{t=0}^{n} \frac{\alpha_t NCF_t}{(1+k_f)^t}$$

Where α_t = risk adjustment factor or the certainty equivalent coefficient

And k_f = risk free rate of interest

$$\alpha_t = \frac{Certain\,Cash\,Flow}{Risky\,Cash\,Flow}$$

Chapter 6

Before we proceed lets refresh some basic financial relationships

Suppose Q= Quantity of a product sold by a firm (in units)

P = Price per Unit

F= Fixed Costs of the firm V= Variable cost per unit of the firm

I = Interest paid by the firm T = Tax Rate D= Dividend paid to equity Shareholders

D_p = Preference Dividend paid to preference shareholders

From above We can write

Sales Revenue = Q x P =QP Total Variable Cost = Q x V =QV

Contribution = Sales Revenue – Total Variable Cost

= QP-QV

Contribution = Q (P-V) (1)

Operating Profit =Contribution –Fixed Costs (1a)

Operating Profit= Q (P-V)-F (2)

Operating Profit is also known as "Earnings before Interest & Taxes" or EBIT

Therefore ***EBIT = Q (P-V)-F*** (3)

Profit Before Tax = EBIT-Interest= EBIT –I = Q (P-V)-F- I (4)

Profit After Tax = Profit before Tax –Tax (**Tax = Profit before Tax X Tax Rate**)

= Profit before Tax – Profit before Tax x Tax Rate

= {Q (P-V)-F –I} – {Q (P-V)-F- I } x T

Profit After Tax= {Q (P-V)-F- I} (1-T) (5)

Profit Available to Equity Shareholders = Profit After Tax – Preference Dividend

Profit Available to Equity Shareholders = {Q (P-V)-F- I} (1-T) - D_p (6)

It may be emphasized here that dividend on preference shares is paid from after tax profits but before paying any dividend to equity shareholders.

If no. of shares issued to equity shareholders = N

Then, Earnings Per Share (EPS) = Profits Available to Equity shareholders/N

EPS = [{Q (P-V)-F- I} (1-T) - D_p]/ N (7)

In order to clearly understand the concept of leverage it is absolutely necessary that the student learns all the above equations from (1) to (7) by heart.

$$Degree\ of\ operating\ Leverage\,(DOL) = \frac{\%\,change\ in\ EBIT}{\%\,change\ in\ sales}$$

$$DOL = \frac{\Delta EBIT\,/\,EBIT}{\Delta Sales\,/\,Sales}$$

$$DOL = \frac{Q(P-V)}{Q(P-V)-F} = \frac{Contribution}{EBIT}$$

% change in EBIT = DOL X % change in Sales

$$Degree\ of\ Financial\ Leverage\,(DFL) = \frac{\%\,Change\ in\ EPS}{\%\,Change\ in\ EBIT}$$

$$DFL = \frac{\dfrac{\Delta EPS}{EPS}}{\dfrac{\Delta EBIT}{EBIT}}$$

$$DFL = \frac{Q(P-V)-F}{\{Q(P-V)-F-I\} - \dfrac{Dp}{(1-T)}} = \frac{EBIT}{Earnings\ before\ Taxes}$$

This equation may also be written as

$$DFL = \frac{EBIT}{EBIT - I - \frac{Dp}{(1-T)}} = \frac{EBIT}{Earnings\ before\ Taxes}$$

$$Degree\ of\ Total\ Leverage\ (DLT) = \frac{\%\ change\ in\ EPS}{\%\ change\ in\ Sales}$$

This can be rewritten as

$$DTL = \frac{\%\ change\ in\ EPS}{\%\ change\ in\ EBIT} \times \frac{\%\ change\ in\ EBIT}{\%\ change\ in\ Sales}$$

Or DTL = DFL x DOL

It can also be calculated by

$$DTL = \frac{Q(P-V)}{EBIT - I} = \frac{Contribution}{Earnings\ before\ Tax}$$

$$Financial\ Break\ Even\ Point = 1 + \frac{D_p}{(1-T)}$$

Where, I = Interest paid, D_p = Preference Dividend, T = Tax Rate

Mathematically the indifference point can be obtained as follows:

Let indifference point EBIT be denoted by EBIT*, then

$$\frac{EBIT - (1-T)}{N_1} = \frac{(EBIT * - I)(1-T) - D_p}{N_2}$$

Chapter 9

Cost of Debentures

➤ ***Cost of capital of redeemable debentures:*** Cost of redeemable debentures is calculated by applying following formula:

$$B_0 = \sum_{t=1}^{n} \frac{INT_t}{(1+k_d)^t} + \frac{B_n}{(1+k_d)^n}$$

Where B_0 = Net Cash inflows at the time of issue

INT = Annual Interest Payment

B_n = Cash outflow at the time of maturity.

Sometimes principal too is amortized periodically. In that case principal is repaid periodically with interest then cash outflow includes interest and principal. Then formula for calculating cost of debentures is given below:

$$B_0 = \frac{INT_t + B_t}{(1+k_d)^t}$$

Where INT_t and B_t are periodical payments of interest and principal.

- **_Cost of Capital of Perpetual Debentures:_** Cost of perpetual debentures can be ascertained by applying following formula.

$$k_d = \frac{I}{B_0}$$

Where k_d = cost of capital of perpetual debentures before tax, I = annual interest payment, B_0 = net cash inflow at the time of issue.

The above cost is before tax and to get after tax cost we will have to adjust this with tax i.e. ***after tax cost of capital of debentures*** $k_d(1-T)$ where T is the tax rate.

Cost of Preference Shares

- ***Cost of capital of preference share capital is calculated by applying following formula:***

$$P_0 = \sum_{t=1}^{n} \frac{PD_t}{(1+k_p)^t} + \frac{P_n}{(1+k_p)^n}$$

Where P_0 = Net Proceeds on issue of shares
PD = Annual preference dividend
P_n = Cash outflow at the time of redemption
k_p = Cost of preference shares
n = Years of redemption.

Cost of Equity Shares

- ***Constant Growth Model***: If dividend on equity shares is growing at a constant rate i.e. g then we cab calculate cost of equity shares under this model. As we all know that in case of equity shares if dividend is growing at a constant rate g then value of equity share is

$$P_0 = \frac{D_1}{k_e - g}$$

where D_1 is expected dividend after year 1;

then $D_1 = D_0(1+g)$

after solving above formula we get cost of capital of equity shares

$$k_e = \frac{D_1}{P_0} + g$$

Where k_e = cost of capital of equity shares, P_0 = present market value of shares, g = growth rate.

we can get growth rate by applying this formula i.e. **g = b * r** where b is retention ratio and r is return on equity.

➢ ***Zero Growth Dividend Model***

$$k_e = \frac{D_1}{P_0}$$

Where k_e = cost of equity share capital, D_1 = expected dividend at the end of year1, P_0 = current market price of the share.

➢ ***Different Growth Rates in Dividend***

$$P_0 = \sum_{t=1}^{n} \frac{DIV_0 (1+g_s)^t}{(1+k_e)^t} + \frac{DIV_{n+1}}{k_e - g_n} * \frac{1}{(1+k_e)^n}$$

Where P_o = current market price, DIV_0 = current dividend, g_s = growth for n years, g_n = perpetual growth beginning from n + 1 year.

➢ ***Cost of Equity Capital through CAPM Model***

$$k_e = R_f + \beta (R_m - R_f)$$

where k_e = Cost of capital of equity capital

R_f = Risk free interest rate

β = A measure of Non – diversifiable risk

R_m = Return from market.

➢ ***Weighted Average Cost of Capital:***

$$WACC = k_e W_e + k_p W_p + k_d W_d$$

Where WACC = weighted average cost of capital, k_e = cost of equity capital, W_e = proportion of equity capital, k_p = cost of preference shares, W_p = proportion of preference capital, k_d = cost of debt capital, W_d = proportion of debt capital.

Chapter 10

➢ ***Walter's Model (Relevance Theory)***

$$P_0 = \frac{D}{k_e} + \frac{\frac{r}{k_e}(E - D)}{k_e}$$

Where P_0 = Current Market Price, D = Dividend per Share, E = Earnings per Share, r = Rate of Return,

k_e = Cost of Equity.

- ***Gordon's Model (Relevance Theory)***

$$P_o = \frac{D_1}{k_e - g}$$

Where P_o = Current Market Price, D_1 = Dividend per Share of next year, k_e = Cost of Equity, g = Growth rate in dividend.

- ***Traditional Model (Relevance Theory)***

$$P = m \times \left(D + \frac{E}{3} \right)$$

P = market price of the share, m = a multiplier, D = dividend per share, E = earnings per share

Chapter 11

- Gross working capital = Total current assets
- Net working Capital = CA- CL
- Gross Operating Cycle = Inventory Conversion Period (ICP) + Average Collection Period (ACP)
- Inventory Conversion Period = Raw Material Conversion Period (RMCP) + work in process Conversion Period (WIPCP) + Finished goods Conversion Period (FGCP)
- Net Operating Cycle = Gross Operating Cycle – Creditors Payment Period (CPP)

The net operating cycle is also known as ***Cash Conversion Cycle.***

The formulae for calculating various components of operating cycle are as follows

$$RMCP = \frac{Average\ Raw\ Material\ Inventory}{Annual\ Raw\ Material\ Consumption / 360}$$

$$WIPCP = \frac{Average\ WIP\ Inventory}{Annual\ Cost\ of\ Production / 360}$$

$$FGCP = \frac{Average\ finished\ goods\ Inventory}{Annual\ Cost\ of\ Goods\ Sold / 360}$$

$$ACP = \frac{Average\ Debtors}{Annal\ Credit\ Sales / 360}$$

$$CPP = \frac{Average\ Creditors}{Annual\ Credit\ Purchase\ /\ 360}$$

- ***Computation of Working Capital***

Various items of current assets and current liabilities are computed as follows:

1. Raw Material Stock:

$$Raw\ Material\ Stock = \frac{Budgeted\ Production\ in\ Units\ x\ Material\ Cost\ Per\ Unit}{360\ /\ 52\ /\ 12} \times RMCP$$

2. Work in Process Stock

$$WIP\ Stock = \frac{Budgetd\ Production\ in\ Units\ x\ Unit\ WIP\ Costs}{360\ /\ 52\ /\ 12} \times WIPCP$$

3. Finished Goods Stock

$$FG\ Stock = \frac{Budgetd\ Production\ in\ Units \times Unit\ Cost\ of\ Production}{360\ /\ 52\ /\ 12} \times FGCP$$

4. Debtors

$$Debtors = \frac{Budgeted\ Credit\ Sales\ in\ Units\ x\ Unit\ Cost\ of\ Sales}{360\ /\ 52\ /\ 12} \times ACP$$

5. Creditors

$$Creditors = \frac{Budgeted\ Creddit\ Purchases\ x\ unit\ Purchases\ Cost}{360\ /\ 52\ /\ 12} \times CPP$$

6. Outstanding Expenses

$$Outstanding\ Expenses = \frac{Budgeted\ Production\ in\ Units\ x\ per\ unit\ expenses}{360/52/12} \times Lag\ in\ payment\ of\ outstanding\ expenses$$

Here, RMCP = Raw Material Conversion Period

WIPCP = Work in Process Conversion Period

FGCP = Finished Goods Conversion Period

ACP = Average Collection Period

CPP = Creditors Payment Period

Chapter 13

- ***EOQ model***

Total Costs = Carrying Costs + Ordering Costs

= Average Inventory x Annual carrying cost per unit + No. of orders in a year x ordering cost per order

= Q/2 x C + A/Q x S

Economic Order Quantity:

$$Q^* = \sqrt{\frac{2AS}{C}}$$

Where, A = annual consumption of inventory

S = cost of placing an order or setup costs

C = annual carrying costs per unit

Q = Order Quantity

Q^* = Economic Order Quantity

Chapter 15

$$\text{Cost of Trade Credit} = \frac{\%\ \text{discount}}{1\text{-}\%\ \text{discount}}\ x\ \frac{365}{\text{Credit - Discount Period}}$$

Contents

Unit 1 : Introduction

Unit - 2 : Investment Decision

Unit 3 : Financing Decision

Unit-1

Introduction

CHAPTER 1 Financial Management: An Overview

Learning Objectives:

By the end of this chapter and having completed the essential reading and activities, you should be able to:

- Understand the Concept of Finance
- Have an understanding of Scope and objectives of finance
- Differentiate Between Profit maximization vs. Wealth maximization
- Grasp the Functions of Finance Manager in Modern Age
- Spell out the Financial decision areas
- Handle the application of the concept Time Value of Money
- Understand the relationship between Risk and Return

To start with...

It is said that finance is lifeblood of business. And finance managers in business firms are one of the influential and highly paid executives. Ever wondered why?

As future manager's we must understand the concept of finance in business firms and also know how finance is interrelated with functions like marketing, human resources, production etc.

In this chapter, we will not only know the aspects outlined above but also discuss things about firm's manifold objectives.

1.1 Concept of Finance

Welcome to the world of finance. In this journey you shall learn the skills needed to handle the most interesting phenomenon on earth, i.e., "money". Isn't money interesting? Sure it is. It is something; which; perhaps can do almost anything for you. Also it is something for which perhaps you will do almost anything!

The term ***finance*** has many meanings. Even a layman will tell you that finance means something related to money. The most common meaning of finance is "money used to run a business, activity or a project". Here finance implies "funds". Another way finance is understood is "provision of funds". Haven't you heard people say "I want to buy a car, and I will go to my bank to ***finance*** it"? We all know that here we are talking about arranging sufficient money (by taking a loan) so that the car can be purchased.

In the context of a business or a firm, Finance also means the art and science of "financial management". Let's understand what is meant by financial management in the context of a firm.

Finance is often called the lifeblood of a business. The term "financial management" refers to the process of acquiring, utilizing and controlling funds for use in business in such a way that the owners of business get richer. Owners will get richer when their wealth is maximized. We shall deal with the concept of wealth maximization later in this chapter.

1.2 Scope and Objectives of Finance

1.2.1 Scope

Having discussed what is understood by the term "finance" lets now look at the scope. Here we shall try to identify the areas in which finance plays a role. The identification of areas in which finanace plays a role comes under "scope" of finance.

Think of any business organization or a firm. Think of what are broad spheres of activity of this firm. You shall see that a firm uses funds to create a set up whereby it supplies goods or services to its clients with a view to earn profits. If we take the example of a manufacturing company then we may broadly divide its activities in three categories:

1. Finance activities- all activities related to arranging, using and keeping control over funds.
2. Production Activities- all activities related to creating the goods or services for clients.
3. Marketing Activities- all activities related to satisfying the needs and wants of customers and making the product available to them.

In real life, all these activities affect each other. The decisions taken in one area have effect on the other & How does this happen?

Essential Learning Background Box-1

Before we proceed it would be a good idea to discuss what we mean by "firm" and "owners". The word **"firm"** means any business organization. On the basis of ownership any business organization can be divided into three forms. The simplest one is "sole proprietorship". In this form the business is owned by a single person. For example; college canteen is a sole proprietorship concern. Another type of firms is known as "partnership". Here the business is owned by more than one person known as "partners" and they share the profits and losses in the ratio of their investment. As per Indian law the number of partners in a firm cannot exceed 20.

The third form of business organization is known as "company" form. However, company is of two types, viz. ***"private limited"*** and ***"public limited"***. In a **private limited** company, the numbers of people that can form it are minimum two and maximum 50. These people who have contributed funds to form the company are called "shareholders" of the company. In a private limited company there are restrictions on selling of shares by one shareholder to other. The **"public limited"** company is one where the minimum number of shareholders is seven and maximum can be unlimited. That is why it is called public limited. Also there is no restriction on transfer of shares from one share holder to another.

How to identify whether a company is public or private? It is not difficult. Just look at the name of the firm. If the name contains the words "(P) limited" or Pvt. Limited then it is a private limited company. For example Rohit Surfactants Private Limited. In case of a public limited company, only the words "limited" will be found. For example "Reliance India limited".

In the study of finance generally, and in this book particularly, we talk from the point of view of a public limited company and its shareholders. Throughout this book, unless specified otherwise, whenever the word "firm" is used it should be understood as a public limited company.

First let us understand better what is meant by finance activities. Have you ever thought how a firm arranges money or funds? Do you remember the concept of balance sheet taught to you in previous semester? The balance sheet had two parts, liabilities and assets. The liabilities are nothing but names given to various sources of funds for the firm. A firm can get funds by two ways. It can either get it from its owners or it can borrow it from lenders. When funds are obtained from owners then it is called "Equity" or Equity Capital or Shareholders Capital or simply capital. Whereas when funds are obtained from lenders it is known as "debt". These are two broad types. In both these cases the firm issues "securities" to the providers of funds.

What are these securities? In case of Equity, these securities are known as ordinary shares or preference shares. In case of debt, these securities are known as debentures or bonds. Generally debentures and bonds refer to the long term sources of debt. There are many other types of debt which are taken for a relatively shorter duration. They are shown under the current liabilities heading of balance sheet, e.g., sundry creditors, bills payable, provisions etc.

Where does the firm issue these securities? It does so in what is called "Primary Market". However, anybody who has acquired these securities can sell it to somebody else. This is done in "Secondary Market". An example of secondary market is "Stock exchange".

So these are the ways by which the firm obtains funds. Now what does it do with these funds? It employs these funds in obtaining various assets and stocks and also in day to day running of the company. The uses of these funds are shown in the asset side of the balance sheet.

Why does firm acquire assets like plant, machinery, land, building and stocks? It does so to produce the goods and services that it wants to sell in the market.

Now let us see how finance function is intertwined with other activities of the firm. The production activities involve using plant and machinery to produce the firm's products. Any decision taken in the production department will affect the finances of the firm. For example if production department wants to hire a team of technical operators for its new machinery, then the salary and wages of these new employees have to be paid and it increases the costs of the firm. Now costs will be directly the concern of finance department. Similarly if production activities require new latest technology machinery in place of existing one, the finance department shall be involved for arranging funds at a reasonable cost.

The relationship between finance activities and marketing activities can also be understood with a few examples. Launch of a new sales promotion campaign is the decision of marketing department but it will involve huge financial outlay and finance department is involved. Another example is allowing credit sales. Suppose the marketing department is negotiating with a large client for bulk order. The client wants to purchase goods on credit and promises to pay after say, 35 days. Here the marketing department cannot proceed with the decision without consulting finance since funds shall be locked up for a period. In fact in such situations, generally firms have pre determined credit policies.

So we may see that the scope of finance is very wide and reaches almost all the areas of firm's activities. However we must remember that finance function does not always become a constraint in the way of other departments. In fact, financial considerations become more important when firm is not doing well. In good times with firm having surplus cash, financial considerations become less important in many decision situations.

Activity 1

Log on to the internet and visit the website of any limited company of your choice. Download the latest financial statements. Take a printout. Now against each entry in the Profit and Loss account write the functional area (e.g. Marketing, Finance, Production, HR etc.) it most probably belongs to. For example: the item "salary & wages" belongs to Human Resources. Can you see how different functional areas of the firm are interconnected and affect the financial position collectively?

1.2.2 Objectives: Profit Maximization vs. Wealth Maximization

In this section we shall learn about the objectives of finance or financial management. Before this first let's understand what the objectives of a business firm are. Generally the objectives of business firms are set by top management. These objectives can be anything like becoming market leader, customer satisfaction, increasing market share, employee satisfaction etc. Often the top management sets more than one objective of the firm. Based on these objectives, the firm sets its long term strategy and policies.

However, for a long time now, earning more and more profits has been considered the most important objective of the firm. This is also known as Profit Maximization Objective of the firm. This objective is also considered to be the objective of financial management.

What is Profit Maximization? We know Profit is difference between Sales (also known as "Revenue") and Costs. Therefore if a firm maximizes its Revenues and minimizes its costs then as a result profits will be maximized. Economic theory also supports this objective as a logical behavior of firm. It is believed that it is perfectly in the self-interest of the owner/manager of the firm to maximize its profits. And in a free market, if every person is allowed to take care of her own self interest, the interest of the society shall automatically be taken care of. Therefore, profit maximization is a valid objective of the firm.

Economic theory further says that in an environment of competition, the firm that tries to achieve profit maximization objective is more likely to survive.

However of late it has been argued that this concept suffers from many weaknesses. Some of the criticisms of this profit maximization hypothesis are:

1. Earlier the business firms were mainly sole proprietorships or on partnership basis. Then the concept of profit maximization was still ok. But we know that most of the firms today are "companies" and they are not owned by a single individual but a group of shareholders. The shareholders do not get benefitted by profit maximization if they do not receive dividends and their share price is not increasing.
2. Profit maximization objective assumes perfect competition which does not hold good in today's imperfect markets.

3. It is not clear that which year's profits are to be maximized? Current years or future years? It is sometimes possible to increase current year's profits at the cost of future profits.
4. Recall that profit is an accounting concept. Two different accountants may calculate different amount of profits and both may be right! Therefore this hypothesis becomes weak since definition of profits itself is ambiguous.
5. Profit maximization is a short term objective. It may affect the long term stability of the firm.
6. Profit maximization objective does not take into consideration the risk factors that the firm is facing.
7. Profit maximization considers the interest of its owner only. However modern firm has many stakeholders like government, employees, clients, creditors, suppliers, banks etc. Profit maximization objective fails to take into account their interests.
8. Profit maximization does not take into account the social responsibility of business. In order to maximize profits the firm may start producing such goods and services which may not be healthy for the society.

Hence this concept is rejected in favor of a new hypothesis known as Wealth Maximization or Shareholder's wealth maximization. Now the question is what is Wealth? Wealth is defined as the net present value of any action.Net present value of any action is the difference between the present value of its benefits and present value of costs. It may be noted that here benefits are not defined as profits, but cash flows (The difference between cash flows and profits are discussed in later chapters). If the present value of benefits is more than the costs, then wealth will increase and otherwise it will decrease. Any financial decision that increases the wealth is accepted and otherwise it is rejected. In case of more than one mutually exclusive (means only one out of many can be chosen) project, the project with the highest net present value should be chosen.

Now the owners of modern firm are shareholders. Their wealth increases if their gains from their shares increase. The gains from shares are earned in two ways. One , in the form of a share of profits earned by the firm-known as dividends- and two, by the increase in the prices of their shares. Since in the modern firm, managers and owners are not the same persons, management must try to maximize the wealth of its share holders.

Therefore the managers need to take those decisions that have a positive net present value, because only then the wealth of shareholders shall increase. In order to obtain the present value of future benefits, discounting is done at an appropriate discount rate. If risks of a decision are high, then higher discount rate is chosen. If risks are lower than a lower discount rate may be applied.

We can see that wealth maximization is a better objective of management (financial management also) than profit maximization for a number of reasons:

1. It does not assume perfect competition in markets.

2. It is in line with the economic welfare of the owners.
3. It considers risk along with returns.
4. It takes into account long term stability and survival of the firm.
5. It takes into account all future cash flows, dividends and earnings per share of the firm.
6. It does not ignore the interests of other stakeholders like government, society, banks, creditors etc since their interests are protected if the firms value increases in the long run.
7. Modern firm has more than one objective like enhancing the market share, exploring new markets etc. Wealth maximization objective takes care of other objectives as well.

The shareholder's wealth is maximized when the value of their shares are maximized. The value of their shares depends on the market price of the shares. The market price of the shares shall go high if the market thinks that the financial decisions of the manager's of the firm are correct and do not put the survival of the firm at risk.

1.3 Functions of Finance Manager in Modern Age

The finance manager's position lies between the firm and the market for raising funds (known as financial markets). Firm is interested in obtaining real assets like land, building, plant, machinery, stocks etc. For this the firm needs money. Firm takes money from providers of funds in the financial markets and in return for funds issues securities to these providers. What are securities? Securities are written promise by the firm that it has taken funds and it shall return them with interest. For providers of capital these securities become "Financial Assets".

Traditionally the finance manager's functions can be divided into two parts:

1. Treasurer Function
2. Controller Function

As a treasurer of the firm the finance manager is supposed to arrange for funds at a reasonable cost for both short as well as long term. After arranging funds the treasurer is also responsible for putting the cash to good use in order to maximize returns. He is also supposed to maintain relationship with different players in the financial markets, banks, creditors, suppliers etc.

As a controller the finance manager is responsible for maintaining proper systems and procedures of accounting and finally preparing the financial statements of the firm in line with the regulatory (means as prescribed by various government agencies) guidelines. The controller is also responsible for taking care of tax obligations of the firm. Various regulators require periodic returns from the firm. This is also the responsibility of the controller.

In small companies the role of treasurer and controller are discharged by the same person. In medium sized companies these roles may be played by two different persons. In very large corporations there might be another person who acts as a head of both treasurer and controller, known as Chief Financial Officer (CFO). CFO is not only required to head finance function but also has general managerial responsibilities and often he is the part of the **Board of Directors.**

Other responsibilities of the finance manager are:

Functions	Description
1.Arranging Long Term Funds	Making programs for arranging funds, maintaining investor relations and creating a secondary market for firm's securities
2.Arranging Short Term Funds	Maintaining a smooth supply of working capital funds, maintaining relations with banks and financial institutions
3.Custody	Keeping firms monies and securities in safe custody
4.Credit Management	Making credit policies, ensuring follow up and collections
5.Investments	Ensuring proper investments to maintain liquidity and solvency
6.Insurance	Providing adequate insurance coverage for firms human and physical assets at a reasonable cost and reliability
7. Taxation and Compliance	Ensuring adequate tax administration policies , and taking care of all government guidelines and regulations
8.Financial Reporting	Preparation of various financial statements that reflect a true and fair view of business
9.Evaluation and Consulting	Keeping constant communication with various levels of management and integrating the objectives of other functions with financial function
10.Economic Appraisal	To appraise continuously economic, social forces and government influences and to interpret their effects upon business
11.Liquidity	To maintain sufficient funds to meet the obligations of the firm
12.Performance Measurement	To identify parameters to measure the financial and operating performance of the firm
13.Price Setting	To help the management in setting correct economic price for its products and services
14. Forecasting	To forecast profits and cash flows for various internal and other purposes

However these are traditional roles of finance manager. Of late there have been tremendous changes in the economic environment. We are witnessing an all-round shift in business models, increased competition, faster paced markets and increased investor awareness coupled with improvement in information and communication technologies. In the new economy the role of finance manager has ceased to be that of a number cruncher. Now increasingly the CFO is being viewed as a "strategist". The days of accountant CFO are over and new Super CFO is the order of the day. The CFO is being viewed as a co-pilot with the CEO, helping him in formulating and implementing enterprise wide strategy to create maximum shareholder value. The traditional treasury and control function are only a starting point these days. The CFO is expected to do a lot more. The evolution of the modern CFO can be summed up as follows:

Levels	Roles	Description
Level 1	Accounting, Control and Treasury	Preparation of final statements, income tax returns, arranging funds from financial markets, creating systems and procedures for control, preparing budgets, credit management
Level 2	Mergers & Acquisitions, Risk Management	Identifying potential takeover opportunities, integrating human assets with physical assets , identifying the sources and extent of risk and taking measures to mitigate them, making organization risk intelligent and not offloading risk on third parties
Level 3	Strategic Perspectives	Finalizing business plans with CEO, providing necessary information inputs in strategic decision making
Level 4	Inter disciplinary approach (supply chain, innovation)	Minimizing operating cost involved in the supply chain, creating reliable supply chain, making use of new financial instruments to achieve the goal of maximizing shareholders wealth
Level 5	Shareholder Relations	Handling analysts, investor meets, ensuring proper and efficient investor services, creating a market for firms securities

Courtesy: Kashyap V R and Mridula E, Evolution of CFO, ICFAI university press

CFOs of tomorrow shall be expected to drive responsive performance management architecture, implement resilient governance structures, provide essential, round the clock controls and oversee dynamic risk management. They are expected to improve efficiencies and cut the current cost base by investing in new technologies, key integration of processes and managing people across business. They are also faced with implications arising from International Accounting Standards, Real Time Reporting, and compliance with Sarbanes-Oxley Act, regaining confidence and corporate governance practices.

The new age finance manager has to look beyond the processing of financial statements and managing the funds. He will have to effectively manage shareholder value and have an increasing awareness and improve performance. He will be a strong personality who will also try to act as a guardian of financial information, a steward, a compliance officer, strategist, guardian of corporate conscience and a powerful entity in the corporate structure, all combined.

1.4 Financial Decision Areas

Broadly there are three areas of financial decision making. They are:

1. Investment Decisions
2. Financing Decisions
3. Dividend Decisions

Let us discuss these areas one by one:

1.4.1 Investment Decisions

In order to generate returns for its shareholders funds, the firm has to invest them in profitable projects. Investments are an ongoing activity in a firm. They are made in new projects as well as for replacing an existing asset whose productivity has gone down with time. The new investment may be on a small scale like purchasing new machinery or constructing a new building, or it may be a large one like setting up a new plant. The decision to acquire an existing entity is also an investment decision. So we may say that investment decisions relates to careful selection of viable and profitable investment proposals, allocation of funds to the investment proposals with a view to maximizing the value of firm's shares. These decisions are also known as **Capital Budgeting Decisions**. In these decisions the key question is that the firm should be able to generate returns which are at least equal to return expected by the suppliers of funds for the project. This minimum rate is known as **"Hurdle Rate"** or **"Cut Off"** rate. Often this is also known as "opportunity cost of capital".

The choice of appropriate rates shall also depend on the riskiness of the project. Whenever a investment proposal is studied the future profitability or cash flows are analyzed. However since these cash flows relate to the future we cannot be certain whether they will actually be realized. This uncertainty associated with future returns brings an element of risk in projects. The finance manager must consider this risk. This risk will be different for different projects. For high risk project the **hurdle rate used will also be high and vice versa.**

1.4.2 Financing Decision

Refer to the section 1.1 in which concept of finance has been discussed. Remember the meaning of finance as in "provision of funds". Financing decisions relate to the choice of sources of funds. The key question is "which source of funds should be used?".This choice depends on the cost of funds from a particular source and its riskiness. Often, more than one source of funds is used .Then the key question becomes "in what ratio different sources of funds should be used? We already know that there are mainly two sources of funds for a firm; Equity and Debt. Equity is generally high cost but low risk source of funds. Why? This is because the firm has to pay to equity holders only when it has earned sufficient profits to cover all other expenses. These payments to shareholders out of **profits are known as dividends**. Therefore the firm does not have to worry about paying to equity holders when it is not earning sufficient profits. Also the money raised by way of Equity is a permanent source and is not required to be paid back (Except in case of buyback of shares). That is why Equity is called **low risk**. But it is high cost because there are no tax benefits available on dividend payments. In other words dividends are not tax deductible expenses.

However in case of debt, the situation is reversed. Debt is high risk but low cost source of fund. It is low cost because interest paid on debt is a tax deductible expense. But it is high risk since the interest on debt has to be paid whether the firm has earned profits or not. Also it is compulsory that the firm pays back the amount of debt taken after a specified period.

Given these characteristics of the **debt and equity**, the firm has to choose a ratio of debt and equity in such a way that the cost of capital is minimized at the given level of risk. If the firm has chosen the minimum cost combination of debt and equity at a given level of risk, then this combination is known as **Optimum Financing Mix** for the firm. In this scenario the value of the firm shall be maximized.

It may be noted that apart from risk and cost, there are some other factors also which are considered before choosing between debt and equity. These factors are loan covenants (restrictions on borrower put by the lender), control over decision making, flexibility and regulatory guidelines.

1.4.3 Dividend Decision

We know that "Profit" of "Net Profit" of a firm is calculated by deducting all the expenses and taxes from sales. Now who should take this profit? Obviously this profit belongs to the shareholders of the firm. But entire profit earned by a firm is often not paid to shareholders. This is because of regulatory reasons and also because some portion of profit is kept within the firm for financing its investments and growth. Therefore we may conclude that only a portion of profits are paid to the shareholders. This portion is known as dividends. The question is "how much proportion of profits should be paid back to the shareholders and how much should be kept back in the firm?" The proportion to be paid as dividends is known as "**payout ratio**" whereas the proportion to be retained is known as **"Retention Ratio"**.

The decision regarding payout ratio and retention ratio is known as **Dividend Decision**. The objective of choosing a particular payout ratio is that the value of the firm's shares should be maximized. Often this decision is made on the basis of available investment opportunities to the firm. If the firm has new projects that can generate high returns (at least higher than what shareholders can earn if they invest the money somewhere else) then the firm would like to retain a higher proportion of profits. Otherwise it would like to distribute it to shareholders. In both the scenarios the objective is to maximize the value of firm's shares.

Therefore the optimum dividend policy is the one that maximizes the value of firm's shares. Other factors considered for determining payout ratio and includes dividend stability, bonus shares and cash dividends in practice.

To conclude we may say that all the three decisions of investment, financing and dividend payout are not independent of each other. They affect each other and should therefore be viewed together by the finance manager. He should consider the impact of all the three decisions simultaneously.

Summary

- To a layman, the term "finance" means "funds" or "provision of funds". In the context of a business or a firm, finance also means the art and science of "financial management". Finance is often called the lifeblood of a business.
- The term "financial management" refers to the process of acquiring, utilizing and controlling funds for use in business in such a way that the owner's wealth is maximized.
- **Firms broadly have three kinds of activities:** Finance activities, Production Activities, Marketing Activities. In real life, all these activities affect each other.
- Funds can be obtained by two ways: Equity (Owner's funds) and Debt (Outsider's funds). In both these cases the firm issues "securities" to the providers of funds. Firm employs these funds in obtaining various assets and stocks and also in day to day running of the company.
- Finance function is closely intertwined with other functions of the firm.
- Financial considerations become important when firm is not doing well. In good times with firm having surplus cash, financial considerations become less important in many decision situations.
- Earlier, earning more and profits has been considered the most important objective of the firm. This is also known as Profit Maximization Objective of the firm. This objective is also considered to be the objective of financial management.
- Over the years it has been accepted that the objective of the firm is **"Wealth Maximization"** and not profit maximization. Wealth maximization if consistent with the long-term survival of the firm.
- The finance manager's position lies between the firm and the market for raising funds (known as financial markets). Firm is interested in obtaining real assets like land, building, plant, machinery, stocks etc. For this the firm needs money.

- Traditionally the finance manager's functions can be divided into two parts: Treasurer Function, Controller Function
- In small companies the role of treasurer and controller are discharged by the same person. In medium sized companies these roles may be played by two different persons. In very large corporations there might be another person who acts as a head of both treasurer and controller, known as Chief Financial Officer (CFO). CFO is not only required to head finance function but also has general managerial responsibilities and often he is the part of the board of directors.
- The traditional roles of finance manager have undergone tremendous changes of late. The role of finance manager has ceased to be that of a number cruncher. Now increasingly the CFO is being viewed as a "strategist". The CFO is being viewed as a co-pilot with the CEO, helping him in formulating and implementing enterprise wide strategy to create maximum shareholder value.
- CFOs of tomorrow shall be expected to drive responsive performance management architecture, implement resilient governance structures, provide essential, round the clock monitoring and control.
- Broadly there are three areas of financial decision making. Investment Decisions, Financing Decisions, Dividend Decisions.
- Investment decisions are concerned with where to put money, financing decisions are concerned with how to arrange money and dividend decisions are concerned with how much earnings to distribute amongst shareholders.

Test Your Understanding

State whether the following statements are true/false

1. Public limited company can have minimum 2 members and maximum 50.
2. In a company marketing manager need not care about the finance manager and vice versa.
3. Earlier, the goal of the firm was profit maximization, but now-a-days it is wealth maximization.
4. There are three decision areas in finance: a) Investment Decisions b) expenses Decision and c) Financing Decision.
5. To go for an expansion of the existing production capacity is an example of investment decision.
6. It is said that dividend decision is actually a financing decision.
7. For a sole proprietorship firm, there is no difference between profit maximization and wealth maximization.
8. If the words Pvt. Limited are found in the name of a company then it is a private limited company, whereas if the words "(P) Limited" are found in the name of a company then it is a public limited company.

9. "Public limited" and "Public sector" are two names for the same thing.
10. Dividend decision means deciding on the proportion of profits to be distributed as dividend to the shareholders.

Answers : 1. F 2. F 3.T 4.F 5.T 6.T 7.T 8.F 9.F 10.T

Multiple Choice Questions

1. What do you think is the goal of financial management? **(UPTU 2010)**

a) Maximization of Profit b) Expanding Market
c) Maximization of Shareholder d) None of the above

2. Financial Assets are: **(UPTU 2010)**

a) Investment in Securities b) Investment in Tangible Assets
c) Investment in both a) and b) above d) None of the above.

3. What is ignored in Profit Maximization? **(UPTU 2009)**

a) Time Value of Money b) Risk
c) Net Value d) Wealth

4. Which of the following is not a function of finance manager?

a) Mobilization of funds b) Deployment of funds
c) Control over use of funds d) To decide about the product mix of the firm.

5. The number of members in a public limited and a private limited company, respectively can not be less than :

a) 7 and 2 b) 2 and 7
c) 5 and 7 d) 2 and 5

6. SKS Ventures Limited is a:

a) Sole Proprietorship Firm b) Private Limited Firm
c) Public Limited Firm d) Partnership Firm

7. Which of the following is related to control function of the financial manager?

a) To advertise the public issue of the firm
b) To negotiate with bankers for a loan
c) To analyze variance between standard costs and actual costs.
d) To estimate the future cash flows from a project under consideration.

Answers : 1. c 2. c 3. b 4. d 5. a 6. c 7. c

Chapter Review Questions

1. Write down the objectives of financial management. **(UPTU 2006)**

2. Explain how the objective of wealth maximization is superior to profit maximization? **(UPTU 2006)**
3. The Goal of Capital Management is the maximization of long term or long term earnings to present shareholders. Comment **(UPTU 2005)**
4. "Finance is the life and blood of industry". Elucidate the statement with suitable examples. **(UPTU 2007)**
5. Define financial management and discuss its objectives. **(UPTU 2007)**
6. What do you understand by "wealth" in wealth management objective? **(UPTU 2007)**
7. Give the functions of Finance Manager in today's world. Do you think it needs rethinking in the period of depression? **(UPTU, 2010)**
8. "The role of finance manager in today's world is not just a treasurer and controller, but a strategist too." Comment.
9. "Profit is not an operationally feasible criterion for financial decision making." Comment. **(DU 2006, 2010)**
10. "Financial Management is nothing but managerial decision making in asset mix, capital mix and profit allocation." Comment. **(DU 2006)**
11. Investment, financing and dividend decisions are all inter- related. Comment. **(DU 2007)**
12. Explain 'Profit Maximisation' and 'Wealth Maximisation' goals. Which is superior in your opinion and why? **(DU 2007)**
13. What are the basic financial decisions? How do they involve risk-return trade off? **(DU 2008)**

References

1. Brealey, Richard A & Myres, Stewart C. (2007), Tata McGraw Hill, New Delhi
2. ICAI study Material on Financial Management, The Institute of Chartered Accountants of India, New Delhi.
3. Khan, M Y & Jain (2007) P K, Financial Management, Tata McGraw Hill, New Delhi
4. Pandey, I M (2009). Financial Management, Vikas Publishing House, New Delhi
5. Van Horne, James C. (2007), Financial Management & Policy, Pearson Prentice Hall, New Delhi
6. Work book on "Financial Management for Managers": The Institute of Chartered Financial Analysts of India, Hyderabad.

CHAPTER 2 Time Value of Money

Learning Objectives:

By the end of this chapter and having completed the essential reading and activities, you should be able to:

- Understand that value of money changes with time
- Obtain future value of a single amount of money today (single cash flow)
- Obtain Present Value of single amount of money in future (single cash flow)
- Obtain future value of a series of cash flows
- Obtain present value of a series of cash flows
- Differentiate between nominal and effective rate of interest
- Apply time value concepts in real life, viz., EMI calculation, loan amortization etc.

To start with...

Rohit is a fresh MBA and has joined a Top Bank as assistant manager through campus selection. On his first day after a brief induction he meets a client Mrs. Sharma who wants to take a ` 8,00,000 loan to buy the latest car from a top auto company. She wants to repay the loan in equated monthly installments (EMIs) over a period of 5 years. She wants to know the EMIs at the prevailing interest rate of 12% p.a. Mrs. Sharma is a tough customer! She also wants to know how EMIs shall change if interest rates change to 10% and 14% respectively.

As a manager you need certain tools and techniques to suitably advise your clients like Mrs. Sharma. This chapter seeks to equip you with such tools and many more! Even if you do not plan to major in finance, the tools in this chapter shall be handy for your personal financial planning. For example you will be able to correctly estimate how much you need to save every month to be able to finance your three year old daughter's medical college education when she clears the PMT exam tomorrow!

2.0 Introduction

Time value of Money is the central concept of finance. Any one aspiring to build a career in finance must have a thorough grasp over this concept. What does this concept mean?

Suppose I give you two options:

1. Take ₹ 2,000 rupees from me now

OR

2. Take ₹ 2,000 rupees from me next year

Which option shall you chose? The answer is obvious. You will take the first option. Why? ***It is because you consider ₹ 2000 received today more valuable than the same ₹ 2,000 received tomorrow.***

Consider another situation:

1. Take ₹ 10,000 now

OR

2. Take ₹ 11,000 next year

Now what is your choice? If I give you additional information that interest rate on bank deposits is 10 % per annum, then what will be your answer? Perhaps you will say that you are now comfortable with either of these options. ***That means you find ₹ 10,000 of today having the same value as ₹ 11,000 of tomorrow.***

From both these examples we can conclude that the same money will have different values or worth at different points in time. Or in other words, a rupee today is worth more than a rupee tomorrow. What it means is that money has time value. The value of money will change with time.

This is the concept of time value of money and in important and useful concept of finance. With the help of this concept, we are able to compare money received at different points of time in future. For example, suppose you are analyzing whether to invest in project A that involves more investment now and gives returns for ;say; 5 years or in project B that involves same investment now but gives lower returns, but for longer duration, i.e., 10 years? In order to arrive at a correct decision you will need to compare returns from both the options. However, how can you compare returns when they are happening at different points of time? Project A is giving returns only for five years whereas project B is giving returns for 10 years. As we shall see later, we can answer these kinds of (and many more) questions with the help of the concept of time value of money.

Before we proceed, let us understand the reasons why money has time value. The important reasons are:

1. **Future Uncertainties:** Money receivable today is certain but money to be received tomorrow has an element of uncertainty. Nobody knows what will happen tomorrow. Because of this natural uncertainty related with future money today has more value than money of tomorrow.
2. **Inflation:** We all live in an inflationary environment. Inflation means that same money can buy more goods today than in future. That is, the purchasing power of money declines when inflation is present. Therefore, the money today is more valuable than money tomorrow.
3. **Preference for present consumption:** Most of us prefer consumption today than at a later date in future. There is a saying that a "bird in hand is better than two in the bush".
4. **Reinvestment:** We prefer money today than money tomorrow because we can invest today's money at the market interest rate and earn returns in future. For example if bank interest rate is 10% per annum for one year deposit then ₹ 1,000 invested today will become ₹ 1,100 next year. In this scenario, it is obvious that ₹ 1,000 of today will be more valuable than the same ₹ 1,000 of tomorrow.

After studying the reasons why money has time value let us understand the time value techniques that can help us in taking various financial decisions.

Let us take another example similar to the previous one in this chapter in which you had to decide between two different payment options. One option was having ₹ 10,000 today and the other option was taking ₹ 11,000 one year from now. In this scenario perhaps you will be indifferent between the options. You may opt for either of the choices because you think that the worth of ₹ 11,000 one year from now is same as worth of ₹ 10,000 today. Here ₹ 1000 (₹ 11,000 - ₹ 10,000) is the additional amount that you will be getting if you chose the second option. This additional ₹ 1000 is the amount, because of which, you consider that ₹ 11,000 to be received one year from now has the same worth as ₹ 10,000 of today. You are ready to accept the difference of one year between the two options because of this ₹ 1,000. **This ₹ 1,000 therefore is called the time value of money.**

In other words, the Time value of money is its rate of return, which the firm can earn by reinvesting its present money. This rate of return can also be understood as a **"required rate of return"** to make equal the worth of money of two different time periods.

But this example was simple enough. You could take the decision based on your gut feeling. In so many other situations, gut feeling may not be enough. You shall need a sound technique wherein you are able to compare the worth of money being received or paid at two different points in time. Also you would like to know "exactly" by how much amount tomorrow's money is **worth more** or **less than** today's money.

Fortunately, two such techniques are available for our rescue. They are known as techniques of compounding and discounting. In compounding, we find out the value of today's money for a future time period and then compare it with the future money. The technique of discounting is the opposite of it. In discounting, we find out what is the worth of tomorrow's money today and then compare it with today's money.

Let us understand it in detail. Take our example above. These two cash flows ("cash flow" means any payments or receipts) of ₹ 10,000 today and ₹ 11,000 tomorrow can be compared only after adjusting them in the following two ways. For the sake of understanding let's express "today" as time T_0 and "tomorrow" as time T_1.

So the only way these two payments can be compared is:

1) Expressing ₹ 10,000 in terms of worth of T_1. Or in other words, compounding it at the required rate of return.

   ₹ 10,000------- (**compounding** adjustment) ———→ ₹ 11,000

   T_0 ———————————————— T_1

2) Expressing ₹ 11,000 in terms of worth of T_0. Or in other words, discounting at the required rate of return.

   ₹ 10,000 ←——(**discounting** adjustment) ---------------------₹ 11,000

   T_0 ———————————————— T_1

The conclusion is that "monies of different time periods can be compared only after adjusting them by discounting or compounding them with reference to the required rate of return"

Let us now learn the techniques of compounding and discounting in greater detail. Before proceeding further, let us introduce some notations:

Value of money at time T_0 = "Present" value of money = PV

Value of money at time T_1 = "Future" value of money = FV

These concepts are not new. In fact if you recall your school level mathematics, you shall remember the concept of compound interest and simple interest. The concept of compound interest is being utilized to link the FV and PV.

The FV is nothing but the value of PV after a time gap. Due to the presence of interest rate or the required rate of return the FV can be calculated as PV plus interest earned during the given time gap.

2.1 Future Value of a Single Flow

Mathematically the relationship between FV and PV can be expressed in the form of an equation. Suppose time gap between FV and PV is given as "n" *time periods compounding in years, ½ years, quarter years, daily etc for* and the interest rate or required rate of return is given as "r" per *time period of compounding*, then the equation that links FV and PV is:

$$FV = PV(1+r)^n \quad \text{Equation (1)}$$

Here we should be clear about the *time period.* This time period can be one year, six months, three months or one day. Note that one year may be expressed as "annual" or "per annum", six months may be expressed as "half yearly", three months can be expressed as "quarterly" or "per quarter" and one day can be expressed as "daily" in practice.

Example 1: What is the future value of a sum of ₹ 10,000 five years from now, if the required rate of return is 12 per cent per annum?

Solution:

Here given PV = ₹ 10,000

n = 5 years

r = 12 % per annum

Putting these values in equation $FV = PV(1+r)^n$

$FV = 10{,}000(1+0.12)^5$

(Remember whenever percentages are used in mathematical calculations first they need to be converted in decimals by dividing them by 100, e.g., 12% will become 12/100 = 0.12)

$FV = 10{,}000(1.12)^5$

FV = 10,000(1.7623)

FV = ₹ 17,623

That means ₹ 10,000 become ₹ 17,623 in five years if the interest rate is 12 % per annum.

You might be wondering what actually is "compounding". In finance, compounding means the interest is paid not only on the original sum or PV or Principal, but also on the amount of interest earned each period.

Take the Example 1. In this example the time period given is in "years" and rate of interest is also given in terms of "per annum". What it means is that the compounding is done after every one year. In other words, interest is calculated for first year on the original sum or PV of ₹ 10000. Then this interest is added to the PV; and then the interest for second year is calculated on the total of PV plus first year's interest. For the third year again, the interest is calculated on PV plus first year's interest plus second year's interest. This process goes on until the given time duration of five years.

We can understand it better with the following table:

End of Year	PV (principal)	Interest @ 12%	Total
1	10,000	1,200	11,200
2	11,200	1,344	12,544
3	12,544	1,505	14,049
4	14,049	1,685	15,734
5	15,734	1,888	17,623

You may observe the following important features from this table:

1. Interest figure is changing for every year though the rate remains the same at 12%! How is this happening? It happens due to the process of compounding. For the first year interest is calculated only on the PV, i.e. ₹ 10,000 @ 12%. However, for the second year the interest has been calculated on ₹ 11,200 which is nothing but ₹ 10,000 plus the interest of first year ₹ 1,200. This process goes on for each of the remaining years.
2. Second important lesson is that PV for the year two is actually the FV (Or "Total") at the end of year 1.

In this example, it was not mentioned when the compounding is done. In the absence of information we assumed that it was done "annually" or per annum. Therefore, the time duration 5 years and rate 12 % per annum may be put straight away in our formula.

$$FV = PV(1+r)^n \qquad \text{Equation (1)}$$

Where n= number of time periods of compounding

r = interest rate or required rate of return per time period.

However, sometimes compounding may not be done annually but half yearly or quarterly or with some other frequency. In such cases, if the interest rate and time periods are given on annual basis then we cannot use them directly. First we need to convert them in terms of our equation.

The only change we have to make is to convert the time period given in terms of number of time periods of compounding and annual rate into rate per time period. This adjustment is done by using the following formula:

Number of time periods of compounding = time period given x frequency of compounding

Required rate of interest per time period = rate given/ frequency of compounding

After this we can straight away put these values in our equation. But before we proceed we should understand the frequency of compounding. It may be defined as number of times compounding is done in a year. Suppose the compounding is done annually then frequency will be 1. For other periodicities the frequency will be as follows:

Compounding Frequency	Frequency
Annual	1
Half Yearly	2
Quarterly	4
Monthly	12
Daily	365
Continuous	Infinite[1]

[1]For infinite compounding the formula is $FV = PVe^{rn}$, where e = 2.71828.

Example 2: Find out the future value of a sum of ₹ 15,000 after 5 years if the required rate of return is 16% and compounding is done quarterly.

Given PV = ₹ 15,000

Since compounding is done quarterly we cannot put the values of 5 years and 16% in our formula for n and r. Therefore we need to convert these values suitably for our formula.

Since compounding is done quarterly the frequency of compounding is 4.

No. of time periods n = time period x frequency of compounding

= 5 x 4

n = 20

Similarly, r = rate per annum/frequency of compounding

= 16/4

= 4 per cent

Putting these values in equation 1

$$FV = 15{,}000\,(1+ .04)^{20}$$

$$= 15{,}000\,(2.191)$$

$$= ₹\ 32{,}865$$

Now you might be wondering that this simple formula involves a lot of calculations! Do not worry. Help is at hand. There exist tables (given in the appendix of this book) which give you pre-calculated values of $(1+r)^n$ for different values of r and n. All you have to do is to ascertain what are your r and n, and refer the table for the value. Let's learn how we can do it.

For using these tables mentioned above, we will make a slight change in equation 1.

As per equation 1, $FV = PV\left(1+r\right)^n$

Here $(1+r)^n$ is the factor that when multiplied by PV, converts it into FV. We will call this factor as Future value interest factor or FVIF. We will write it in our formula as FVIF(r,n). Therefore our equation 1 now becomes:

$$FV = PV \times FVIF\left(r,n\right) \qquad \text{Equation (2)}$$

Where FVIF(r,n) is future value interest factor for r and n

Pre calculated values of FVIF are available in FVIF table in the appendix. The columns represent the various interest rates and the rows represent time periods. Suppose we want to find the value of FVIF for our example 2 above, we see that at quarterly compounding the values of r and n are 4 % and 20 respectively. Therefore we want to find out the value of FVIF (4%, 20).

So to obtain the value of FVIF (4%, 20) in the FVIF table first go down the first column and go to n = 20, then in front of this move horizontally, and stop at the value under 4% column. You will see that the value is 2.191.

Now straight away you can use this value in equation 2.

FV = 15,000 x FVIF (4%, 20)

= 15,000 x 2.191

= ₹ 32,865

2.2 Present Value of a Single Flow

The process of calculating present values is the reverse of the process of calculating future values. That means, we will learn that if we are given the future value of an investment, we will learn what amount of money should be invested today to realize that future value. This amount of money that must be invested today is called the **present value**.

What we are interested in is how to determine the amount of money that must be invested today, earning an interest rate of r for n periods, in order to produce a **specific future value**. This can be done by solving the future value equation no 1 given earlier:

As per equation no 1, $FV = PV\left(1+r\right)^n$

Rearanging we get

$$PV = \frac{PV}{\left(1+r\right)^n} \qquad \text{Equation (3)}$$

$$= FV(1+r)^{-n}$$

The term in brackets is equal to present value of Re 1; that is it indicates how much should be invested today, earning an interest rate of r, in order to have Re 1, n periods from now.

The process of computing the present values is also known as "discounting". Therefore, the present value is sometimes referred to as the **discounted value** and the interest rate is referred as **discount rate.**

Two things that must be remembered about present value is that, one, the greater the number of periods over which interest could be earned, the less amount must be invested today for a given future value to be received in future, i.e., the lower the present value. Two, the higher the rate that can be earned on any amount invested today, the less must be invested today to obtain a specified future value.

Again just like the future value tables, there exist present value tables to reduce unnecessary calculations. The formula in equation 3 can be converted as follows to be able to use the present value tables. (The procedure for finding values in present value tables for different values of r and n remain the same as future value.)

As per equation 3 $FV = PV\left(1+r\right)^{n}$

Replacing $(1+r)^{-n}$ with PVIF (r,n) we get,

$$PV = FV \; x \; PVIF\left(r,n\right) \qquad \text{Equation (4)}$$

Example 3

A father wants to keep ready a sum of ₹ 1,00,000 for his son's MBA education after three years when becomes a graduate. How much money he should invest now if the interest rate is 10 %.

Here the present value of ₹ 1,00,000 needs to be found out for r= 10% and n = 3 years.

Substituting these values in equation 4, we get:

PV = ₹ 1,00,000 x PVIF (10%, 3)

Looking up the value of PVIF (10%, 3) in the present value tables we get PVIF (10%, 3) = 0.751

PV = ₹ 1,00,000 x 0.751

= ₹ 75,100

That means ₹ 75,100 should be invested today at 10 % to obtain a value of ₹ 1,00,000 three years from now.

2.3 Effective Rate of Interest vs. Quoted Rate of Interest

Now, since we are familiar with the concept of compounding and different frequencies of compounding, we can see that if compounding is done more than once a year, then we get more interest than what we get if compounding is annual or once a year. This is so because when compounding is done more than once a year we earn interest on interest as well.

Now suppose you see two advertisements of a bank deposit. The advertisement says that the interest will be 12 per cent per annum compounded quarterly in bank A. The second advertisement says that the interest on deposit will be 12 per cent compounded annually in bank B. Since you are familiar with the concept of compounding now, your choice will be bank A. Why? Interest quoted by both the banks is the same 12% since compounding is quarterly in bank A, at the end of the year you will get more interest than bank B; which is also quoting the same interest rate but compounding annually.

We can find out exactly how much interest you will get in bank A. This "actual" interest that you will get is known as **effective rate of interest** or annual **percentage yield**.

If we represent effective rate of interest as r_e, then the formula is:

$$(1+r_e)=\left(1+\frac{r}{m}\right)^m \qquad \text{Equation (5)}$$

Where r_e = Effective rate of interest

r = nominal or quoted rate of interest per annum

m= number of compounding periods in a year

In our example of bank A, r = 12%, and m = 4 (compounding is quarterly), we can see that the value of r_e comes out to be 12.68%,by equation 5. So effectively the rate is higher than the quoted rate of interest.

Activity 1

Go to the nearest branch of any commercial bank. Get the savings schemes detais of Fixed and Recurring Deposits. Find out from the bank officer the frequency of compounding of interest rates. After that calculate the maturity value of a notional FD of ₹ 10000 after 1) One Year, 2) Two Years and 3) Five Years. Do the same with the Recurring Deposit scheme for a notional monthly sum of ₹ 1000 (After reading sec 1.5.3 below) . Also calculate the effective interest rate and compare them with the quoted interest rates. What do you observe?

2.4 Future Value of a Series of Equal Cash Flows (Annuities)

Having understood the calculation of future value of a single flow, now let's consider more than one flow. You must have heard of **recurring deposit scheme of banks**. In this scheme an equal amount of money is deposited at regular intervals (generally every month) and after a specified period (1 year or more), the depositor gets the money with interest.

This type of payment (or receipt) where an **equal amount is paid (or received) at regular intervals is known as annuity.** When the first flow of this series occurs at the end of one period from now, it is known as **ordinary annuity**. If the first flow occurs at the beginning of first period, it is known as **annuity due.**

First let's take the case of ordinary annuity. Graphically, an ordinary annuity can be represented as follows:

Example 4

Time	Year 0	Year1	Year2	Year3	Year 4
Flows		1,000	1,000	1,000	1,000

This is an example of ordinary annuity in which a flow of ₹ 1,000 occurs at the end of each year for four years. How can we find the value of this annuity at the end of four year as shown above, if the required rate of return is 14%? In other words, what is the future value of this stream of equal cash flows at the end of four years?

We can think of this annuity or a stream of cash flow as four different single cash flows of ₹ 1,000 each. In the preceding section we have learnt that how to calculate the future value of a single cash flow. Therefore if we calculate the future values of these four different single cash flows and add it , then we will obtain the future value of the annuity. We have calculated the values in the following table:

Year	Flow	FV formula	FV amount
0	Nil	-----	------
1	1,000	1,000 FVIF (14%, 3)	1,482
2	1,000	1,000 FVIF (14%, 2)	1,300
3	1,000	1,000 FVIF (14%, 1)	1,140
4	1,000	1,000 FVIF (14%, 0).	1,000
Total			**4,922**

So, the future value of the annuity in example above is ₹ 4,922.

There exist a shorter way of finding future value of annuity. We can simply use the formula

$$FVA = A\left[\frac{(1+r)^n - 1}{r}\right] \qquad \text{Equation (6)}$$

Where FVA = Future value of an ordinary annuity

A = Equal annual payments

r = interest rate per time period

n =number of time periods

In our example above, A = 1,000, r = 14% and n = 4 years, putting these values in equation 6, we get FVA = ₹ 4,922. Again we can see that calculations can get cumbersome with this formula. An easy way is to use.

There exist tables for annuity, just like we discussed in the previous section for a single flow. In the case of annuity, the multiple of $\left[\frac{(1+r)^n - 1}{r}\right]$ has been calculated at different combination of values of r and n. This factor can be expressed as FVIA (r, n). Then the formula in equation 4 becomes:

$$FVA = A\,x\,FVIA(r,n) \qquad \text{Equation (7)}$$

Where $FVIA(r,n) = \left[\frac{(1+r)^n - 1}{r}\right]$

The procedure of finding value of FVIA (r,n) remains the same as in case of the table of single flow. Now let us attempt to find the future value of annuity of our example above with the help of equation 7:

Here A = ₹ 1,000, r = 14% and n = 4

Substituting these values in equation 7, we get:00

FVA = 1,000 x FVIA (14%, 4)

From Appendix, the value of FVIA (14%, 4) is 4.922, putting this value in above equation we get:

FVA = ₹ 4,922 which is the same as obtained above.

As described above this was the case of ***ordinary annuity.*** However, when the first flow occurs at the beginning of the period then the annuity is known as **annuity due.**

The formula for finding the future value of annuity due is:

$$FVA_{due} = A\,x\,FVIA(r,n)\,x(1+r) \qquad \text{Equation (8)}$$

Sometimes, annual amount A grows by a fixed rate per year. This is known as growing annuity. In such a case the formula for future value of annuity becomes:

$$FVA_{Growing} = A_1\left[1-\left(\frac{1+g}{1+r}\right)^n\right] \qquad \text{Equation (9)}$$

Where g = growth rate in annual payments per period

A_1 = First annual payment

After discussing future value, let us understand the concept of sinking fund factor.

2.4.1 Sinking Fund Factor

Another concept related with future value of annuity is **"sinking fund factor"**. First, let us understand what is "sinking fund". As you will study in later chapters, when a company issues debentures, it has to redeem (repay) these debentures at the end of a given duration. In order to be able to meet this payment obligation, firm creates a sinking fund in which equal amount of money is deposited at regular intervals so that a pre determined sum can be withdrawn at the end of a specified period.

Simply put, sinking fund is a fund in which equal amount of money is deposited at regular intervals so that, after a given time period, the sum total of money deposited and interest on these deposits will equal a target amount .

Perhaps now you understand what a sinking fund is. Now the next question is what **"sinking fund factor"** is.

For , let's go back to equation 6.

$$FVA = A\left[\frac{(1+r)^n - 1}{r}\right]$$

We can rewrite this equation as:

$$A = FVA \Big/ \left[\frac{(1+r)^n - 1}{r}\right]$$

$$A = FVA \times \frac{r}{(1+r)^n - 1}$$

Here, the expression $\frac{r}{(1+r)^n - 1}$ is called **SINKING FUND FACTOR**.

We can also express sinking fund factor in a different way:

As per equation 7, $FVA = A \times FV1A(r,n)$

Or $A = FVA \times \frac{1}{FVIA(r,n)}$

Here the expression 1/FVIA (r,n) is called sinking fund factor.

$$A = FVA \times sinking\ fund\ factor(r,n) \qquad \text{Equation (7a)}$$

$$sinking\ fund\ factor = \frac{1}{FVIA(r,n)} \qquad \text{Equation (7b)}$$

Therefore, we can say that sinking fund factor is reciprocal of FVIA or future value interest factor for annuity.

If we put the value of FVA =Re 1. Then equation 7a becomes

$A = 1 \times sinking\ fund\ factor(r,n) = sinking\ fund\ factor$

Where A is equal periodic cash flows.

Therefore, sinking fund factor can also be defined as **the amount of money to be deposited in each period at an interest rate of r per period to get ₹ 1 at the end of n years.**

Example 5

What amount of money should be deposited each year to get ₹ 50,000 at the end of 5 years at 12% interest rate.

Let's find out sinking fund factor here

Sinking fund factor = 1/FVIA (r, n) = 1/FVIA (12%,5) = 1/ 6.353 = 0.1574

So by definition, we need to save ₹ 0.1574 each year to get Re 1 at the end of 5 years at 12%. So the amount of money to be deposited each year to get ₹ 50,000 = 50,000 * Sinking Fund Factor

= 50,000 * 0.1574 = ₹ 7,870.

2.5 Present Value of a Series of Equal Cash Flows (Annuities):

The procedure of finding out the present value of annuity is similar to that of future value. Let's consider the Example again.

Time	Year 0	Year 1	Year 2	Year 3	Year 4
Flows		1,000	1,000	1,000	1,000

Again, this is an example of ordinary annuity in which a flow of ₹ 1,000 occurs at the end of each year for four years. In the previous section we calculated the future value of this annuity at the end of four years, if the required rate of return is 14%?

Now, in this section, we will learn to calculate the value of this stream of cash flows at the beginning of four year period , i. e., at the point "year 0" or today. In other words, we wish to compute the present value of this stream of equal cash flows at the ***beginning*** of four years?

Again, just like the previous section, we can think of this annuity or a stream of cash flow as four different single cash flows of ₹ 1,000 each.In the preceding section 2.2, we have learnt that how to calculate the present value of a single cash flow. We can think of the annuity in this Example as a combination of four single cash flows occurring at the end of year 1, 2, 3 and 4 respectively. Therefore if we calculate the present values of these four different single cash flows and add it , then we will obtain the present value of the annuity. We have calculated the values in the following table:

Year	Flow	PV formula	PV amount
0	Nil	-----	------
1	1,000	1,000 PVIF(14%,1)	877.19
2	1,000	1,000 PVIF(14%,2)	769.47
3	1,000	1,000 PVIF(14%,3)	674.97
4	1,000	1,000 PVIF (14%,4)	592.08
Total			**2,914 Approx.**

So, the present value of the annuity in example above is ₹ 2,914.

You must be thinking that like previous cases, there must exist a shorter way of finding present value of annuity. You are right. The formula for directly obtaining the present value of annuity is:

$$PVA = A\left[\frac{(1+r)^n - 1}{r(1+r)^n}\right] \qquad \text{Equation (8)}$$

Where PVA = Present value of an ordinary annuity

A = Equal annual payments

r = interest rate per time period

n =number of time periods

In our example above, A = 1,000, r = 14% and n = 4 years, putting these values in equation 8, we get PVA = ₹ 2,913.70. Again we can see that calculations can get cumbersome with this formula. Do not worry. Here also help is at hand.

There exist tables for annuity, just like we discussed in the previous section for future value of annuity. In the case of present value of annuity, the multiple of $\frac{(1+r)^n - 1}{r(1+r)^n}$ has been calculated at different combination of values of r and n. This factor can be expressed as PVIA (r, n). Then the formula in equation 8 becomes:

$$PVA = A \times PVIA(r,n) \qquad \text{Equation (9)}$$

Where $PVIA\,(r,n) = \frac{(1+r)^n - 1}{r(1+r)^n}$

The procedure of finding value of PVIA (r,n) from the table in the appendix remains the same as in case of the table of FVIA(r,n).

Now let's attempt to find the present value of annuity of our example above with the help of equation 8:

Here A = ₹ 1,000, r = 14% and n = 4

Substituting these values in equation 8, we get:

PVA = 1,000 x PVIA (14%, 4)

From Appendix, the value of PVIA (14%, 4) is 2,914, putting this value in above equation we get:

PVA = ₹ 2,914 which is the same as obtained above.

Activity 2

Consider the present value of annuity obtained in the example given above (secion 2.4). Now consider this to be a single cash flow occuring today.Calculate the future value of this single flow after four years at an interest rate of 14%. Now compare your answer with the future value of annuity example in section 2.3.What do you observe?

As described above this was the case of ordinary annuity. However, when the first flow occurs at the beginning of the period then the annuity is known as annuity due.

The formula for finding the Present Value of annuity due is:

$$PVA_{due} = A x PVIA(r,n) x(1+r) \quad \text{Equation (10)}$$

Sometimes, annual amount A grows by a fixed rate per year. This is known as growing annuity. In such a case the formula for present value of growing annuity becomes:

$$PVA_{growing} = \frac{A}{r-g}\left[1-\left(\frac{1+g}{1+r}\right)^{n}\right] \quad \text{Equation (11)}$$

Where g = growth rate in annual payments per period

A = First annual payment

After discussing present value of annuity let us understand the concept of capital recovery factor.

2.5.1 Capital Recovery Factor

This is a concept similar to sinking fund factor. Capital recovery factor is the amount of money that can be withdrawn at the end of each period for n year, if Re 1 is deposited today at an interest rate of r% per year.

It is the reciprocal of PVIA (r,n).

As per equation 9: $PVA = AxPVIA(r,n)$

$$PVA = A \times PVIA(r,n)$$

We can rewrite it as: $$A = PVA * \frac{1}{PVIA(r,n)} = PVA * Capital\ Recovery\ Factor$$

So $$Capital\ Recovery\ Factor = \frac{1}{PVIA(r,n)}$$ Equation (10a)

Where $$PVIA(r,n) = \frac{(1+r)^n - 1}{r(1+r)^n}$$

Putting value of PVIA (r,n) in equation 10a, we get

$$Capital\ Recovery\ Factor = \frac{r(1+r)^n}{(1+r)^n - 1}$$

Example 6

Mrs. Nafeesa deposits ₹ 1,00,000 for five years at 12 % rate of interest. How much money in equal amounts can she withdraw each year so that she has nil balance left at the end of five years?

Let's find the Capital Recovery Factor first.

Capital Recovery Factor = 1/PVIA (r,n) = 1/PVIA (12%, 5) = 1/ 3.605 = 0.2774

That means if she deposits Re 1 today, then she can with draw Re 0.2774 each year for five years and her balance will be nil at the end.

Therefore, if she deposits ₹ 1,00,000 today she can with draw 1,00,000 * 0.2774 = ₹ 27,740 each year to leave nil balance at the end of five year period.

2.6 Present Value of A Perpetuity

Perpetuity is an annuity that does not end. It continues indefinitely. In real life there are **very few examples of perpetuity**. One example may be the irredeemable preference shares. As you will learn in later chapters, the preference shares carry a fixed rate of dividend each year. If they are irredeemable (Irredeemable means the issuing company will not repay the original investment of preference shareholder), they can be considered as an example of perpetuity.

How to find the present value of perpetuity? Let's consider the equation 8 again:

$$PVA = A\left[\frac{(1+r)^n - 1}{r(1+r)^n}\right]$$

This formula gives us the present value of annuity. Since, perpetuity is also an annuity with n=∞, we may rewrite the above equation as follows:

$$\text{Present Value of Prepetuity} = \lim_{n \to \infty} A\left[\frac{(1+r)^n - 1}{r(1+r)^n}\right]$$

$$\text{Present value of Prepetuity} = \frac{A}{r} \qquad \text{Equation (11)}$$

Example 7

An insurance company offers that on deposit of a sum X at the time of retirement, it will pay ₹ 10,000 annually as pension to a policyholder as long as he lives. If the interest rate is 10% per annum, what should be the value of X?

Since the company will pay ₹ 10,000 per annum indefinitely (we do not know how long the policy holder will live), it is a case of perpetuity. Therefore, the value of X will be nothing but the present value of the perpetuity. So putting values of A (₹ 10,000) and r (10%) in the equation 10, we get:

Present value of perpetuity (X) = 10,000/0.10 = ₹ 1,00,000.

Similarly, we may also find the present value of a growing perpetuity. If perpetuity is growing at the rate of g% per annum, the present value may be given by the following formula:

$$\text{Present value of growing Prepetuity} = \frac{A}{r-g} \qquad \text{Equation (12)}$$

Illustrative Solved Examples

1. **You invest ₹ 6,000 a year for 3 years and ₹ 8,000 a year for 7 years thereafter at interest rate of 15% p.a. What will be the maturity value at the end of 10 years?**

Solution:

This problem has two components, first is ₹ 6,000 deposited for three years. Then ₹ 8,000 deposited for 7 years.

Graphically we can show the cash flows as follows:

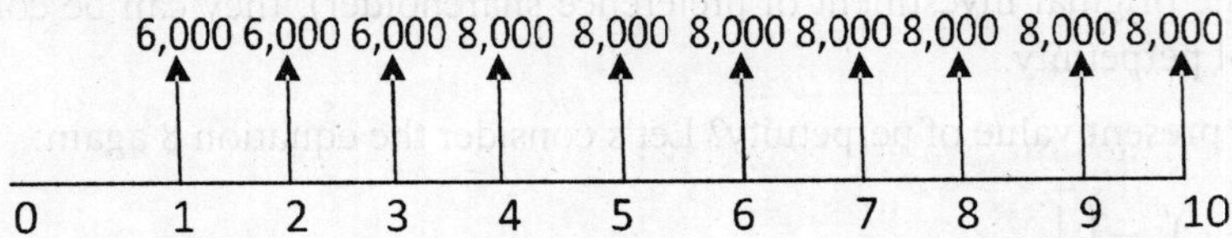

We have to find the value at maturity, i.e., future value at the end of 10 years. The *total future value* at any point is the sum total of all *component future values* taken together. Let us see what these *component future values* are:

1) Future value of an annuity of ₹ 6,000 at the end of three years.

2) Future value of value obtained in 1) at the end of 10 years.

3) Future value of ₹ 8,000 annuity, starting from the end of 4th year and ending at the end of 10th year.

We can find the answer by adding future values obtained in 2) and 3) above.

Let us calculate 1) first:

1) To find out value of ₹ 6,000 annuity at the end of three years, we will consider only the highlighted portion of the diagram above.

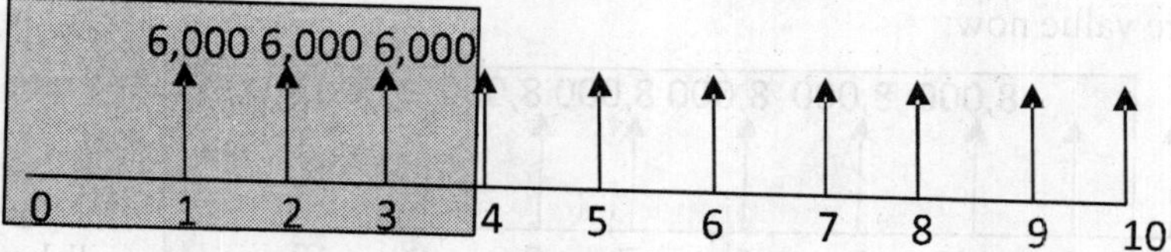

Now, it is simple to compute.

The formula for future value of annuity is:

$$FVA = A \times FVIA(r,n)$$

Putting A = ₹ 6,000 and r = 15% and n = 3 years, we get

$$FVA = 8{,}000 \times FVIA(15\%,7)$$

From future value of annuity table, we get the value of FVIA (15%, 3) = 3.473. Putting this value in equation above, we get:

$$FVA = 8{,}000 \times 11.067$$

We get FVA = ₹ 20,838

sNow let us calculate 2) as described above. The value of ₹ 20,838 obtained from 1) above can be considered as a lump sum at the end of three years. Graphically, we can show it as follows:

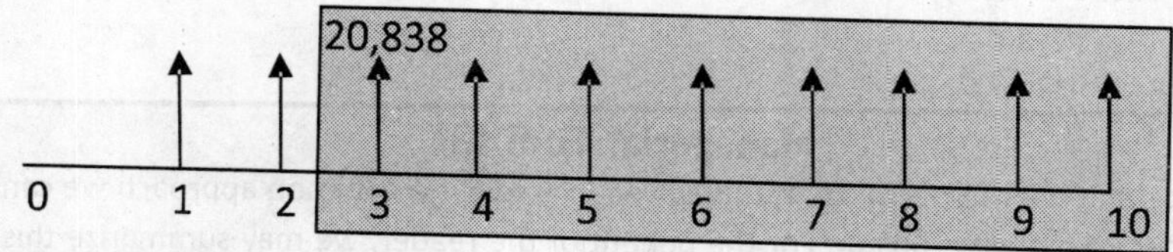

Now, we need to find the future value of ₹ 20838, beginning from end of three years till the end of 10 years, i.e., 7 years. As highlighted above in the diagram, we can use the formula:

$$FV = PV\ FVIF(r,n)$$

Putting, PV = ₹ 20,838 and r =15% and n = 7 years, we get

$$FV = 20{,}838\ FVIF(15\%,7)$$

Consulting the future value table for a lump sum in the appendix, we get FVIF (15%,7) = 2.660. Putting this value in above equation, we get,

$$FV = 20{,}838 \times 2.660$$

Solving, we get, FV = ₹ 55,429.08 (2)

Now , we just need to calculate 3) as described above. Graphically we can show that we need the following future value now:

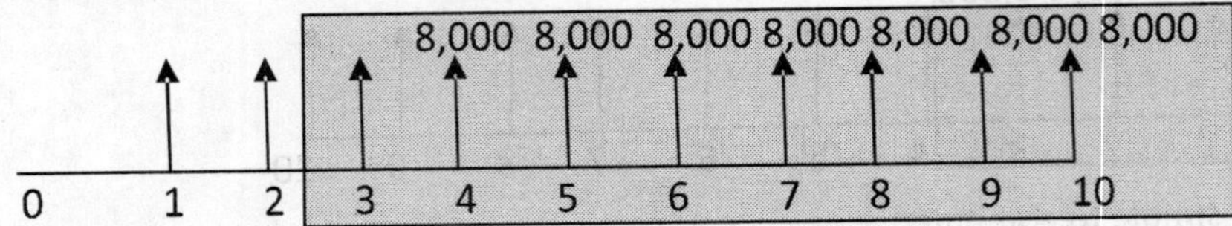

This again has become simple now. It is nothing but finding the future value of an annuity of ₹ 8,000 starting at the end of 4th year and ending at the end of 10th year, i.e., for 7 years.

We can easily use the formula:

$$FVA = A \times FVIA(r,n)$$

Putting values of A = 8,000, r = 15% and n =7 years, we get:

$$FVA = 8{,}000 \times FVIA(15\%,7)$$

Putting value of FVIA (15%,7) = 11.067 from the future value table, we get:

$$FVA = 8000 \times 11.067$$

FVA = ₹ 88536 (3)

Now, as discussed, our answer is the sum of 2) and 3) above. Therefore:

The maturity value of the given cash flow stream = ₹ 55,429.08 + ₹ 88,536 = ₹ 1,43,965.08

Managerial Tool Kit

Another learning that we can derive from this solved example is a common approach we can adopt for solving time value of money problem. For the benefit of the reader, we may summarize this approach as follows:

1) First, draw a timeline to show all the cash flows.
2) If the formula is directly applicable, then solve.
3) If the formula is not directly applicable, then break up the time line into separate components in such a way that we can apply a formula to each component individually.
4) Now solve and; to obtain the total value at any time point; add all the component values.
5) This approach is applicable to present as well as future value problems.

2. **You invest ₹ 15000 at the end of year 1, ₹ 20,000 at the end of year 2 and ₹ 50,000 at the end of each year from 3rd year to 10th. Calculate the PV of this stream if the discount rate is 10%.**

Solution:

We can solve this problem first by drawing a time line of all given cash flows:

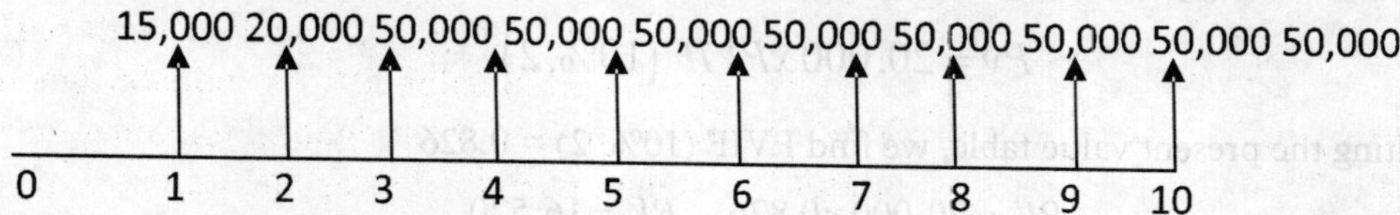

We have to find out the present value of all the cash flows at time 0.As we cannot directly apply any of the formula, we must figure out different components of present value. The desired answer can be arrived at by computing the sum total of :

1) Present value of ₹ 15,000 for one year
2) Present value of ₹ 20,000 for two years
3) Present value of annuity ,at the end of two years, of ₹ 50,000 starting from the end of 3rd year and ending at 10 years
4) Present value of the value obtained in 3) above considering it as a single flow happening at the end of two years.

Let us solve each one by one.

1) This is simple. We have to find the present value of ₹ 15,000. Graphically it can be shown as follows:

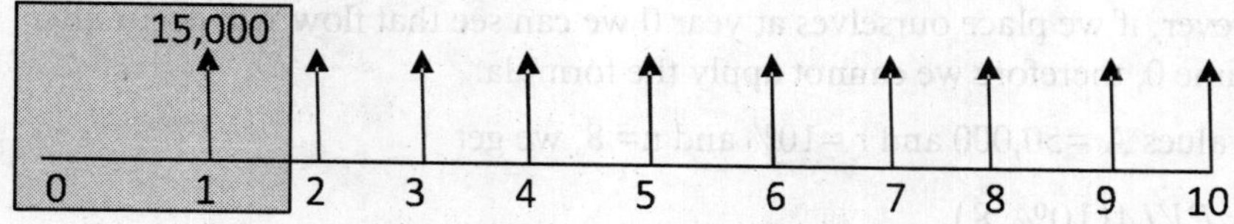

This can be found out by the formula , $PV = FV \, x \, PVIF\left(r,n\right)$

Putting, FV = 15,000, r = 10% and n =1, we get $PV = 15{,}000 \, x \, PVIF\left(10\%,1\right)$

Consulting the present value table for a single flow from the appendix, PVIG (10%,1) = 0.909

$$PV = 15{,}000 \, x \, 0.909$$

$$PV = 13635$$

2) For solving 2) as described above, the time line will look like as follows:

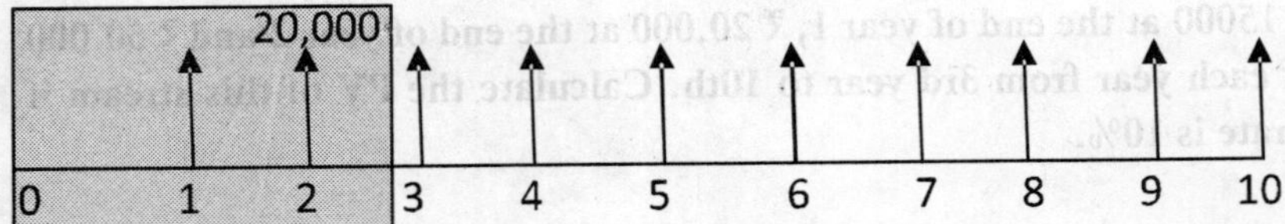

Just like 1), finding present value of ₹ 20000 for two years is simple.

$$Pv = 20,000\, xPVIF(10\%,2)$$

Consulting the present value table, we find PVIF (10%, 2) = 0.826

$$PV = 20,000\, x\, 0.826\ ,\ PV = 16,520$$

3) Now let us find out value as described in 3) above. The timeline will look like as follows:

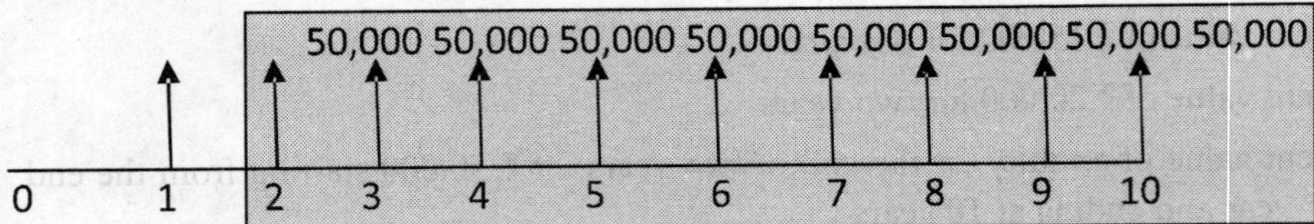

One important feature of the highlighted portion is that, we are trying to find the present value of this annuity at year 2 in the time line. Why cannot we get the present value of this ₹ 50,000 directly at year 0? It is because the formula for present value of annuity $PVA = A\, x\, PVIA(r,n)$ applies only when first cash flow in the annuity begins one year from now. If we are standing at year 2, then this condition is satisfied and we can apply the formula. However, if we place ourselves at year 0 we can see that flow will occur after three years from time 0, therefore we cannot apply the formula.

Now putting the values A =50,000 and r =10% and n= 8, we get

$$PVA = 50,000\, x\, PVIA(10\%,8)$$

Consulting the PVIA table in appendix, we get PVIA(10%,8) = 5.335, Therefore, PVA = 2,66,750

Now as described in 4) above, we have to find the present value of this sum of ₹ 2,66,750, considering it as a single flow happening at time 2.

4) Graphically, it can be showed as:

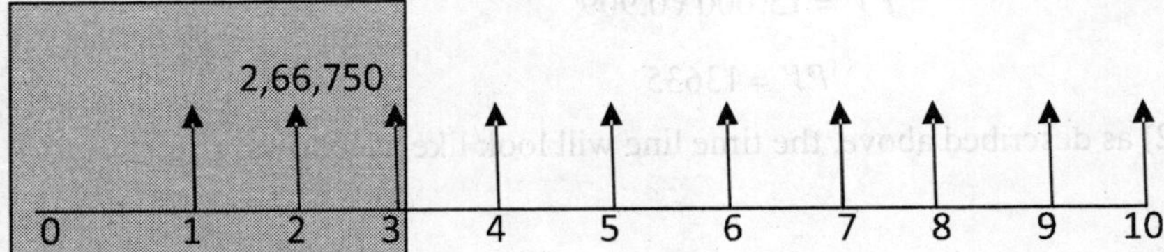

Here, we have to find the present value at time 0. We can compute it by the formula:

$$PV = FV\,x\,PVIF(r,n)$$

Putting FV = 266750 and r = 10% and n = 2, we get $PV = 2,66,750\,x\,PVIF(10\%,2)$

Now putting PVIF (10%, 2) = 0.826, we get, $PV = 2,66,750\,x\,0.826$ = **2,20,335.5**

As discussed already, our answer will be the sum total of values obtained in 1), 2) and 3). We get 13,635 + 16,520 + 2,20,335.5 = 2,50,490.50

This is the answer.

3. **Dr V P Singh is going to retire soon. His employer gives him two options; A lifetime annuity ₹ 25,000 for as long as he lives, or a lump sum amount of ₹ 2,00,000.If he expects to live for 20 years and Interest rate is 12%, which option is better for him?**

Solution:

Let us suppose Option A: Lifetime Pension of ₹ 25,000 per annum

Option B: Lump sum of ₹ 2,00,000

In order chose the better option between A and B, we will first calculate the present value of all the cash flows related to Option A and compare it with ₹ 2,00,000 of Option B. Needless to say that we will chose the option giving the higher present value.

So let us calculate the present value of Option A:

Here the cash flow is ₹ 25,000 per year for life time. But since Dr Singh expects to live for only 20 years, we will consider this cash flow as an annuity for 20 years.

We can compute the Present value of the annuity with the formula:

$$PVA = A\,x\,PVIA(r,n)$$

Putting A = ₹ 25,000, r = 12% and n = 20 years. We get:

$$PVA = 25,000xPVIA(12\%,20)$$

From PVIA table, PVIA (12%, 20) = 7.469 and solving, we get $PVA = Rs1,86,785$

So the present values of Option A = ₹ 1,86,785

Present value of Option B = ₹ 2,00,000

Obviously, Dr V P Singh should choose Option B since it offers higher present value.

4. **Atul is planning to buy 2,000sq ft land for ₹ 50,000 by taking a bank loan.He will repay it in 20 EMIs of ₹ 9,200. What compound interest rate shall he be paying?**

Solution

Since Atul is getting ₹ 50,000 today and will pay it back In annual instalments of ₹ 9,200 for 20 years. This is equivalent to an annuity of 20 years with cash flows of ₹ 9,200 per annum and present value as ₹ 50,000.

From the present value formula for annuity, we know that $PVA = A\,x\,PVIA(r,n)$

Putting PVA = ₹ 50,000, A = 9,200, n = 20 we get, 50,000= $9,200\,x\,PVIA(r,20)$

Solving, we get

PVIA (r, 20) = 5.4347

Now, we have to find the value of r from this equation. Till now we used to look up the value of PVIA in the table with given r and n. This time it's a little different. Now we have to find r, given PVIA and n. How do we do this?

For this, first we go to the PVIA table and go straight to the row containing the given number of years. This in our case is 20 years. In this row we move horizontally and reach the value of PVIA that is closest to the given PVIA value. Once we locate such PVIA value, we move upwards in the column containing that PVIA value and stop at the interest rate at the top of the column.

Let us go to the PVIA table in appendix and go to the row for 20 years. Now we see that PVIA = 5.4347 is not there. The closest value of PVIA that we observe is 5.628 at r= 17% and 5.353 at r = 18%.

That means, PVIA (17%, 20) = 5.628

PVIA (18%, 20) = 5.353

Since our value of PVIA = 5.4347 lies between 5.628 and 5.353, we can conclude that our that value of "r" that we are looking for also lies between 17% and 18%.

Now, we are just one-step short of our answer, i.e., the exact value of r.

We can calculate it by the following formula:

$$r = 17\% + \frac{PVIA(17\%,20) - PVIA(r\%,20)}{PVIA(17\%,20) - PVIA(18\%,20)}$$

Putting values, we get:

$$r = 17\% + \frac{5.628 - 5.4,347}{5.628 - 5.353}$$

Therefore, r = 17.70 %.

5. **How much do you need to invest now at interest rate of 11% p.a. to have a perpetual income of ₹ 22,000 from the beginning of the 15th year?**

Solution

The timeline for this problem looks like below:

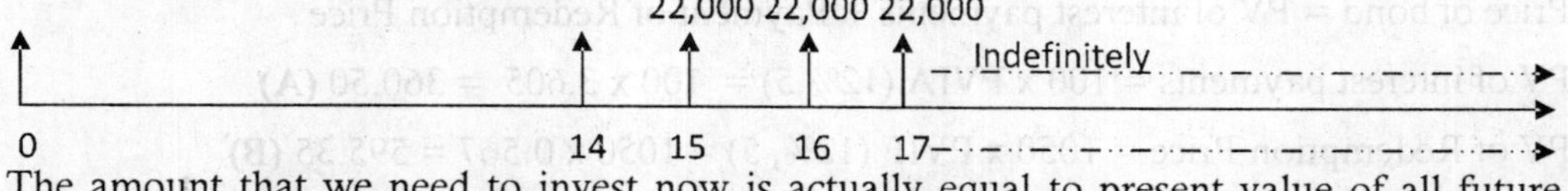

The amount that we need to invest now is actually equal to present value of all future cash flows that we will get back. We can find out this present value in two steps:

Step 1: Finding the present value of perpetuity of 2,200 at time 14.

Step 2: Finding the present value of the amount calculated above for fourteen years.

For step 1 we need to use the formula for present value of perpetuity, i.e.,

$$PVA_{Perpetuity} = \frac{A}{r}.$$

We are given, A = ₹ 22,000 and r= 11%, putting these values in equation, we get

$$PVA_{Perpetuity} = \frac{22,000}{0.11} = 2,00,000$$

Now in step 2, we will calculate the present value of ₹ 2,00,000 obtained above by considering it as a lump sum at time 14.We can compute this present value by $PV = FV\,x\,PVIF(r,n)$. Putting FV = ₹ 2,00,000, r = 11% and n = 14 years, we get $PV = 2,00,000\,x\,PVIF(11\%,14)$. Now Consulting the PV table in the appendix, we get PVIF (11%,14) =0.232, plugging this value in the equation we finally get

$$PV = 2,00,000\,x\,0.232$$

This is our answer, i.e., we need to invest ₹ 46,400 now in order to get a perpetual income of ₹ 22,000 indefinitely, beginning from 15th year.

6. **As a potential investor, you are considering the purchase of a bond that pays 10% per year on face value of ₹ 1,000. The bond will mature in 5 years at a premium of 5%. What price you should be willing to pay if you require 12% rate of return.**

Solution:

The price that we will be willing to pay will be nothing but the present value of all future payments that we will receive from our investment. We will get two types of payments.

First will be the interest component of 10% x ₹ 1,000 = ₹ 100 for five year beginning from the end of first year. Actually, it is nothing but an annuity of ₹ 100 for five years.

Second, at the end of five years the company will redeem our bond with a premium of 5% on the face value of ₹ 1,000. That means we will get a lump sum of ₹ 1,000+ 5% x 1,000 = ₹ 1,050 at the end of five years.

As already noted, the price of the bond is equal to sum total of present value of all future payments, we may write that:

Price of bond = PV of interest payments + Payment of Redemption Price

PV of interest payments = 100 x PVIA (12%,5) = 100 x 3.605 = 360.50 **(A)**

PV of Redemption Price = 1050 x PVIF (12%, 5) = 1050 x 0.567 = 595.35 **(B)**

Price of the bond = (A) + (B) = ₹ 955.85

7. You deposit ₹ 2,500 per year at the end of each year for next 20 years in an account that yields 10% p.a. How much you could withdraw at the end of each of the next twenty years following your last deposit.

Solution

We can arrive at the solution in a two-step procedure. First, we need to find the Future value of an annuity of ₹ 2,500 at the end of 20 years. Then considering this value as the present value at the end of 20 years, we need to obtain the annual installment of another annuity, again for 20 years.

As per step 1, we need the future value of an annuity of ₹ 2500 for 20 years at an interest rate of 10%. We can compute it by the formula $FVA = A\,x FVIA(r,n)$ putting values, we get $FVA = 2{,}500\,x\,FVIA(10\%,20)$ Solving, we get FVA = 1,43,187.50.

Therefore, we have accomplished the step 1. Now, as discussed, for step 2, we will consider ₹ 1,43,187.50 as present value of annuity of twenty years, beginning from the 21st year. We can accomplish this by the help of the formula. $PVA = A\,x PVIA(r,n)$.

Putting values, we get, $Rs\,14{,}31{,}87.50 = A\,x\,PVIA(10\%,20)$. Solving with the help from the present value for annuity table in the appendix, we get, $A = Rs\,16{,}818$.

8. A ₹ 20,00,000 plant expansion is to be financed as follows; 15% down payment and remainder is borrowed at 9% interest. The loan is to be repaid in 8 equal installments starting 4 years from now. Find the amount of each equal annual installment.

Solution

Given, 15% of ₹ 20,00,000 = 3,00,000 is paid as down payment.

Loan taken = 85% of ₹ 20,00,000 = ₹ 17,00,000

Graphically, we can show the problem as follows. Let us suppose that the firm has to pay eight installments of amount A to repay the loan completely.

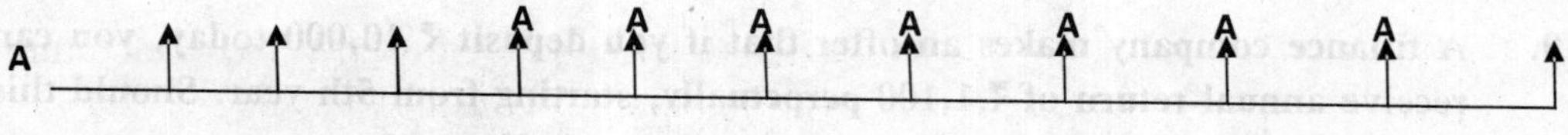

We may consider the amount of loan taken (₹ 17,00,000)as the present value at time zero. It will be equal to the present value of all payments made to repay it. But as we can see the formula for present value of annuity can not be directly applied. However, we may apply the formula in two steps.

Step 1: Finding the present value of annuity of equal amounts A at time point 3 (as shown graphically below)

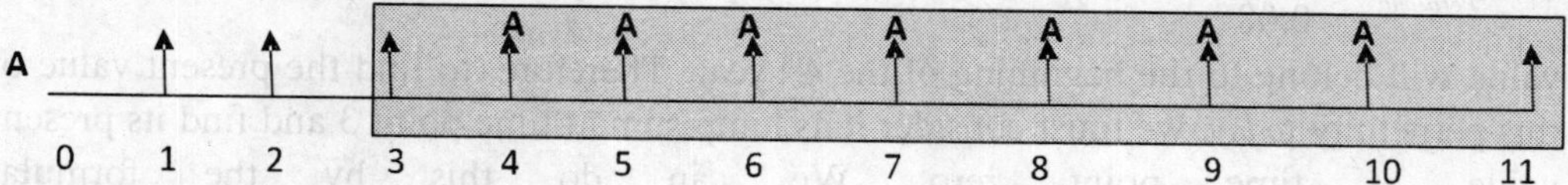

As we can see, now for the highlighted portion of the diagram, it is possible to apply the formula for present value of annuity. We know that $PVA = A\,x\,PVIA(r,n)$ **Putting values of r = 9% and n = 8, we get .**

$PVA = AxPVIA(r,n)$

Next, we can consider the PVA obtained above as a lump sum at time point 3. Now we can find the present value of this lump sum at time point 0. Graphically:

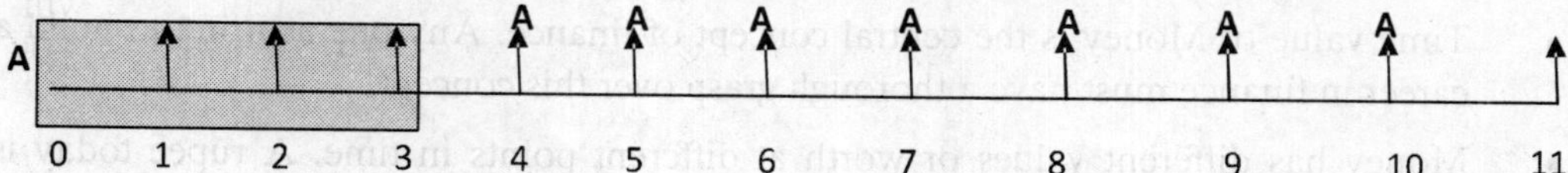

Now, we can find out the present value of a lump sum by the formula $PVA = AxPVIA(r,n)$.

Putting values of FV = $A\,x\,PVIA(9\%,8)$**, r = 9% and n= 3, we get**

$PV = A\,x\,PVIA(9\%,8)\,x\,PVIF(9\%,8)$

As discussed earlier, this PV will be equal to the amount of loan taken, i.e., ₹ 17,00,000. Therefore:

₹17,00,000 = $A\,x\,PVIA(9\%,8)\,x\,PVIF(9\%,8)$

Putting values of PVIA and PVIF from relevant tables from appendix and solving, we get $A =$ ₹397845.1

9. A finance company makes an offer that if you deposit ₹ 10,000 today, you can receive annual return of ₹ 1,100 perpetually, starting from 5th year. Should this offer be accepted if the rate of interest preference is 8% p.a.?

Solution

From the formula of present value of perpetuity, $PVA_{Perpetuity} = \frac{A}{n}$, we can find the present value of perpetuity. Putting the values A = ₹ 1,100 and r = 8%, we get, $PVA_{Perpetuity} = \frac{1,100}{0.08}$ = **₹ 13,750.** But since the perpetuity starts from 5th year, this present value will belong to the beginning of the 4th year. Therefore, to find the present value of this perpetuity *today,* we must consider it as lump sum at time point 3 and find its present value at time point zero. We can do this by the formula, $PV = FV \; x \, PVIF(r,n)$, where, FV = ₹ 13,750, r= 8% and n = 3 years. Substituting these values and solving we get PV =₹10,917.. Now this amount is higher than the amount of deposit that has to be made, i.e., ₹ 10,000.

Therefore, we may accept the offer since present value of inflows is higher than the present value of outflow.

Summary

- Time value of Money is the central concept of finance. Any one aspiring to build a career in finance must have a thorough grasp over this concept.
- Money has different values or worth at different points in time. A rupee today is worth more than a rupee tomorrow. The value of money will change with time.
- With the help of this concept, we can compare money received at different points of time in future.
- The reasons why money has time value are 1) Uncertainties related to future 2) Inflation leading to loss of purchasing power 3) Preference for present consumption 4) Opportunity to earn returns by investing money.
- Time value of money is the rate of return, which the one can earn by reinvesting one's present money. This rate of return can also be understood as a "required rate of return" to make equal the worth of money of two different time points.
- In order to find out the exact value of money at a point of time different from present, there are some techniques available. These are called techniques of compounding and discounting. In compounding, we find out the value of today's money for a future time period and then compare it with the future money. The technique of discounting is the opposite of it. In discounting, we find out what is the worth of tomorrow's money today and then compare it with today's money.

- Compounding and discounting both can be done for a lump sum as well as a series of payments.
- When cash flow occurs more than once a year, the effective rate of return will be higher than the quoted rate.
- Payment (or receipt) where an equal amount is paid (or received) at regular intervals is known as annuity. When the first flow of this series occurs at the end of one period from now, it is known as **ordinary annuity**. If the first flow occurs at the beginning of first period, it is known as **annuity due.**
- A concept related with future value of annuity is "sinking fund factor". Simply put, sinking fund is a fund in which equal amount of money is deposited at regular intervals so that, after a given time period, the sum total of money deposited and interest on these deposits will equal a target amount . Sinking fund factor can be defined as amount of money to be deposited in each period at an interest rate of r per period to get Re 1 at the end of n years. It is the reciprocal of FVIFA (r,n)
- Capital recovery factor is the amount of money that can be withdrawn at the end of each period for n year, if Re 1 is deposited today at an interest rate of r % per year. It is the reciprocal of PVIA (r, n).
- A special type of annuity is called Perpetuity. Perpetuity is an annuity that does not end. It continues indefinitely.

Test Your Understanding

State whether the following statements are true (T) or False (F)

1. Money has time value because a person forgoes something certain today for something uncertain tomorrow.
2. The uncertainty factor increases with time – the distant the cash flows, the more uncertain they become.
3. If the compounding period is lower, effective rate of interest is higher.
4. The interest rates tend to increase as inflation rises.
5. One of the reasons for money having time value is that individuals prefer future consumption to current consumption.
6. In case of annual compounding the nominal rate of interest is equal to the effective rate of interest.
7. For correct financial decisions it is essential to consider time value of money because most financial problems at corporate and individual level involves cash flows occurring at different points in time.
8. Given a principal amount of ₹ 15,000 to be invested for one year, it is better to invest in a scheme that offers 12% annual compound interest than investing in a scheme that earns 12% simple interest.

9. A bank that pays 14% interest compounded annually pays a higher effective rate of interest than a bank that pays 14% interest compounded quarterly.
10. The formula for effective rate of interest (re) is- $r_e = (1+r/m)^n - 1$.
11. A regular is defined as the one in which a series of equal periodic cash flows t occur at the beginning of each period.
12. Frequency of compounding does not affect interest earned.
13. Maximum effect of compounding is observed when money is compounded on a daily basis.
14. Present value of an unequal stream of cash flows can be calculated with the help of present value of annuity table.
15. While investing money it is always beneficial to obtain a higher frequency of compounding.
16. Increased frequency of compounding is equivalent to decrease in compounding period.
17. Effective rate of interest depends on the compounding period.
18. In simple interest, interest for each year in same.
19. The process of determining present value is often called discounting.
20. A perpetuity is an annuity that continues for 1,000 years.
21. The present value of any future sum is inversely related with rate of interest.
22. The compound value of any sum invested today varies directly with rate of interest (r) and time period (n).
23. Money has time value because a sum of money to be received in future is more valuable than the same amount today.
24. The process of compounding assumes discounting at same rate over the given time horizon.
25. Compounding over the same time period, ordinary annuity will have lower future value than annuity due.
26. Annuity tables can be used to handle all types of cash flows.
27. For a given rate of interest(r) and given number of years (n), the present value annuity factor will be greater than future value annuity factor.
28. In future value tables, all values are greater than 1.
29. Present value of annuity due is equal to present value of ordinary annuity x (1 + r).
30. The price of any asset today is the present value of the entire cash flow stream associated with the asset.
31. An annuity is defined as a stream of constant cash flows occurring at regular intervals of time.
32. A perpetuity is an annuity that continues for ever i.e., till infinity.

33. The present value of a mixed stream of cash flows is the sum of the present values of the individual cash flows.

Answers : 1.T, 2. T, 3. T, 4. T, 5. F, 6. T, 7. T, 8. F, 9. F, 10. F, 11. F, 12. F, 13. F, 14. F, 15. T, 16. T, 17. T, 18. T, 19. T, 20. F, 21. T, 22. T, 23. F, 24. T, 25. T, 26. F, 27. F, 28. T, 29. T, 30. T, 31. T, 32. T, 33. T

Multiple Choice Questions

Choose the correct alternative out of the given

1. The compound interest on ₹ 8,000/- for 5 years at 12% compounded yearly is: **(UPTU, 2009)**

   a) ₹ 4,900 b) ₹ 5,100

   c) ₹ 6,100 d) ₹ 5,500

2. Time value of money arises from :

   a) preference of future consumption to present consumption.

   b) Certainty of Money today than money tomorrow

   c) Higher worth of money today than money tomorrow in terms of purchasing power.

   d) Possibility of earning risk free return on money invested today.

   e) (b), (c) and (d) above.

3. Given an investment of ₹ 50,000 for a period of one year, it is better to invest in a scheme that pays:

   a) 15% interest compounded annually b) 15% interest compounded quarterly

   c) 15% interest compounded monthly d) d. 15% interest compounded daily

4. Give the compounded value of ₹ 1000 invested @ 10% p.a. for three years **(UPTU 2010)**

   a) ₹ 1,000 b) ₹ 2,000

   c) ₹ 1,331 d) None of the above

5. To find the present value of a sum of ₹ 1,00,000 to be received at the end of each year for the next 10 years at 15% rate, we use:

   a) Present value of a single cash flow table b) Present value of annuity table.

   c) Future value of a single cash flow table d) Future value of annuity table

6. Sinking fund factor is the reciprocal of:

   a) Present value interest factor of a single cash flow.

   b) Present value interest factor of an annuity.

   c) Future value interest factor of a single cash flow.

d) Future value interest factor of an annuity.

7. If the effective rate of interest compounded quarterly is 16%, then the nominal rate of interest is :

   a) 14.6% b) 15%

   c) 14.8% d) 15.12%

8. If the interest rate on a loan is 1% per month, the effective annual rate of interest is :

   a) 12% b) 12.36%

   c) 12.68% d) 12.84%

9. If a loan of ₹ 30,000 is to be paid in 5 annual installments with interest rate of 12% p.a. then the equal annual installment will be;

   a) ₹ 7,400 b) ₹ 8,100

   c) ₹ 7,812 d) ₹ 8,322

10. X took a housing loan of ₹ 20,00,000. The loan is to be redeemed in 120 monthly installments of ₹ 25,000 each to be paid at the end of each month. What is the implicit interest rate per annum.

    a) 8.68% b) 8.50%

    c) 9.70% d) 9.25%

11. The difference between effective annual rate of interest with monthly and quarterly compounding, when nominal rate of interest is 15% is;

    a) 0.16% b) 0.17%

    c) 0.29% d) 0.21%

12. A bond has a face value of ₹ 10,000 and a coupon rate of 10%. It will be redeemed after 4 years at 10% premium. Find the present value of bond at a required rate of 12:

    a) ₹ 10,020.80 b) ₹ 9,600.72

    c) ₹ 9,800.84 d) ₹10,200.12

13. State bank offers 12% nominal interest for a three year fixed deposit to senior citizens. If the compounding is done quarterly, then effective annual rate of interest is :

    a) 12.25% b) 12.55%

    c) 12.46% d) 12.52%

14. Ram Kumar deposits ₹ 2,000 at the end of every month in a bank for 5 years. If the interest rate offered by bank is 8% p.a. compounded monthly, the accumulated sum Ram Kumar will get after 5 years will be:

    a) ₹ 1,96,802 b) ₹ 1,46,953

c) ₹ 1,41,507 d) ₹ 1,24,752

15. You invest ₹ 1,500 at the end of year one and ₹ 2,000 at the end of second year and ₹ 5,000 each year from third to tenth. Find the present value of stream at discount rate of 10%
    a) ₹ 25,062 b) ₹ 24,712
    c) ₹ 26,502 d) ₹ 24,242
16. If you take a loan of ₹ 1,00,000 today and return ₹ 1,41,170 after 4 years to clear off the loan, what effective annual interest rate is paid by you:
    a) 12% b) 10%
    c) 9% d) 12.8%

Answers : 1. c , 2. e, 3. d, 4. c, 5. b, 6. d, 7. d, 8. c, 9. d, 10. a, 11. d, 12. a, 13. b, 14. b, 15. a, 16. c

Practice Problems

1. If Avinash deposits ₹ 1, 50,000 now a company is offering to pay ₹ 20,000 annually for a period of 10 years. What is implicit interest rate in this offer?
2. Assume an annual rate of interest of 15%. Deepshikha has a debt to pay and bank has given her a choice of paying ₹ 1,000 now or some amount X five years from now. What is the maximum amount X can be for her to be willing to shift payment for five years?
3. Sunil has deposited ₹ 2, 00,000in a bank that pays interest @ 8% p.a. How much can he withdraw at the end of every year for a period of 25 years, so that there is no balance left in the end?
4. In order to accumulate ₹ 25,000 at the end of 10th year, how much you should invest at the beginning of each year if r = 10%?
5. You have borrowed a car loan of ₹ 50,000 from your employer. The loan requires 10% interest and five equal year end payments. Draw up a loan amortization schedule.
6. Calculate the PV of an annuity of ₹ 5,000 receivable for 35 years, if the first receipt occurs after 15 years. Take discount rate as 12%.
7. Akshay takes a bank loan of ₹ 10,000 to purchase a scooter. He has to pay an installment of ₹ 500 p.m. for next 2 years. What is the implied interest rate?
8. You deposit a sum of ₹ 10,000 with a bank at 12%. If you want to withdraw ₹ 1,500 every year, for how long can you do this?
9. Ten years from now Mr. X will start receiving a pension of ₹ 3,000 a year. The payment will continue for 16 years. How much is the pension worth now at 10%?

10. A deposit is made in a bank that earns 10% compounded half yearly. It is desired to withdraw ₹ 50,000 three years from now and ₹ 70,000 five years from now. What is the size of initial deposit?
11. You want to buy a new television for ₹ 10,000 on an installment basis. A shopkeeper offers to you that you can make the payment at 13% per annum in four yearly installments as follows:

Principal	₹ 10,000
Interest of 4 years	₹ 5,200 (10,000 x 0.13 x 4)
Total	₹ 15,200
Installment	₹ 15,200/4 = ₹ 3,800

What interest rate is being earned by the shopkeeper?
12. You want to buy a house costing ₹ 20 lakh. You approach a housing finance company and finance 50% of cost. Finance company charges interest @ 1% per month. You can pay ₹ 12,000 per month towards loan amortization. Calculate maturity period of loan. For installment No. 72, calculate interest portion and principal portion.
13. A company has debentures of ₹ 50 lakh to be repaid after 7 years. How much should the company invest in a sinking fund earning 12% in order to be able to repay debentures?
14. Abhijeet borrows ₹ 80,000 for a music system at a monthly interest rate of 1.25%. The loan is to be repaid in 24 equal monthly installments, payable at the beginning of each month. Calculate the amount of each installment.
15. You deposited ₹ 70,000 in your Recurring Deposit A/C for 15 years at 8% interest. How much you will get on maturity.
16. Shailesh would need ₹ 100, 5 years from now. How much amount should he deposit he should make in his bank account if the interest rate is 10% per annum.
17. A finance company offers to triple your money in 10 years. What is the effective rate of interest implicit in the offer?
18. The EPS of Accent Ltd. was ₹ 3 ten years ago. Today it stands at ₹ 4.02. What is the compounded annual growth rate the firm has achieved?
19. A company has advertised that it can take any person to moon at a cost of ₹ 100 Lakhs. I can save ₹ 5 lakhs every year. How long I will have to wait if my savings earn interest @ 12% p.a. Assume that the company shall not increase its price tag.
20. Mr. X borrows ₹ 1, 00,000 at 8% interest. Equal annual payments are to be made for 6 years. However, at the time of 4th payment, X decides to pay off the entire loan. Find equal annual installment. Also, calculate the amount to be paid at the end of 4th year.

21. Devesh wishes to accumulate ₹ 80,00,000 by the end of 5 years by making equal annual deposits at the end of each year over the next 5 years. Assuming 7 percent rate of return, how much should he deposit at the end of each year to accumulate ₹ 80,00,000.

Answers : 1. 5.6%, 2. ₹ 2,011.36, 3. ₹18,736, 4. ₹ 1,426, 6. ₹8,364, 7. 18.15%, 8. 14.2 years, 9. ₹9,954, 10. ₹80,285, 11. 19.14%, 12. 180 months, ₹7, 964, ₹4, 054, 13. ₹4.96 lakhs, 14. ₹3,831, 15. ₹19,00,648, 16. ₹ 16.38, 17. 11.61%, 18.3%, 19.10.8 years, 20. ₹21, 631.53, ₹60,206, 21.₹ 1,39,106

Review Questions

1. Why does money have time value? Discuss.
2. Explain how "Time Value of Money" is applied in taking financial decisions? **(UPTU 2006)**
3. "Cash flows of two years in absolute terms are incomparable". Give reasons in support of your answer.
4. Explain Annuity, PV factor and Perpetuity with reference to Investment and Financing decision.
5. Explain the difference between effective rate of interest and nominal rate of interest with the help of a suitable example.
6. What role does "compounding" play in time value of money? Give an example to illustrate the power of compounding.
7. Explain
   (i) "Money has no time value" **(DU)**
   (ii) Techniques of compounding and discounting and identical. **(DU)**

References

1. Brealey, Richard A & Myres, Stewart C. (2007), Tata McGraw Hill, New Delhi
2. ICAI study Material on Financial Management, The Institute of Chartered Accountants of India, New Delhi.
3. Khan, M Y & Jain (2007) P K, Financial Management, Tata McGraw Hill, New Delhi
4. Pandey, I M (2009). Financial Management, Vikas Publishing House, New Delhi
5. Van Horne, James C. (2007), Pearson Prentice Hall, New Delhi
6. Website of Institute of Certified Financial Planners, New Delhi
7. Work book on "Financial Management for Managers": The Institute of Chartered Financial Analysts of India, Hyderabad.

CHAPTER  Risk & Return Analysis

Learning Objectives:

By the end of this chapter and having completed the essential reading and activities, you should be able to:

- Understand the Concept of Return of a single asset
- Know the different ways in which returns are understood
- Understand Risk and handle its measures in case of a single asset
- Compute return in portfolio context
- Measure risk in portfolio context
- Decompose portfolio risk into its components
- Have working knowledge relationship between Risk and Return
- Have introductory understanding of Capital Asset Pricing Model

3.0 Introduction

Risk and Return are most fundamental concepts of finance. It is vital that we have a crystal clear understanding of these. Let's start with the Return first:

3.1 Return of a Single Asset

What does return mean to a layman? Most probably, to anyone, return represents what one gets over and above one's initial investment. Let's take an example.

Suppose you buy a house today for ₹ 10,00,000Since you don't need it for living yourself, you decide to rent it out. You get a tenant ready to pay ₹ 6,000 per month as rent. This arrangement works fine for one year. However, at the end of the year you get a foreign job offer and you are wondering who will take care of the house when you are gone. You decide to sell the house before you leave. You get a buyer and strike a deal. You sell the house for ₹ 12,00,000. Now can you calculate your total Rupee return from this transaction of buying and selling the house?

Initial investment: ₹ 10,00,000

Rent Received : ₹ 72,000 (₹ 6,000 for 12 months) (x)

Profit due to increase in price of asset: Sale Price – Purchase Price

₹ 12,00,000- ₹ 10,00,000

₹ 2,00,000 (y)

Total Rupee Return from the house= Rent Earned during the year+ Change in Price

= (x) + (y)

=₹ 72,000 + ₹ 2,00,000

=₹ 2,72,000

We can see that on an investment of ₹ 10,00,000 the house has given you a total rupee return of ₹ 2,72,000 . In this amount ₹ 72,000 come from cash income earned from the house and ₹ 2,00,000 come from the change in the price of the asset. It may be noted that in this particular example the change in the price of the asset is positive therefore you make a profit on sale. It is also possible that at the time of sale you do not get a buyer willing to pay more than ₹ 9,50,000 for the house!

If this happens, then rather than profits, you will incur a loss on sale. And your total rupee return will be calculated as follows:

Total Rupee Return= Rental Income + Change in Price

= ₹ 72,000 (as before) + {₹ 9,50,000(sale price)-₹ 1,00,000 (purchase price)}

= ₹ 72,000-+ (- 50,000)

(-50,000 means you have incurred a loss of ₹ 50,000 due to change in price)

Total Rupee Return = ₹ 22,000

This is a simple example of a house. But if you understand this example, you will be able to understand the concept of return for any type of asset, viz. shares, bonds, deposits etc.

Let's put our learning from the example in a generalized form that shall apply to any type of asset.

Going back to our example we can write that:

Total Rupee Return from House = Rental Income + Change in Price (also known **as "Capital gain/Loss)**

Generalizing the above for any type of asset:

Total Rupee Return from an asset = Cash Income from asset + Capital Gain/Loss (z)

Most of the time we would like to know how our return fares vis a vis our investment. For this purpose, we need a measure that compares our rupee returns with our initial investment. This is obtained by "percentage returns". **"percentage returns" is nothing but Total Rupee Return expressed as a percentage of our initial investment.**

% Return = Total Rupee Return x 100 / Initial Investment- (z')

In our house example; percentage return will be ₹ 2,72,000x100/₹ 10,00,000 = 27.2%

Now look carefully at the equation (z). The first component of the return is cash income. In case of the house it was rental income received from the house. In case of other assets the cash income shall be:

Asset	Cash Income
House Property	Rent
Shares	Dividend
Debentures	Interest

The capital gains/losses will simply be the difference between the sale price and purchase price in case of all assets.

What can we conclude from the above?

1. Total Rupee return from an asset has two components. First, the cash income and second the Capital Gains/Losses.
2. If we divide total rupee returns by our initial investment and multiply by 100, we get % return.

% returns can also be divided into two components. Consider equation z' again:

% Return = Total Rupee Return x 100 / Initial Investment

= (Cash Income + Capital gain or loss) x100/Initial Investment

$$= \frac{Cash\ Income \times 100}{Initial\ Investment} + \frac{(Capital\ Gain\ or\ Loss) \times 100}{Initial\ Investment}$$

= Income Yield + Capital gains/loss yield

This is another way of expressing total % returns.

3.1.1 Average Rate of Return

Till now we were considering the income and capital gains earned during a one year period. What if we hold the asset for more than year? Let's say five years. In this case we can calculate returns for each year by the previous method. Lets say we get the returns R_1, R_2,R_3, R_4,R_5 for each of the five year period. What is the average annual return that we earned?

Average annual Return= Sum of R_1, R_2, R_3, R_4,R_5/ 5

Or more generally, Average annual return for R_1, R_2, R_3, ...R_n will be expressed as

Average annual return $\frac{1}{n}\sum_{i=1}^{n} R_i$

3.1.2 Holding Period Returns and Compounded Annual Return

Suppose you hold an asset for four years and in each of the year you have earned 12%, 6%, 14% and 11% returns annually. Now you want to know your overall returns for the total period for which you hold the asset (In this case its 4 years). This return is known as **"Holding Period Return"**.

Holding period return is calculated as follows:

Suppose you had invested one rupee at the beginning four years ago. Each year you earned 12%, 6%, 14% and 11% returns respectively. At the end of four years the amount of one rupee grows like this:

Beginning: ₹ 1

Value at the end of one year= Initial investment (1+ 0.12) = 1(1.12) = 1.12

Value at the end of two years = 1.12 (1+0.06) = 1.1872

Value at the end of three years = 1.1872 (1+0.14) = 1.3534

Value at the end of four years = 1.3534 (1+0.11) = 1.5022

We can calculate the above directly also from the following:

Value at the end of four years = (1+0.12) (1+0.06) (1+0.14) (1+0.11) = 1.5022

If we subtract our initial investment of ₹ 1 from our total value after four years, i.e., 1.5022, we get

0.5022 or 50.22% returns. This is our holding period return for a period of four years.

However, we may be interested in knowing what was our Compounded annual return if we earned 50.22 % return in four years? This can be calculated by obtaining the ***geometric mean*** of returns as follows:

$$\text{Compounded annual return} = \sqrt[4]{(1+0.12)(1+0.06)(1+0.14)(1+0.11)} - 1$$

$$= 0.1071 \text{ or } 10.71\ \%$$

3.2 Risk

Risk is something that we all are familiar with. In our day to day lives, we face different types of risks . We take necessary precaution to manage these risks as well. For example, in rainy season we carry an umbrella when we go to the market. This is to prevent the risk of getting wet if it rains. When we travel, we hide some cash secretly in our clothes for use in case our pocket is picked etc.

How can we define risk? Risk is the possibility that the actual outcome will be different from the expected outcome. Actual outcome can happen in three ways. One, it is exactly like the expected outcome. In this case there is no risk. Two, the actual outcome may be worse than the expected outcome. Three, the actual outcome may be better than the expected outcome. Situation two and three are the situations involving risk.

But here you may be wondering that in situation three, the actual outcome is better than the expected outcome, so why it is also considered as risk? The answer is that "Risk" includes both the scenarios, i.e., BETTER ACTUAL OUTCOMES AND WORSE ACTUAL OUTCOMES. When actual outcome is better than the expected it is called "upside" risk. When it is worse, then we call it "downside" risk.
While studying risk and risk management, we generally focus on "downside" risk.

Often you hear the term "uncertainty". What is uncertainty? Is it the same as Risk?

No it is not. We must have clear idea of difference between certainty, uncertainty and risk. Certainty is a situation where there is a 100% chance of happening of something. **Risk** is a situation where it is known that there might be many outcomes possible, each having different probabilities. However, we do not know which of these outcomes will actually take place.

On the other hand, **uncertainty** is a situation when even the probable outcomes are not known i.e. we are absolutely clueless about what is going to happen.

Though we must have a clear idea about the distinction between risk and uncertainty, in real life often both these terms are used to convey the same meaning.

Talking about risk, the risk does not depend only on the different probabilities of each possible outcome. It also depends on the magnitude of each outcome. In the following sections, we shall study the measurement of risk.

3.2.1 Risk of a single asset

Carefully look at the table below. It contains five years past annual returns for two companies A and B. If you want to invest in either of these which one will you prefer?

Year	Company A	Company B
2006	20%	14%
2007	3%	16%
2008	18%	13%
2009	10%	15%
2010	24%	17%
Average Return	*15%*	*15%*

So both the companies' average past return is 15%. But perhaps you chose company B. Why? When in the past both the companies have offered equal average rate of return why should we prefer B over A? This means there is something more than just the return that has affected our decision.

Look closely at the pattern of past return of both the firms. In case of firm A the returns have been fluctuating wildly year by year. The returns of company A have fluctuated between 3% and 22%. Whereas in case of firm B, the returns have moved in a very narrow corridor, ranging between 13% and 17%. Therefore, since the past average returns of both the firms are the same, it is the variability of returns in firms has affected our choice and we have chosen firm B over firm A. In other words, if two different firms are offering same returns, then a rational investor shall prefer the firm whose returns have less variability over time.

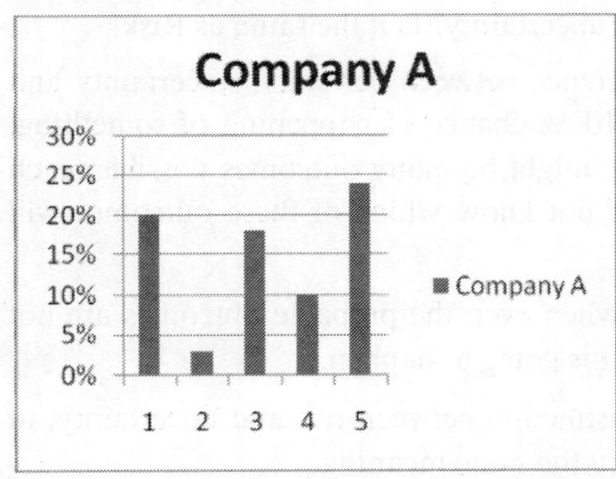

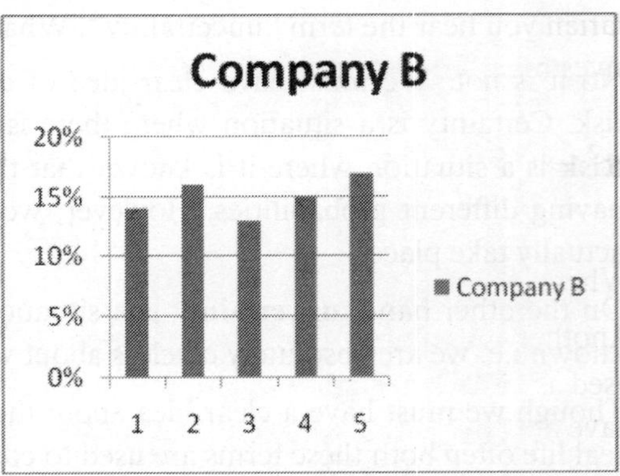

This variability of returns is what is known as risk in the world of finance. Risk is also defined as **the possibility that the actual outcomes shall be different from the expected outcomes.** The greater the variability, the greater is the risk associated with the particular investment.

In case of the example above, you could assess variability just by visual inspection. However, it is not always the case. When the data points are large or, on visual inspection, variability looks more or less equal between different companies, we need a measure to calculate exactly the variability of returns of each option.

Since variability represents the riskiness of an asset, the measures to calculate variability shall be used as a measure of risk.

Most commonly, there are three measures used to compute variability or risk of investments.

First is called the **Range** (Remember your statistics class in the previous semester.) Range is defined as the difference between the highest and lowest values in a data set. For instance, in the example above what is the range of returns of firm A and firm B?

	Company A	**Company B**
Highest Return	22%	17%
Lowest Return	3%	13%
Range (Highest-Lowest)	19%	4%

As expected, the firm A has a range of 19% where as the firm B has a range of 4%. Since higher the value of range higher is the variability, we can conclude that investment in company A is riskier than company B.

Though range is pretty simple to compute it suffers from many limitations. The biggest shortcoming of range as a measure of risk is that it takes into account only the extreme values and does not capture the information contained in the other remaining values. This leads to incorrect results sometimes.

Another measure that does not suffer from this limitation of range is known as the variance. It is represented by σ^2. If R_1, R_2, R_3, ...R_n are past returns of an investment for n years, the variance shall be computed as follows:

$$\sigma^2 = \frac{1}{n-1}\sum_{1}^{n}\left(\overline{R} - R_i\right)^2 \qquad \text{Equation (*)}$$

Where $\overline{R}$ is the average or mean return.

Another measure of risk which is more intuitively appealing and perhaps most widely used is called standard deviation. Standard deviation is represented by σ. Perhaps you have already guessed, it is nothing but square root of variance.

$$Standard\ deviation(\sigma) = \sqrt{Variance(\sigma^2)}$$

From equation (*) we can write that :

$$\sigma = \sqrt{\frac{1}{n-1}\sum_{1}^{n}\left(\overline{R} - R_i\right)^2}$$

Let's find out the values of variance and standard deviation for our example above. The standard deviation of firm A shall be as follows:

$$Variance\ A = \frac{1}{4}\{(15-20)^2 + (15-3)^2 + (15-18)^2 + (15-10)^2 + (15-24)^2\}$$

$$\sigma_A^2 \ = \ 0.71\%^2 \quad \underline{Yields} \quad \sigma_A = 8.43\%$$

Similarly for company B

$$Variance\ B = \frac{1}{4}\left\{(15-14)^2 + (15-16)^2 + (15-13)^2 + (15-15)^2 + (15-17)^2\right\}$$

$$\sigma_B^2 \ = \ 0.02\%^2 \quad \underline{Yields} \quad \sigma_B = 1.58\%$$

We can summarize the above as follows:

	Company A	Company B
Average Return	15%	15%
Range	19%	4%
Variance	$0.71\%^2$	$0.02\%^2$
Standard Deviation	8.43%	1.58%

We can clearly see that that company A has higher riskiness than company B. Our conclusion is supported by all the three measures of risk.

3.2.1.1 Historical Data vs Future Data

In the previous example we have used past or historical data available for company A and company B. Based on our calculations with this past data we have obtained average return and standard deviation. But our decision to invest in either of these companies will be affected by the future performance of these companies, not the past. Though possible, it is not necessary that the future performance shall be just like the past performance. Therefore it makes more sense to estimate likely future returns for these companies under different economic scenarios and then calculate the return and risk.

The return computed from the estimates of future return is known as "expected return". It is equivalent to the "mean return" calculated in case of historical data. The formulae used to obtain expected return and risk are as follows:

$$Expected\ Return\ E(R) = \sum_1^n P_i R_i$$

$$\text{Variance } \sigma^2 = \sum_1^n P_i \{E(R) - R_i\}^2$$

$$Standard\ devience(\sigma) = \sqrt{Variance(\sigma^2)}$$

Here R_i represents returns, E(R) is the expected return and P_i represent the probability of obtaining a particular return R_i.

To best illustrate how the expected return, the variance and the standard deviation are calculated with future data, let us consider a simple example:

Suppose you own a single share in company A which has a current market value of 10 and you expect that the future possible value of the share and the dividends at the end of the period are those set out below.

Market Conditions	**Probability**	**end share price**	**End dividend**	**Total end return**
Favorable	0.2	15.00	1.50	(16.5 – 10.0) 65%
Normal	0.6	12.50	1.00	(13.5 – 10.0) 35%
Unfavorable	0.2	7.50	0.50	(8.0 – 10.0) 20%

You will notice that under favorable market conditions, the total return will be 65%, under normal market conditions 35% and under unfavorable market conditions, –20%. Also notice that the sum of probabilities in different conditions comes out to be 1.

The Expected Return R is calculated by multiplying each total period end outcome R_i by the probability P_i associated with its market condition and summing;

Expected Return =E(R) = P1 R1+ P2 R2+ P3 R3

= 0.2 × (0.65) + 0.6 × (0.35) + 0.2 × (–0.2)

= 0.30 (i.e. 30%)

The Variance, which measures how much each individual outcome differs from the average (or in other words variance measures dispersion and volatility) is calculated by multiplying each end period return R_i minus the expected return by E(R) the probability P_i associated with the market condition and summing;

$$\text{Variance } \sigma^2 = \sum_{1}^{n} P_i \left\{ E(R) - R_i \right\}^2$$

Variance = $0.2 \times (0.65 - 0.3)^2 + 0.6 \times (0.35 - 0.3)^2 + 0.2 \times (-0.2 - 0.3)^2$

= 0.076 (i.e. 7.6%)

The Standard Deviation is simply calculated as the square root of the variance;

Standard Deviation = $\sigma = \sqrt{Variance(\sigma^2)}$ = 0.276

There is also another measure of risk. It is called coefficient of variation. It is defined as risk per unit of return. It is helpful when choosing between two independent risky assets;

this is the co-efficient of variation. Its use in this context assumes constant marginal utility, which may be acceptable over a short range.

Co-efficient of Variation = standard deviation / R (or E(R) as the case may be) = 0.276 / 0.30 = 0.92

Thus a rational investor when choosing between two heterogeneous investments will prefer the one with the lower co-efficient of variation – the lower risk per unit of return.

It should be clear at this point; that other things being equal, investors will prefer an investment giving the highest expected return for a given level of risk or one that has the lowest risk for a given level of expected return.

For instance, if you were told that the return on a share is expected to be 20% and you have been given three risk ratings, 30%, 15% and 10%; assuming that the 10% risk rating is associated with the lowest risk, then you will select this level of risk for the given level of return.

3.3 Risk & Return in a Portfolio Context (More than One Asset)

What is a portfolio? A portfolio is a combination of two or more things. In financial management, the portfolio means the combination of two or more assets or securities. For example, if I have invested in the shares of Company A, Company B and Company C and also I have put some money in Bank Fixed Deposit, then this collection of my investments is called a portfolio. If someone asks me what are different assets in my portfolio, then I will simply answer that my portfolio consists of shares of company a, company B, company C and bank fixed deposit.

Hardly any one puts all his money in a single asset or a single class of assets. We can say that almost every one has his or her unique investment portfolio.

In sections 1 and 2 we learnt to calculate return and risk in case of a single asset. In this section we shall learn to calculate return and risk in case of a portfolio. In other words, we will learn to calculate risk and return when we are dealing with a combination of two or more assets.

3.3.1 Portfolio Return

If a portfolio has n assets, each having an expected return $E(R_1), E(R_2), E(R_3)..................E(R_n)$, the expected return of the portfolio, $E(R_p)$, can be found by the formula:

$$E(R_p) = \sum_{l}^{n} w_i E(R_i), \quad where \sum_{i}^{n} w_i = 1$$ Equation (3.1)

Where, w_i = weights of security i. Weights can be calculated simply by dividing the amount of money divided in the particular security by total amount invested in the portfolio.

We can rewrite the above equation as:

$$E(R_P) = w_1E(R_1) + w_2E(R_2) + w_3E(R_3)..............w_nE(R_n) \quad \text{Equation (3.2)}$$

Example 1

Dr. Meenal Yadav is a savvy investor and has created a portfolio of her investments. Her portfolio has the following assets:

Security	**Investment**	**Expected Return**
Shares of Tata Motors	₹ 50,000	16%
Shares of HLL	₹ 1,00,000	18%
SBI Fixed Deposit	₹ 50,000	10%
Total	**₹ 2,00,000**	

Calculate the expected return from the portfolio.

Solution:

First we will calculate weights of the different assets in the portfolio. We know that :

$$W_i = \frac{Amount\ invested\ in\ security\ i}{Total\ Portfolio\ Value}$$

Putting values of different securities in this formula; we get:

$$W_{tata\ moters} = \frac{50,000}{2,00,000} = 0.25,\ w_{HLL} = \frac{1,00,000}{2,00,000} = 0.50,\ w_{SBI} = \frac{50,000}{2,00,000} = 0.25,$$

(It should be noted here that sum of all portfolio weights is always equal to 1.)

That is, $w_{tata\ moters} + w_{HLL} + w_{SBI}$ **= 1.**

Now, we can apply the equation 3.2.

Putting values, we get: $E(R_P) = 0.25 \times 16\% + 0.50 \times 18\% + 0.25 \times 10\% = 15.5\%$

3.3.2 Portfolio Risk

Risk in case of a single asset is denoted by σ^2, or variance. In case of portfolio also, total risk is measured by σ^2. The formula for computing total risk σ^2 for a portfolio of n assets is :

$$\sigma_p^2 = \sum_{1}^{n} w_1^2 \sigma_1^2 + 2\sum_{i=1}^{n}\sum_{j=1}^{n} w_i w_j \operatorname{cov}_{ij}$$ Equation (3.3)

Where Cov_{ij} represents covariance of returns between two assets, i and j. Covariance is calculated by the formula:

$$COv_{ij} = \rho_{ij}\sigma_i\sigma_j$$ Equation (3.4)

Where ρ_{ij} Correlation between security i and j

We hope you have still not *entirely* forgotten your statistics course from the first semester. In case you have, help is at hand. ρ_{ij} (Pronounced as "rho") indicates whether, and to what extent, the returns between any two securities move in the same direction. It can take values between – 1 to + 1. When ρ_{ij} is positive, it indicates that the returns on both the securities rise as well as fall together. However, when ρ_{ij} is negative, it means when returns on one security increases, the returns on other security decreases.

Putting value of cov_{ij} **in equation 3.3, we get**

$$\sigma_p^2 = \sum_{i=1}^{n} w_i^2 \sigma_i^2 + 2\sum_{i=1}^{n}\sum_{j=1}^{n} w_i w_j \rho_{ij}\sigma_i\sigma_j$$ Equation (3.5)

In case of a portfolio consisting of two securities, we can write the formula for expected return and variance with the help of equation 3.1 and 3.5

Expected return of two security portfolio $E(R_P) = w_1 E(R_1) + w_2 E(R_2)$,

Variance of two security portfolio:

$$\sigma_p^2 = w_1^2\sigma_1^2 + w_2^2\sigma_2^2 + 2w_1 w_2 \rho_{12}\sigma_1\sigma_2$$

Example 2

Shyamsharan is a very astute investor. He has created a two security portfolio as follows:

Investment	**% of total portfolio**	**Expected Returns**	**Standard Deviation**
Shares	75	17%	10%
Bonds	25	10%	9%

It has been found that the correlation between shares and bonds is -0.75. Calculate the expected return and risk of this portfolio.

We know that:

$$E(R_P) = w_1 E(R_1) + w_2 E(R_2)$$

Putting values, we get $E\left(R_p\right) = .75x17\% + .25x10\%$ = 15.25%

Further, for variance, the formula is $\sigma_p^2 = w_1^2\sigma_1^2 + w_2^2\sigma_2^2 + 2w_1w_2\rho_{12}\sigma_1\sigma_2$

Putting values, we get $\sigma_p^2 = (0.75)^2\,10^2 + (0.25)^2\,9^2 + 2$ x 0.75 x 0.25 x (-0.25) x 10 x 9

Solving, we get $\sigma_p^2 = 36$

Therefore, $\sigma_p = 6$

3.3.3 Diversification and Portfolio Risk

Before we proceed, first let us understand the term "diversification". Diversification means "to diversify" or "to have something of different types". In financial management, diversification means investing in more than one type of asset. When a portfolio has more than one type of asset, or different assets of the same type, it is called a diversified portfolio.

Look at the above example closely. Is it a diversified portfolio? The answer is yes because it has two different types of assets, namely, shares and bonds.

The more important question is "Is there any benefit of diversification?" Your guess is correct. Yes, there are benefits of diversification. How?

Let us go back to the above example. Suppose Mr. shyam sharan had decided to invest 100% of his money in shares. What would be the portfolio return and risk in that case? It would be 17% and 10%. On the other hand, if Mr shyam sharan had put all his money in bonds, then? Now the portfolio return and risk would be 10% and 9%.

Now look at his actual portfolio of 75% shares and 25% bonds. What is the risk and return of this portfolio? We have just calculated that portfolio return is 15.25% and risk is 6%.The standard deviation of the portfolio is only 6 whereas the standard deviation of the components of this portfolio are 10 and 9!

That means, the risk of the portfolio is less than its components! How is that possible?

Well, it is very much possible. Look at the formula for portfolio risk. What are the factors on which the portfolio risk depends? It depends on:

1) Weights of individual securities (w_1, w_2 etc)

2) Standard deviation of individual securities σ_1, σ_2 *etc.*

3) Correlation coefficient of securities. ρ_{ij}

Now, each of the term w_1, w_2 $\sigma_1 and \sigma_2$ was positive. Then how could σ_p or portfolio risk reduce? Well, the answer is ρ_{ij} . The portfolio risk went down because both the securities had a negative correlation. That means, if we combine securities with a negative correlation with each other then we can reduce the risk of the portfolio. This phenomenon is known as risk reduction by diversification.

The detailed treatment of concept of portfolio diversification is outside the scope of this text book. However, for the benefit of the reader, some general conclusions are given here:

1. The measurement of portfolio risk requires information regarding the variance of individual securities and covariance between securities.
2. Three factors determine portfolio risk; variances of the individual securities, the co variances between the pairs of the securities and the proportions of total fund invested in securities.
3. As the number of securities increase in a portfolio, the impact of the covariance of the securities rather than their individual variance affects the portfolio risk.

A question arises here. If we keep adding securities to our portfolio, then will the risk of portfolio keep decreasing? A lot of research has taken place on this. It has been found that as we increase the number of securities in a portfolio, the incremental reduction in the risk keeps decreasing. After about 20-25 securities, the risk reduction becomes verv small, so small that we may neglect it.

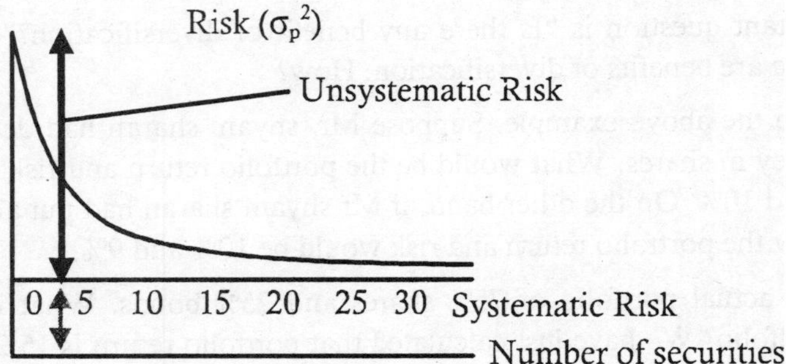

As we can see in the above graph, as the number of securities in a portfolio approaches 15 and above, the amount of risk reduction with each additional security becomes very small. This leads to another important conclusion. That is, the risk of a portfolio can not be reduced below a certain level (shown by small arrow in the above graph), how so ever the number of securities we may add.

That means, when we add securities in a portfolio, due the effect of diversification, risk gets reduced. However, out of the total risk of the portfolio, some risk always remains and can not be removed by further diversification.

This portion of the total risk, that we can not completely diversify away, is known as systematic risk. It is also called market risk or non-diversifiable risk. The portion of risk which we could remove by diversification is known as Unsystematic risk or diversifiable risk.

Therefore we can conclude that:

Total Risk = Systematic Risk + Unsystematic Risk

The systematic risk is the risk due to the factors external to the firm. The firm has no control over it and it has to live with these factors. In other words, systematic risk arises from the economic environment the firm operates in. All firms have to bear this risk. For example, state of the economy, inflation etc.

However, Unsystematic risk arises from factors specific to or internal to the firm. For example, management competency, technology, labor relations etc. This risk can be diversified away by choosing securities which have negative correlation with each other.

It has been proven, that in the context of a portfolio, it is the only the systematic risk that matters, not the total risk. Why? It is because the unsystematic portion of the total risk can be completely eliminated by diversification. But not the systematic risk. Therefore the portfolio investor should be concerned with the systematic risk only.

Before we proceed, it would be useful to have a snapshot of various types of risks that a firm faces:

3.3.4 Sources (Types) of Risks

The returns from investing in a company's securities depend on many factors. The most important among these factors are profits. The profits are at risk from many sources. These sources of risks are of many types. Some of the important types of risks that a firm faces are;

1. Interest Rate Risk

This risk originates from movement of interest rates. If affects the firms in two ways. First it affects the interest cost of funds borrowed. For example, if a firm has taken a term loan on floating interest rate, then its interest costs will shoot up if interest rate rises.

Second, it affects the value of assets and liabilities of the firm. For example, if a firm has made fixed rate investments, then if the interest rates in the market increase, the value of these investments goes down. The exposure to interest rate risk depends on the asset-liability structure of the firm. Firms with floating rate liabilities shall have a higher exposure than firms with fixed rate liabilities.

2. Default Risk

When a firm sells its goods and/or services on credit, it may or may not get back its dues from the customers. Default risk refers to the chance that the firm will be unable to recover its dues from its debtors. The debtors (customers who have purchased the goods and services on credit) may default due to either their inability or their unwillingness.

3. Exchange Risk

Increasingly, the markets around the world are getting integrated. Owing to this, firms have to face the exchange risk. Exchange risk may be defined as the possibility of adverse effect on firm's assets, liabilities and income due to movement of interest rates. It may be noted that if a firm is not operating in foreign markets then it shall not face exchange risk. Even a firm with 100% domestic sales may face exchange risk. For example, if rupee appreciates against dollars, then a product can be imported at cheaper rates, affecting the sales of domestic firm selling the same product.

4. Financial Risk

It is the converse of default risk. In default risk, the possibility of loss arose from the customer's not making payment of their dues towards the firm. Whereas, the financial risk means the firm's inability to pay its dues towards creditors. If this happens, then the firm will suffer a great loss of goodwill, increased costs and even closure. As we will see in later chapters, financial risk increases with increase use of borrowed funds (debt).The main reasons for financial risk are liquidity risk and faulty capital structure.

5. Business Risk

This may also be called environmental risk faced by the firm from either its internal environment or external environment. Examples for risks arising from external environment are change in government policy, changes in customer preferences, slowdown in economy, instable law and order etc.

Examples of risks arising from internal factors are death of a key managerial employee, strike, breakdown of plant, turnover of key personnel etc.

6. Liquidity Risk

It refers to the inability of the firm to meet its financial obligations on time owing to non availability of ready cash or liquidity. Liquidity risk arises both in case of poor liquidity or excess liquidity. A firm may be very profitable, but it might have sold on credit heavily and its funds might be blocked in debtors. In this case it may fail to repay its creditors.

When a firm has surplus liquidity, unless it finds profitable avenues to deploy these funds, it will incur an opportunity cost affecting its profitability adversely.

7. Market Risk

It is also known as Price Risk. It refers to erosion of market value of a firm's investments due to market movements. This is not an absolute risk in itself because it arises due to combined effects of many other types of risks, especially, interest rate risk and exchange risk.

8. Marketability Risk

It is a type of liquidity risk. It refers to firm not being able to sell its marketable assets on their fair value. The sale of marketable assets is not always due to distress factors or due to a need for liquidity to repay liabilities. However, when the firm is facing marketability risk when it is selling its assets for liquidity purposes, marketability risk leads to liquidity risk.

3.3.5 Measures of Systematic and Unsystematic Risk

We know that the measurement of total risk is done by variance (or standard deviation). We may write:

Total risk of a security i = σ^2

Systematic Risk of Security = $\beta_{im}^2\sigma_m^2$ Equation (3.3.3)

Where, β_{im} is called beta of security. It is given by the formula

$$\beta_{im} = \frac{Cov_{im}}{\sigma_m^2}, \quad \text{Equation (3.3.4)}$$

and σ_m^2 is known as variance of the market portfolio.

Another formula for beta is;

$$\beta_{im} = \frac{\rho_{im}\sigma_i\sigma_m}{\sigma_m^2} = \frac{\rho_{im}\sigma_i}{\sigma_m} \quad \text{Equation (3.3.5)}$$

This formula for beta applies to a single asset. In case we are interested to find out the value of portfolio beta, we may use the following formula:

$$\beta_{portfolio} = \sum_{i=0}^{n} w_i\beta_{im} \quad \text{Equation (3.3.6)}$$

That is, the portfolio beta is nothing but weighted average of betas of individual assets of portfolio.

Similarly, once we have obtained beta of portfolio beta, we may obtain systematic risk of the portfolio as well with the help of equation 3.3.3, by replacing individual beta with portfolio beta, we get:

$$Systematic\ risk\ of\ portfolio = \beta^2{}_{portfolio}\sigma_m^2 \quad \text{Equation (3.3.7)}$$

Putting value of portfolio beta from equation 3.3.6, we get

$$Systematic\ risk\ of\ portfolio = \sigma_p^2 - \left(\sum_{i=o}^{n} w_i\beta_{im}\right)^2 \sigma_m^2 \quad \text{Equation (3.3.8)}$$

We know that, unsystematic Risk of Portfolio = Total Risk – Systematic Risk

$$Unsystematic\ risk\ of\ portfolio = \sigma_p^2 - \left(\sum_{i=o}^{1} w_i\beta_{im}\right)$$

3.3.5.1 Interpretation of beta

As already explained, beta is a measure of systematic risk of a security. Beta of market index is 1. On the other hand securities may have beta values more than or less than 1.

But other securities may have beta values more or less than 1 and sometimes, equal to 1. How do we make sense of if we are given beta value of a security? Suppose a security has beta 1.3. It means that if the stock market rises by 10%, the security will rise by 13%. Similarly, if the market falls by 10%, the security returns will fall by 13%.

We may say that:

$$\%\, change\ in\ security\ returns = \beta\ x\ \%\, change\ in\ market\ returns$$

Securities with beta more than 1 are called aggressive securities because their systematic risk is more risk than average market risk. Securities with beta less than 1 are called defensive securities as their systematic risk is less than average market risk. As already pointed out, sometimes a security will have beta exactly equal to one. Such securities are called neutral securities as their systematic risk is equal to average market risk. Can we have a security with zero beta? The answer is yes. These are the securities whose returns are not affected by the movement in market returns. They are also called risk free securities. Generally government securities (bonds issued by central and state government) fall into this category.

Can beta be negative also? The answer is again yes. The returns of negative beta securities will move in the opposite direction of the movement of market returns. Gold as an investment is generally found to have negative beta.

3.3.6 Relationship between Risk and Return

Introduction to Capital Asset Pricing Model (CAPM)

Why does one invest in risky assets like shares when risk free securities (government securities) are available? Are the investors fools? No, they are not. When ever an investor invests in a risky asset, he expects that he will get some ***extra return*** which will be more than the return on a risk free asset. For him this extra return is some kind of compensation for taking extra risk by investing in a risky asset and not in risk free security.

This extra return is known as Risk Premium.

Risk Premium =Expected Return from a risky investment – Expected return from risk free security.

So, you would agree that we all take extra risk in the hope of earning risk premium. Suppose rate of return on risk free securities is r_f and rate of return on a portfolio or risky assets, for example, a market portfolio is r_m. Then, obviously $r_m > r_f$. Why? It is because why would you invest in the risky market portfolio if it does not offer returns more than the risk free security?

Now we can see that:

1) By investing in a market portfolio (beta =1), the investor expects an extra return (or Risk Premium) of $r_m - r_f$

2) By investing in risk free security (beta = 0), the investor expects zero risk premium $\left(r_f - r_f = 0\right)$

How can we calculate the expected risk premium when investor invests in securities that have beta values other than 0 and 1?

The solution to this problem was given by three economists in 1960 (Sharpe, Lintner an Treynor), which became famous as **Capital Asset Pricing Model (CAPM).**

According to this model,

$$Expected\ rosk\ primium\ on\ risky\ asset = beta\ x\ expected\ risk\ primium\ on\ market\ portfolio$$

Suppose the expected return on the risky asset is equal to "r", then expected risk premium on risky asset becomes $\left(r - r_f\right)$ we have already seen that expected risk premium on market portfolio is equal to $r_m - r_f$

Therefore, the above relationship of CAPM becomes:

$$\left(r - r_f\right) = \beta\left(r_m - r_f\right)$$

OR $\quad r = r_f + \beta\left(r_m - r_f\right)$

This is a very important relationship in finance. Understand it well and do not forget it.

Illustrative Solved Examples

1. **The following table gives dividend and share price data for Excellent Products Limited.**

Year	Dividend per Share	Closing Share Price
2000	3.00	15.50
2001	3.00	17.25
2002	3.00	22.50
2003	3.50	20.60
2004	3.50	25.50
2005	3.75	25.50
2006	4.00	27.00
2007	4.00	28.25
2008	4.00	32.00
2009	4.50	36.00
2010	4.50	39.00

Calculate:

a) **The annual rates of return**

b) **The mean rate of return**

c) **The variance**

d) **The standard deviation of returns**

Solution:

a) **The annual rates of return can be computed as follows:**

Year	Dividend per Share	Closing Share Price	%Annual Rate of Return	
2000	3.00	15.50		
2001	3.00	17.25	{3.00+(17.25-15.50)100}15.50 =	30.65
2002	3.00	22.50	{3.00+(22.50-17.25)100}17.25 =	47.83
2003	3.50	20.60	{3.00+(20.60-22.50)100}22.50 =	7.11
2004	3.50	25.50	{3.50+(25.50-20.60)100}20.60 =	40.78
2005	3.75	25.50	{3.75+(25.50-25.50)100}25.50 =	14.71
2006	4.00	27.00	{4.00+(27.00-25.50)100}25.50 =	21.57
2007	4.00	28.25	{4.00+(28.25-27.00)100}27.00 =	19.44
2008	4.00	32.00	{4.00+(32.00-28.25)100}28.25 =	27.43
2009	4.50	36.00	{4.50+(36.00-32.00)100}32.00 =	26.56
2010	4.50	39.00	{4.50+(39.00-36.00)100}36.00 =	20.83

b) Mean return can be calculated by taking the average of the returns column above: = (30.65+47.83+7.11+40.78+14.71+21.57+19.44+27.43+26.56+20.83)/10 = 25.69%

c) **Variance can be calculated in the following manner:**

Year	Annual Rate of Return	Annual Return -Mean Return	Square of Annual Return - Mean Return
2000			
2001	30.65	4.95	24.55
2002	47.83	22.14	489.97
2003	7.11	-18.58	345.20
2004	40.78	15.09	227.59
2005	14.71	-10.98	120.67
2006	21.57	-4.12	16.99
2007	19.44	-6.25	39.02

2008	27.43	1.74	3.04
2009	26.56	0.87	0.76
2010	20.83	-4.86	23.59
Mean Return	25.69		
Sum			**1,291.38**

We know that:

$$variance = \sigma^2 = \frac{1}{n-1}\sum_{1}^{n}\left(\overline{R} - R_i\right)^2$$

Putting values $\sum_{1}^{n}\left(\overline{R} - R_i\right)^2 = 1291.38$ from the table and n=10, we get

$\sigma^2 = 143.48$

d) We know that:

$$standard\ deviation(\sigma) = \sqrt{\text{variance}(\sigma^2)}$$

Putting value of $\sigma^2 = 143.48$, we get:

$\sigma = 11.97\%$

2. The shares of little star ltd. Are expected to provide following returns under various economic conditions:

Scenario	Probability	Expected Return
Recession	0.4	-8%
Normal Growth	0.4	6%
High Growth	0.2	18 %

Calculate the expected return and standard deviation of this stock.

Solution

We know the formula for expected return is

$$Expected\ return E(R) = \sum_{1}^{n} P_i R_i$$

Putting values from the table we get:

$$Expected\ return\ E(R) = 0.4\,x(-8\%) + 0.4\,x\,6\% + 0.2\,x\ \ 18\%$$

Solving, we get

$Expected\ return\ E(R) = 2.8\%$

Variance $\sigma^2 = \sum_{1}^{n} P_i\{E(R) - R_i\}^2$

Putting Values we get,

$\sigma^2 = 0.4\{2.8\% - (-8\%)\}^2 + 0.4\{2.8\% - 6\%\}^2 + 0.2\{2.8\% - 18\%\}^2$

$Solving\ we\ get, \sigma^2 = 97$

$Standard\ deviation(\sigma) = \sqrt{variance(\sigma^2)}$

$Putting\ value\ of\ \sigma^2, we\ get\ \sigma = 9.84$

3. The standard deviation of XYZ Limited stock is 25% and its correlation coefficient with the market portfolio is 0.45. The expected return from market is 17% with a standard deviation of 20%. If the risk free rate is 5%, calculate the required rate of return on XYZ stock.

Solution

We know that $\beta_{im} = \frac{\rho_{im}\sigma_1\sigma_m}{\sigma_m^2} = \frac{\rho_{im}\sigma_i}{\sigma_m} = \frac{\rho_{im}\sigma_i}{\sigma_m}$

Given, $\rho_{im} = 0.45$, $\sigma_i = 25\%$, $\sigma_m = 20\%$, Putting these values in above equation we get:

$\beta_{im} = \frac{0.45 x 25}{20} = 0.5626$

Having calculated beta, we can now use capital asset pricing model to find the required rate of return:

$r = r_f + \beta(r_m - r_f)$

We have, $r_f = 5\%, \beta = 0.5625\ and\ r_m = 17\%$ **putting these values in the CAPM equation, we get** $r = 11.75\%$

4. There are two stocks A and B for which following data is available:

Expected return on stock A	=	**10 %**
Expected return on stock B	=	**18 %**
Standard Deviation of Stock A	=	**3 %**
Standard Deviation of stock B	=	**6 %**

Mr. G P Agrawal wishes to create a portfolio of these two stocks by taking them in equal proportions. Calculate the expected portfolio return and standard deviation if correlation between these two stocks is 0.6.

Solution

We know that portfolio return can be calculated by the formula:

$$E(R_P) = w_1 E(R_1) + w_2 E(R_2)$$

Given $w_1 = 50\%, E(R_1) = 10\%, w_2 = 50\%, E(R_2) = 18\%,$ putting these values in above equation we get:

$$E(R_P) = 50\% x 10\% + 50\% x 18\%$$

$$E(R_P) = 14\%$$

We also know that, Variance of two security portfolio:

$$\sigma_p^2 = w_1^2 \sigma_1^2 + w_2^2 \sigma_2^2 + 2 w_1 w_2 \rho_{12} \sigma_1 \sigma_2$$

We have, $w_1 = 50\%, w_2 = 50\%, \rho_{12} = 0.6, \sigma_1 = 3\%, \sigma_2 = 6\%$, Putting these values in the formula above we get:

$$\sigma_p^2 = 16.65$$

We know that:

$$\text{Standard deviation}(\sigma) = \sqrt{Variance(\sigma^2)}$$

$$Therefore, Standard\ deviation(\sigma) = 4.08\%$$

Summary

- Return represents what one gets over and above one's initial investment.
- Total Rupee Return from an asset can be broken down into two components. Cash Income from asset and Capital Gain/Loss.
- "Percentage returns" is nothing but Total Rupee Return expressed as a percentage of our initial investment. Percentage returns can also be expressed as sum of Income Yield and Capital gains/loss yield.
- If we hold an asset for more than a year, then average return is the arithmetic average of annual returns of different years.
- Overall returns for the total period for which you hold the asset is known as "Holding Period Return".

- Compounded annual return (CAGR) is obtained by finding geometric mean of returns.
- Risk is the possibility that the actual outcome will be different from the expected outcome. Actual outcome can happen in three ways. One, it is exactly like the expected outcome. In this case there is no risk. Two, the actual outcome may be better than the expected outcome (upside risk). Three, the actual outcome may be worse than the expected outcome (down side risk). Situation two and three are the situations involving risk. While studying risk and risk management, we generally focus on "downside" risk.
- Risk and uncertainty are not the same. Risk is a situation where it is known that there might be outcomes possible, each having different probabilities. So in Risk, we do not know which of these outcomes will actually take place. On the other hand, uncertainty is a situation when even the probable outcomes are not known. In uncertainty we are absolutely clueless about what is going to happen. However, often, both these terms are used to convey the same meaning.
- In the world of finance, risk is the variability of returns. Variability of returns or Risk of a single asset can be measured by many methods, e.g., range, variance and standard deviation. Out of these three standard deviation is most commonly used.
- When we are dealing with historical data, we use past returns to calculate risk and return. When are interested in what might be future return and risk, we use probability distribution of returns to calculate returns and risk.
- There is also another measure of risk. It is called coefficient of variation. It is defined as risk per unit of return. It is helpful when choosing between two independent risky assets.
- A portfolio is a combination of two or more things. In financial management, the portfolio means the combination of two or more assets or securities.
- Portfolio Return is weighted average of returns of individual component securities of a portfolio.
- Portfolio Risk is also measured by standard deviation or variance. For calculating portfolio risk we need standard deviation of individual securities in addition to the weights of individual securities in the portfolio and covariance between the securities.
- In finance, diversification means investing in more than one type of asset. When a portfolio has more than one type of asset, or different assets of the same type, it is called a diversified portfolio.
- The risk of a portfolio can be reduced by diversification if the component securities of a portfolio have negative correlation with each other. However, risk reduction by diversification is possible only up to a point. This is so because total risk is

composed of systematic and unsystematic risk. Unsystematic risk can be diversified away but systematic risk can not be.

- A firm faces many types of risk. Some of the major ones are interest rate risk, default risk, exchange risk, financial risk, business risk, liquidity risk, market risk and marketability risk etc.
- Systematic risk can be measured by beta coefficient. Beta of market index is 1. On the other hand securities may have beta values more than or less than 1. Securities with beta more than 1 are called aggressive securities because their systematic risk is more risk than average market risk. Securities with beta less than 1 are called defensive securities as their systematic risk is less than average market risk.
- Investors invest in risky assets in order to earn some extra returns which is called risk premium. Risk Premium =Expected Return from a risky investment – Expected return from risk free security.
- Capital asset pricing model provides a framework for linking risk and return.

Test Your Understanding

State whether the following statements are true or false

1. Market risk an example of Non-systematic risk.
2. Systematic Risk is also known as diversifiable risk.
3. Expected return on a security is sum of products of probability and related returns.
4. Risk and uncertainty are one and the same things.
5. Return on an asset is composed of cash income and capital gain/loss.
6. The covariance between any two securities is equal to the product of correlation between them and standard deviation of each security.
7. Beta of market portfolio is equal to zero.
8. For achieving risk reduction through diversification, it is important to have securities with negative correlation in the portfolio.
9. The main benefit of diversification is increase of expected returns.
10. Beta of a security can never be negative.

Answers : 1. F, 2. F, 3. T, 4. F, 5. T, 6. T, 7. F, 8. T, 9. F, 10.F

Multiple Choice Questions

1. Risk free security has a

   a) 1.0 beta b) 2.0 beta

   c) 0.0 beta d) 0.5 beta

2. CAPM provides a framework for measuring risk. Identify the correct risk.

(UPTU 2010)

a) Portfolio Risk b) Market Risk

c) Systematic Risk d) None of the above

3. If an investment produces annual return of 12% in first year, 7% in second year and 10% in the third year, what is the annual return over three years?

a) 9.65% b) 9.42%

c) 9.67% d) None of the above

4. If the expected return on a portfolio having two assets is 16% and the return on one asset (having 40% weight in the portfolio) is 20%, then return on the other security is:

a) 18% b) 13.33%

c) 20% d) None of the above

5. If the coefficient of correlation between A and B is 0.4, the covariance between them is 0.8 and standard deviation of B is 0.2, the variance of A should be·

a) 100 b) 5

c) 10 d) 0.01

6. Beta is a measure of :

a) Systematic risk b) Unsystematic Risk

c) Total Risk d) None of the above

7. If the beta of a security is less than 1, then it would be called:

a) A defensive security b) An aggressive security

c) A neutral security d) None of the above

8. Which of the following is a non-diversifiable risk:

a) Strike in a factory b) Slow down in economy

c) Poor management of the company d) None of the above

9. Portfolio beta is:

a) Calculated as the weighted average of individual security betas.

b) Calculated as the arithmetic average of security betas

c) Is a measure of portfolio risk

d) both a) and c) above.

10. Risk premium on Capital Asset Pricing Model is given by:

a) $[\beta \times (r]_m - r_f)$ b) r_f

c) $[(r]_m - r_f)$ d) None of the above

Answers : 1.c 2.c 3.a 4.b 5.a 6.a 7.a 8.b 9.d 10. a

Practice Problems

1. An asset is expected to return the following rates of return between the years 2010 to 2018. What is the 9 year holding period return?

Year	2010	2011	2012	2013	2014	2015	2016	2017	2018
Return(%)	15	17	6	18	20	23.50	22	25	22

Also calculate the compound annual return for this period.

2. The distribution of returns for a share X and market is given as follows:

	Returns (%)	
Probability	**Market**	**Share X**
0.4	20	15
0.3	16	19
0.3	-17	0

Calculate the following for both share X and market:

a) Expected Return

b) Standard Deviation

c) Variance

3. The risk-free return is 8% and market return is 17%. You are considering to invest in a stock X. The Stock X has a beta of 1.4. Currently it is selling for ₹ 35. The expected dividend for stock X in the coming year is ₹ 5. What is the growth rate expected in stock X?

4. Ms Rubina has the following stocks in her portfolio:

Stocks	Beta	Proportion of investment (%)
Uco Bank	1.24	10%
UTI Gold Share	-0.11	20%
Bombay Dyeing	0.8	5%
RIL	1.1	15%
Infosys	1.3	30%
Suzlon Energy	1.1	20%

If the risk free rate is 5% and the return on market portfolio is 16%, calculate the expected return on her portfolio.

5. Mr Abhishek Pandey bought one share of High Growth Limited for ₹ 3,000 two years ago. He received ₹ 95 and ₹ 165 as dividend for the last two years. This year he sold the share for ₹ 4,020. Calculate the holding period return of Mr Abhishek Pandey on this share.

6. The standard deviation of return on security A is 19% and market returns is 14%. Calculate the beta of security A in each case if the covariance between security A and the market is as follows:

a) $\rho_{Am} = +0.80$

b) $\rho_{Am} = +0.50$

c) $\rho_{Am} = +0.30$

7. A portfolio consists of three securities A, B and C. The details are as follows:

	A	B	C	Correlation
Expected Return	20%	15%	22%	
Standard Deviation	16%	19%	31%	
Weights in Portfolio	20%	50%	30%	
Correlation				
AB				+ 0.60
BC				-0.20
AC				+0.80

Calculate the risk and return of this portfolio.

8. A portfolio consists of two securities A and B. The details are as follows:

	A	B
Expected Return	18%	22%
Standard Deviation	13%	19%
Weights in Portfolio	50%	50%

a) If the investor desires to have a standard deviation of 14% for this portfolio, what should be the correlation coefficient between A and B.

b) Based on your answer in a), what will be the standard deviation of this portfolio if the weights of the securities is 30% and 70% respectively.

c) If the desired standard deviation is 12% and securities A and B have weights 30% and 70% respectively, what should be the correlation coefficient between A and B.

9. The risk free rate of return is 7% and the expected return on a stock is 17%. The beta of the stock is 1.3.

Applying CAPM, what should be the return on the market portfolio?

10. Ms Monika Negi has started a manufacturing business of automobile parts. It is an all equity firm. The beta of her company's stock is 1.4. the risk free rate is 6% and the market premium is 11%. She is considering another project which is expected to generate a return of 22%. If this project is same level of risk as her existing business, should she accept the new project?

Chapter Review Questions

1. What is risk? Give various types of risks. How do these affect investment?

(UPTU 2010)

2. What is risk? Is it the same thing as uncertainty? Give various types of Risks.

(UPTU 2009)

3. What are the various kinds of risks associated to business operation? How the risks are measured.
4. Explain risk and return analysis.
5. What is return? Discuss its various components. Should we include unrealized capital gains and losses while computing returns?
6. Write notes on the following:
   a) Holding Period Return125%
   b) Expected rate of return
7. What is a portfolio? Explain how the risk and return of a portfolio is measured.
8. Explain the concept of Systematic and Unsystematic Risk with the help of suitable examples.
9. What is beta? How it is calculated? Also explain how it is interpreted?
10. What is the relationship between risk and return? Give a brief introduction of CAPM.
11. What is Risk- Return trade-off in financial decision-making? **(DU 2005)**

References

1. Brealey, Richard A & Myres, Stewart C. (2007), Tata McGraw Hill, New Delhi
2. Damodaran, Aswath. (1994). Damodaran on Valuation, John Wiley & Sons, New York
3. ICAI study Material on Financial Management, The Institute of Chartered Accountants of India, New Delhi.
4. Khan, M Y & Jain (2007) P K, Financial Management, Tata McGraw Hill, New Delhi
5. Pandey, I M (2009). Financial Management, Vikas Publishing House, New Delhi
6. Van Horne, James C. (2007),Financial Management & Policy, Pearson Prentice Hall, New Delhi
7. Work book on "Financial Management for Managers": The Institute of Chartered Financial Analysts of India, Hyderabad.

Unit-2

Investment Decision

CHAPTER 4 Capital Budgeting

Learning Objectives:

By the end of this chapter and having completed the essential reading and activities, you should be able to:

- Explain the nature of capital investments
- Understand the process of Appraisal of projects
- Apply Techniques of Capital Budgeting
- Decide why a technique is suitable to a given situation and why not

4.0 Introduction

We are familiar by now that the goal of the firm is to maximize the value of its shares. This is also known as shareholder's wealth maximization. How can the firm achieve this goal? One of the ways this goal is achieved is by investing firm's resources in assets that generate more returns than its cost of funds. Where do firms invest?

Firms invest their resources in both short term and long term assets. The process of deciding on suitable long term investments is known as Capital budgeting.

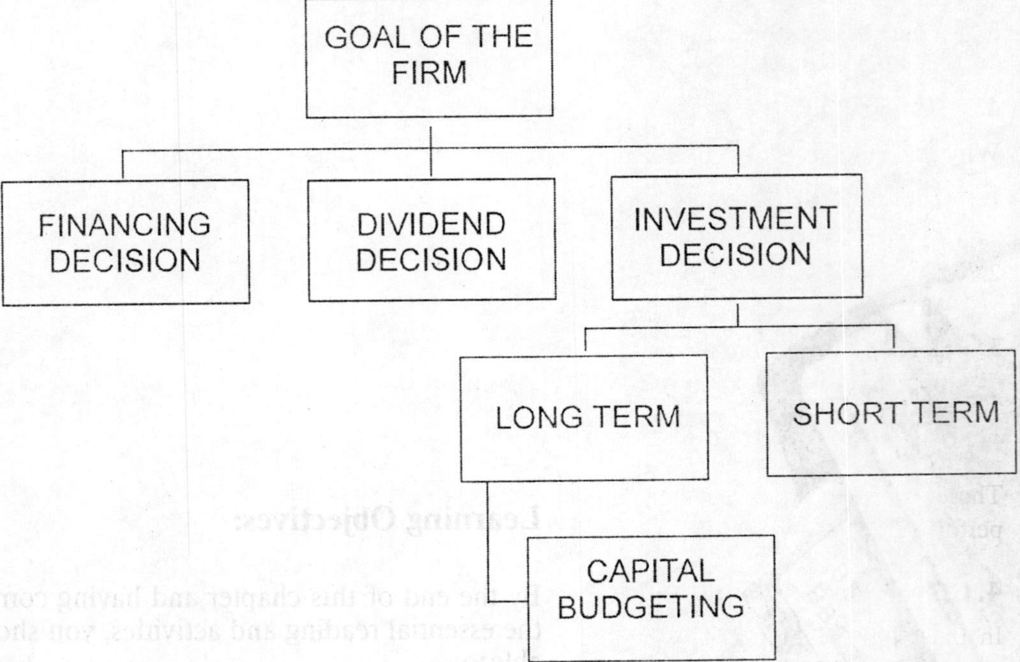

Capital budgeting is primarily concerned with ***sizeable*** investments in ***long-term*** assets. What are these long term assets?

They can be *tangible* like plant, machinery and equipment or *intangible* like new technology, patents, trade-marks and R & D.

Consider a few more examples:

- Reliance announces setting up of a power plant in Dadri in UP.
- Tata Motors proposes to set up a new plant at Gujarat to manufacture its dream car which will cost less than ₹ 1 Lac.
- The vice-chairman of Sri Lakshmi Public Charitable Trust announced setting up of a new business school near its existing campus in Faizabad.

These are a few examples of company's investment decisions. These decisions are also known as Capital expenditure Decisions or Capital Budgeting Decisions.

Capital budgeting or Capital budgeting decision may be defined as the company's decision to invest its current funds most efficiently in long term assets in anticipation of an expected flow of benefits over a series of years.

These decisions are considered very important because:

1. They affect firm's strategic position many years hence. This means these decisions affect the firm's risk-return profile for a large number of years.
2. They involve huge amount of money and may be critical to firm's performance for a number of years.
3. Once taken, these decisions can be reversed only with a huge cost. Therefore, practically they are irreversible.
4. They are difficult to take since almost always more than one alternative is present.

Why are these decisions so difficult to take? There are many reasons:

1. It is difficult to quantitatively express (put in numbers) all the costs and benefits related to an investment in a plant, machinery etc.
2. The benefits of such capital expenditure will come only in future. And we all know that future is very uncertain.
3. In these decisions costs are incurred NOW but the benefits occur only IN FUTURE! So to analyze these decisions, it becomes necessary to bring all the cost and benefits on a common time frame first. (Remember your Time Value of Money class?)

These decisions start with identification of investment opportunities and end with performance review after the project is implemented.

4.1 Overview of Capital Budgeting Process

In the highly simplified flow chart on the next page, each stage of capital budgeting process has been depicted. We can see that capital budgeting is a multi faceted activity. Let us now have a look at each stage of the flow chart.

4.1.1Strategic Planning: A strategic plan is firm's roadmap into future. This plan helps to translate the goals of the firm into specific policies and objectives. It helps to set priorities in the operational matters. The vision and mission statements of the firm are covered in strategic planning itself.

However, as you may see in the flow chart, strategic planning gets feedback from preliminary screening, accept/reject and post implementation review. Based on the feedback, it may be sometimes necessary to change the future direction of the firm. In this case the strategic plan will accordingly change.

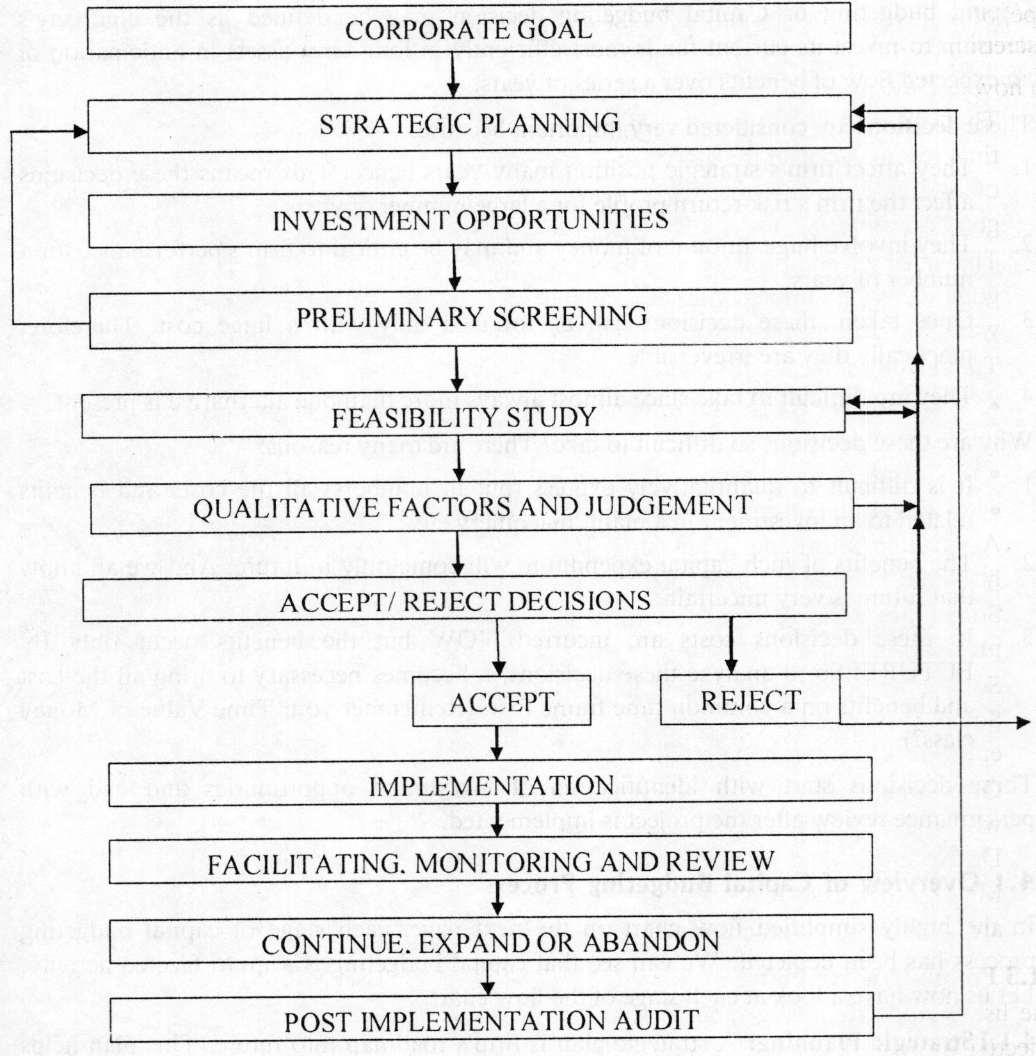

Capital Budgeting Process

4.1.2 Identification of investment opportunities

It is a critical stage in capital budgeting. The potential investment opportunity has to fit with the strategic plan and firm's mission and vision. However, sometimes a potential opportunity may be so attractive that changes in vision and mission are made to accommodate it.

However, identification of potential investment opportunities is often difficult. There are so many options to choose from!

Some investments are mandatory in nature due to health, regulatory and safety considerations. The firm has to make them in order to remain in business. Except these type, other investments are made for growth, cost savings etc. Such investments are called discretionary investments.

So how to chose these discretionary investment options? Here are some suggestions:

a) The firm may identify and shortlist industries where demand exceeds supply. Then the firm may look at the level of capacity utilization in that industry, the profitability of existing units and new projects under implementation. Success of Maruti cars is a good example.

b) The study of end-product and bye-products of various industries can give various good ideas.(Example: Mini Steel plants were set up to use steel scrap which was a waste for large steel firms)

c) Trend studies like the following may also suggest some investment opportunities:
   - Trends in exports and imports during last five years to see potential investment opportunities.
   - Trends in social tastes and preferences
   - Trends in consumption patterns abroad

d) A sick unit represents a potential investment opportunity to an entrepreneur who has the capability of turning it around. (example : Malvika steel in Jagdishpur,)

e) Sometimes existing firms may resort to forward integration. For example, a textile producer may start its own ready made garment unit.

f) Sometimes investment opportunities are identified by informal sources as well. Some very good investment ideas can come during casual chit chat between employees at water cooler/ office canteen!

g) Government's industrial policy and laws are a good source to find out projects where government subsidies and incentives are available. For example, Industries Development and regulations) Act, Income Tax Act, and Foreign Exchange Management Act. It has always been a smart business practice to set up projects in area that are government priority.

4.1.3 Preliminary screening

The list of opportunities generated from above should further be scrutinized. Here, the objective is not to conduct a very detailed analysis. The intention is to apply some decisions criteria to short list a few projects that are *prima facie* (means "In the first glance") desirable.

These rules of thumb that can be applied are the availability of physical and financial resources, compatibility with governmental policies, availability of raw material, size of market, risk characteristics (effect of business cycle, seasonal effects etc).

In this stage often the "gut-feel" or judgment of experienced management plays a crucial role.

4.1.4. Feasiblitiy Study

Feasibility study discloses whether the project is technically feasible, economically viable and financially sound.

In this stage a detailed project report (DPR) is prepared for the project passing out of preliminary screening stage. In DPR all marketing, technical, financial and economic aspects are discussed. Usually, the DPR also contains fairly specific estimates of project costs, means of financing, schedule of implementation, estimates of profitability based on projected sales and production costs, estimates of cost and benefits stream in terms of cash flows, debt servicing capability of the project and social profitability. The ultimate decision whether to go in for the project or not and how to finance it, is taken after this study.

4.1.5 Implementation

This is a very critical stage since here the plans are converted into action. This stage is very time consuming, highly complicated, filled with tension and risky. In this stage many different parties are involved. This stage involves architects, contractors, equipment suppliers, bankers, engineers etc. The most critical aspect of this stage is continuous monitoring and corrective action in case of deviations.

Inadequate monitoring may result in project delays and cost overrun. To avoid these delays a) the project should be well formulated so that all aspects of the project are covered and targets are set on time. b) Specific responsibilities are assigned to project managers for completing the project within the defined time-frame. c) Network techniques like PERT/CPM should be used.

4.1.6 Post Implementation Audit

It is like a post mortem of the project after implementation. This is an integral and vital part of project management because: 1.It gives very important feedback on project appraisal and strategy formulation. 2. It tells us how realistic were the assumptions while formulating the project 2.It is a valuable tool for decision making in future.

4.2 Aspects of Project Appraisal

Project appraisal includes four types of appraisal:

1. Market Appraisal
2. Technical Appraisal
3. Financial Appraisal
4. Economic Appraisal

4.2.1 Market Appraisal

Viability of a project will depend how much surplus it generates year by year. This will further depend on how much growth the products register in the market and the size of the market. Market appraisal seeks to asses this.

In addition, market appraisal also seeks to answer the questions like: a) what is the expected growth rate in the market b) What will be the project's share of the total market

To answer these questions, the market analysts need data on:

- Past and present consumption trends and Consumer Requirements
- Present and Prospective supply positions and import & exports
- Competitive structure
- Elasticity of Demand
- Production Constraints

Managerial Tool Kit

The question is how to get such data? There are many professional agencies publishing well researched industry reports. One such agency is CRIS-INFAC. Its reports are available in soft and hard copy versions. Databases like PROWESS database from CMIE also come in handy for market appraisal.

4.2.2 Technical Appraisal

This stage is especially critical when the project involves use of new technology. In this stage, appraisal of all technical issues after the commissioning of projects is done. It includes analysis of availability of required raw materials, availability of utilities like power, water etc , appropriateness of the plant design and layout, the proposed technology vis-à-vis the alternative technologies available, flexibility of the scale of operations, plant-size , the technical specifications and assembly line balancing.

4.2.3 Economic Appraisal

Economic appraisal means finding out the costs and benefits to the society due to the project. It is also known as Social Cost Benefit Analysis (SCBA). In this an effort is made to adjudge whether the project is desirable from social point of view. Some of the issues considered in this analysis are:

- Impact of the project on the distribution of income in the society
- Impact of the project on the level of savings and investment in the society
- Contribution of the project in socially desirable objectives like self-sufficiency, employment etc.

4.2.4 Financial Appraisal

As students of finance we must be GOOD at all the aspects of project appraisal. However, we must be VERY GOOD at Financial Appraisal:

Assumptions in Financial Appraisal

- The benefits from the project are measured by Cash Inflows and the costs will be measured by Cash outflows
- these cash flows occur only once a year
- The risk characterizing the project is similar to the risk complexion of on-going projects of the firm.

The first assumption is made to simplify the calculations; the second is made to clarify the concepts of financial appraisal to students in a simple manner. What about the third assumption? Do not worry. Wait till the chapter on cost of capital. After that it will be clearer to you. For now, just accept it as it is.

Financial Appraisal involves following two steps:

Step 1: Defining the stream of cash flows (both inflow and outflows) associated with the project.

Step 2: Analyzing the cash flow stream to determine whether the project is financially viable or not.

Let us see these steps in detail.

4.2.4.1 Step 1: Determination of Cash Inflows and Outflows

The first step in financial appraisal is determining costs of and benefits from the project. Remember, all cost and benefits must be measured in terms of *cash flows* and not profits. Why?

This is because the in calculation of profits (PAT), we deduct non-cash items also like depreciation, from sales. Due to this, profit figure does not correctly reflect the cash position.

Therefore, we make some adjustment in PAT go calculate cash flow. How?

We add back all non-cash charges like depreciation which have been deducted for the purpose of calculating profits to PAT. This gives us the value of cash flows.

2. Taxes are mandatory payments. Therefore, we will consider cash flows after tax (CFAT) only.

3. We consider only those cash flows (both inflows and outflows) that are relevant to suppliers of long term funds (debt and equity both).

The basic idea is to find out:

a) amount of long-term funds (debt + equity) is required for project and

b) How much cash surplus, belonging to suppliers of long term funds (debt + equity), project will generate, after meeting all other cash expenses.

4. Because of point no. 3 above, interest on long term loans must not be deducted for determining cash inflows. The reason is that for discounting cash flows we will use post tax cost of funds for the project. Now deducting interest on long term loans from cash inflows and then discounting these cash inflows again with long term cost of funds would be double counting.

5. We measure all costs and benefits only in incremental terms.

6. Benefits from the project under review accruing to other aspects of business should also be considered.

7. Sunk costs (means costs that already have been incurred) must be ignored.

8. Opportunity costs of using firm's existing resources must be considered.

9. The share of existing overhead costs which will be shared by project must be considered.

Now let's understand the application of these principles:

Mini Case 1

Karan, an engineer with 10 years of experience, and Arjun, an MBA with 7 years of experience, are evaluating a project. They have estimated the total outlay on the project as follows:

Plant & Machinery	₹ 40 lacs
Working Capital	₹ 30 lacs

The proposed scheme of financing is as follows:

Equity Capital	₹ 20 lacs
Term Loan	₹ 30 lacs
Trade Credit	₹ 10 lacs
Working Capital Advance	₹ 10 lacs

The project has an expected life of 10 years. Plant & Machinery will be depreciated by straight line method. The expected annual sales would be ₹ 100 lacs, and cost of sales (including depreciation but excluding interest) is expected to be ₹ 70 lacs per year. The tax rate of the company will be 50 percent. Term loan will carry 16 % interest and will be repaid in 5 equal annual installments, beginning from the end of the first year. Working capital advance will carry an interest rate of 18 percent and is expected to be renewed each year.

Define the cash flows for the first three years from the long term funds point of view:

	Year	0	1	2	3
A	Investment	(50.00)			
B	Sales		100.00	100.00	100.00
C	Operating Costs (excluding depreciation)		66.00	66.00	66.00
D	Depreciation		4.00	4.00	4.00
E	Interest on working capital advances		1.8	1.8	1.8
F	Profit Before Taxes		21.20	21.20	21.20
G	Tax		10.6	10.6	10.6
H	Profit After Tax		10.6	10.6	10.6
I	Initial Flow	(50.00)			
J	Operating Flow (H + D)		14.60	14.60	14.60
K	Net Cash Flow(I + J)	(50.00)	14.60	14.60	14.60

Working Notes:

1. The investment has to be considered from the point of view of suppliers of long term funds. In our case, we find that ₹ 20 lacs out of the investment of ₹ 30 lacs in current assets are financed by way of trade credit and working capital advance. The difference of ₹ 10 lacs is called working capital margin. Working capital margin is the contribution of the suppliers of long term funds towards working capital. Therefore the investment outlay relevant from the long term fund point of view will be investment in plant and machinery plus working capital margin.= ₹ 50 lacs.
2. Since depreciation is a non cash charge which has to be added to the PAT, this charge must be disclosed separately in the cash flow statement and not clubbed together with operating costs. Also, the depreciation charge relevant here is the one which is relevant from IT Act 1961.
3. While interest on long term debt must be excluded because of our assumptions (see the assumptions for calculating cash flows), interest on short-term bank borrowing must be included in the cash flow statement.

In the above mini case we have defined the cash flows for the first three years of project's life. But in practice the cash flows are defined:

- over the entire life of the project, or
- A specific time period if project is too long.

In both these cases, estimated salvage value of fixed assets as well as current assets (working capital) must be included in cash flow computations. Salvage value means value obtained when something is sold after use, for example: scrap value or value obtained from kabari etc. Salvage value is included as "Terminal Flow" in the last year on the time horizon (time horizon means the expected life of the project in years).

Let's take another mini case:

Mini Case 2

Amar Enterprises Limited is considering a capital project. The project would involve ₹ 120 lakhs investment in Plant and Machinery and ₹ 75 lakhs in working Capital. The firm wants to make good use of booming stock market and raise the funds from the market to the maximum. It plans to raise ₹ 80 lakhs equity, ₹ 45 lakhs debentures. It is expecting to get supplier's credit of 25 lakhs and ₹ 45 lakhs from commercial banks.

The project is estimated to last for 8 years. The firm follows WDV method of depreciation at 20% for plant and machinery. Sales are expected to be at ₹ 200 lakhs per annum. The cost of sales (including depreciation but excluding interest) is likely to be ₹ 100 lakhs a year. The company falls into a tax bracket of 50%. It is expected that at the end of 8 years, salvage value of plant and machinery will be equal to book value. The investment in current assets will be fully recovered. The debenture will have a coupon rate of 15 percent per annum. They will be repaid in six annual installments beginning end of third year. Working capital limit from commercial banks will be renewed each year and will attract in interest rate of 16%. It will be fully liquidated after 8 years. Supplier's credit is also expected to be uniformly available throughout the eight year period. However, it will be fully paid back at the end of the eighth year.

You are requested to compute the cash flows for this project from long term funds point of view. Ignore the effect of tax shields on depreciation.

Solution:

	Year	0	1	2	3	4	5	6	7	8
A	**Investment**	-125.00								
B	**Sales**		200.00	200.00	200.00	200.00	200.00	200.00	200.00	200.00
C	**Cost of Sales**		76.00	80.80	84.64	87.71	90.17	92.14	93.71	94.97
D	**Depreciation**		24.00	19.20	15.36	12.29	9.83	7.86	6.29	5.03
E	**PBIT (B-C-D)**		100.00	100.00	100.00	100.00	100.00	100.00	100.00	100.00
F	**Interest on ST Bank Borrowings**		7.20	7.20	7.20	7.20	7.20	7.20	7.20	7.20
G	**PBT (E-F)**		92.80	92.80	92.80	92.80	92.80	92.80	92.80	92.80
H	**Tax (50% of G)**		46.40	46.40	46.40	46.40	46.40	46.40	46.40	46.40
I	**PAT (G-H)**		46.40	46.40	46.40	46.40	46.40	46.40	46.40	46.40
J	**Net Salvage Value of Fixed Assets**									20.13
K	**Net Salvage Value of Current Assets**									75.00
L	**Repayment of Trade Credit**									25.00
M	**Payment of ST bank borrowings**									45.00
N	**Net Cash Flow (A+I+D+J+K-L-M)**	**-125.00**	**70.40**	**65.60**	**61.76**	**58.69**	**56.23**	**54.26**	**52.69**	**51.43**

The procedure of obtaining cash flows can be summarized as follows:

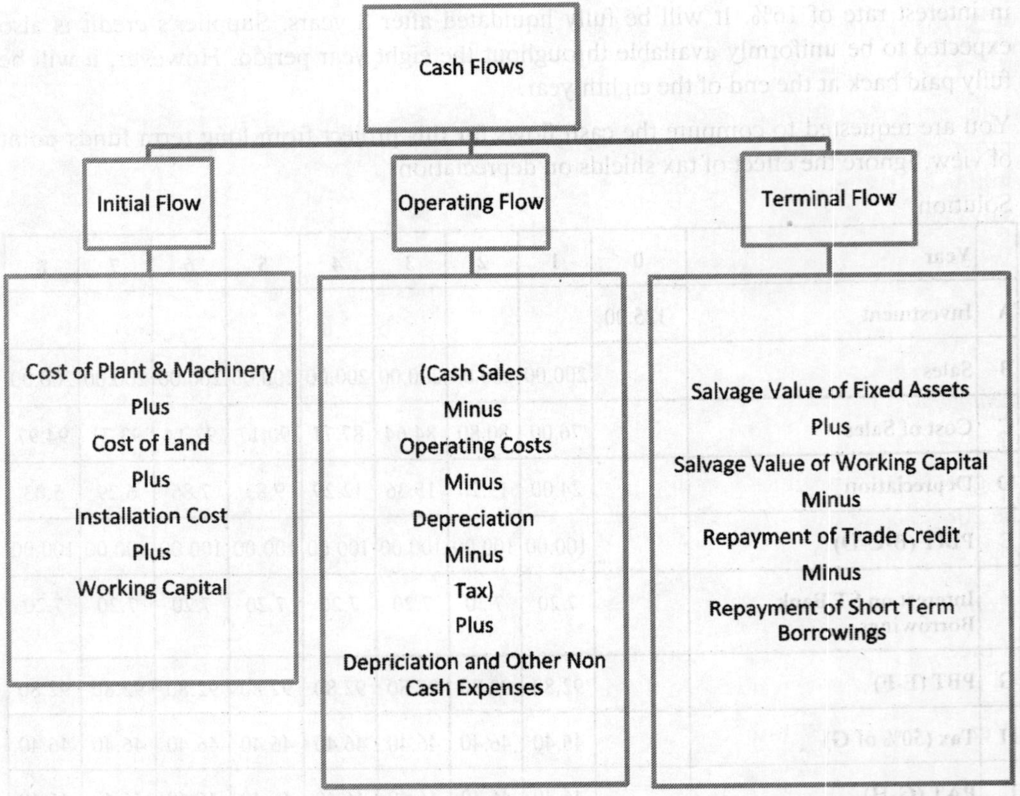

Once we have correctly estimated these cash flows, step 1 of financial appraisal is complete. The next step is to apply a suitable appraisal criterion on these cash flows.

4.2.4.2 Step 2: Appraisal Criteria

There are a number of criteria that can be employed to study the financial desirability of a project. Broadly they can be divided into two categories: Non-Discounting Criteria and Discounting Criteria.

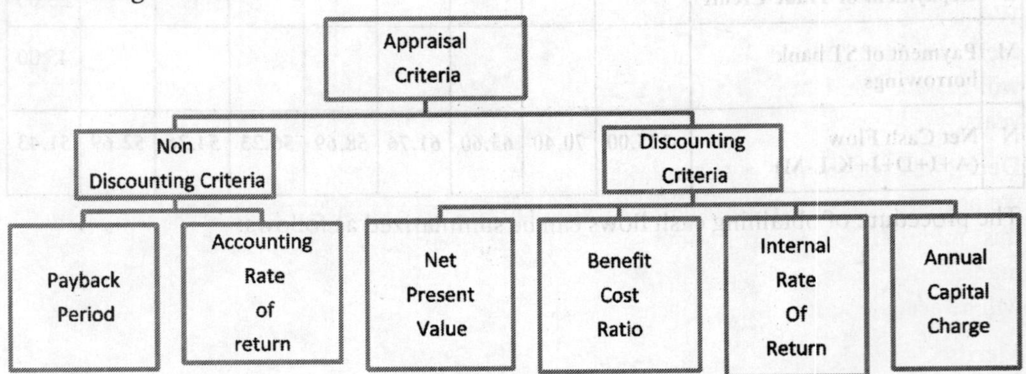

4.3 Techniques of Financial Appraisal

4.3.1Payback Period

It is the simplest and most widely used appraisal criterion for evaluating investments proposal. Payback period can be defined as the length of time required to recover the initial outlay in a project. In computation of payback period, we normally disregard salvage values, if any.

When annual cash inflows are constant the formula for calculating payback period is:

$$\text{Payback Period} = \frac{\text{Initial investment}}{\text{Constant annual cash flow only after taxes}}$$

Example 1

If a project requires an initial outlay of ₹ 20 lacs and has a life of 5 years, and is expected to generate a constant annual inflow of ₹ 8 lacs, the payback period of the project would be 20/8 = 2.5 years.

The procedure of calculating payback period will change if cash inflows are not constant.

Example 2

If the project is expected to generate an inflow of ₹ 4 lac, 6 lacs , 7 lacs, 9 lacs , 12 lacs and 14 lacs in successive years then the payback period is calculated as follows:

Year	Cash Flow	Cumulative Cash Flow	Amount of Initial Investment yet to be recovered
0	-20	-	20
1	4	4	16
2	6	10	10
3	7	17	3
4	9	26	Zero

We need only three lacs in fourth year to recover our initial investment completely. And there is a cash flow of 9 lacs in fourth year. Therefore, we may estimate that ₹ three lacs will be recovered in 3/9 = 0.33 years. Therefore, the payback period is 3 + 0.33 = 3.33 years.

Decision Criterion: Now calculating the payback is not the end. How to decide whether we accept a project whose payback period we have calculated? The decision criterion in this method is comparing the payback period to a cut-off period decided by the management. The projects which have a payback less than or equal to the cut-off period will be accepted and others rejected.

Merits

1. It is simple in both concept and application.

2. It helps to identify and reject risky projects by favoring those projects which generate more money in initial years.

3. It is better than accounting rate of return since it considers cash flows and not accounting profits.

Demerits

1. It fails to consider time value of money

2. The cutoff is chosen in an arbitrary manner which may result in choice of some bad short duration projects and rejection of some good long duration projects.

3. It fails to consider all cash flows over the life of the project.

4. Since the application of the payback period criterion leads to discrimination against projects which generate substantial cash inflows in later years, the criterion can not be considered as a measure of profitability.

To incorporate time value of money criteria in payback period, **discounted payback period** method can be used. Here if a project generates a cash flow of A every year and the initial investment is equal to I, and if discount rate is given by k, then discounted payback period "n" will be calculated from:

A * PVIFA (k, n) = I

Example 3

Suppose in the example 1, the discount rate is 10%, find the discounted payback period.

Putting values in the formula, we get:

8 x PVIFA (10, n) = 20

Solving, we get, n = payback period = 3.02 years. Earlier, the simple payback period was calculated as 2.5 years.

The discounted payback period will be longer than the simple payback period because of discounting.

Now which method is better in these two? Well, the only advantage of discounted payback over simple payback is that it considers time value of money. All other shortcomings of simple payback remain the same.

4.3.2Accounting Rate of Return (ARR)

It is defined as a tool which measures profitability of the investment proposals. Also known as the return on investments (POI) or average rate of return (ARR) and measured in terms of percentage.

ARR = Average profit after tax / average book value of investments

After ARR is calculated, what is the decision criterion?

Decision Criterion: The decision criterion for ARR is comparing it with some predetermined cut-off or with some other benchmark like industry average. If project ARR is higher than the cut-off (or benchmark), we accept the project. Otherwise we reject it.

ARR can also be used to rank projects when more than one investment option is being considered. The project with the higher ARR will be preferable to the one with lower ARR.

Example 4

Year	0	1	2	3
Investment	1,00,000			
Sales Revenue		1,40,000	1,20,000	90000
Operating Expenses(excluding depreciation)		80,000	60,000	50000
Depreciation		40,000	35,000	25000
PBIT		20,000	25,000	15000

Average Annual Income= 20,000+25,000+15,000/3

= ₹ 20,000

Average Net Book Value of Investments

= (1,00,000+0)/ 2

= 50,000

Average rate of return = (20,000/50,000) * 100

= 40 per cent

So the firm will accept the project if it is higher than the cut-off set by the management.

Merits

1. It is simple and easy to calculate.
2. It is easily understood by the businessmen who are used to understanding rates rather than other numbers.
3. It considers the returns over the entire life of the project hence serves as a measure of profitability (Unlike payback which is only a measure of capital recovery).

Demerits

1. It does not consider time value of money.
2. It is calculated with accounting income and not cash flows after taxes.
3. Finally the firm using ARR must decide a cutoff ARR which is generally chosen in an arbitrary manner. The current book returns of the whole firm may be an

inappropriate cut-off since it may be very high or very low. Due to this, we may end up accepting bad projects and rejecting good projects.

4. It does not allow the fact that profits can be reinvested.

4.3.3 Net Present Value (NPV)

Remember the chapter on time value of money? You are already comfortable with the concept of present value. The Net Present Value is an extension of that concept. NPV is nothing but present value of all cash inflows minus the initial investment.

$$NPV = \sum_{t=1}^{n} \frac{CF_t}{(1+k)^t} + \frac{S_n + W_n}{(1+k)^n} - I$$

Here, CF_t = cash inflow at the end of year t.

S_n = salvage value of fixed assets

W_n = salvage value of working capital in the nth year

I = Initial Investment

Decision Criterion: The decision rule for NPV is: Accept if NPV > 0 and reject if NPV < 0. It seldom happens that NPV is exactly equal to zero. If it is so, it means we can remain indifferent between choosing and not choosing the project. But actually if NPV is positive but close to zero then one must be cautious. This only means that the project should be studied more thoroughly. Even a slight adverse variation in cash flows may turn the project into an unacceptable one.

Example 5

Consider the following stream of cash flows. Compute the NPV if the discount rate is 12 per cent.

Year	0	1	2	3	4
Cash flow	(1,00,000)	30,000	35,000	40,000	40,000

Solution:

$$NPV = \frac{30000}{(1+0.12)^1} + \frac{35000}{(1+.012)^2} + \frac{4000}{(1+0.12)^3} + \frac{4000}{(1+0.12)^4} - 100000$$

NPV = ₹ 4115 = + ve

We may accept the project since NPV is positive.

Merits

1. Like all DCF techniques, it considers time value of money.
2. Like all DCF techniques, NPV considers cash flows for the entire life of the project.
3. NPV, by definition, is contribution to the net wealth of the shareholders. Therefore, maximizing NPV is also consistent with the objective of shareholder wealth maximization.

Demerits

Generally people are more comfortable in interpreting a rate of return. For example they will understand fully if we say "Project X generates 13% annual rate of return". However, NPV value obtained is difficult to interpret for most. This seems to be the only drawback of NPV. Still, NPV is better than almost any other criterion.

4.3.4 Benefit Cost Ratio or profitability index

This technique is a variant of NPV technique. It is defined as follows:

$$BCR = \frac{PV}{I}$$

Where BCR= Benefit cost ratio

PV = Present value of all cash inflows

I = Initial Investment

Another variant of BCR is NBCR.

$$NBCR = \frac{NPV}{I}$$

Putting formula NPV = PV – I, in above, we get NBCR = (PV- I)/ I

Or, NBCR = (PV/I) - 1

NBCR = BCR –1

Decision Criterion

Decision Rule for BCR is

If BCR >1 (NBCR > 0) Accept the project

If BCR< 1 (NBCR < 0) reject the project

Example 6

In the previous example of NPV let's calculate the BCR and NBCR.

Solution:

From the previous example, we get

$$PV = \frac{30000}{(1+0.12)^1} + \frac{35000}{(1+.012)^2} + \frac{4000}{(1+0.12)^3} + \frac{4000}{(1+0.12)^4} = 104115$$

I = 100000

BCR = PV/I = 1,04,115/1,00,,000 = 1.04 > 1, therefore accept.

NBCR = BCR -1 = 1.04-1 = 0.04 = +ve, therefore accept.

Merits

1. Like all DCF techniques, it considers time value of money.

2. Like all DCF techniques, BCR considers cash flows for the entire life of the project.
3. In fact, BCR has all the merits of NPV. In fact in some situations it is even better than NPV. Suppose two projects, have the same NPV of ₹ 40,000, but project A requires initial investment 60,000 and project B requires initial investment of 30,000. NPV will rank both the projects equally. But BCR will favor project B. It is so since BCR measures present value per rupee of outlay. It is considered useful for ranking a set of projects in order of decreasingly efficient use of capital.

Demerits

1. BCR is found inferior in case of mutually exclusive projects.
2. The biggest limitation of BCR is that it does not allow comparison of a combination of small projects with a large one.
3. If investment is taking place more than once then BCR can not be used.

4.3.5 Internal Rate of Return (IRR)

It is the rate of return at which the NPV of the project is equal to zero. IRR can also be defined as the rate of discount at which the present value of all cash inflows is equal to the present values of all outflows.

In NPV calculations, we need the rate of discounting beforehand. However, in case of IRR the rate has to be found out which will make NPV equal to zero.

We may write the formula for IRR, by putting NPV = 0.

$$NPV = \sum_{t=1}^{n} \frac{CF_t}{(1+k)^t} + \frac{S_n + W_n}{(1+k)^n} - I = 0$$

$$I = \sum_{t=1}^{n} \frac{CF_t}{(1+k)^t} + \frac{S_n + W_n}{(1+r)^n}$$

Therefore, r is the IRR in the above equation.

Decision Rule: To use the IRR as an appraisal criterion we require information about the cost of capital or funds employed in the project. If we define IRR as r and cost of funds as k then the decision rule is accept the projects which have r greater than k. and reject when r is less than k.

If r > k, accept. Otherwise, reject. Also can write

Accept IRR > cost of capital

Reject IRR > cost of capital

Example 7

Following are the cash flows of a project A. If cost of capital is 16%, advise whether the firm should accept the project.

Year	Cash Flows (in lacs)
0	(15)
1	7
2	7
3	5
4	2

Solution: First, we may calculate the IRR of the project.

As per the equation, if IRR = r, then r can be found by solving:

$$15 = \frac{7}{(1+r)^1} + \frac{7}{(1+r)^2} + \frac{5}{(1+r)^3} + \frac{2}{(1+r)^4}$$

By, trial and error, or using EXCEL, we get r = 18%. Now, given k = 16%, obviously r>k. Therefore, we may accept the proposal since IRR is higher than cost of capital.

Merits

1. It takes into account time value of money.
2. It considers the cash flow stream over the entire investment horizon.
3. Like ARR, it can be understood easily by those businessmen who are in the habit of thinking in terms of rate of return on capital employed.
4. Unlike NPV, IRR does not require cost of capital (or Discount rate) as an input in computation. It produces a rate of return itself. In fact, in case of IRR, cost of capital enters later while applying decision criterion.

Demerits

1. This criteria works well with simple projects where there is a single cash outflow followed by one or more cash inflows. The signs of cash flows in **simple projects** look like this:

   "- + + + + + + +"

   In such cases when we solve the formula for IRR, we get a single IRR.

   But in complex projects, where there is more than one cash outflow, IRR fails.

   The signs of cash flows in case of ***complex projects*** look like this:

   "- + + + - + +"

   As we can see, here there are two changes of signs in cash flows. First, in the year 1 (from –ve to + ve) and second, in fourth year (from +ve to –ve). It means there is one more cash outflow in fourth year. Projects having more than one change of sign in cash flows are known as complex projects.

In complex projects, on solving the formula, we get more than one IRR. Hence, we can not decide which one is the correct IRR.

Project	Year 0	Year 1	Year 2	Year 3	Year 4	IRR
A	-20	5	10	15	15	34%
B	-10	-10	15	15	15	40%
C	-10	5	-10	20	20	44%, 200000%

In above table we can see that projects A and B are simple investments and therefore will result in unique IRR. But in case of project C there two IR₹ since their cash flow changes sign more than once. For such projects IRR can not be a meaningful criterion.

2. The IRR criteria can be misleading when the decision maker has to choose between mutually exclusive projects that differ significantly in terms of outlays.
3. IRR, by definition, also represents the rate at which the cash inflows are reinvested. This aspect can be easily seen in calculation of IRR. However, this feature is one of the important weaknesses of IRR. Suppose two projects have IR₹ 14% and 19 % respectively. It means the firm is able to reinvest the cash flows from first project at 14% and at 19% in case of second project. Don't you find it amusing? How can the same firm have the ability to reinvest its funds at two vastly different rates?

Conclusion: In spite of these limitations, the IRR is one of the most used criterions. All financial institutions insist that for the projects involving very huge investments the DPR must contain IRR calculation.

Essential Background Reading Box

1. **Mutually Exclusive Projects:** When we have to decide on one and only one of the projects out of many, such projects are called mutually exclusive. It means accepting one would lead to automatic rejection of others. For example, you want to buy a car and there are three choices available in your budget. If you decide on car A, car B and C get automatically rejected, since you will buy only one of the cars.
2. **Contingent Projects:** They are projects which are accepted or rejected if some other project is accepted or rejected. They are contingent upon (depend on) some other project's acceptance or rejection. For example, you will consider constructing a garage in your house only if you are buying a car. You will not need a garage if you do not buy a car. So construction of garage is contingent upon buying a car. One of the projects is dependent on other.

NPV vs IRR: Which is better?

In evaluating projects with NPV and IRR methods, many a time both the methods give same recommendations. In other words, often if a project is accepted/rejected by NPV method, it also gets accepted/rejected by IRR method. However, sometimes we see situations where a project is accepted by NPV but rejected by IRR or vice versa. What should we do in such situations? Should we accept the result of NPV or IRR?

In this section we would try to answer this question.

4.3.6 NPV Vs IRR

First, let us look at situations where both the methods give same accept/reject results.

Situations when NPV and IRR give similar results

NPV and IRR methods always give same results in case of usual projects with a single cash outflow and subsequent cash inflows. Such projects are known as "conventional projects".

If we draw a plot between the NPV and discount rates for a project, it will look like this:

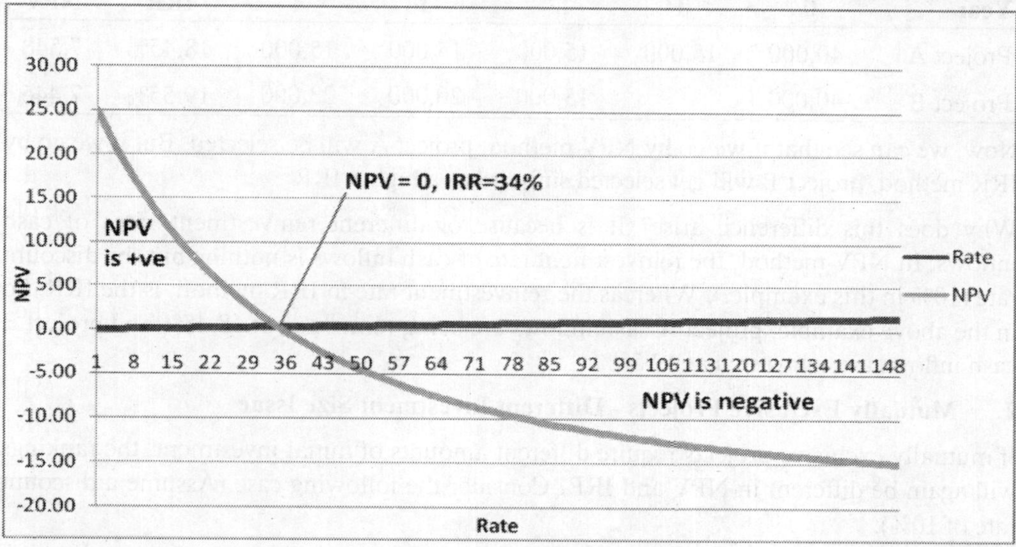

In the above plot, NPV is on Y axis and discount rate is on X axis. We can see that NPV remains positive till the discount rate is less than 34%. At 34%, NPV is zero. This is the IRR of the project. After 34%, NPV is negative.

Now, if we are evaluating the above project with NPV method, we will accept it so long as it is positive.

Also, if we are using IRR method, then we will accept the project when IRR is greater than the cost of capital. In the above case, the project will be accepted till cost of capital is less than 34%, by IRR method. However, we can see in the plot that so long as the discount rate is less than 34 %, NPV is also positive. This means for discount rates less than 34%, both NPV and IRR are giving same recommendation of "Accept".

For discount rates more than 34%, IRR will reject the project, by definition. And, for discount rates more than 34%, NPV is also negative. Again both the methods have given the same recommendation "Reject".

Therefore we can see that NPV and IRR give same results in this case.

Situations Where NPV and IRR give different results

1. Mutually Exclusive Projects - Reinvestment Rate Issue

In case of mutually exclusive projects, the results of NPV and IRR may be different. What it means is that, if we rank projects based on NPV and IRR, these rankings will not be the same. A project ranked high by NPV may get a low rank by IRR.

Consider the following situation where the firm has to chose either the project A or B. Assume the discount rate as 10%.

Year	0	1	2	3	4	IRR	NPV
Project A	-40,000	15,000	15,000	15,000	15,000	18.45%	7,548
Project B	-40,000		15,000	20,000	23,000	19.55%	7,446

Now, we can see that if we go by NPV method, project A will be selected. But if we go by IRR method, project B will get selected since it has a higher IRR.

Why does this difference arise? It is because of different reinvestment rates of cash inflows. In NPV method, the reinvestment rate of cash inflows is nothing but the discount rate (10% in this example.). Whereas the reinvestment rate in IRR method, is the IRR. So in the above example, project A cash inflows are being reinvested at 18.45% and project B cash inflows are reinvested at 19.55%.

2. Mutually Exclusive Projects - Different Investment Size Issue

If mutually exclusive projects require different amounts of initial investment, the rankings will again be different in NPV and IRR. Consider the following case (Assume a discount rate of 10%):

Year	0	1	IRR	NPV
Project A	-1,000	3,000	200.00%	1,727
Project B	-5,000	9,000	80.00%	3,182

Why does it happen? It is because in case of IRR, we would prefer project A because it generate higher returns in percentage terms. Percentage IRR indicates return on per rupee of investment. IRR will give a measure of return per rupee of investment, regardless of the size of investment. Where as, in NPV, the result is an "absolute" rupee value. This absolute value obtained in NPV does not reflect the return generated per rupee of investment, but total addition to the wealth of the shareholders.

Therefore, NPV has given higher rank to project B. The NPV is higher because of higher investment amount in case of project B.

3. Multiple IRR in case of complex investments

This point has already been discussed in the section on demerits of IRR.

Conclusion

So what is the conclusion? Whether NPV is better or IRR?

First situation was of mutually exclusive projects. There is a critical weakness of IRR method observed here. In IRR, the reinvestment rate will be higher if the project has high IRR, and lower, if project has low IRR. This is a very unrealistic situation as discussed earlier. This problem is not there in NPV. It is definitely more realistic to assume that the firm will be able to reinvest its cash flows at the going required rate of return.

Also, we know that NPV is a measure of net wealth generated from a project. We have already seen that the objective of the firm is shareholder's wealth maximization. Therefore, we would choose project with higher NPV as it would mean higher increase in the wealth of shareholder, even if its IRR is lower.

Second situation was where the initial investment between two projects is different. Here again, since our objective is shareholder's wealth maximization, we would choose the project with higher NPV rather than IRR.

In the last situation of multiple IRR, we have seen that it is a very critical weakness of IRR method.

Therefore, we can conclude that theoretically, NPV method is far superior to the IRR method. This is mainly because it is consistent with the objective of the firm (shareholder's wealth maximization).

However, in practice, IRR is a very popular tool and is found usually reliable too. Why? Chiefly because as stated earlier, interpreting a rate of return given by IRR is easier for most of us than interpreting the absolute value of NPV. Also, IRR does not require "cost of capital" or "required rate of return" for its calculation.

Managerial Tool Kit

Feeling confused? Not sure where to use NPV or IRR? Here are some rules of thumb:

If the projects are not mutually exclusive, or do not have more than one change of sign in cash flows, use IRR with confidence.

However, whenever you are dealing with mutually exclusive projects or complex projects, be cautious. Either use IRR by modifying it for reinvestment rate, or use NPV. With NPV, you are almost always safe. Annual capital charge (ACC) may also be used.

4.3.7 Annual Capital Charge

This appraisal criterion is used for evaluating mutually exclusive projects or alternatives which provide similar service but have differing patterns of costs and often unequal life spans, e.g., choosing between fork-lift transportation and conveyor belt transportation.

The calculation involves two steps:

Step 1: Determine the present value of investment and operating costs.

Step 2: Divide this present value by PVIFA (k, n) where n represents life span of the project. The result is known as annual capital charge or equivalent annual cost.

Decision criterion: We will choose the machine whose Annual capital charge is lower.

Example 8

Pawan Putra Limited, is evaluating two alternative machines, A and B. while the two machines have the same purpose, system A has the life of 7 years while system B has life of five years. The initial outlay and operating costs are given as follows:

Year	A	B
0	15,00,000	1,20,000
1	1,50,000	2,50,000
2	1,75,000	3,10,000
3	2,00,000	4,00,000
4	2,50,000	4,75,000
5	3,00,000	5,00,000
6	3,50,000	
7	3,00,000	

If cost of capital is 12 percent, which machine is a better investment? Assume net salvage value to be zero.

Solution:

First we will find out the present value of all costs of both the machines.

Present value of costs of machine A=

$$= 1500000 + \frac{150000}{(1+0.12)^1} + \frac{175000}{(1+0.12)^2} + \frac{200000}{(1+0.12)^3} + \frac{250000}{(1+0.12)^4} + \frac{300000}{(1+0.12)^5} + \frac{350000}{(1+0.12)^6} + \frac{300000}{(1+0.12)^7} = 2675817.01$$

Similarly, in case of machine B,

Present value of costs =

$$1200000 + \frac{250000}{(1+0.12)^1} + \frac{310000}{(1+0.12)^2} + \frac{400000}{(1+0.12)^3} + \frac{475000}{(1+0.12)^4} + \frac{500000}{(1+0.12)^5}$$

= 1371517.92

Now, can we take a decision based on the present values of costs of these machines? No, not yet. Why? It is because the lives of these two machines are different. A has a life of 7 years while B has a life of 5 years.

Therefore, the next step is to find the annual capital charge of both. To obtain annual capital charge, first we create a fake annuity whose present value will be equal to the present value of cost of machines. Now using a discount rate of 12%, we can easily get the value of annual payments of this annuity. This annual payment is nothing but annual capital charge.

For machine A, using the annuity formula as described above, we get:

PVA = A x PVIA (12%, 7)

Putting values we get, for machine A:

2675817.01 = *A x PVIA* (12%, 7)

Putting Values, we get A= Annual Capital Charge = 5,60,487.13 for machine A.

Similarly, for machine B, Annual Capital Charge = 3,80,472.42

Now, since the annual capital charge of machine A is higher, we will choose machine B.

Managerial Tool Kit

Whenever only cost data (outflows) is available, including the initial investment and other annual expenses, Annual Capital Charge method should be used for appraisal.

Illustrative Solved Examples

Q 1. Maruti Nandan Limited is considering modernization of its plant. The firm is considering two machines, out of which one has to be purchased. The firm sells all its products on cash. Its required rate of return (cost of capital) is 12%. The firm falls into the 30% tax bracket. Relevant details about both the machines are as follows:

	Machine A	**Machine B**
Investment Required	5,00,000	5,00,000
Projected Sales	8,00,000	7,00,000
Manufacturing Costs		
Direct Materials	64,000	84,000
Direct Labor	75,000	60,000
Factory Overheads	85,000	84,000
Administrative Overheads	**30,000**	**15,000**
Selling & Distribution Costs	15,000	15,000
Estimated Economic Life	3 Years	4 Years
Salvage Value	60,000	35,000

The firm follows straight line method of depreciation. Advise which machine is more profitable based on Payback Period Criterion.

Solution

We may calculate the payback period of the machine as per the following computations:

		Machine A	Machine B
1	Investment Required	5,00,000	5,00,000
2	Sales	8,00,000	7,00,000
3	Less Costs		
4	Direct Materials	64,000	84,000
5	Direct Labor	75,000	60,000
6	Factory Overheads	85,000	8,000
7	Depreciation	1,46,667	1,16250
8	**Administrative Overheads**	**30,000**	**15,000**
9	Selling & Distribution Costs	15,000	15,000
10	Interest on Capital	60,000	60,000
11	Total Costs (3+4+5+6+7+8+9+10)	4,75,667	4,34250
12	Profit Before Tax (2-11)	3,24,333	2,65,750
13	less Taxes @ 30%	97,300	79,725
14	Profit After Tax (12-13)	2,27,033	1,86,025
15	Add Depreciation	1,46,667	1,16,250
16	Net Cash flow (14+15)	3,73,700	3,02,275
17	Payback Period (1/16)	1.34 Years	1.65 Years

Since machine A has a shorter payback period, we would prefer it over machine B.

Case Study

Q2. A limited company is considering the purchase of a new machine. The machines, A and B are available. From the following information relating to the two machines ascertain which of the two machines will be more profitable. The average rate of income tax may be taken at 50%.

	Machine A	Machine B
	(₹)	(₹)
Cost of each machine	1,00,,000	1,60000
Working Life	4 years	6 years
Salvage Value	Nil	Nil
Earnings before taxes		
Year 1	20,000	16,000
Year 2	30,000	28,000

Year 3	40,000	50,000
Year 4	50,000	60,000
Year 5	Nil	36,000
Year 6	Nil	26,000

Solution:

In solving this problem we would obtain payback period of each machine. For calculating payback period we need cash flow calculations first:

Cash Flow Calculation of Machine A

	Machine A	Year 1	Year 2	Year 3	Year 4
1	EBIT	20,000	30,000	40,000	50,000
2	Less Tax @ 50%	10,000	15,000	20,000	25,000
3	PAT (1-2)	10,000	15,000	20,000	25,000
4	Add Depreciation	25,000	25,000	25,000	25,000
5	Cash Flow (3+4)	35,000	40,000	45,000	50,000

Since cash flows are not of equal amount each year, we need to obtain cumulative cash flows to calculate payback period:

Year	Cash Flow	Cumulative Cash Flow
1	35,000	35,000
2	40,000	75,000
3	45,000	1,20,000
4	50,000	1,70,000

As we can see that ₹ 100000 of investment in machine was recovered sometime in the 3 rd year. Therefore, payback period should be between 2 and 3 years:

Payback period = 24 months (2 years) + {(1,00,000-75,000)/1,20,000}x12 months = 26.5 months

Similarly, for machine B, the calculation shall be as follows:

	Machine A	Year 1	Year 2	Year 3	Year 4	Year 5	Year 6
1	EBIT	16,000	28,000	50,000	60,000	36,000	26,000
2	Less Tax @ 50%	8,000	14,000	25,000	30,000	18,000	13,000
3	PAT (1-2)	8,000	14,000	25,000	30,000	18,000	13,000
4	Add Depreciation	26,667	26,667	26,667	26,,667	26,667	26,667
5	Cash Flow (3+4)	34,667	40,667	51,667	56,667	44,667	39,667

Again, to calculate payback period, we need to calculate cumulative cash flows:

Year	Cash Flow	Cumulative Cash Flow
1	34,667	34,667
2	40,667	75,333
3	51,667	1,27,000
4	56,667	1,83,667
5	44,667	2,28,333
6	39,667	2,68,000

As we can see, the investment of ₹ 1,60,000 is recovered between 3rd and 4th year. Therefore, we may calculate the payback period as follows:

Payback period = 36 months (3 years) + {(1,60,000-1,27,000)/1,83,667} x 12 months = 38.15 months.

Since payback period of machine A is shorter, we would prefer the machine A.

Q3. Rudrawatar Limited purchases 12000 tubes @ ₹ 4.00 per tube from its suppliers for packing its "Dentaglow" brand of toothpaste. However, the new GM (production) feels that if the firm produces these tubes on its own it will incur a cost of ₹ 3.50 (excluding depreciation). The machinery will cost ₹ 20000 and the applicable depreciation rate is 20% pm on WDV basis. The machine is expected to last for five years. The firm falls in the tax bracket of 40% and its required rate of return is 10%. The salvage value of machine after five years is nil. What is your recommendation to the firm?

Solution

First let us compute the cash flows associated with purchase of new machine:

Savings in cost due to own manufacturing =12000 x (4-3.5)= 6000 per year

Computation of Cash Flows:

Year	0	1	2	3	4	5
Initial investment	-20,000					
Savings		6,000	6,000	6,000	6,000	6,000
Depreciation		-4,000	-3,200	-2,560	-2,048	-1,638
Profit before Tax		2,000	2,800	3,440	3,952	4,362
Tax @ 40%		800	1,120	1,376	1,581	1,745
Profit After tax		1,200	1,680	2,064	2371	2,617
PAT+ Depreciation		5,200	4,880	4,624	4,419	4,255

Now, the required rate of return is 10%, therefore, we may compute the NPV of buying the new machine as follows:

$$NPV = -20,000 + \frac{5200}{(1+0.10)^1} + \frac{4880}{(1+0.10)^2} + \frac{4624}{(1+0.10)^3} + \frac{4419}{(1+0.10)^4} + \frac{4255}{(1+0.10)^5} = -2105$$

Since, the NPV is negative; we can not accept the project. The recommendation is to continue purchasing the tubes from supplier rather than manufacturing in-house.

Q4: Suppose in the above problem, the machine has a salvage value equal to its book value at the end of five years. What would be your recommendation now?

Solution

The machine has salvage value now; therefore, the NPV calculation will include the present value of salvage value five years from now. As given, salvage value is equal to the book value after five years; it can be obtained by subtracting the total depreciation of five years from the purchase price.

Book value after five years = Purchase Price- Total depreciation charged in five years

= 20,000- (4,000+3,200+2,560+2,048+1,638)

= 6554

$$NPV = -20,000 + \frac{5200}{(1+0.10)^1} + \frac{4880}{(1+0.10)^2} + \frac{4624}{(1+0.10)^3} + \frac{4419}{(1+0.10)^4} + \frac{4255}{(1+0.10)^5} + \frac{6554}{(1+0.10)^5} = 1964$$

Now, the NPV is positive. Therefore, we recommend discontinuing the purchases from supplier and going for manufacturing in house.

Q5. Tarak Limited is considering two independent projects A and B. The cash flows associated with these are as follows:

Year	0	1	2	3	4	5
Project A	-60	18	22	25	30	12
Project B	-70	13	24	30	35	41

The company has a debt to equity ratio of 5:2. The cost of debt is 14% on pre tax basis and cost of equity is 28%. The applicable tax rate is 40%.

Advise the company which of these projects is better on the basis of NPV criterion.

Solution

First, we will calculate the WACC of the firm:

WACC = post tax cost of debt x proportion of debt + cost of equity x proportion of equity

= 14% (1-0.4) x 5/7 + 28% x 2/7

= 14%

This WACC will be our required rate of return from these projects. Now we can calculate the NPV of these projects as follows:

$$NPV_A = -60 + \frac{18}{(1+0.14)^1} + \frac{22}{(1+0.14)^2} + \frac{25}{(1+0.14)^3} + \frac{30}{(1+0.14)^4} + \frac{12}{(1+0.14)^5}$$

Solving, we get $NPV_A = 13.59$

Similarly, for project B:

$$NPV_B = -70 + \frac{13}{(1+0.14)^1} + \frac{24}{(1+0.14)^2} + \frac{30}{(1+0.14)^3} + \frac{35}{(1+0.14)^4} + \frac{41}{(1+0.14)^5}$$

Solving, we get $NPV_B = 22.14$

Now, since $NPV_B > NPV_A$, project B should be accepted.

Q6. Jaya Limited is considering purchase of a machine costing ₹ 300000. It has a useful life of 5 years with no salvage value. Following details are available:

Year	**1**	**2**	**3**	**4**	**5**
Profit Before Depreciation & Taxes	**100000**	**110000**	**120000**	**130000**	**90000**

The applicable tax rate is 40% and depreciation is charged at the rate of 20% by WDV method. Find out the IRR of the project.

Solution

First we will calculate the cash flows as follows:

Computation of Cash Flows:

Year	1	2	3	4	5
Profit Before Depreciation & Taxes	1,00,000	1,10,000	1,20,000	1,30,000	90,000
Depreciation	60,000	48,000	38,400	30,720	24,576
Profit Before Tax	40,000	62,000	81,600	99,280	65,424
Tax @40%	16,000	24,800	32,640	39,712	26,170
Profit After Tax	24,000	37,200	48,960	59,568	39,254
PAT+ Depreciation	84,000	85,200	87,360	90,288	63,830

Therefore, IRR can be calculated as the rate of discount such that NPV = 0

Let's say IRR = k, then

$$0 = -300000 + \frac{84000}{(1+k)^1} + \frac{85200}{(1+k)^2} + \frac{87360}{(1+k)^3} + \frac{90288}{(1+k)^4} + \frac{63830}{(1+k)^5}$$

By trial and error, we get k = 11.82%.

Q7. Kampoonji Limited has a limited investment budget of ₹ 30 lakhs. It is considering three projects X, Y and Z. Out of this projects Y and Z are mutually exclusive. The estimated life of all the projects is 1 year. The other details are as follows:

Project	Investment Required	NPV
X	15	7
Y	16	8
Z	14	6

Prepare a report for the management, giving your recommendations with reasons.

Solution

The report is as follows:

Combinations	Investment	NPV	Remarks
X and Y	31	15	Investment required exceeds budget, rejected.
X and Z	29	13	Investment within budget, recommended.
Y and Z	30	14	Though within budget, not feasible as Y and Z are mutually exclusive.

Therefore, the combination X and Z are recommended.

Q8. Aayush Limited has ₹ 1500000 capex budget. It has got the following investment options with other details:

Proposed Project	Investment Required	Benefit Cost Ratio
P	2,00,000	0.98
Q	6,50,000	1.25
R	6,00,000	1.08
S	5,00,000	1.30
T	2,50,000	1.20
U	7,00,000	1.28

If these projects are indivisible then give your recommendations as to which projects should be accepted.

Solution

First of all, we would rank the projects on the basis of benefit cost ratio:

Proposed Project	Investment Required	Benefit Cost Ratio	Rank
S	5,50,000	1.3	1
U	7,00,000	1.28	2
Q	6,50,000	1.25	3
T	2,50,000	1.2	4
R	6,00,000	1.08	5
P	2,00,000	0.98	6

Now let us also rank the projects on the basis of NPV. We know that NPV = (BCR-1) x Initial Investment. Therefore:

Proposed Project	Investment Required	Benefit Cost Ratio	NPV	Rank
U	7,00,000	1.28	196000	1
S	5,50,000	1.3	1,65,000	2
Q	6,50,000	1.25	1,62,500	3
T	2,50,000	1.2	50,000	4
R	6,00,000	1.08	48,000	5
P	2,00,000	0.98	-4,000	6

As we can see both the methods have given same rankings. Therefore, in the capital budget of ₹ 1500000, we can select projects S, U and T. This will consume the entire budget and the total NPV generated will be ₹ 4,11,000.

Summary

- Firms invest their resources in both short term and long term assets. The process of deciding on suitable long term investments is known as Capital budgeting. These long term investments are made with the objective of shareholder's wealth maximization.
- Capital budgeting is primarily concerned with ***sizeable*** investments in ***long-term*** assets. Long terms assets include *tangible assets* like plant, machinery and equipment or *intangible assets* like new technology, patents, trade-marks and R & D. These decisions have special significance because 1) These decisions affect the firm's risk-return profile for a large number of years.2) They involve huge amount of money and may be critical to firm's performance for a number of years.3) Once taken, practically they are irreversible. 4) They are difficult to take since almost always more than one alternative is present.
- Capital budgeting decisions are difficult since a) It is difficult to quantitatively express (put in numbers) all the related costs and benefits. b) The benefits of such capital expenditure will come only in future which is uncertain. c) To analyze these decisions, it becomes necessary to bring all the cost and benefits on a common time frame first.
- These decisions start with identification of investment opportunities and end with performance review after the project is implemented.
- Project appraisal involves a)Market Appraisal b) Technical Appraisal c) Financial Appraisal d)Economic Appraisal.

- Some important assumptions in financial appraisal are a)The benefits from the project are measured by Cash Inflows and the costs will be measured by Cash outflows b)these cash flows occur only once a year c)The risk characterizing the project is similar to the risk complexion of on-going projects of the firm.
- Essentially financial appraisal is a two step process a) Defining the stream of cash flows (both inflow and outflows) associated with the project and b) Analyzing the cash flow stream with the help of appraisal criterion to determine whether the project is financially viable or not.
- Appraisal criteria are divided into two types 1) Discounting Techniques and 2) Non Discounting Techniques.
- First non discounting technique is payback period. It is the length of time required to recover the initial outlay in a project. We accept the projects which have payback period more than a pre-specified number. Another variant of payback period is discounted payback period.
- Second non-discounting technique is Accounting Rate of Return (ARR). ARR is defined as average profit after tax divided by average book value of investments. If ARR is higher than some predetermined cut-off rate, projects are accepted.
- First discounting technique is Net Present Value (NPV). It is present value of all cash inflow minus value of investment outlay. Project is accepted if NPV is positive.
- Second discounting technique is Benefit Cost Ratio (BCR), also known as Profitability Index (PI). It is present value of all cash inflows divided by the investment outlay. Project is accepted if BCR is greater than 1.
- Next discounting technique is very popular Internal Rate of Return (IRR). It is the rate of return at which the NPV of the project is equal to zero. IRR can also be defined as the rate of discount at which the present value of all cash inflows is equal to the present values of all outflows. We accept the project when IRR is greater than cost of capital.
- NPV and IRR may give different recommendations in different circumstances.
- Annual Capital Charge is another appraisal criterion used for evaluating mutually exclusive projects or alternatives which provide similar service but have differing patterns of costs and often unequal life spans. It is found out by 1) determining the present value of investment and operating costs.2) dividing this present value by PVIFA (k, n) where n represents life span of the project. The result is known as annual capital charge or equivalent annual cost. Then we choose the machine whose Annual capital charge is lower.

Test Your Understanding

State whether the following statements are true or false

1. IRR is the rate of discount at which NPV is negative.
2. Payback period is a discounted cash flow method of appraisal.
3. Accounting Rate of Return is a Non DCF method of appraisal.
4. NPV and IRR methods always give same recommendations.
5. NPV is the best method to appraise the capital projects.
6. In IRR, reinvestment rate of higher IRR projects are higher and that of lower IRR projects are lower.
7. If a project's cash flows have more than one change of sign, then it will have a unique IRR.
8. Two projects X and Y have IR₹ 12% and 13% respectively. The cost of capital is 16%. We would select project Y since it has higher IRR.
9. While estimating project cash flows, we always consider interest on both short and long term loans.
10. In NPV method, the cash flows are assumed to be reinvested at cost of capital.
11. The rankings of BCR and NPV will always be the same.
12. IRR is superior to NPV since it is expressed in percentage and can be easily understood by most.
13. In case of mutually exclusive projects, the one with higher NPV should be chosen, not the one with higher IRR.
14. Discounted payback period method is inferior to Simple payback period method.
15. Despite its weaknesses, IRR is a popular method in practice.

Answers :1.F 2.F 3.T 4.F 5.T 6.T 7.F 8.F 9. F10.T11. F12.F 13.T 14.F 15. T

Multiple Choice Questions

1. Which is not Payback method? **(UPTU 2009)**

   a) Pay-off method　　b) Payout method

   c) Recoupment Period Method　　d) None

2. Capital Budgeting deals with

   a) Cash Management　　b) Management of Working Capital

   c) Managing Fixed Assets　　d) None of the above

3. A project has investment of ₹ 120000 and yield annual cash flow of ₹ 12000 for 12 years. Find out payback period: **(UPTU 2009)**

   a) 15 years　　b) 10 years

c) 19 years d) None

4. Which of the following will be affected by Taxation of a project? (UPTU 2009)
   a) Project Earning
   b) Weighted average cost of capital
   c) Further investment incentives of the project
   d) All of the above
5. When a project should be accepted under profitability index: (UPTU 2009)
   a) When PI > 1 b) When PI < 1
   c) When PI = 0 d) None of the above
6. Non discounting method of capital budgeting is: (UPTU, 2010)
   a) PV method b) IRR
   c) Profitability Index d) Accounting Rate of Return
7. IRR of a project is the rate where NPV tends to: (UPTU, 2010)
   a) Zero b) More than 1
   c) Less than 1 d) 1
8. When a project will be accepted, if the IRR rule is applicable: (UPTU 2010)
   a) IRR> k b) IRR < k
   c) IRR is greater than or equal to k d) None
9. Estimates of future cash flows should not include:
   a) Income tax receipts and payments
   b) Projections of cash flows for continuing use of asset
   c) Net cash flow from salvage value
   d) None of these.
10. The IRR method assumes that intermediate cash flows are reinvested at:
    a) IRR b) Cost of Capital
    c) Risk free rate of return d) Cost of debt
11. In capital budgeting appraisal, the cash flows are computed from:
    a) Long term funds point of view
    b) Short Term funds point of view
    c) Both Long and Short term points of view
    d) None of these
12. Which of the following are true about NPV?
    a) It considers all the cash flows

b) It gives more weight to distant flows than near-term flows

c) It considers time value of money

d) Both a) and c) are true.

13. If in a project the BCR is equal to 1, then IRR is:

a) More than discount rate b) Less than discount rate

c) Equal to discount rate d) None of these

14. Net Salvage Value of Fixed assets is equal to:

a) Excess of salvage value over book value

b) Excess of book value over salvage value

c) Scrap value

d) Scrap value less any income tax paid on excess of scrap value over book value

15. Which of the following is true:

a) If BCR > 1 and NBCR < 0, accept b) IF BCR > 1 and NBCR > 0, accept

c) If BCR < 1 and NBCR > 1, reject d) If BCR<1 and NBCR < 1, accept.

Answers 1. b, 2.c, 3.b, 4.d, 5.a, 6.d, 7.a, 8. a, 9. a, 10. a, 11.a, 12. d, 13. c, 14. d, 15.b

Practice Problems

1. Cash blow Limited is considering a project with the following details

Initial Investment	**₹ 50,0000**
PBDT	
Year 1	**₹ 1,25,000**
Year 2	₹ 1,40,000
Year 3	₹ 1,70,000
Year 4	₹ 2,50,000
Year 5	₹ 3,75,000

The company falls in the tax bracket of 40%. The estimated economic life of the asset is 5 years. The required rate of return for the firm is 10%.

Calculate:

1) NPV

2) IRR

3) Benefit Cost Ratio

4) Net Benefit Cost Ratio

5) Payback Period

6) Accounting Rate of Return

2. Konfusion Limited is investing in a machinery costing ₹ 2 Crore. The cash flows from the project have been forecast as follows:

Year	Cash Flow
0	(2 Cr.)
1	40 lakh
2	60 lakh
3	65 lakh
4	70 lakh
5	100 lakh

Later it was discovered that the calculation of cash flows is incorrect. In place of a depreciation of 20% on WDV basis, the finance manager had charged depreciation at 10% on SLM basis. The required rate of return for the company is 15% and it falls in 30% tax bracket.

Calculate:

a) Revised cash flows

b) NPV

c) IRR

3. A company is planning to purchase new machinery and it has shortlisted two machines. It has to purchase only one of the two. The details are as follows:

	Machine A	Machine B
Purchase Price	₹ 75,000	₹ 50,000
Operating Cost year 1	₹ 15,000	₹ 20,000
2	₹ 15,000	₹ 25,000
3	₹ 20,000	₹ 30,000
4	₹ 25,000	₹ 35,000
5	₹ 25,000	
6	₹ 40,000	
7	₹ 40,000	

Both the machines have no salvage value. Advise which machine is to be purchased if the required rate of return is 16%.

Q4. Calculate the net benefit cost ratio for the following two projects:

	Year 0	Year 1	Year 2
Project A	-90,000	60,000	50,000
Project B	-1,20,000	80,000	70,000

The required rates of return are:

a) 13% b) 16% c) 20%

At what rates these projects should be accepted?

Q5. Badal Do Limited is considering replacement of its fully depreciated machine by a new one costing ₹ 150000. The current market value of the old machine is ₹ 20000 and the salvage value after six years is zero. The salvage value of the new machine after six years is ₹ 16000. With the use of new machine, the sales are expected to increase by 20000 per annum and operating expenses to decrease by 12000 per annum. If the company follows a 30% WDV depreciation policy, its cost of capital is 12% and attracts a tax rate of 30%, should the company replace the existing machine?

Q6. The cash flows of two mutually exclusive projects are as under:

Year	Project A	Project B
0	-40,000	-20,000
1	13,000	7,000
2	8000	13,000
3	14,000	12,000
4	12,000	
5	11,000	
6	15,000	

1) Estimate the NPV of project A and B using 15% as hurdle rate.
2) Estimate the IRR of both the projects.
3) Why is there a conflict between both the criteria?
4) Which criterion would you chose and why? Which project would you ultimately recommend?

7. On the basis of the data given below calculate. (i) ARR on projects A & B (ii) Pay back period for A & B. Depreciation has been charged on straight line basis and estimated life span of both projects is 5 years.

Item	Project A	Project B
Cost	₹ 56,125	₹ 56,125

net income after depriciation & taxes (in ₹)

Year	Project A	Project B
1	3375	11375
2	5375	9375
3	7375	7375
4	9375	5375
5	11375	3375

Review Questions

1. What is capital budgeting? List various methods of capital budgeting. Give merits and demerits of NPV method. **(UPTU 2007, 2009)**
2. What are various DCF techniques being applied for capital budgeting decisions? **(UPTU 2006)**
3. Explain why NPV is superior to IRR?(UPTU, 2005, DU 2006, DU 2008)
4. Write down the factors affecting investment decision? **(UPTU 2005)**
5. What is the need for capital budgeting?(UPTU, 2007)
6. Explain the procedure of capital budgeting. **(UPTU 2007)**
7. Explain clearly the payback method of evaluating alternative capital expenditure decisions. **(UPTU 2007, DU 2006, 2007, 2008, 2010)**
8. Distinguish between Internal Rate of Return and Accounting Rate of Return with the help of an example.
9. Explain the method of IRR. How is it calculated? Also give its merits and demerits.
10. Explain with an example the method of Profitability Index (PI). What is the relationship between PI and NPV? **(DU 2009)**
11. Explain distinctive features of capital budgeting decisions? **(DU)**
12. What are the steps involved in the calculation or IRR in the case of uneven cash in flows? **(DU)**
13. What do you mean by incremental cash flows. **(2005)**
14. Why do we focus on cash flows rather than on profits while evaluating capital budgeting decisions? **(DU 2005)**

Case Study 1 (UPTU, 2010)

Acclaim entertainment, Inc. is a mass marketer of interactive entertainment software whose games can be played on such well-known video game systems as Ninja and Sega. Some of their more successful games include Martal Kombat 1 and 2, NBA jam1 and 2. Maximum Carnage,Virtual Bart (Simpson), and NFL Quarterback. Acclaim has also obtained licenses from True Lies, Batman Forever, and Spiderman. Presently, Acclaim has licensing agreements with three industry leaders: Sony computer entertainment of America (SCE), Ninja, and Sega.

Acclaim is currently in the design/production stage of a new version of Martal Kombat, since the previous versions of the game were extremely successful acclaim is not greatly concerned with the acceptance of the game by the general public. It is concerned, however, with the hardware platform that should be chosen to distribute the game. Since licensing agreement are extremely short term, acclaim wonders which of the three hardware companies should carry Mortal Combat. For example, the licensing agreement with SCE expires in December two years from now. The Ninja agreement expires in December this year and the Sega contract expires in December of next year. While these contracts expire and have traditionally been renewed or extended in the future.

A further consideration involves the costs charged by each company. SEC Ninja and Sega charge their licensees a fixed amount per unit based on chip configuration, memory capacity, and market price. This charge covers manufacturing, printing and packaging of the unit, as well as a royalty for the use of their respective names, proprietary information and technology, Furthermore, these charges are subject to adjustment at the discretion of SCE, Ninja and Sega. To offset the expenses of licensing fees, acclaim must speculate on the ability of the three hardware platforms to access enough end users to make their games profitable. Ninja and Sega hold a greater share of the market, but SCE charges lower licensing fees.

In general, the product life cycle in the interactive software business is from one month up to eighteen months with the majority of sales occurring within the first three months after introduction.

Acclaim's management has assembled the following projected net cash flows associated with the distribution of Martal Kombat. These net cash flows reflect all licensing fees, productions costs, advertising expenditures, revenues, etc. From the table given below answer the following questions:

Year	Cash Flow (in millions)		
	SEC	Ninja	Sega
0	-₹ 40	-₹ 40	-₹ 40
1	₹ 34	₹ 44	₹ 41
2	₹ 10	₹ 16	₹ 18
3	₹ 5		₹ 4
4	₹ 1		

Questions:

a) What is the payback period for Martal Kombat when marketed under the three different hardware companies? Assuming a required payback period of 1 year, which company would you allow to carry the new product?

b) Assuming a discount rate of 10%, what is the net present value (NPV) under each system? Under which system, if any, would you be willing to produce Martal Kombat?

c) What are the Internal Rates of Return (IRR) under each marketer? Which marketer(s) has/ have accepted IR₹

Case Study 2 (UPTU, 2010)

The management of a manufacturing company is planning to replace an old machine which has been in use for the last six years by a new and improved model of a similar machine which has a record of improved output. Give your opinion in regard to the proposal form the following data. Support your answer with arguments:

	Old machine (₹)	New Machine (₹)
Purchase Price	90,000	180000
Annual Expenses on:		
a) Power Consumption	10,500	12,000
b) Consumable Stores	6,000	7,500
c) Repairs & Maintenance	7,500	6,000
Labor cost per running hour	3	3.75
Units of output per hour	60	90
Machine Running Hours	2,000	2,000
Material Cost per Unit	40 paise	40 paise
Selling price per unit	1.00	1.00
Estimated Life (Years)	10	10

Case Study 3 (DU 2005)

Ankit Manufacturing Co. Ltd. owns a machine which is six years old and has an estimated remaining life of two years. The following cash flow estimates have been made for the machine:

End of Year	Net Cash flow	Salvage Value
6	-	₹ 1,20,000
7	₹ 80,000	₹ 60,000
8	₹ 50,000	Nil

Management wants to determine whether the machine should be retained for one more year or two or more years. The Company's required rate of return is 10%. Use NPV method.

The present value of the one rupee at 10% for different years is given below:

Year	1	2	3	4	5	6	7	8	9	10
	0.909	0.826	0.751	0.683	0.621	0.564	0.513	0.467	0.424	0.386

Case Study 4 (DU 2006)

A company is considering the replacement of an existing obsolete machine. It is faced with two alternatives:

(i) To buy machine A which is similar to the existing machine.

(ii) To buy machine B which is more expensive and has higher capacity.

The cash flows after tax at the present level of operations for the two alternatives are as follows:

After Tax, Cash Flows (in Lakhs of ₹) at the end of year:

Year	A	B
0	-25	-40
1	–	10
2	5	14
3	20	16
4	14	17
5	14	15

Cost of capital is 10%. Calculate:

(i) Net present value

(ii) Profitability Index.

Advise the company about the better alternative.

Case Study 5 (DU 2007)

Corporation whishes to replace its existing machine. The following information is available:

Existing Machine:

Purchased 2 years ago

Remaining life = 6 years

Salvage value = ₹ 500

Current book value = ₹ 2,600

Realizable Market Value = ₹ 3,000

Depreciation – Straight Line method

New Machine:

Capital Cost of = ₹ 8,000

Estimated useful life = 6 years

Estimated Salvage value = ₹ 800

The replaced machine would permit an output expansion. As a result sales is expected to rise by ₹ 1,000 per year. Operating expenses would decline by ₹ 1,500 per year. It would require an additional inventory of ₹ 2,000 and would cause an increase in Accounts Payable by ₹ 500. Assume a Corporate tax of 40% and cost of capital of 18%, should the machine be replaced? Use differential approach for calculations:

PV of an annuity of Re.1 for 6 years is 3.498. The PV factor @ 18% is as follows:

Year	1	2	3	4	5	6
PV factor	0.847	0.718	0.609	0.516	0.437	0.370

References

1. Brealey, Richard A & Myres, Stewart C. (2007), Tata McGraw Hill, New Delhi
2. Damodaran, Aswath. (1994). Damodaran on Valuation, John Wiley & Sons, New York.
3. Dayananda, Don et al (2002), Capital Budgeting: Financial Appraisal of Investment Projects, Cambridge University Press, London
4. Khan, M Y & Jain (2009) P K, Financial Management, Tata McGraw Hill, New Delhi
5. Kishore, Ravi. M (2009), Financial Management, Taxmann Publications, New Delhi
6. Mukherjee, D D (2006). Credit Appraisal, Risk Analysis And Decision Making, Snow White Publications Pvt. Ltd., New Delhi
7. Pandey, I M (2009). Financial Management, Vikas Publishing House, New Delhi
8. Study Material & Work book on "Financial Management for Managers": The Institute of Chartered Financial Analysts of India, Hyderabad.
9. Van Horne, James C. (2007),Financial Management & Policy, Pearson Prentice Hall, New Delhi

CHAPTER 5 Risk Analysis in Capital Budgeting

Learning Objectives:

By the end of this chapter and having completed the essential reading and activities, you should be able to:

- Understand risk in capital budgeting context
- Carry out quantitative measurement of risk
- Apply various risk assessment techniques in capital budgeting
- Know when to use a particular technique and why. Also, why not?

5.0 Introduction

We may remember that in the section on project evaluation, we start with defining cash flows from the project over a period of time. At that time it is assumed that these cash flows will occur in future with certainty. We express no doubt at all about it. We simply take these cash flows as given.

However, in real world this may not be the case. The actual cash flows from a project may be very - very different from the ones that we have estimated. This might happen because of the fact that our calculation of cash flows is always based on some assumptions about the future which may or may not turn out to be true always.

For example, if we are building a new plant for product A and want to arrive at the future cash flows for next 5 years then we may need expected sales data for this product for next 5 years. Suppose we estimate that the future sales will be as follows:

(₹ Lakhs)

Year	1	2	3	4	5
Sales	15	16	18	24	30

However, are we sure that actual sales of the product A shall be exactly like this in coming five years? No, we can not be sure. Why? This is because this estimate of sales is based on our assumption about the state of economy. If the economic conditions turn out to be the same as we anticipated then this sales estimate will be true. But, if the economic conditions turn out to be different tomorrow, then sales may be better or worse than these estimates.

Therefore, since we can not forecast cash flows associated with a project with certainty there is always an element of risk that our forecasts may prove to be wrong in future. ***We can say that risk arises in project evaluation since we can not anticipate the occurrence of the possible future events with certainty, and consequently, can not make any correct predictions about the cash flow sequence.***

What are the sources of these risks? These risks arise because of various possible events that may take place in future. These events may happen in any of the following areas:

1. **The overall economy**: The factors are related to the overall level of business activity. They might be affected by events like external and internal political situation, government's monetary and fiscal policies and social conditions etc.

2. **The Industry:** A particular industry may be affected with factors peculiar to it, e.g., rise in material costs, wages etc.

3. **The Company:** The factors particular to a company like, natural disaster, strike etc.

In more formal terms, we may say that risk associated with an investment may be defined as the variability that is likely to occur in the future returns from the investment. A project shall be considered more risky if the variability of returns from it is higher. We already know that these risks can be measured by standard deviation and coefficient of variation.

However, there are various methods to handle risk in capital budgeting. Some of these are:

Measurement of Risk in Capital Budgeting:

Though there exist many tools to measure risk in capital budgeting but two popular measures are discussed here:

5.1 Standard Deviation (Absolute Measure of Risk)

This is a measure of risk which is more intuitively appealing and perhaps most widely used. Standard deviation is represented by σ. Perhaps you have already guessed, it is nothing but square root of variance.

Let us say that n possible levels of cash flows are CF_1, CF_2, CF_3 ....CF_n. Also let the probability of these cash flows be P_1, P_2, P_3..............P_n. Let the mean of these cash flows be given by $\overline{CF}$. The mean cash flow may also be called expected cash flow and is given by:

$$Expected\ cash\ flow\ \overline{CF} = \sum_{1}^{n} P_i CF_i$$

The variance and standard deviation respectively are given by:

$$\text{Variance}\ \sigma^2 = \sum_{1}^{n} P_i \left\{CF_1 - \overline{CF}\right\}^2$$

$$\text{Standard Deviation}(\sigma) = \sqrt{Variance\,(\sigma^2)}$$

Higher the standard deviation associated with a project, higher will be the variability and therefore higher the risk.

If two projects have same mean (expected cash flow) but different standard deviations, then the project having higher standard deviation will carry higher risk.

Let us understand this by an example:

Project A

CF_i	$\overline{CF}$	$CF_i - \overline{CF}$	$(CF_i - \overline{CF})^2$	P_i	$P_i(CF_i - \overline{CF})^2$
6000	25200	19200	368640000	0.2	73728000
45000	25200	-19800	392040000	0.4	156816000
30000	25200	-4800	23040000	0.2	4608000
				$\sum_{1}^{n} P_i\{E(R)-R_i\}^2$	235152000
				σ (project A)	15334.66661

Project B

CF_i	$\overline{CF}$	$CF_i - \overline{CF}$	$(CF_i - \overline{CF})^2$	P_i	$P_i(CF_i - \overline{CF})^2$
55000	25200	-29800	888040000	0.2	177608000
26000	25200	-800	640000	0.4	256000
19000	25200	6200	38440000	0.2	7688000
				$\sum_{1}^{n} P_i\{E(R)-R_i\}^2$	185552000
				σ (project B)	13621.74732

In the above example, both the projects have the same mean. Now, since the project B has lower standard deviation than project A, it has lower variability of cash flows. In other words, project B is less risky than project A, therefore preferable.

5.2 Coefficient of Variation (Relative Measure of Risk)

In the above example, the comparison of riskiness of these projects was easier since both had the same expected (or mean) cash flow. However, it becomes difficult to compare the standard deviation of two projects if their expected cash flow is also different. In such a case, we use a measure of risk called coefficient of variation.

$$\text{Co-efficient of Variation} = \frac{\text{standard deviation}}{\overline{CF}}$$

Sometimes coefficient of variation may also be express as a percentage. In this case the formula becomes:

$$\text{Co-efficient of Variation (\%)} = \frac{\text{standard deviation}}{CF} \times 100$$

Coefficient of variation enables comparison between two projects with different expected cash flows. This is because it measures risk per unit of mean. So, even if means are different, risk per unit of mean shall always be comparable.

Example 1

Two projects A and B have the following expected cash flows and standard deviation:

	Project A	Project B
Expected Cash Flow	40,000	1,35,000
Standard Deviation	24,000	1,12,000

Which project is riskier?

Since the expected cash flows are different, we cannot compare the standard deviations directly.

However, we may use the coefficient of variation. Calculating, we get:

Coefficient of variation of project A = 24,000/40,000 = 0.60

Coefficient of variation of project B = 1,12,000/1,35,000 = 0.82

Since, the coefficient of variation of project B is higher than project A; we conclude that project B has higher risk than project A.

We have already learnt that risk in capital budgeting arises due to variability in expected cash flows. Therefore, the finance manager can not say with certainty that his cash flow projection is going to be true in reality as well.

Due to this inherent unpredictability, it would be better for the finance manager to forecast more than one set of cash flows under different assumptions.

5.3 Techniques of Risk Analysis

1. Payback
2. Risk Adjusted Discount Rate
3. Certainty Equivalents
4. Sensitivity Analysis
5. Simulation
6. Decision Tree Analysis

5.3.1 Payback Period

We have already discussed **payback** and its calculation. We noted that payback is the number of years when the capital investment of the firm will be fully recovered. It is a very popular method amongst the businessmen. This method automatically selects the projects with shorter payback periods. This method actually does not look at the profitability of the projects but their ability to return the capital quickly. Also, this method favors short term projects which may be less risky than long term projects.

However, the payback period method actually takes care of a possible, but, not always likely; risk of sudden business closure after a few years. This scenario is theoretically possible but not always likely. This might happen in case of sudden flood, earthquake etc. These disasters may happen but no one does business by anticipating these calamities. The day to day concern is not some big disaster but more likely event of actual cash flows going wrong and not tallying with projected cash flows. Also, this method does not take care of time value of money.

5.3.2 Risk Adjusted Discount Rate

Let us look at another way of handling risk, known as the **risk adjusted discount rate method**. We know that

$$NPV = \sum_{i=0}^{n} \frac{CFi}{(1+k)^i} - I$$

Here, we know that k is the required rate of return. It is also known as discount rate. Now, we also know that if the project A is more risky than project B then, to compensate for the additional risk, the required rate of return on project A shall be more than project B.

That means the investors shall demand a risk premium on the more risky projects than the less risky ones. Now, let us imagine the discount rate k as the sum of two different parts. One, a risk free rate which is constant and the other, a risk premium which increases/decreases as the risk increases/decreases.

$$k = k_f + k_r$$

Where, k_f is risk free rate and k_r is the risk premium.

Now, if we feel the project is risky we may increase the value of k and re-calculate NPV.

Sometimes companies follow a discount rate policy specifying different risk premiums for projects with different riskiness. It may look like this:

Routine maintenance capex- No Risk	Zero risk premium
Modernization capex- Low Risk	4% risk premium
Expansion capex- Moderate Risk	6% risk premium
Diversification capex- High Risk	8% risk premium

As we can see, this approach is a commonsense approach to handling risk in investment appraisal by adjusting the minimum required rate of return to reflect the riskiness of the project.

Merits

1. This method is simple in application and is easy to understand.
2. Also, it encourages an investor to be sensitive towards risk.
3. It actually produces a decision advice in the form of risk-adjusted NPV.

Demerits

1. There is no fool proof method to calculate risk premium. It may differ from person to person.
2. It assumes that investors are risk averse which may not always be the case.

5.3.3 Certainty Equivalent

Another method of handling risk is **certainty equivalent.** If we look at the equation above carefully we will find that the by using risk adjusted discount rate we have done adjustment in the denominator. We can also incorporate risk by making adjustment in the numerator.

Let us say an investor expects a cash flow of ₹ 100000 next year as per his best estimate. But he feels that there is a chance that he may not realize this estimate. So, to be on the safe side, he does not use ₹ 100000 in his analysis. Instead, to be on the safe side, he uses ₹ 80000 as the expected cash flow. So, by applying a correction factor of 0.8 (= 80,000/1,00,000) he has become more certain of his estimates. This is known as certainty equivalent.

We may write the formula for NPV with certainty equivalent method as:

$$\sum_{i=0}^{n} \frac{CFi}{(1+k)^{i}} - I$$

Where α_t = risk adjustment factor or the certainty equivalent coefficient

And k = risk free rate of interest.

α_t can be calculated as the ratio of Certain Cash Flow to Risky Cash Flow.

The problem with certainty equivalent approach is that the value of coefficient α_t is likely to vary from project to project. Also, when the forecaster knows that this method is being used by the top management, he may actually inflate her estimates beforehand in anticipation of a reduction by certainty equivalent factor.

The concept would be clearer with an example:

Example 2

The projected cash outflows of a project are as follows:

Year 1 ₹ 50,000

Year 2	₹ 90,000
Year 3	₹ 70,000

The promoters feel that these cash flows may not actually materialize and want to convert them to certainty equivalents. The risk adjustment factor for year 1 is 75%, year 2 is 80% and year 3 is 90 %. The risk free rate is 12%. If the initial investment is ₹ 120000, advise whether the project can be accepted or not?

Solution:

First we will convert the estimated cash flows to certainty equivalent:

Year	Cash Flow	Risk Adjustment	Certainty Equivalent Factor
Year 1	₹ 50,000	75%	₹ 37,500
Year 2	₹ 90,000	80%	₹ 72,000
Year 3	₹ 70,000	90%	₹ 63,000

Initial investment is ₹ 120000; therefore NPV will be equal to:

NPV = -1,20,000 + 37,500 PVIF (12%, 1) +72,000 PVIF (12%, 2) + 63,000 PVIF (12%, 3)

= ₹ 14,037

Since, NPV with certainty equivalents is positive, we may accept the project.

Another method of risk analysis is sensitivity analysis. It is also known as "what if" analysis. What is sensitivity analysis?

5.3.4 Sensitivity Analysis

We are aware that in any project appraisal the first step is to determine the cash flows. How do we determine cash flows? We first forecast sales. Sales are calculated as quantity demanded multiplied by sales price. Then there are a number of cost items that are deducted from the sales to arrive at profit. After this only we may determine cash flows. So, we may see that calculation of cash flows depends on a large number of variables. If our forecast of any of these variables goes wrong, the resultant cash flows will change. Since the resultant cash flows will change, our calculation of NPV and IRR will also change.

Since the future is uncertain and any of the variables may actually turn out to be different from our forecast, a better idea would be to develop three different forecasts for different scenarios. These scenarios may be a) optimistic b) pessimistic c) normal.

The NPV is recalculated in these different scenarios or different assumptions. This method of recalculating NPV or IRR by changing the forecast is called sensitivity analysis.

Sensitivity analysis is a way of analyzing change in the project's NPV (or IRR) for a given change in one of the variables. It indicates how sensitive a project's NPV (or IRR) is to change in particular variables. The steps involved in sensitivity analysis are as follows:

1. Identification of all those variables which have an influence on the project's NPV (or IRR).
2. Definition of the underlying (mathematical) relationship between the variables.
3. Analysis of the impact of the change in each of the variables on the project's NPV.

Sensitivity analysis has the following advantages:

1. It compels the decision maker to identify the variables which affect the cash flow forecasts. This helps him in understanding the investment project in totality.
2. It indicates the critical variables for which additional information may be obtained. The decision maker can consider actions which may help in strengthening the week spots in the project.
3. It helps to expose inappropriate forecasts, and thus guides the decision maker to concentrate on relevant variables.

Its weaknesses are as follows:

1. It does not provide clear cut results. The term optimistic and pessimistic could mean different things to different persons in an organization. Thus, the range of values suggested may be inconsistent.
2. It fails to focus on the interrelationship between variables. For example, sale volume may be related to price and cost. A price cut may lead to high sales and low operating cost.

Managerial Tool Kit

The sensitivity analysis can be performed easily with the help of Excel spreadsheet. First, create a projected profitability statement (or NPV calculation) in Excel 2007. Make sure that you do not hardcode (**hardcode** means directly inputting the value in a cell rather than obtaining it with a formula) the sales value and profits. Use formulas to calculate sales, total variable costs, contribution and profits etc. Now the effect of changes in any one variable can be analyzed by going to data ⟶ what if analysis⟶Goal Seek. Then the reader may follow the instructions in Goal Seek dialogue box and analyze the effect of change in variables one by one. Try it and see your confidence soaring.

5.3.5 Simulation

Simulation means mimicking reality. Simulation is the name given to a statistical technique as well. In this technique, we make use of predetermined probability distributions and random numbers to make an estimate of risky outcomes.

Simulation is similar to sensitivity analysis. However, simulation is far more comprehensive. In sensitivity analysis, we could estimate the impact of change in only one of the key variables on NPV. Whereas, in simulation, we can see the impact of changes in ALL key variables on NPV within one run only. These runs are called iterations also.

Simulation is superior to sensitivity analysis on other counts as well. Simulation does consider the interaction among variables. It also considers the probabilities of change in variables.

What is the outcome we get in simulation analysis? We get a probability distribution of NPVs (All possible values of NPV along with their probabilities). Once we have the probability distribution we can obtain the mean and standard deviation of these values. These values coming out of simulation exercise are more reliable estimates of likely risk-return profile of the project.

Now, the question is how simulation exercise is conducted in practice? Following is a summary of steps in a typical simulation exercise.

1. The simulation exercise begins with a clear cut definition of the problem. This definition should also be as precise as possible to avoid ambiguity.
2. Then the variables associated with the problems should be identified.
3. The numerical relationship between variables should be clearly spelt out. This relationship is also known as "model" or "formulae".
4. Develop a probability distribution for each of the variables specified.
5. Run the experiment with the aid of a computer package that can select values of different variables based on some assigned random number and put it into the formula to calculate the NPV.

The outcome of above exercise is a probability distribution of all possible NPVs. Here a question arises. What should be the discount rate to be used to calculate the NPVs in a simulation exercise? Well, it is time to be surprised. The discount rate to be used here is the risk free rate.

Surprised? Ok, here is the logic. The simulation exercise takes into account the possible changes in values of all variables. Or in other words the simulation exercise already has taken care of variability of various values. This variability is nothing but the risk. Now if we use the risk adjusted discount rate, it will be equivalent to double counting.

In summary, since simulation has already taken care of variability of cash flows, we use risk free rate to compute the NPV.

Now let us look at the merits and demerits of simulation:

Merits

1. Simulation is very handy when problems are so complex that mathematical modeling is not useable.
2. It is far more comprehensive than sensitivity analysis.
3. It is not very quantitatively complicated and therefore is easy to understand by people with non mathematical background as well.

4. It comes in very handy if the variables under consideration fail to be fitted into standard distributions like Poisson, Normal Exponential etc.
5. Simulation can handle both dependence and independence among variables.

Demerits

1. Model often becomes too complex to handle.
2. The probability values assigned to various variables are subjective in nature.
3. Simulation is not an optimization technique. It does not actually answer the question that whether the project should be accepted or not. It produces another probability distribution and that is it.
4. Simulation is costly and time consuming since it requires mountains of data to handle.

5.3.6 Decision Tree Analysis

A decision tree is a diagrammatic representation in the form of a tree which indicates the magnitude, probabilities and inter-relationship of all possible outcomes. This diagram looks like the branches of a tree. Therefore, it is called decision tree approach.

Often decisions related to investment in projects are not one-time decisions like "accept" or "reject". In real life, the success of a project depends on its future cash flows. The decision tree analysis helps a manager in assessing the impact of future events on the projects cash flows.

Decision trees are particularly useful in the following two situations:

1) When decisions at a point of time affect the decisions of the firm at a later date in future.
2) When decisions related to a project have to be made sequentially. It is normally the case in complex investment decisions.

Decision trees are constructed from left to right. Each branch shows the probability and the value of a possible outcome.

We can understand the decision tree method better with the aid of an example:

Example 3: Ram Bharose Limited is considering a project which has an initial investment of ₹ 500000. The project will last for two years only. The probability distribution of cash inflows from the project are as follows:

Year 1

Cash Inflow	Probability
2,00,000	0.4
3,00,000	0.3
4,00,000	0.3

The cash inflows in year 2 depend on the cash inflows in year 1. The probability distribution of year 2 inflows is as under:

Year 2

Year 1 Inflow = ₹ 2,00,000		Year 1 Inflow = ₹ 3,00,000		Year 1 Inflow = ₹ 4,00,000	
Cash inflow	**Probability**	**Cash inflow**	**Probability**	**Cash inflow**	**Probability**
3,50,000	0.2	3,00,000	0.3	1,50,000	0.1
4,00,000	0.5	3,50,000	0.3	3,00,000	0.8
4,50,000	0.3	4,00,000	0.4	2,00,000	0.1

If the discount rate is 12%, calculate the expected NPV of the project with the help of decision tree analysis.

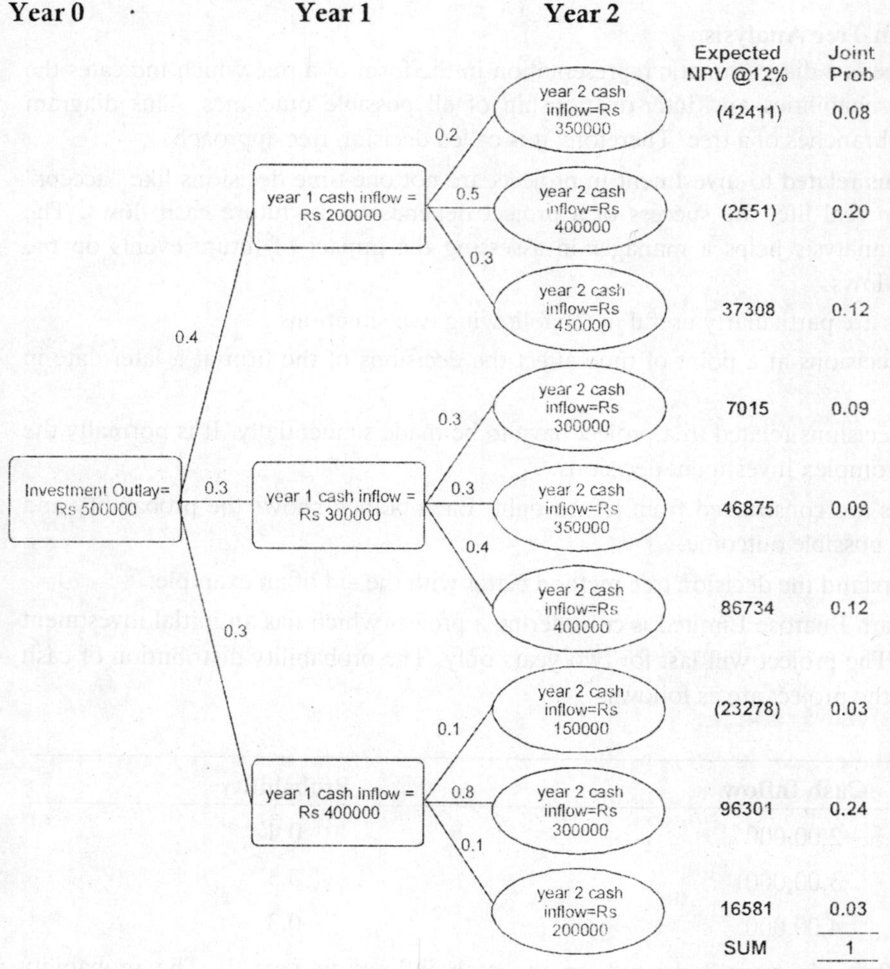

In the above diagram, the expected NPV has been calculated by discounting the cash flows 12%. The joint probabilities have been calculated by multiplying the individual probabilities of a particular path. For example, for first path, the individual probabilities are 0.4 for year 1 and 0.2 for year 2. So the joint probability is 0.08 (0.4 x 0.2). Finally, the expected NPV has been calculated by multiplying the NPV of a path with its joint probability.

We may write the formula for expected NPV as follows:

$$\overline{NPV} = \sum_{i=1}^{n} P_i \times NPV_i$$

Where, $\overline{NPV}$ is expected NPV. P_i is joint probability of ith path and NPV_i is the NPV related to ith path. Here it may be seen that $\sum P_i = 1$.

The beauty of decision approach is that it considers all possible cash flows along with their probabilities. Also, the best and worst possible NPVs can be easily seen in the diagram. In the above diagram we see that the best possible NPV is ₹ 96,301 and worst possible NPV is (₹ 23,278).

Merits and Demerits of decision tree analysis

Merits

1. Decision trees help link the present decisions with future. This can be useful for managers in choosing the strategy that is most beneficial.
2. Decisions trees bring clarity to by clearly depicting various cash flow possibilities and associated risks.
3. The decision trees are simpler to understand because they are in graphic format. (Remember "a picture is worth a thousand words"?)

Demerits

1. Decision trees may become so very complex so very quickly that the analyst may lose interest.
2. As more and more variables and interdependence between them is included the calculations may become very cumbersome and complicated.

Illustrative Solved Examples

1. **Samvedansheel Limited is considering a project to manufacture a new product A. The projected profitability statement for the project is as follows:**

Sales (3000 units @ ₹ 10)		**₹ 30,000**
Variable Cost		
Material	**₹ 6,000**	
Labor	**₹ 4,500**	**₹ 10,500**
Contribution		**₹ 19,500**
Less Fixed Costs		**₹ 10,000**
Profit		**₹ 9,500**

Conduct a sensitivity analysis for the project.

Solution: The sensitivity analysis yields the following conclusions:

1) The profits will be wiped out if the sale price/sales quantity goes down by more than 31.8%.
2) If the material costs increase by 158% the profits will be zero.
3) If the labor costs increase by 211 %, the profits will be wiped out.
4) The project will become a loss making one if the fixed costs increase by more than 95%.

We can conclude that sales units and price are most sensitive and need careful consideration.

2. **Kapish Limited is considering investment proposals at Salasar and Menhdipur. At Salasar, the company has to choose between proposals A and B and at Menhdipur the choice is between project C and D.The following details are available:**

For Salasar:

	Expected NPV	Standard Deviation
Project A	₹ 3,00,000	₹ 1,50,000
Project B	₹ 3,00,000	₹ 2,50,000

For Menhdipur:

	Expected NPV	Standard Deviation
Project C	₹ 3,50,000	₹ 1,80,000
Project D	₹ 4,00,000	₹ 3,50,000

Can you advise the company about which project is better at each location?

Solution

Salasar

Here the NPV of both the projects A and B are the same. Therefore, we should choose the project that is less risky. Standard deviation is a measure of risk. Therefore the less risky project will be the one which has lower standard deviation. Hence we would choose the project A.

Menhdipur

Here both projects C and D have different, expected NPV and risk. We can apply the coefficient of variation in such cases.

Coefficient of Variation (C) = Standard Deviation/Expected NPV

= 1,80,000/3,50,000 = 0.51

Coefficient of Variation (D) = 3,50,000/4,00,000 = 0.87

Since coefficient of variation of Project D is higher than Project C, we choose project C, since it is less risky of the two.

3. **Anjani Limited is considering a project with the following details:**

Initial Investment	**₹ 2,00,000**
Cash Inflow (year 1-4)	**₹ 70,000**
Discount Rate	**12%**

Conduct a sensitivity analysis and find out which of the following is most sensitive:

a) **Cash Inflow**

b) **Discount Rate**

c) **Initial Investment**

Solution

We find that the NPV of the project = -2,00,000+ 70,000 PVAF (12%, 4) = 12,614.45

Let's check sensitivity of each component:

a) By using goal seek function as described above in Managerial Tool Kit above, we get that NPV = 0, if cash inflow go down to 65846.88. In percentage terms:

(70,000-65,846.88)/ 70,000 = 5.9%

So if cash flows decrease by 5.9 % the NPV will become zero.

b) Again by using the procedure in a), we see that if discount rate increases to 15%, the NPV becomes zero.

In percentage terms:

(15%-12%)/12% = 25% increase in discount rate will bring the NPV down to zero.

c) Now, by applying the procedure used in a) and b) above, we see that the NPV becomes zero if initial investment increases to ₹ 2,12,614.45. In percentage terms, if initial investment increases by 6.3%, NPV becomes zero.

Conclusion: we find that the cash flows are most sensitive since only 5.9% change in them will bring the NPV down to zero.

4. **Tapaneya Limited is looking for a diversification opportunity and has finally shortlisted the following two projects:** **(DU 2007 Adapted)**

	Project A		Project B	
	Cash Flow	Certainty Equivalent	Cash Flow	Certainty Equivalent
Year 0	-1,20,000		-1,50,000	
Year 1	60,000	0.7	85,000	0.60
Year 2	75,000	0.9	90,000	0.75
Year 3	90,000	0.6	1,00,000	0.50

The risk free rate on 10 year benchmark g-sec is 6%.

Which project has?

a) Higher NPV

b) Lower Risk

Solution

NPV of the project A can be calculated as follows:

Project A:

1 Year	2 Cash Inflow	3 Certainty equivalent	4 Adjusted Cash Inflow (column3 x column2)
1	60,000	0.7	42,000
2	75,000	0.9	67,500
3	90,000	0.6	54,000

NPV (A) = -1,20,000+ 42,000 PVIF (6%,1) + 67,500 PVIF(6%,2) + 54,000 PVIF (6%,3)

= 25,036

Similarly, for Project B

1 Year	2 Cash Inflow	3 Certainty equivalent	4 Adjusted Cash Inflow (column3 x column2)
1	85,000	0.6	51,000
2	90,000	0.75	67,500
3	1,00,000	0.5	50,000

NPV = -1,50,000+ 51,000 PVIF (6%, 1) + 67,500 PVIF (6%, 2) + 50,000 PVIF (6%,3)

= 169

Therefore, we conclude that the NPV of project A is higher.

c) Now to find out which of the two projects is riskier, let us have a closer look at the certainty equivalent coefficients. These coefficients are higher in case of project A than project B. That means the company is more certain of project A than project B. Therefore, project B is riskier.

5. For calculating risk adjusted discount rates firms employ different methods. Pawansut Limited believes that the coefficient of variation is the best indicator of riskiness of a project. It also uses the risk adjusted discount rates for evaluating its investments. It has developed a chart listing appropriate discount rates for a given level of coefficient of variation:

Coefficient of Variation	Discount Rate
2.8-2.4	22%
2.4-2.0	20%
2.0-1.6	18%
1.6-1.2	16%
1.2-0.8	14%
0.8-0.4	12%
Below 0.4	10%

The company is considering three investment proposals at present. The coefficients of variation for these projects X, Y and Z are 2.37, 1.44 and 0.25. What should be the risk adjusted discount rate for these projects?

Solution:

From the table, we can deduce that the risk adjusted discount rate shall be as follows:

Project	Coefficient of Variation	Discount Rate
X	2.37	20%
Y	1.44	16%
Z	0.25	10%

Summary

- In project appraisal we start with estimating cash flows. However, since we make some assumptions, the actual cash flows from a project may turn out to be very - very different from the ones that we have estimated.
- Therefore, since we can not forecası cash flows associated with a project with certainty there is always an element of risk that our forecasts may prove to be wrong in future.
- The sources of risk in capital budgeting may exist in a) The Overall Economy b) The Industry c) The Company.
- The risks in capital budgeting can be measured by a) standard deviation and b) coefficient of variation.
- There are various techniques of risk analysis in capital budgeting. These techniques are : 1) Payback 2. Risk Adjusted Discount Rate 3. Certainty Equivalents 4. Sensitivity Analysis 5. Simulation 6. Decision Tree Analysis
- Payback method favors projects which return the investment the quickest. It is based on the assumption that the earlier the investment is returned, the less risky it is.
- Another techniques of risk analysis is Risk Adjusted Discount Rate. In this the discount rate for project appraisal is bifurcated into risk free rate and risk premium. The risk premium is kept higher for projects with higher risk.
- The next technique of risk analysis is Certainty Equivalent. It is reflected by certainty equivalent factor which is equal to ratio of Certain Cash Flow to Risky Cash Flow.
- Sensitivity Analysis is another very important technique of risk analysis. Sensitivity analysis is a way of analyzing change in the project's NPV (or IRR) for a given change in one of the variables. It indicates how sensitive a project's NPV (or IRR) is to change in particular variables.
- The next technique is Simulation. In simulation we make use of predetermined probability distributions and random numbers to make an estimate of risky outcomes.
- Decision Tree Analysis is also a very useful technique of risk analysis. A decision tree is a diagrammatic representation in the form of a tree which indicates the magnitude, probabilities and inter-relationship of all possible outcomes. This diagram looks like the branches of a tree.

Test Your Understanding

State whether the following statements are true or false

1. If a project has positive NPV, then firm should always invest immediately.
2. If we are using simulation, we do not need to calculate the discount rate (or the project's opportunity cost of capital).
3. NPV in case of certainty equivalent method is calculated using risk free rate of return.
4. If two projects have same expected NPV, then we may select the project with the higher coefficient of variation.
5. We can identify the critical variables in a project's success through sensitivity analysis.
6. Risk in capital budgeting arises from variability of future cash flows.
7. A simulation model cannot handle data that does not fit a standard mathematical distribution.
8. Payback period is only an appraisal criterion, not a risk assessment tool.
9. Risk adjusted discount rate is equal to firm's opportunity cost of capital plus risk premium.
10. Decision tree exercise becomes simpler with inclusion of more variables.

Answers : 1. F 2.T 3.T 4.F 5.T 6.T 7.F 8.F 9. T 10.F

Multiple Choice Questions

1. If risk of a project is higher, the risk adjusted discount rate will be:

   a) Higher b) Lower
   c) Will not change d) None of these.

2. The ratio of certain cash flow to risky cash flow is known as:

   a) Risk adjusted discount rate b) Certainty equivalent
   c) Scenario Analysis d) None of these

3. The coefficient of variation is equal to:

   a) Mean per unit of standard deviation b) Standard deviation per unit of mean
   c) Standard deviation squared d) None of these

4. The variability in estimated cash flow arises from:

   a) Economy wide factors b) Industry wide factors
   c) Company specific factors d) All of these

5. If risky cash flow is 80,000 and certain cash flow is 40,000, then certainty equivalent is

   a) 0.5 b) 2

   c) 2.5 d) None of these

6. Which of these statements are true:

   a) Risk and uncertainty are the same

   b) In a risky situation the probabilities of different outcomes is known

   c) In an uncertain situation the probabilities as in b) are not known

   d) Both b) and c) are true.

7. Sensitivity analysis allows us to see the effect of

   a) Change of one variable at a time

   b) Change of more than variable at a time

   c) Only large changes in one variable

   d) None of these

8. The outcome of a simulation exercise is:

   a) NPV b) Probabilities

   c) Probability distribution of NPVs d) None of these

9. Which of the following is/are the advantages of Decision Tree analysis:

   a) Clarity b) Comprehensiveness

   c) Graphic Depiction d) All of these

10. In all the risk management techniques, it is generally assumed that investors are:

    a) Risk averse b) Risk Neutral

    c) Risk Seeking d) None of These

Answers: 1. a 2.b 3.b 4.d 5.a 6.d 7.a 8.c 9.d 10.a

Practice Problems

1. Amongst the pairs of projects given below, find out which one is acceptable?

		Expected NPV	Standard deviation
Pair 1	Project A	3,000	900
	Project B	3,000	1,000
Pair 2	Project A	40,000	10,000
	Project B	57,000	10,000
Pair 3	Project A	3,700	1,259
	Project B	4,600	1,436

Pair 4	Project A	15,000	6,000
	Project B	30,000	12,000

2. Narsinh Limited is considering two mutually exclusive projects. The details are as follows:

	Project X		Project Y	
Year	Cash flow	Certainty Equivalent	Cash Flow	Certainty Equivalent
0	-2,00,000	1.00	-4,00,000	1.00
1	40,000	0.8	79,000	0.8
2	65,000	0.9	1,34,000	0.7
3	79,000	0.7	1,67,000	0.8
4	80,000	0.7	1,99,000	0.7
5	1,20,000	0.5	2,45,000	0.5

If the yield on 10 year benchmark govt. securities is 7%, which of these project is acceptable?

3. A company has projected the following profitability statement for a new project.

Sales	5000 units @ 15/- per unit		75000
Variable Costs			
	Material Cost@ 2/-	10,000	
	Labor Cost @ 1/-	5,000	
	Over head cost @1.5/-	7,500	22,500
Contribution			52,500
Fixed Costs (out of which SLM depreciation is 2000)			20,000
Profit Before Tax			32,500
Tax @ 30%			9,750
Net Profit			**22,750**

If the company has a discount rate of 12% and the initial investment required for the project is 90,000. If the expected life of the project is 5 years, calculate its NPV. Also conduct sensitivity analysis and find out which of the cost factors is most sensitive.

4. A company has the following probability distributions for its cash flows from a project under consideration:

Year 1		Year 2	
Cash Inflow	**Probability**	**Cash Inflow**	**Probability**
35000	0.6	50,000	0.3
		70,000	0.6
		80,000	0.1
48000	0.4	66,000	0.2
		85,000	0.4
		98,000	0.4

The initial investment required for the project is ₹ 90,000. The discount rate is 12%. Draw a decision tree and calculate:

1) Expected NPV

2) Probability that the NPV will be positive.

5. Akshar Limited is considering a project with an initial investment of ₹ 50,000. The project has an estimated life of one year. Following is the probability distribution of Sales units, sale price and variable cost.

Sales units	Probability	Sale Price	Probability	Variable Cost	Probability
3,000	0.4	120	0.3	40	0.35
40,000	0.3	150	0.6	70	0.25
50,000	0.3	170	0.1	75	0.40

Conduct a simulation exercise with 10 runs. Use random numbers generated from RAND function in Excel 2007. (Hint: Type "=RANDBETWEEN (00, 99)" in any cell and press enter, then select this cell and drag down to select 29 more cells.). Find out the average profits after this exercise.

Review Questions

1. Explain the term "Risk" in capital budgeting decisions. **(UPTU 2005, 2006)**
2. Explain the technique "Certainty Equivalent" approach in capital budgeting decisions.
3. Explain the role of standard deviation and coefficient of variation in measuring risk in capital budgeting decisions. **(UPTU 2005)**
4. "Risk and Uncertainty are integral part of capital budgeting". Comment.

(UPTU 2007)

5. Why is risk important in capital budgeting? Explain various methods of measurement of risk.
6. What is sensitivity analysis? Describe its merits and demerits.
7. Compare the certainty equivalent method and risk adjusted discount rate method. Also, describe their merits and demerits.
8. Describe the decision tree approach with the help of an example. Also list out its merits and demerits.
9. Differentiate between Risk- adjusted Discount Rate and Certainty Equivalent methods of incorporation of risk in capital budgeting. **(DU 2008, 2010)**

Case Study

Mohit has recently joined RD Limited as a management trainee (finance). He was very eager to apply in his work, the techniques he learnt in his MBA. It had been two weeks since he had joined and he was now starting to feel fairly familiar with his work and colleagues. He had been working hard for last two weeks. Now, he felt he deserved a break. This weekend he was planning to watch a movie with a special friend.

Saturday came and Mohit was getting ready to pick up his friend and go to the INOX. As he was getting out of his apartment, his cell phone rang. It was his boss. How fast can you reach office? He asked. Mohit sank. Office? Uh..sir..actually uh…he groped for the right words to convey to his boss he was not available. Listen Mohit....its very urgent…I understand you might have plans…sorry can't help it…I am expecting you in about an hour in my office, and with this phone was disconnected. Mohit swore.

Well, come on in…his boss beamed as he saw Mohit. Don't look so sullen. My wife has already given me a piece of her mind when she learnt I was coming to office. What was so urgent sir?

His boss explained to him that the company was considering an investment proposal and was fairly convinced of its potential. However, the firm wanted to assess the riskiness of the proposal as well. The management had strong belief in the certainty equivalent and risk adjusted discount rate methods. Mohit was expected to prepare a report on the riskiness of the project using both these methods.

Here you go…he put forward a sheet that had relevant data.

Year	Cash Flow	Certainty Equivalent Factor
0	-3,00,000	1.00
1	50,000	0.8
2	60,000	0.9
3	95,000	0.7
4	1,25,000	0.85
5	17,05,000	0.75

The yield on 10 year benchmark dated securities is ruling at 7%. The firm's opportunity cost of capital for this project is 12%. Based on the probability estimates of NPV, the coefficient of variation was 1.21. The company used the following table for risk adjusted discount rate:

Coefficient of Variation	Risk Premium over cost of capital
2.8-2.4	6%
2.4-2.0	5%
2.0-1.6	4%
1.6-1.2	3%
1.2-0.8	2%
0.8-0.4	1%
Below 0.4	0%

Mohit was expected to include the following in his report:

1) NPV based on certainty equivalent method
2) NPV based on risk adjusted discount rate method
3) Explain the difference in results, if any, obtained from these two methods.
4) Compare the merits and demerits of both the methods.

References

1. Brealey, Richard A & Myres, Stewart C. (2007), Tata McGraw Hill, New Delhi
2. ICAI study Material on Financial Management, The Institute of Chartered Accountants of India, New Delhi.
3. Khan, M Y & Jain (2007) P K, Financial Management, Tata McGraw Hill, New Delhi
4. Kishore, Ravi. M (2009), Financial Management, Taxmann Publications, New Delhi
5. Pandey, I M (2009). Financial Management, Vikas Publishing House, New Delhi
6. Van Horne, James C. (2007),Financial Management & Policy, Pearson Prentice Hall, New Delhi

CHAPTER 6 EBIT-EPS Analysis

Learning Objectives:

By the end of this chapter and having completed the essential reading and activities, you should be able to:

- Understand the concept of leverage in finance
- Differentiate between different types of leverage, viz., operating, financial and total
- Compute the numerical measures of leverage
- Assess the implication of leverage on the firm and shareholders
- Conduct EBIT-EPS analysis of a firm
- Apply the concept of indifference point in EBIT-EPS analysis

To start with...

One of the most vexing questions before a finance manager is "what proportion of debt and equity will be most beneficial for the firm". "This is equivalent to asking how much debt the firm should employ". We will study the various theories on the capital structure in later chapters. However, in this chapter, we shall learn to approximately compute the effect of a certain level of debt on the wealth of our shareholders. After all, the ultimate objective of all financial decisions is just one: Shareholders wealth maximization.

6.0 Introduction

We know that amongst the decision areas in finance, financing decisions are one of the most crucial ones. As you may recall, financing decisions imply the choice of sources of funds. You may also recall that broadly there are only two categories of sources of funds, namely, Owner's Funds (or Equity) and Outsider's funds (Debt or debt capital).

This chapter on leverage analysis prepares a background for the financing decision of the firm. Before we describe what is meant by the term "LEVERAGE", it would be useful to revisit a very important characteristic of the both the sources of funds described above.

We know that all the providers of funds require a return on the funds they have provided. In case of Owners funds (Equity) the return provided by the firm is in the form of dividends. However, it should be remembered that the quantum of dividend that the firm will pay is not fixed. It may vary from year to year depending on the firm's profits and various other considerations. Therefore we can call equity a source of fund which does not have a fixed or constant cost to the firm.

What about Outsider's funds (Debt)? The return paid by the firm to providers of debt capital is known as **"interest".** Unlike equity, the rate of interest to be paid by the firm is fixed at the time of raising the debt by the firm. Therefore debt is a fixed cost source of funds. The firm has to pay the agreed interest to its debt providers irrespective of whether it has earned a profit or not!

So the point is, different sources of funds have different type of costs. Some have fixed costs viz. debentures, term loans, preference shares etc. whereas some others do not have fixed costs; like equity.

Can we categorize other expenses (like salary, wages, fuel, material etc., also known as operating expenses) also in the category of fixed and variable? Perhaps you already know the answer from your management accounting course. All the other expenses can also be classified into fixed or variable. However, some expenses are semi variable, i.e., partly fixed and partly variable. They can also be broken down into fixed and variable components.

In summary, all the expenses of the firm, either financial expenses (cost of different sources of funds) or non-financial expenses (manufacturing/production/selling and distribution etc.) can be divided into two categories, fixed and variable.

Having distinguished between the fixed and variable expenses of a firm, now we are set to define leverage. Leverage can be defined as the employment of assets and sources of funds having fixed costs by the firm. In other words, if a firm has presence of fixed costs in its expenses, we can say that the firm is having "leverage".

Leverage can be categorized in two categories viz. financial leverage and operating leverage. Financial Leverage refers to presence of fixed financial costs in the firm (e.g. interest, preference dividend etc.). Operating Leverage refers to presence of fixed operating (non-financial) costs in the firm.

The combined effect of financial and operating leverage is known as Combined Leverage or Total Leverage.

However, it is not enough to say that leverage is present or absent in a firm. As managers, we must be able to precisely measure the degree of leverage present. In the sections that follow, we will learn the techniques to precisely measure the degree of leverage. One by one we will learn how to obtain degree of operating, financial and total leverage.

Essential Background Reading Box-1

Before we proceed lets refresh some basic financial relationships.

Suppose Q= Quantity of a product sold by a firm (in units)

P = Price per Unit

F= Fixed Costs of the firm V= Variable cost per unit of the firm

I = Interest paid by the firm T = Tax Rate D= Dividend paid to equity Shareholders

D_p = Preference Dividend paid to preference shareholders

From above We can write

Sales Revenue = Q x P =QP Total Variable Cost = Q x V =QV

Contribution = Sales Revenue – Total Variable Cost

= QP-QV

Contribution = Q (P-V) (1)

Operating Profit =Contribution –Fixed Costs (1 a)

Operating Profit= Q (P-V)-F (2)

Operating Profit is also known as "Earnings before Interest & Taxes" or EBIT

Therefore ***EBIT = Q (P-V)-F*** (3)

Profit Before Tax = EBIT-Interest= EBIT –I = Q (P-V)-F- I (4)

Profit After Tax = Profit before Tax –Tax (Tax = **Profit before Tax X Tax Rate**)

= Profit before Tax – Profit before Tax x Tax Rate

$= \{Q (P\text{-}V)\text{-}F - I\} - \{Q (P\text{-}V)\text{-}F\text{-} I \} \times T$

Profit After Tax $= \{Q (P\text{-}V)\text{-}F\text{-} I\} (1\text{-}T)$ (5)

Profit Available to Equity Shareholders = Profit After Tax – Preference Dividend

Profit Available to Equity Shareholders $= \{Q (P\text{-}V)\text{-}F\text{-} I\} (1\text{-}T) - D_p$ (6)

It may be emphasized here that dividend on preference shares is paid from after tax profits but before paying any dividend to equity shareholders.

If no. of shares issued to equity shareholders = N

Then, Earnings Per Share (EPS) = Profits Available to Equity shareholders / N

$$EPS = [\{Q (P\text{-}V)\text{-}F\text{-} I\} (1\text{-}T) - D_p] / N \quad (7)$$

In order to clearly understand the concept of leverage it is absolutely necessary that the student learns all the above equations from (1) to (7) by heart.

6.1 Operating Leverage

Operating leverage can be defined as presence of fixed operating costs in the cost structure of the firm. What is the effect of operating leverage from a manager's point of view? We know that firm's operating profit (EBIT) depends on sales. If there is a change in sales then the operating profit will also change. But if operating leverage is present, then the change in EBIT (operating profit) will be larger than the change in firm's sales.

In other words, presence of operating leverage ***magnifies*** the change in EBIT due to a change in sales. That is, if sale ***increases*** by; say; 5%, then due to presence of operating leverage, the EBIT will increase by more than 5%. Similarly, if sale ***decreases*** by 5%, then EBIT will decrease by more than 5%.

Let's understand it by an example:

Suppose a company ABC Ltd. Sells 10000 units of its product at a price of 10/- per unit. It incurs a variable cost of ₹ 5/- per unit and a fixed cost of ₹ 30000-00. What is change in its Operating Profit (EBIT) if sales 1) decrease by 20% and 2) increase by 20%.

Table A

	Effect of Operating Leverage	**Sales change by -20%**	**Current Sales**	**Sales change by +20%**
1	**Sales**	80,000	1,00,000	1,20,000
2	**Variables Costs**	40,000	50,000	60,000
3	**Contribution (1-2)**	40,000	50,000	60,000
4	**Fixed Costs**	30,000	30,000	30,000
5	**EBIT (3-4)**	10,000	20,000	30,000
6	**Change in EBIT**	-50%		+50%

As we can see, the EBIT has changed by 50% for a change of 20% in the sales. That means, EBIT has changed more than change in Sales. This has happened due to the presence of fixed costs or Operating Leverage.

Here a question arises. If a firm does not have fixed operating costs in its cost structure, then, by definition, it should not have operating leverage. In this case, for a given change in sales, the EBIT should not change more than change in sales. In fact, if there are no fixed operating costs (or no operating leverage), the change in EBIT will be equal to change in sales.

Let's demonstrate this for the example above, this time assuming no fixed costs.

As you can see in the table below, fixed costs have been assumed to be nil. Now if the sales changes by 20% (either increases or decreases), in both the cases, the EBIT also changes by exactly the same amount, i.e., 20%.

Table B

	Effect of Operating Leverage with no fixed cost	**Sales change by -20%**	**Current Sales**	**Sales change by +20%**
1	**Sales**	80000	100000	120000
2	**Variables Costs**	40000	50000	60000
3	**Contribution (1-2)**	40000	50000	60000
4	**Fixed Costs**	0	0	0
5	**EBIT (3-4)**	40000	50000	60000
6	**Change in EBIT**	**-20%**		**+20%**

After seeing how the operating leverage works, let's address our next concern. We mentioned earlier that we can not simply say that leverage is present or not in a firm. As managers we should have tools to precisely measure the degree of operating leverage. It is calculated by the following formula:

$$Degree\ of\ operating\ Leverage\,(DOL) = \frac{\%\,change\ in\ EBIT}{\%\,change\ in\ sales}$$

Here it may be noted that DOL will always be more than 1 whenever there is presence of fixed operating costs in the cost structure of the firm and vice versa.

$$DOL = \frac{\Delta EBIT\ /\ EBIT}{\Delta Sales\ /\ Sales}$$

(Putting the values from Essential Background Reading Box-1 and simplifying) we get:

$$DOL = \frac{Q(P-V)}{Q(P-V)-F} = \frac{Contribution}{EBIT}$$

It may be noted that DOL is always greater than 1 because, due to the presence of fixed costs, the %change in EBIT is more than the % change in sales.

Now what does DOL signify?

1. DOL enables us to compute the possible change in EBIT for a given change in sales. The value of DOL represents % change in EBIT for 1% change in Sales. For example, if DOL is calculated to be "3", it means that for one percent change in sales, EBIT will change by 3%.

   % change in EBIT = DOL X % change in Sales

2. DOL is a measure of Business Risk or Operating Risk. Business risk refers to the risk of firm not being able to earn enough revenue to cover its fixed operating costs. A high DOL would mean high business risk. In this case, if sales are rising, then a high DOL firm will see accelerating profits. But if sales go down, a high DOL firm will see rapid decrease in profits.

6.2 Financial Leverage

Financial leverage refers to use of those sources of funds by the firm which have a fixed charge. The examples of these fixed financial charge sources are Debentures, Term Loans, Preference Shares etc. When financial leverage is present, and if there is a change in Operating Profit (EBIT) of the firm, then due to financial leverage, there will be a larger change in the earnings available to shareholder. Therefore, just as we saw in case of operating leverage, financial leverage acts to magnify the change in shareholder's earnings due to a change in EBIT , in the same direction.

It may be pointed out here that presence of financial leverage is also known as "trading on equity" in finance literature. IT is so because financial leverage refers to use of debt capital by the firm and debt providers provide funds to the firm on the strength of its equity capital. Why? This is so because equity capital will earn as a insurance for the debt provider's interest payments if the firm is not able to earn sufficient income (EBIT). Therefore, a firm with higher equity is generally able to get higher debt. It is equivalent to "trading on equity".

Coming back to the effect of magnification of shareholder's earnings due to the presence of financial leverage, let's understand why does this happen. Whenever a firm uses fixed charges sources of funds then it has to earn sufficient EBIT to be able to pay to providers of these funds. Firm earns this EBIT on its total assets. Whenever the firm is able to earn more return on its assets than the cost of fixed charges sources of funds, some profits will be left after payment of fixed financial charges. These leftover profits belong to equity shareholders and thereby, their returns get increased without any additional investment of funds by them. This results in magnification of shareholders earnings due to financial leverage. The similar phenomenon works in opposite direction when the firm earns less return on its assets than the fixed financial charges. Since the firm is legally bound to pay its fixed financial charges, it has to pay them even if its EBIT is not sufficient. The firm has no alternative but to meet this shortage in EBIT from shareholder's earnings. Therefore shareholders' earnings get reduced more than the change in EBIT.

Let's demonstrate the operation of financial leverage with the aid of an example.

Suppose a firm XYZ limited has current level of EBIT of ₹ 1,00,000. This firm has the following capital structure:

Equity Capital (10000 shares of ₹ 10 each)	₹ 1,00,000
15 % Debentures	₹ 1,00,000
10% Preference Shares	₹ 1,00,000

In this case the firm has to pay fixed financial charges as follows:

Interest on Debentures (15% X 1,00,000)	₹ 15,000
Dividend on Preference shares (10% X 1,00,000)	₹ 10,000

It may be remembered here that interest will be paid from pre-tax earnings whereas preference dividend will paid out of Profit After Tax.

The effect of leverage can be demonstrated as follows:

Table C

	Effect of Financial Leverage	EBIT changes by -20%	Current EBIT	EBIT Changes by +20%
1	EBIT	80000	100000	120000
2	Interest	15000	15000	15000
3	Profit Before Tax (1-2)	65000	85000	105000
4	Tax @ 30%	19500	25500	31500
5	Profit After Tax (3-4)	45500	59500	73500
6	Preference Dividend	10000	10000	10000
7	Shareholder's Earnings (5-6)	35500	49500	63500
8	% Change	-28.28%		+28.28%
9	EPS (7/No of shares)	3.55	4.95	6.35
10	% changes in EPS	-28.28%		+28.28%

As you can see, when there is a change of + 20%, there is a change of + 28.28 % in shareholder's earnings (or EPS). This more than proportionate change in EPS due to a change in EBIT is due to the presence of Financial Leverage.

Here, again, a question arises. If a firm does not have fixed financial costs like interest and preference dividend in its cost structure, then, by definition, it should not have any financial leverage. In this case, for a given change in EBIT, the EPS should not change more than the change in EBIT. In fact, if there are no fixed financial costs (or no financial leverage), the change in EPS will be equal to change in EBIT.

Let's demonstrate this for the example above, this time assuming no fixed financial costs.

As you can see in the table below, fixed financial costs have been assumed to be nil. Now if the EBIT changes by 20% (either increases or decreases), in both the cases, the EPS also changes by exactly the same amount, i.e., 20%.

Table D

	Effect of Financial Leverage with no fixed financial costs	**EBIT changes by -20%**	**Current EBIT**	**EBIT Changes by +20%**
1	EBIT	80000	100000	120000
2	Interest	0	0	0
3	Profit Before Tax (1-2)	80000	100000	120000
4	Tax @ 30%	24000	30000	36000
5	Profit After Tax (3-4)	56000	70000	84000
6	Preference Dividend	0	0	0
7	Shareholder's Earnings (5-6)	56000	70000	84000
8	% Change	-20.00%		+20.00%
9	EPS (7/No of shares)	5.6%	7	8.4
10	% changes in EPS	-20.00%		+20.00%

It is not enough just to see the presence of financial leverage. As managers we must be able to calculate precisely how much financial leverage exists in a firm. This can be done with the help of formula for "Degree of financial Leverage" as in the case of Operating Leverage.

$$Degree\ of\ Financial\ Leverage\,(DFL) = \frac{\%\,Change\ in\ EPS}{\%\,Change\ in\ EBIT}$$

This is equation no. (A).

It may be noted that the DFL will always be more than 1 whenever there is presence of financial leverage and vice-versa.

$$DFL = \frac{\frac{\Delta EPS}{EPS}}{\frac{\Delta EBIT}{EBIT}}$$

Putting Values from Essential Background Reading Box-1 and simplifying we get

$$DFL = \frac{Q(P-V)-F}{\{Q(P-V)-F-I\} - \frac{Dp}{(1-T)}} = \frac{EBIT}{Earnings\ before\ Taxes}$$

This equation may also be written as

$$DFL = \frac{EBIT}{EBIT - I - \frac{Dp}{(1-T)}} = \frac{EBIT}{Earnings\ before\ Taxes}$$

This is equation no. (B)

Let's calculate DFL with the help of formula in equation A, by putting values from our first example:

$$DFL = \frac{\%\,Change\ in\ EPS}{\%\,Change\ in\ EBIT} = 28.28/20 = 1.41$$

DFL can also be calculated by putting values in equation (B) from current data in Table C.

$$DFL = \frac{100000}{100000 - 15000 - \frac{10000}{(1-0.30)}}$$

$$\text{DFL} = 1.41$$

Now let us see what the significance of DFL is:

1. DFL can be used to predict changes in EPS for a given change in EBIT. The value of DFL obtained as above represents the % change in EPS for 1% change in EBIT. For Example if we calculate DFL to be 3 then it means, for a 1% change in EBIT, there will be 3% change in EPS in the same direction as EBIT.
2. DFL is also a measure of financial risk of a firm. Financial risk refers to the possibility that the firm will not be able to meet its fixed financial commitments like interest. A failure to do so has serious consequences for the firm since the providers of debt capital have the legal recourse to get the firm wound up to recover their dues. Higher the DFL, higher the financial risk. Though in case the EBIT is rising, the equity holders shall get higher return as well because of the financial leverage.

6.3 Degree of Total Leverage

The degree of total leverage is defined as % change in EPS for 1% change in sales. It can be computed as follows:

$$Degree\ of\ Total\ Leverage\,(DLT) = \frac{\%\,change\ in\ EPS}{\%\,change\ in\ Sales}$$

This can be rewritten as

$$DTL = \frac{\%\,change\ in\ EPS}{\%\,change\ in\ EBIT} \times \frac{\%\,change\ in\ EBIT}{\%\,change\ in\ Sales}$$

Or

$$DTL = DFL \times DOL$$

It can also be calculated by

$$DTL = \frac{Q(P-V)}{EBIT - I} = \frac{Contribution}{Earnings\ before\ Tax}$$

Interpretation of Degree of Total Leverage:

1. With the help of DTL, we can determine the impact on EPS by a given % change in sales revenue. For example if we calculate DTL to be "2.6" for a firm, then it means that for a 1% change in sales revenue, the EPS will change by 2.6% in the same direction as the sales revenue.
2. DTL represents the degree of total risk faced by the firm since it is obtained by a product of DOL and DFL and they represent operating risk and financial risk respectively. The DTL can be used for planning the capital structure also. For example, if a firm wants to undertake a project which has a high level of operating risk(high DOL), then in order to keep the total risk of the firm (DTL) at the same level, the firm has to chose a financing plan which has a low DFL. The total risk can be retained at acceptable levels by choosing the financing plan appropriate to the riskiness of the new projects. Therefore, it is clear that for risky projects, it is more advisable for the firm to go in for low financial leverage (more equity, low debt) in order to keep total risk within acceptable level.

   However, in case of low risk projects with high degree of certainty about their revenues and lower element of fixed cost (low DOL), the firm may adopt a financing plan with high leverage (debt financing-high DFL) and the total risk of the firm will still remain within acceptable limits.

6.4 EBIT-EPS Analysis

For raising funds, a firm has many options like equity, preference shares, debentures, term loan etc. The choice of a particular combination of sources of funds is known as capital structure decision of the firm. How does the firm decide which combination of different sources is the best for it?

EBIT-EPS analysis is one of the methods that can help a manager decide the best combination of different sources of funds. In this method, in line with the objective of shareholder's wealth maximization, EPS is calculated under different financing plans (different combinations of sources of funds) by assuming EBIT at a certain level. Then the option which promises highest EPS is chosen as the best option.

This can be better understood with the help of an example:

Let's suppose a firm has projected an EBIT of ₹ 3,00,000 for its new project. Currently the firm has ₹ 5,00,000 (50,000 shares of ₹ 10 each) of equity and it needs to raise additional ₹ 5,00,000 for the new project. Let's suppose the firm is considering the following options:

1) Raising entire ₹ 5,00,000 from equity by offering 50000 shares of ₹ 10 each
2) Raising 50% of ₹ 5,00,000 from equity and remaining 50% from 8% debentures
3) Raising the entire ₹ 5,00,000 from 8% debentures
4) Raising 60% of ₹ 5,00,000 from equity and 40% from 6% preference shares
5) Raising entire amount from 8% preference shares

In order to decide, we need to calculate the EPS under different options of financing. It can be done from the following table:

Table E

	EBIT-EPS Analysis under different financing plans	**Plan 1 (100% Equity)**	**Plan 2 (50% Equity, 50% Debt)**	**Plan 3 (100% Debt)**	**Plan 4 (60% Equity, 40% Pref. Shares)**	**Plan 5 (100% perference shares)**
1	No of equity shares before new project	50000	50000	50000	50000	50000
2	New Equity shares to be issues	50000	25000	0	30000	0
3	Total no. of equity shares post project (1+2)	100000	75000	50000	80000	50000
4	EBIT	300000	300000	300000	300000	300000
5	Interest	0	20000	40000	0	0
6	Profit Before Tax (4-5)	300000	280000	260000	300000	300000
7	Tax @ 30%	90000	84000	78000	90000	90000
8	Profit After Tax (5-6)	210000	196000	182000	210000	210000
9	Preference Dividend	0	0	0	12000	40000
10	Profit available to equity shareholders (7-8)	210000	196000	182000	198000	170000
11	EPS (9/3)	2.10	2.61	3.64	2.48	3.40

We can see from the table that the EPS is highest under plan 3. Therefore under the assumed EBIT of ₹ 3,00000, out of the given options, the option of 100 % debt is the best one because it results in highest EPS.

The student has to carefully study the above table. Can you explain why EPS under Plan 5 is lower than EPS under plan 3, whereas in both cases the firm is paying ₹ 40,000 as cost of funds? The answer lies in the fact that in plan 3 funds were raised through debentures at 8%, for which interest of ₹ 40,000 was paid. However, interest is a tax deductible expense. That means we subtract interest from EBIT before paying taxes. Therefore EBIT gets reduced by the amount of interest and tax is saved to the extent of " tax rate X interest expense".

Whereas-in plan 5-funds were raised by Preference shares, again at the rate of 8%. Here also ₹ 40,000 was paid to the preference shareholders. But since preference dividend is not a tax deductible expense, the firm paid higher tax in plan 5. Due to higher tax payout, Earnings available to equity shareholders went down and EPS was only ₹ 3.40.

Having discussed this let us move on to another important concept. It is called Financial Break Even Point.

Financial Break Even Point is defined as the minimum amount of EBIT the firm has to earn so that it is able to pay all its fixed financial charges like interest, preference dividend etc.

At financial break even point, the earnings available to equity shareholders is zero, and so is EPS.

In other words, Financial BEP is equal to the total pre tax fixed financial charges paid by the firm.

Let's see in the above example what are the total fixed financial charges paid by the firm on pre tax basis:

Plan 2 ₹ 20,000

Plan 3 ₹ 40,000

Plan 4 ₹ 17,143

Plan 5 ₹ 57,143

You might be wondering where from this figures ₹ 17,143 and ₹ 57,143 in plan 4 and 5 have come? See, in plan 2 and Plan 3, the firm has to pay interest of ₹ 20,000 and ₹ 40000. Since interest is always paid before taxes so the amount of EBIT needed to pay the interest is exactly equal to interest, i.e., ₹ 20,000 and ₹ 40,000 respectively. However In case of plan 4 and 5, we want to know the minimum level of EBIT which, after paying taxes, will cover the payment of ₹ 12,000 and ₹ 40000 preference dividend respectively , since preference dividend is always a post tax payment.

This can be found out simply by D_p/ (1-T). Now putting values of D_p = ₹12,000 and ₹ 40,000 and T = 30%, we get ₹ 17,143 and ₹ 57,143 respectively.

From this discussion we may conclude that

$$Financial\ Break\ Even\ Point = I + \frac{D_p}{(1-T)} \qquad \text{Equation (F)}$$

Where, I = Interest paid

D_p = Preference Dividend

T = Tax Rate

This leads us to the next crucial concept in EBIT-EPS analysis, known as Indifference Point. Indifference point in EBIT-EPS analysis is known as that level of EBIT at which EPS in different financing plans is equal. At the indifference level of EBIT, the firm may remain indifferent between alternative financing plans since both plans result in same level of EPS.

The question is how to find the indifference point (or in other words, indifferent level of EBIT). This can be done by two methods; 1) graphically and 2) Mathematically.

6.4.1 Indifference Analysis (Graphical Approach)

In graphic approach, we will continue with our example above. In graphic approach, a graph is plotted between EBIT and EPS in different financing plans. The EPS is plotted on the horizontal (X) axis and the EBIT is plotted on the vertical (Y) axis. The plot thus obtained is a straight line. We know that, in order to draw a straight line, we need two points in (x, y) plane. In our case, point x will be represented by EPS and point y will be represented by EBIT.

One set of points (x, y) or (EPS, EBIT) can be obtained directly from Table E as follows:

	Plan 1 (100% Equity)	Plan 2 (50% Equity, 50% Debt)	Plan 3 (100% Debt)	Plan 4 (60% Equity, 40% Pref. Shares)	Plan 5 (100% preference shares)
EPS	2.10	2.61	3.64	2.48	3.40
EBIT	300000	300000	300000	300000	300000

In order to draw graph, we need another set of (EPS, EBIT) points. This again we can take from our analysis in earlier paragraphs related to financial breakeven point. We know that financial breakeven point is that level of EBIT at which EPS is zero. We have already obtained break-even level of EBIT in case of plan 2, 3 ,4 and 5 as ₹ 20,000, ₹ 40,000 ₹ 17,143 and ₹ 57,143 respectively. However, what is the break even level of EBIT in case of plan 1?

Since plan 1 is an all equity plan, there are no interest and preference dividend payable. From the formula given equation (F), the break even level of EBIT or financial break even point is equal to:

$$Financial\ Break\ Even\ Point = 1 + \frac{D_p}{(1-T)}$$

In plan 1, I = 0 and D_p = 0. So break even point = 0 +0/1-0.3 =0

Now we have another set of EPS, EBIT points that can be summarized as follows:

	Plan 1 (100% Equity)	Plan 2 (50% Equity, 50% Debt)	Plan 3 (100 % Debt)	Plan 4 (60% Equity, 40% Pref. Shares)	Plan 5 (100% preference shares)
EPS	0	0	0	0	0
EBIT	0	20000	40000	17143	57143

Now we have two sets of points for (EPS, EBIT) in X-Y plane. The next task is to plot these points and join them. We obtain the following graph:

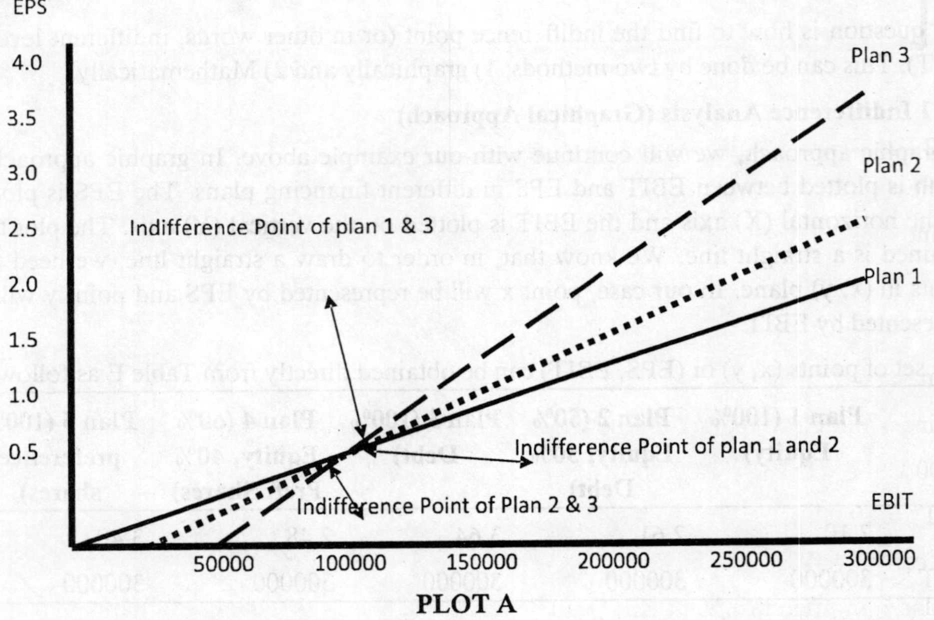

PLOT A

As we can see in the adjoining Plot A, the indifference points can be found at the intersection of the curves. We have used only three plans, namely 1, 2 and 3, for the sake of simplicity. However, these graphs can be drawn for any number of plans, to get indifference points between any two plans.

As we can see, at the indifference point plans 1-2, plans 2-3 and plans 1-3, the EPS under each plan of the pair is the same. If we drop a vertical line from the indifference point on to the horizontal axis, we will get the Indifference EBIT, i.e., the level of EBIT at which the firm can remain indifferent between two alternative plans. This is demonstrated in PLOT B below.

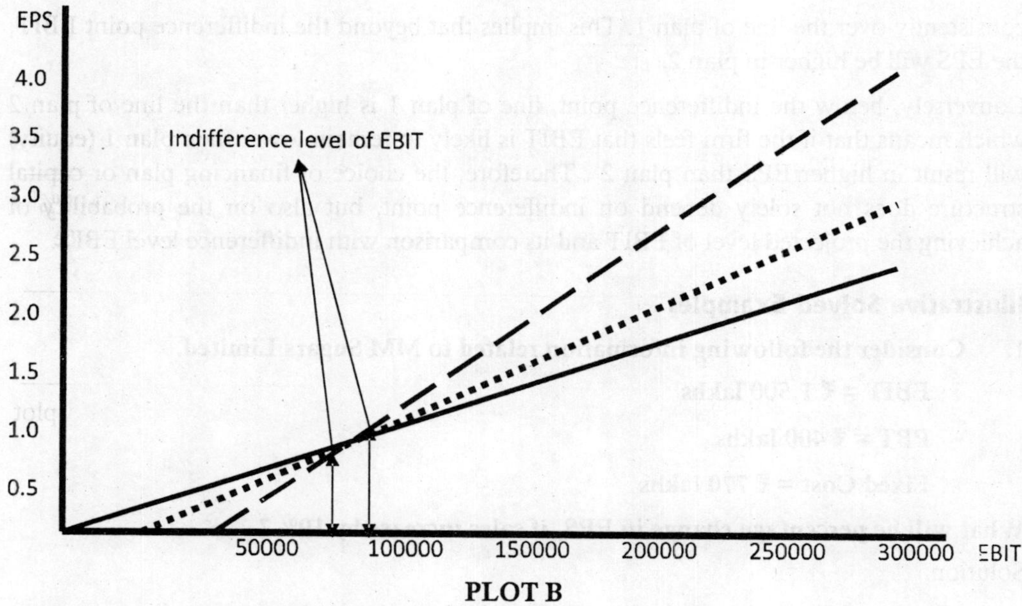

PLOT B

6.4.2 Indifference Analysis (Mathematical Approach)

Mathematically the indifference point can be obtained as follows:

Let indifference point EBIT be denoted by EBIT*, then

$$\frac{EBIT-(1-T)}{N_1}=\frac{(EBIT^*-I)(1-T)-D_p}{N_2}$$

From our example, let's calculate EBIT* for plan 1 and 2.

Putting Values from table E in the above formula: we obtain the following results

75000 EBIT* (1-0.3) = 1,00,000{(EBIT*-20,000) (1-0.3)}

EBIT* = 80,000

This can be verified graphically also.

Similarly, indifference point EBIT can be found out between any pair of financing plans.

Interpretation of EBIT-EPS Analysis

For a prospective manager it is not enough to just be able to calculate these values. Of utmost importance is the interpretation. In order to interpret EBIT EPS analysis, we begin with our projected level of EBIT and compare it with indifference level of EBIT. For example in plan 1 and 2 above, the indifference level of EBIT (80,000) is much lower than projected EBIT of ₹ 3,00,000. What does it mean? It means that if the firm expects strongly that it will achieve the projected level of EBIT then it should go for plan 2, because in plot B, beyond the indifference point, as we can see, line of plan 2 is consistently over the line of plan 1. This implies that beyond the indifference point EBIT, the EPS will be higher in plan 2.

Conversely, below the indifference point, line of plan 1 is higher than the line of plan 2 which means that if the firm feels that EBIT is likely to remain lower then plan 1 (equity) will result in higher EPS than plan 2 . Therefore, the choice of financing plan or capital structure does not solely depend on indifference point, but also on the probability of achieving the projected level of EBIT and its comparison with indifference level EBIT.

Illustrative Solved Examples

1. Consider the following information related to MM Sugars Limited.

EBIT = ₹ 1,500 lakhs

PBT = ₹ 400 lakhs

Fixed Cost = ₹ 770 lakhs

What will be percentage change in EPS, if sales increase by 10% ?

Solution:

Let us find the degree of operating leverage by the formula

$$DOL = \frac{Contribution}{EBIT} = \frac{EBIT + F}{EBIT}$$

$$DOL = \frac{2270}{1500} = 1.51$$

Now, we can find the degree of total leverage by the formula

$$DFL = \frac{EBIT}{Earnings\ before\ Taxes} = \frac{1500}{400} = 3.75$$

Therefore DTL = DOL X DFL = 1.51 X 3.75 = 5.66

We know DTL = % change in EPS/ % change in Sales , therefore:

% change in EPS = 5.66 * 10% = 56.6%

2. AgeBarho Limitied needs ₹ 1 crore for its planned expansion. After this expansion the EBIT is expected to increase to ₹ 18,00,000. To finance the expansion, the company has the following three options:

Option A Debt : ₹ 10,0,0000 (@ 10%)

Option B Debt: ₹ 5,00,00,000 (@ 10% up to ₹ 10,00,000 and @ 14% for over ₹ 10,00,000)

Option C Debt: ₹ 70,00,000 (@ 16% for over ₹ 50,00,000, otherwise as above)

In options B and C the firm will raise the remaining amount through equity by issuing new shares. Its shares are currently trading in the market at ₹ 300. It is expected that the share price will fall to ₹ 250 in the company raises debt for more than ₹ 60,00,000.

If the company falls in the tax bracket of 40%, advise which plan will result in the highest EPS.

Solution

First we will calculate the Interest and no. of shares in each options as follows:

Interest in Option B	10% * 1000000+14% (50,00,000-10,00,000)= ₹ 66,000
Interest in Option C	10% * 1000000+14% (5000000-10,00,000)+ 16% (70,00,000-50,00,000)
No. of Shares in Option A	90,00,000/300 = 30,000
No. of Shares in Option B	50,00,000/300 = 16,667
No. of shares in Option C	30,00,000/250 = 12,000

We can calculate the EPS in different financing options as follows:

	Option A	**Option B**	**Option C**
Equity	90,00,000	50,00,000	30,00,000
Debt	10,00,000	50,00,000	70,00,000
EBIT	18,00,000	18,00,000	18,00,000
Interest	1,00,000	6,60,000	9,80,000
Profit before Tax	17,00,000	11,40,000	8,20,000
Tax @ 40%	10,20,000	6,84,000	4,92,000
PAT	6,80,000	4,56,000	3,28,000
No. of Shares	30,000	16,667	12,000
EPS	22.67	27.36	27.33

We can see that EPS gets maximized in the Option B.

3. **The following are the operating results of a firm:**

Sales (units)	**30000**
Interest per annum	**₹ 35000**
Selling price per unit	**₹ 28**
Tax Rate	**₹ 60%**
Variable Cost per Unit	**₹ 20**
No. of Equity shares	**10,000**
Fixed costs per annum	**₹ 90,000**

Calculate: 1) EBIT 2) EPS 3) Break Even Sales 4) Operating Leverage 5) Financial Leverage

6) Total Leverage

Solution

1	**Sales (30000@ ₹ 28)**		8,40,000
2	**Less variable Cost (30000 @ ₹ 20)**	6,00,000	
3	**Contribution(1-2)**		2,40,000
4	**Less Fixed costs**	90,000	
5	**EBIT**		1,50,000
6	**Interest**	35,000	
7	**EBT**		1,15,000
8	**Less Tax @ 60%**	69,000	
9	**Profits After Tax**		46,000

1) EBIT = ₹ 1,50,000
2) EPS = PAT/ No. of shares = 46,000/10,000 = ₹ 4.6
3) Break Even sales = Fixed Costs/ Contribution Per Unit = 90,000/8 = 11,250 units
4) Operating Leverage = Contribution/EBIT = 2,40,000/1,50,000 = 1.6
5) Financial Leverage = EBIT/ EBT = 1,50,000/1,15,000 = 1.30
6) Total Leverage = DOL x DFL = 1.6 x 1.30 = 2.08

Summary

- Leverage can be defined as the employment of assets and sources of funds having fixed costs by the firm. In other words, if a firm has presence of fixed costs in its expenses, we can say that the firm is having "leverage".
- Leverage can be categorized in two categories viz. financial leverage and operating leverage. Financial Leverage refers to presence of fixed financial costs in the firm (e.g. interest, preference dividend etc.). Operating Leverage refers to presence of fixed operating (non-financial) costs in the firm.
- The combined effect of financial and operating leverage is known as Combined Leverage or Total Leverage.
- If operating leverage is present then for a given change in sales, firm's EBIT (operating profit) will also change by a larger amount. Operating leverage is measured by DOL (Degree of Operating leverage which is equal to ratio of percentage change in EBIT and percentage change in sales. It is always greater than 1.

- DOL is a measure of Business Risk or Operating Risk. Business risk refers to the risk of firm not being able to earn enough revenue to cover its fixed operating costs.
- Financial leverage refers to use of those sources of funds by the firm which have a fixed charge. When financial leverage is present, and if there is a change in Operating Profit (EBIT) of the firm, then due to financial leverage, there will be a larger change in the earnings available to shareholder. Financial leverage acts to magnify the change in shareholder's earnings due to a change in EBIT, in the same direction.
- Financial leverage is measured by DFL (Degree of Financial Leverage). It is calculated as ratio of percentage change in EPS and percentage change in EBIT.
- DFL is also a measure of financial risk of a firm. Financial risk refers to the possibility that the firm will not be able to meet its fixed financial commitments like interest.
- The degree of total leverage is defined as % change in EPS for 1% change in sales.
- DTL represents the degree of total risk faced by the firm since it is obtained by a product of DOL and DFL and they represent operating risk and financial risk respectively. The DTL can be used for planning the capital structure also.
- EBIT-EPS analysis is one of the methods that can help a manager decide the best combination of different sources of funds. In this method, in line with the objective of shareholder's wealth maximization, EPS is calculated under different financing plans (different combinations of sources of funds) by assuming EBIT at a certain level. Then the option which promises highest EPS is chosen as the best option.
- Financial Break Even Point is defined as the minimum amount of EBIT the firm has to earn so that it is able to pay all its fixed financial charges like interest, preference dividend etc. ***At financial break even point, the earnings available to equity shareholders is zero, and so is EPS.***
- Indifference point in EBIT-EPS analysis is known as that level of EBIT at which EPS in different financing plans is equal. At the indifference level of EBIT, the firm may remain indifferent between alternative financing plans since both plans result in same level of EPS.
- Indifference point can be obtained by two methods 1) graphically and 2) Mathematically.

Test Your Understanding

State whether the statements given below are true or false

1. Leverage analysis is a tool to understand the relationship between the composition of source of financing and the value of the firm.

2. Existence of fixed operating costs in a firm implies presence of financial leverage.
3. If operating leverage is present, then the effect of a change in sales on change in EBIT gets magnified.
4. Degree of operating leverage is greater than 1.
5. The presence zero interest debt from friends and relatives in the capital structure would signify financial leverage.
6. Degree of financial leverage is always greater than 1.5.
7. Financial leverage results in more than proportionate change in EPS due to a given change in EBIT.
8. Degree of Total leverage is product of Degree of financial leverage and Degree of operating leverage.
9. Financial leverage is a measure of total risk of the firm.
10. EBIT-EPS analysis can be useful in the capital structure decision.
11. At financial breakeven point the EPS of the firm will be negative.
12. Indifference point and financial break even point are the same.
13. Indifference point is the level of EBIT at which EPS of two different alternatives is the same.
14. Indifference analysis can only be done graphically.
15. Operating leverage is a measure of business risk.

Answers : 1. T 2.F 3.T 4.T 5.F 6.F 7.F 8.T 9.F 10.T 11.F 12.F 13.F 14.F 15.T

Multiple Choice Questions

1. XYZ limited manufactured and sold 30000 units with a variable cost of ₹ 30 per unit and ₹ 60 as selling price. The fixed costs during the period are ₹ 120000. The operating leverage of the firm is:

   a) 1.5 b) 3.0

   c) 1.25 d) 1.23

2. The financial leverage for ABC limited is 1.8. If the EBIT increases by 20%, the EPS will :

   a) Increase by 20% b) Decrease by 20%

   c) Increase by 36% d) Decrease by 36%

3. The DOL of a firm is 1.4 and DFL is 1.8. What is DTL?

   a) 2.50 b) 2.52

   c) 1.8 d) 1.4

4. The financial data for a firm are as follows:

DOL = 4, DFL = 3, Interest expenses = 15 lakhs, Tax Rate = 30%, Variable cost to Sales Ratio = 0.6. What is the EBIT of the firm?

a) 26 lakhs b) 22.5 lakhs

c) 24 lakhs d) 20 lakhs

5. Higher debt in the capital structure will increase;

a) Financial risk b) Operating Risk

c) Total Risk d) None of these

6. EBIT stands for:

a) Earnings before interest and taxes b) Earnings before Income and tax

c) Earning before interest and tax d) None of these

7. What does EPS refer to?

a) Earnings per share b) Earning profit scheme

c) Earning plan scheme d) None of these

8. If EBIT is less than financial break even point, then what will happen? **(UPTU, 2010)**

a) EPS will be negative b) EPS will be positive

c) Cost of debt rises d) No impact on EPS

9. Financial break even point is equal to:

a) $1+\frac{D_p}{1-T}$ b) $1-\frac{D_p}{1-T}$

c) $I+D_p$ d) None of these

10. What kind of firm you would advise a conservative investor to invest in:

a) High DTL b) Low DTL

c) Zero DTL d) None of these

Answers: 1. c 2.c 3.b 4.b 5.a 6.a 7.a 8.a 9.a 10.a

Practice Problems

1. Following details are available from the financial data of a firm.

Degree of Operating Leverage	4.3
Degree of Financial leverage	1.9
Interest	₹ 11,00,000
Contribution Sales Ratio	0.5
Tax Rate	50%

Prepare the income statement.

2. The operating leverage of PeepliLive Ltd. has increased to 1.4 this year from 1.2 last year. However, the fixed costs have also increased by 30% over the previous year. How much contribution has changed over the previous year?
3. The share capital of a company is ₹ 2,00,00,000. The face value of shares is ₹ 10. The capital structure of the company has debt capital of ₹ 11,00,000 at an interest rate of 12%. The firm sells 4,00,000 units of its product every year at a selling price of ₹ 7 per annum. The fixed costs are ₹ 3,00,000 per annum and variable cost is ₹ 4 per unit. The tax rate applicable to the company is 40%. The sales are likely to increase by 15% this year. Find out:
   a) Degree of Operating leverage pre and post increase in sales
   b) Degree of Financial Leverage pre and post increase in sales
   c) Degree of Total Leverage in both the cases
   d) Percentage increase in EPS
4. For a company the following data is available:

EBIT	₹ 2,00,000
Interest	₹ 1,00,000
Contribution	₹ 3,00,000

   If the sales of the company are expected to decrease by 7 %, determine the percentage change in EPS.
5. KBC Limited has a debt of ₹ 36,00,000 at an interest rate of 11%. It is considering expansion and estimates that it would need ₹ 50,00,000. The firm is evaluating three financing plans: a) Raising the entire amount through debt at 12% b) Raising the entire amount through preference shares with 10.5% dividend. C) Raising the entire amount through equity by issuing shares at the price of ₹ 20. The firm has issued 100000 shares. The tax rate applicable to the company is 35%.

   Calculate:
   a) EPS in each of the alternatives if EBIT is 16,00,000 currently.
   b) Prepare an indifference chart for all three alternatives. Also calculate the indifference point mathematically and indicate on the graph.
   c) Advise the company which alternative is the best. Give reasons.
6. Calculate various measures of leverage viz. Operating, financial and total for a firm whose income statement is as follows:

   Income statement for the year ending 31 March, 2010

Sales	12,00,000
Variable Cost	8,65,000
Fixed Cost	1,00,000

EBIT	2,35,000
Interest	1,07,000
Tax (35%)	44,800
PAT	83,200

Option	Equity	Debt	Preference
A	100%		
B	80%	20%	
C	80%		20%
D	50%	50%	
E	50%		50%
F	50%	25%	25%

7. A new company RK Limited is planning its capital structure. It can issue debt at 14% and 10% preference capital. The firm can sell equity shares at ₹ 20 per share. The firm falls in a tax bracket where its tax rate is 40%.The firm needs to raise ₹ 500 lakhs. The company has generated six possible capital structures as follows:

   You are required to:

   a) Plot EBIT-EPS chart over a EBIT range of 15 lakhs to 85 lakhs

   b) Find out the indifference points for Options C & A and E & F.

   c) Advise the company which plan results in maximum EPS.

8. A company is planning to raise ₹ 3,00,000 funds for its new project. It has three financing options. First, it may issue 30,000 shares at ₹ 10 per share. Second, it may issue 15000 shares at ₹ 10 each and 1500 debentures at ₹ 100 each at 15%.Third, It may issue 10000 shares at ₹ 10 each and 2000, ₹ 100 debentures at 16%.

   The profits before tax for the company are a) ₹ 8,000 b) ₹ 15000 and c) ₹ 30,000. Obtain;

   a. EPS in each case

   b. ROE in each case

   c. ROCE in each case

   Also calculate all the above assuming a Tax rate of 40%. Account for the difference in your answers.

9. Soham Limited needs ₹ 2,00,00,000 for its new factory. The expected EBIT is ₹ 2,50,000 per year. The factory can be financed with two alternative financing plans:

   a) 80% equity at ₹ 30 each and 20% debt at 15%.

   b) 50% equity at ₹ 40 each and 50% debt at 16%.

   If tax rate is 40%, which plan is better and why?

Review Questions

1. Explain various types of financial leverages. Do they affect share earning? If yes, how? Explain with the help of an example. **(UPTU 2009)**
2. What is financial leverage? Give its impact on earnings of shares. **(UPTU 2010)**
3. Write a short note on "Indifference Points". **(UPTU 2010)**
4. Explain what Operating Leverage is. **(UPTU 2006)**
5. Explain what is Financial Break point? **(UPTU 2006)**
6. Explain what is financial risk of a firm? **(UPTU 2006, DU 2007, 2008)**
7. Write down the role of leverage in designing the capital structure of a firm. **(UPTU 2005, 2006)**
8. Write down the role of Operating leverage in designing capital structure planning. **(UTPU 2007)**
9. What is total leverage? What does it measure?
10. Explain the concept of indifference point. Why is it called so? Briefly discuss the utility of this concept.
11. Explain with the help of an example how the indifference point is computed in EBIT-EPS analysis.
12. How can break-even analysis be used in financial planning? **(DU 2005, 2006, 2007)**

Case Study 1

DebtMore Industries has experienced rapid growth in sales revenue over the past four years. The company is now operating at 100% of capacity and must expand in order to meet the demand for its new line of video games.

The current financial statements for DebtMore Industries are as follows:

DebtMore Industries
Balance Sheet
as on March 31, 2011
(₹'000)

Liabilities :		Assets:	
Equity Capital	1,000	Net Fixed Assets	16,244
Retained earnings	15,310		
Accounts payable	550	Cash	1,000
Accruals	249	Accounts receivable	2,100
Other current liabilities	1	Inventories	2,766
8% bonds	5,000		
Total	₹22,110	Total	₹22,110

DebtMore Industries
Income Statement
for the year ended March 31, 2011
(₹ '000)

Sales	₹25,002
Cost of Goods Sold	18,252
Gross Margin on Sales	₹ 6,750
Administrative and Selling Expenses	4,000
Earnings before Interest Expense and Taxes	2,750
Interest expense	400
Earnings before tax	₹ 2,350
Taxes	1,011
Net Income	₹1,339

If the firm does not expand, it sales growth will stall at the current ₹25m level or less. If the company undertakes the planned expansion management has identified a probability distribution for possible EBIT levels:

Possible EBIT	Probability
₹2,200	.1
₹2,700	.4
₹3,200	.4
₹3.700	.1

The planned expansion will require DebtMore Industries to raise ₹10,000,000 in new capital. If raised in the form of bonds, the bonds would carry a 6.5% coupon rate. New Equity could be sold for ₹250.00 per share.

Find the EBIT/EPS indifference point. What is the probability that EBIT will be greater than the indifference point? Which method of financing is most likely to maximize earnings per share? What method of financing do you recommend? Why? Discuss the limitations of indifference analysis. Prepare a properly labeled diagram of the EBIT/EPS analysis.

SOLUTION
DebtMore Industries
Indifference Analysis

We can first determine the expected EBIT for next year and using that, determine the standard deviation of that EBIT. These calculations will be useful later when we try to determine the probability that EBIT will be less than, or greater than the indifference point.

Possible EBIT	Probability	Wtd EBIT
₹ 2,200,000	10.0%	₹ 220,000
2,700,000	40.0%	1,080,000
3,200,000	40.0%	1,280,000
3,700,000	10.0%	370,000
	Expected EBIT =	₹ 2,950,000

$$\sigma_{EBIT} = \sqrt{.1(-750^2)+.4(-250^2)+.4(250^2)+.1(750^2)}$$
$$= \sqrt{56250+25,000+25,000+56250}$$
$$= \sqrt{162,500}$$
$$= 403.11$$
$$= Rs403,110$$

Next set up equations for EPS for each alternative source of financing, equate them, substitute in known values and solve for the common EBIT.

Our prediction for EPS at EBIT=₹2,675,000 for the common share financing alternative is

$$EPS_{common} = \frac{(EBIT - I)(1-T)}{n_1 + n_2}$$

$$EPS_{debt} = \frac{(EBIT - I_1 - I_2)(1-T)}{n_1}$$

$$EPS_{common} = EPS_{debt}$$

$$\frac{(EBIT - I_1)(1-T)}{n_1 + n_2} = \frac{(EBIT - I_1 - I_2)(1-T)}{n_1}$$

$$\frac{(EBIT - 400,000)(1-.43)}{100,000+40,000} = \frac{(EBIT - 400,000 - 650,000)(1-.43)}{100,000}$$

$$EBIT = Rs2,675,000$$

$$EPS_{commonshare} = \frac{(Rs2,675,000 - Rs400,000)(1-.43)}{140,000} = Rs9.26$$

$$EPS_{Debt} = \frac{(Rs2,675,000 - Rs1,050,000)(1-.43)}{100,000} = Rs9.26$$

The probability than EBIT will favour Equity financing (ie. be less than the indifference point) is:

$$z = \frac{X - \mu}{\sigma}$$

Where z = the number of standard deviations away from the mean

X = the point of interest

α= the standard deviation of the probability distribution

μ = the mean of the probability distribution

$$z = \frac{2,675,000 - 2,950,000}{403,110}$$

$$= -0.6822$$

The negative sign indicates that the point of interest (X) or (indifference point) lies on the left-hand side of the mean. It lies .6822 of 1 standard deviation away from the mean.

Going to the table for Values of the Standard Normal Distribution Function we find the area under the curve between the point of interest and the mean of the distribution to be:

0.2517 or 25.27%

Therefore the probability that EBIT will exceed the indifference point (favouring debt financing) is 75.17% The probability that EBIT will be below the indifference point (favouring equity financing is (1- .7517) 24.83%.

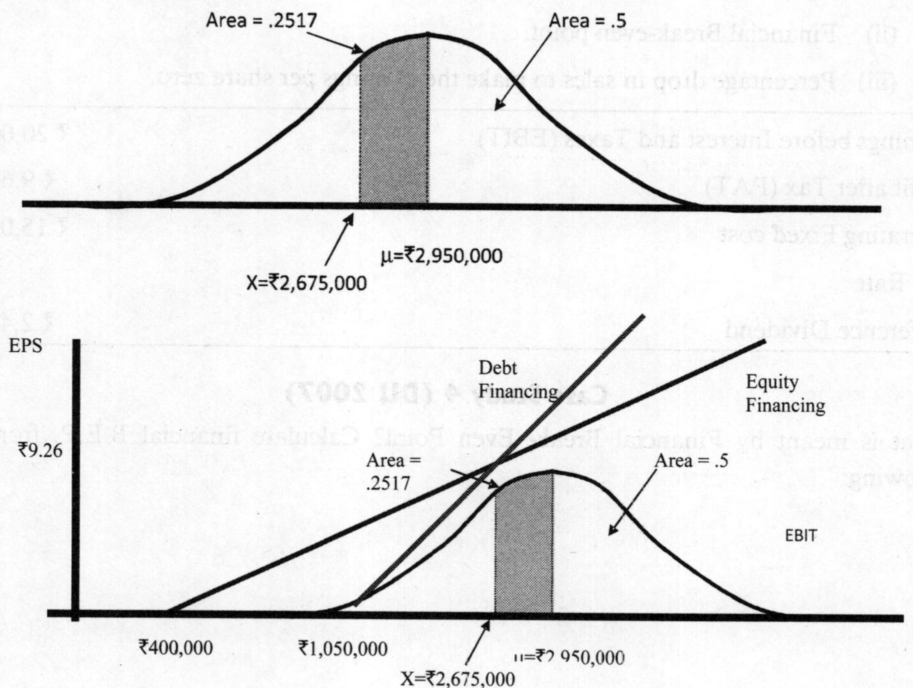

Case Study 2 (DU 2005)

Arvind Textile Mill currently has 10, 00,000 shares of equity outstanding with a market price of ₹ 50 per share. It also has ₹4 crore in 12% bonds. The company is considering a ₹ 5 crore expansion program that it can finance through:

1. all equity shares at ₹ 40 per share or
2. Straight bonds at 15% interest or
3. half equity shares at ₹40 per share and half 15% bonds. You are required to do the following.

   (i) For EBIT level ₹ 2,50,00,000 after the expansion programme, calculate the earnings per share for each of the alternative modes of financing. Assume a corporate tax rate of 50%.

   (ii) What are the indifference points between alternatives?

   (iii) What is your interpretation of the results?

Case Study 3 (DU 2006)

From the following data, calculate:

(i) Operating, financial and combined leverage.

(ii) Financial Break-even point.

(iii) Percentage drop in sales to make the earnings per share zero.

Earnings before Interest and Taxes (EBIT)	₹ 20,00,000
Profit after Tax (PAT)	₹ 9,60,000
Operating Fixed cost	₹ 15,00,000
Tax Rate	40%
Preference Dividend	₹ 2,40,000

Case Study 4 (DU 2007)

What is meant by Financial Break- Even Point? Calculate financial B.E.P. from the following:

(i) Interest p.a. Issue of 1,00,000 equity shares of ₹ 10 each. ₹ 60,000

(ii) Issue of 12% Preference share capital of ₹ 3,00,000 and equity share capital of ₹ 7,00,000 as in (i)above

(iii) 10% Debt of ₹ 4,00,000 and Equity Share Capital of ₹ 6,00,000 as in (i)above.

(iv) Issue of 12% Preference Share Capital of ₹ 2,00,000, 10% Debt of ₹ 3,00,000 and balance by issue of Equity Share Capital as in (i)above.

Find out the EPS in all these situations given that the tax rate applicable to company is 40%. Which option should be preferred by the company?

Preference dividend	₹ 45,000
Tax rate	40%

References

1. Brealey, Richard A & Myres, Stewart C. (2007), Tata McGraw Hill, New Delhi
2. Damodaran, Aswath. (1994). Damodaran on Valuation, John Wiley & Sons, New York
3. ICAI study Material on Financial Management, The Institute of Chartered Accountants of India, New Delhi.
4. Khan, M Y & Jain (2007) P K, Financial Management, Tata McGraw Hill, New Delhi
5. Kishore, Ravi M, (2009), Financial Management, Taxmann Publications, New Delhi
6. Pandey, I M (2009). Financial Management, Vikas Publishing House, New Delhi
7. Van Horne, James C. (2007),Financial Management & Policy, Pearson Prentice Hall, New Delhi
8. Work book on "Financial Management. for Managers": The Institute of Chartered Financial Analysts of India, Hyderabad.

Unit-3

Financing Decision

CHAPTER 7 Long-term Sources of Finance

Learning Objectives:

By the end of this chapter and having completed the essential reading and activities, you should be able to:

- Understand the Concept of Financing Decision and its effects
- Have an understanding of Long Term Sources of Finance
- Differentiate Between Various Long Term Sources of Finance
- Discuss the advantages and disadvantages of Various Long Term Sources of Finance
- Explain Shares and Debentures and their Characteristics

To start with...

Atul is already doing well in his job as Management Trainee (Finance). His immediate boss put him on a new assignment. His company, a housing construction giant Dream Homes Ltd. wants to enter into the construction of shopping malls but the company wants to explore various funding options available to finance this project before taking any investment decision. With the help of given data Atul has to prepare report on company's investment and financing decision.

After preparing his favorable report on investment decision Atul is now preparing his report on financing decision by exploring various long term sources of finance , their availability, feasibility and advantages & disadvantages.

Firms have various long term sources of financing but every source has its limitation, merits, demerits and legal aspects. Firms have to choose that source of finance, which ultimately results in shareholder's wealth maximization.

This chapter describes various sources of long term financing and their properties.

7.0 Financing Decision

We know that a finance manager takes mainly three types of decisions, ***Investment Decision***, ***Financing Decision*** & ***Dividend Decision.*** Investment decisions involve mainly capital budgeting decisions which we have discussed in earlier unit. In dividend decision, decision is taken whether dividend is to be paid or not and if yes, then how much? We shall discuss dividend decisions in next unit.

In this unit we shall discuss financing decisions. We will focus on long term financing, its sources, its impact on capital structure and its cost.

Sources of Finance

Financing means procurement of funds from various available sources. "Sources of finance" are the avenues from where a company may get funds for financing an activity or a project. We may assume that the firm has already decided on the activity or the project. (In other words, firm has already taken an ***Investment Decision).*** Let us take a real life example: if you are planning to own a house but you do not have ample funds then you go to the bank for taking a housing loan to buy or construct the house. In this example, like a finance manager, you take a series of decisions, e.g., decision for owning a house is investment decision, getting housing loan from bank is a financing decision and bank is a source of finance.

Whenever the firm raises funds from a particular source of finance, the firm has to repay them as well. The period of repayment can range from less than one year to indefinite. Based on when the repayment has to be made, the sources of finance can be divided into various three categories:

a) **Long Term Sources** are those where repayment period is usually more than three years (example: debentures) or infinite (example: equity shares).

b) **Medium Term sources** are those where repayment period is usually between one to three years (example: public deposits)

c) **Short term sources** are those where repayment period is usually less than one year (example: cash credit, certificate of deposits etc.)

Here the reader should keep in mind that there is no universally accepted criterion for categorizing something as medium term or long term. Some times a source may be considered a long term source if the repayment period is more than one year! However, every one agrees that sources with less than one year repayment period are short term.

In case of a business firm, for long term financing i.e. to finance its long term assets, firm has many options. It can raise the required funds from either of Equity Shares, Preference Shares, Debentures & Bonds and Term Loans .Firms can also use a combination of two or more out of these sources. Take a look at chart ***A below.***

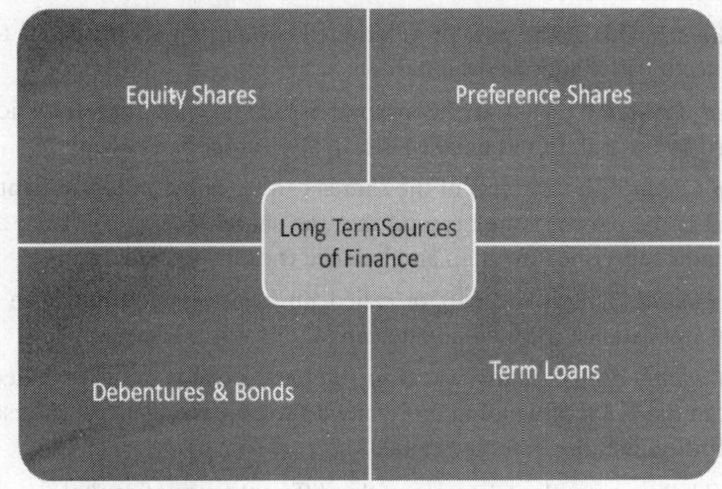

CHART A

Now we shall discuss various sources in detail one by one.

7.1 Equity Shares

As per Companies' Act 1956 "*an equity share is share which is not preference share*". An equity share does not carry any preferential right. Equity shareholders are entitled to dividend and repayment of capital after the claims of preference shareholders are satisfied. Equity shareholders control the affairs of the company and have right to all the profits; left after the preference dividend has been paid.

For understanding the above definition we shall have to know the concept of capital in case of a company. Take an example that Mr. Atul who wants to start a business and total investment for that business is ₹ 10 lacs. Mr. Atul has only ₹ 4 lacs and balance ₹ 6 lacs is to be financed by financial institution like banks. Now Mr. Atul will invest only ₹ 4 lacs from his own funds, this ₹ 4 lacs is called CAPITAL or EQUITY CAPITAL which Mr. Atul (the owner) is going to invest.

Hence we can say that capital is the fund invested by the owners of the business into their business. Capital can be introduced for starting a new business or into an existing business for an expansion. Capital can also be called Promoter's Contribution.

In case of a company, whether public or private, capital is divided into small fractions. These fractions are called shares. And the "capital" is called "share capital" or "Equity Capital". Under Indian law, the share capital is of many types. It can be categorized in the following manner:

a) ***Authorized, Nominal or Registered Capital:*** This is the capital with which the company registers. This capital is mentioned in Memorandum of Association and it is the maximum amount of capital which the company is authorized to raise without amendment in its Memorandum of Association.

b) ***Issued Capital***: This is the part of authorized capital which is offered to the public and balance is called unissued capital.

c) ***Subscribed Capital*** : This is the part of issued capital that is which has been subscribed by the public and balance is called unsubscribed capital

d) ***Called up Capital***: The amount of the shares can be called in installments and called up capital is the part of issued capital that the shareholders have been asked to pay on the shares subscribed by them and balance is called uncalled capital.

e) ***Paid up Capital***: This is the part of called up capital which has been paid by the company and balance is called unpaid capital or calls in arrears.

f) ***Reserve Capital***: If a company wants to reserve a portion of its uncalled capital for raising it in the event of winding up it may do so by passing a special resolution. The reserve portion is called reserve capital.

The CHART B below gives the schemata of the different types of capital.

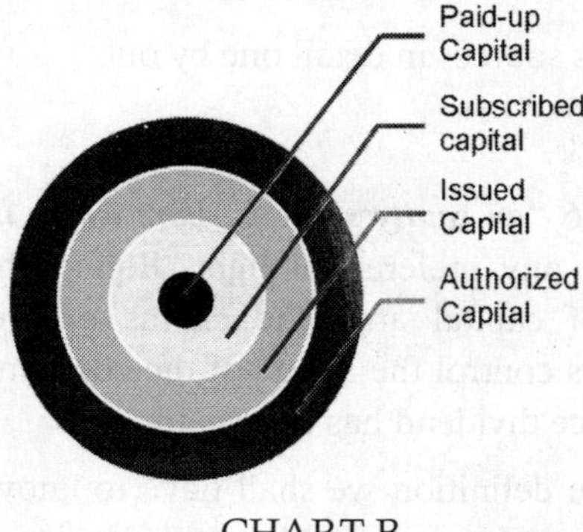

CHART B

Capital may be either in the form of equity shares or equity & preference shares both. Can it also be only in the form of preference shares? The answer is NO.

EQUITY SHARES are the basic sources of finance for any company. It is permanent in nature. Here "Permanent" means Equity shareholders can get back their investment only in the event of winding up of the company. Equity shareholders are the legal owners of the company. It is not a fixed income security like a bond. That means equity shareholders are not entitled to receive fixed interest at regular intervals. The income of equity shareholders is variable in nature because equity shareholders only get dividend. What is dividend? It is that part of profits of a firm that has been paid to the shareholders. Since profits vary from year to year, dividend also varies from year to year. The dividend may be for nil also in a year! Why? It is because payment of dividend depends upon the decision of the board of directors.

The price at which company issues these shares consists of two portions, first is ***Par Value*** & second is ***Premium.*** Par value can also be called Nominal Value or Face Value which normally is ₹ 10 but it may be more than ₹ 10 or less than ₹ 10. Excess of issue price over the nominal value is called premium. If issue price of shares consists of premium then it is called issue of shares at premium. Issue of shares at premium is not mandatory but some times a well established company with big bottom-line (profits) may issues shares at premium.

For understanding the premium; just take a reference of Partnership Accounts. When a new partner enters into an existing partnership firm he brings his capital contribution which includes some portion towards goodwill. The same concept applies to the premium.

7.1.1 Characteristics of Equity Shares

Equity shares have certain inherent characteristics which are explained as below:

Dividend: Dividend is the share of profits which is paid to the equity shareholders. Rate of dividend is decided by the board of directors & it is possible that board of directors decide not to pay any dividend! A company is not ***legally bound*** to pay dividend to its equity shareholders. Rate of dividend is not fixed. In any year, It may be more or less as compared to previous year. Dividend is paid out of residual profits which is arrived after satisfying all the claims like expenses, interest, taxes and dividend payable to preference shareholders by the company.

Dividends are not taxable in the hands of shareholders because as per Income Tax Act 1961 "Dividends received by an equity shareholder from a domestic company is not taxable u/s 115O". But in the hands of the company dividends are not tax deductible because every company has to pay Dividend Distribution Tax on dividend distributed by the company.

Voting Rights: Equity shareholders are the legal owners of the company. They have the power to control the affairs and management of the company through voting rights.

Normally, each equity shareholder has number of votes equal to the number of shares held (However, now a company can issue shares with differential voting rights, i.e., more voting power in proportion to number of shares.)

Equity shareholders can control the affairs of the company by exercising voting power on various resolutions in the general meeting. Equity shareholders may cast their vote against or in favor of any resolution put before them.

Equity shareholders can also control the management of the company through their voting right. Management of the company is in the hands of board of directors. And board of directors is formed by equity shareholders. Directors can be appointed only by equity shareholders. In case any of the directors acts against the interest of the equity shareholders, they can remove him and appoint a new director.

Marketability: Equity shares are marketable securities. A shareholder can sell or transfer his shares to another person. Companies have no control over transferability of equity shares. If shares of the company are listed on a stock exchange then shareholders can sell them through stock exchange. Listing on the stock exchange brings many benefits for the company. For example, it helps companies in raising additional capital. If an investor sells or transfers his shares to another investor, the seller does not require permission from the company. And after transfer, the new investor gets registered with the company and becomes entitled for dividend and other rights and benefits.

Right of pre-emption: Right of pre emption means right to purchase first, and if refused to purchase, then sell the right to another person. In case of a company, existing shareholders have pre emptive rights. If a company wants to issue additional capital then it will have to first offer them to existing shareholders. This ensures that the proportionate shareholding of a shareholder is maintained before and after the issuance of additional capital. How?

Consider this example. If a shareholder owns 5% of equity share then he has the right to subscribe 5% of new shares issued. If a shareholder does not want to subscribe additional capital then he can sell his right of pre emption to another person. The right of pre emption protects shareholders in mainly two ways; firstly it prevents dilution in the earnings of the existing shareholders in the form of dividend and secondly; it prevents dilution in control over the affairs of the company by preventing new investors from purchasing additional issuance of equity shares.

Claims: Equity shareholders are have residual claim over earnings and assets of the company. These shareholders are entitled to dividend only after satisfying all the claims like expenses, interests and taxes etc from the earnings. In case of liquidation, equity shareholders will get their share in the assets of the company if any assets are left after payment to employees, secured creditors, unsecured creditors, preferential creditors and preferential shareholders. In other words, creditors other than equity shareholders are having preferential rights over the assets of the company.

7.1.2 Merits & demerits of equity financing

The following are merits and demerits of equity financing:

Merits

1. **Payment** of dividend is not a legal obligation for a company. It depends upon the board's decision and availability of earnings. In case of company facing financial crises, or not having adequate profits, it may defer payment of dividend. Companies also defer payment of dividend in case it is considering a new project with potential for high returns.
2. **Equity** share capital is a permanent capital in nature. There is no obligation on the company to redeem this capital.
3. **In** case a company goes for debt financing; the financiers may impose certain conditions, restrictions and charge over the company and companies' assets. But in case of equity financing companies are free from these conditions and restrictions.
4. **Though** equity share capital is of permanent nature but now companies; as per Companies Act and SEBI's Guidelines; can buy back their equity shares.

Demerits

1. **Dividends** are not tax deductible and companies have to pay additional "dividend distribution tax" on distributed dividend. But in case of debt financing, interest payment to creditors are tax-deductible.
2. **In** case a company issues new equity shares for financing, it results in dilution of ownership of existing shareholder despite having right of pre emption.
3. **Issuance** of new equity shares may dilute earnings per share because it is possible that earnings may not increase in the same proportion as new shares issued.

7.1.4 Disclosure in Balance Sheet: Equity shares are disclosed in the balance sheet in the following manner: Share capital is shown on the liability side of the balance sheet as below.

Balance Sheet as at 31.03.2010

(₹ in thousands)

Liabilities		
Authorized 500000 equity shares of ₹ 10 each	5000.00	
Issued 300000 equity shares of ₹ 10 each	3000.00	
Subscribed & paid up 240000 equity shares of ₹ 10 each		2400.00

7.2 Preference Shares

As per companies Act 1956 "an ***equity share is share which is not preference share.***" Companies Act does not define equity share but preference share. Preference shares are another kind of shares which are issued by the companies to raise capital. These shares are also an important source of long term financing. These shares have characteristics of equity shares and debt instrument both. In other words , these shares play double role just like our film stars. They are also known as hybrid securities. As per Companies Act 1956 "Preference shares are those which have the following two characteristics. First; these shares have a preferential right to get dividend at a fixed rate. And second, in case of liquidation; these shares have preferential right over the equity shareholders to the return of capital. Preference shares are also called hybrid security. This is because these shareholders get fixed rate of dividend as in case of a debt instrument. And also these shareholders are owners of the company and get dividend like equity shareholders.

7.2.1 Characteristics of Preference Shares

Characteristics of preference shares are explained as below:

Voting Rights: Normally preference shares do not carry voting rights. But in certain circumstances, these shareholders may vote. As per sec. 87(2)(a) of Companies Act 1956 "every member of a company limited by shares and holding any preference shares capital therein shall, in respect of such capital, have a right to vote only on resolution placed before the company which directly affects the right attached to these preference shares. In simple words, preference shareholders can vote only on those resolutions which are, if passed, going to affect their rights. Companies Act recognizes any resolution for winding up of the company, repayment or reduction of its share capital as resolutions affecting the rights attached to preference shares. Preference shareholders can vote on aforesaid resolutions but they can vote on every resolution if the dividend due on such capital or any part of such dividend has remained unpaid in the following situations:

(a) in the case of cumulative preference shares, in respect of an aggregate period of not less than two years preceding the date of commencement of the meeting; and (b) in the case of non-cumulative preference shares, either in respect of a period of not less than two years ending with the expiry of the financial year immediately preceding the commencement of the meeting or in respect of an aggregate period of not less than three years comprised in the six years ending with the expiry of the financial year aforesaid.

Dividend: It is a very important characteristic of preference shares that they get dividend at a fixed rate just like investors in debt instruments get interest. However, like equity shares, company in not legally bound to pay the dividend to the preference shareholders. In case company wants to pay the dividend to the equity shareholders it will have to first pay dividend to the preference shareholders first and then to equity shareholders. In case of cumulative preference shares company will have to first pay cumulative dividend to the preference shareholders and then to equity shareholders. It is also possible that company may pay dividend only to preference shareholders. In simple words if company wants to pay dividend then it should pay first to preference shareholders then to equity shareholders.

Claims: Preference shareholders have preferential right over equity shares be it dividend or redemption of capital. In case of winding up, after paying all debts and satisfying all claims excluding share capital redemption, preference shares get priority over equity shares for receiving any amount left.

Redemption: As per Companies Act "no company shall issue any irredeemable preference shares or redeemable preference shares which are redeemable after a period of twenty years". In other words, now irredeemable preference shares can not be issued and every preference shares shall have to be redeemed within a period of twenty years. Certain conditions, to be satisfied by the company which is going to redeem preference shares, are given below:

- Preference shares must be fully paid.
- Preference shares can be redeemed only out of profits available for dividend or out of proceeds of a fresh issue of shares made for the purpose for redemption.
- Any premium, if payable, on redemption shall have been provided for out of the profits of the company or out of the company's premium account.

If preference shares are going to be redeemed out of profits, an amount equal to nominal value of shares must be transferred to capital redemption reserve account.

7.2.2 Merits & demerits of preference shares financing

The following are merits and demerits of preference shares financing:

Merits

1. ***Payment*** of dividend in case of preference shares is not a legal obligation so companies can defer payment of dividend.
2. ***There*** are limited voting rights available to preference shareholders; therefore, dilution of control over ownership is also limited.
3. ***Since*** rate of dividend is fixed, it provides leverage advantages.
4. ***Dividend*** on preference shares in the hands of shareholders is tax free.

Demerits

1. ***It is mandatory that Companies*** redeem preference shares with in twenty years. In the year of redemption company will face heavy cash outflow.
2. ***Payment*** of dividend is not tax deductible. Conversely companies have to pay tax on dividend.

   Due to non tax deductibility of dividend cost of capital of preference shares is more than the debt instrument.

7.2.3 Disclosure in Balance Sheet

Preference shares are disclosed in the balance sheet in the following manner:

Share capital is shown on the liability side of the balance sheet as below.

Balance Sheet as at 31.03.2009

		(₹ In thousand)
Liabilities		
Preference Shares		
Authorized 300000 preference shares of ₹ 100 each	30,000	
Issued 300000 preference shares of ₹ 100 each	30,000	
Subscribed & paid up 300000 preference shares of ₹ 100 each		30,000

7.3 Debentures

Debentures are a long term debt instrument, issued by the companies for long term financing. Unlike equity and preference shares, debentures do not form part of share capital. Debenture holders are termed as creditors of the company to whom company pays interest at certain rate for a certain period. Interest payment may be quarterly, half yearly or annually. Interest is paid at fixed rate on par value. Par value is the face value of debentures. Debentures may be issued at discount i.e. at less than face value. Bonds are another form of debentures. Most companies in India are issuing bonds for debt financing. After a certain period debentures will have to be redeemed by the companies. In other words we can term debenture as promissory note in which company promises to pay interest and par value to debenture holders. Unlike equity and preference shares debentures are a fixed income security.

Interest payment on debentures is mandatory. There is no option available to companies for nonpayment of debenture interest. In other words, companies are legally bound to pay interest to debenture holders. In case of nonpayment of interest, creditors may sue the company to be declared as insolvent.

Types of debentures:

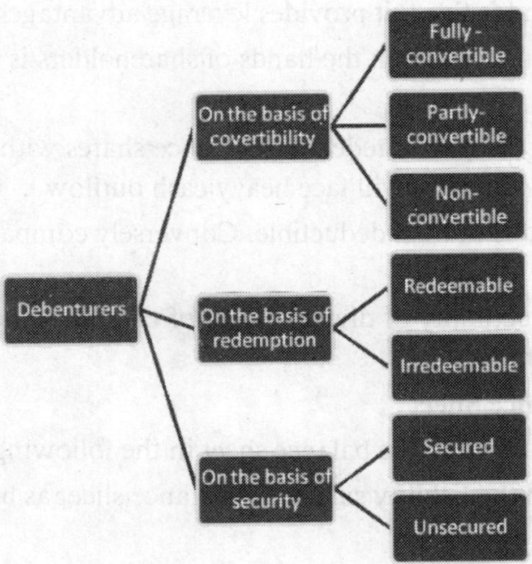

Chart C depicts types of debentures which are issued by the companies.

a) ***Fully-convertible debentures***: The face value Fully-convertible debentures can be converted into other type of security. Normally it is converted into equity shares. These types of debentures are having less coupon rate than non-convertible debentures because this type of debentures have additional feature of convertibility.

b) ***Partly-convertible debentures***: The face value of partly-convertible debentures consists of two parts, one part is convertible and another is non-convertible. In other words, partly-convertible debentures are perfect blend of equity and debt instrument. These debentures are attractive for investors because investors may take advantages available to owners and creditors both. In other words we can term these debentures as hybrid security.

Important: Convertible debentures can be converted at the option of debentures holders or compulsorily. And after conversion, creditors become the owners of the company. A finance manager should take great care while taking decision of conversion because cost of capital of equity shares is more than debentures due to the fact that interest to debentures holders is tax deductible (to be discussed ahead).

c) ***Non-convertible debentures***: These are typical form of debt instrument. The investor gets interest periodically and on maturity he gets face value of debentures. The coupon rate on these debentures is higher than partly or fully convertible debentures because partly or fully convertible debentures contain an additional feature of convertibility.

d) ***Secured debentures***: These debentures are secured against assets of the company in the form of charge over the respective assets of the company. Charge may be in the form of fixed or floating charge over assets of the company. Fixed charge on assets means that claims of debenture holders shall be limited to the value of that asset. Floating charge means debenture holders shall get first their claim from the asset which is secured for them and claim left, if any, shall be discharged from other assets also.

e) ***Unsecured debentures***: These debentures are not secured against any assets i.e. debenture holders do not have any charge over assets of the company. But debenture holders, in case of liquidation, get priority, over and above equity & preference shareholders. In case of unsecured debentures, investor makes investments generally on the basis of the reputation of the company.

f) ***Redeemable Debentures:*** These debentures are redeemed after a certain period of time. To redeem these debentures companies are required to amortize a fixed portion of the total redeemable value of debentures every year in a fund called sinking fund. This is done to enable the firm to have ready funds equal to the total redemption amount.

g) ***Irredeemable Debentures:*** These debentures are not redeemed during the life time of these debentures. These are also called Perpetual Debentures. Companies pay only coupon rate on these debentures.

7.3.1 Characteristics

- It is a credit instrument and holder of this instrument gets interests at periodic intervals and principal at the time of maturity.
- Debentures holders cannot vote because debenture holders are creditors of the company.
- In the event of winding up, debenture holders get priority over shareholders and some other creditors for distribution of assets.
- Debentures are redeemable after a certain period.

As per the guidelines issued by SEBI that No company shall make a public issue of debt instrument (whether convertible or not) unless credit rating is obtained from at least one credit rating agency registered with the board and disclosed in the offer document. In other words no company can issue debentures without obtaining credit rating.

Companies create a sinking fund for redemption of debentures. Sinking fund is a fund in which periodically money is transferred and invested in some security for getting the sum that will be used for redeeming debentures at the time of their maturity.

7.3.2 Merits & demerits of Debenture financing

The followings are merits and demerits of debentures:

Merits

1. ***Cost*** of capital of debentures is less as compared to shares, because interest on debentured are tax deductible (to be discussed in next chapter).
2. ***Control*** dose not dilute in case of debentures because debenture holders are creditors not owners.
3. ***Debentures*** provide a cover in case of inflation, because interest and principal payment is fixed. ***Debenture holders*** are not entitled to get extra returns (interest) in case of extra ordinary profits. This is because commitment towards debentures is fixed in the form of fixed interest and they do not carry voting rights

Demerits

1. ***There*** is certain obligation towards debentures like interest and redemption. Companies are legally bound to pay the interest and to redeem debentures. In case of financial crunch companies can not deny these payments
2. ***At*** the time of redemption, company faces huge cash out flow.
3. ***Companies*** face certain restriction imposed by debenture indenture. Debenture indenture or debenture trust deed is a legal agreement between company and debenture trustee who represent the debenture holders.
4. ***Financial*** leverage created by use of debt financing will adversely affect EPS In case of company is not getting rate of return equal to cost of debentures.

Activity

Get the financial statement of a limited company. In liability side of that financial statement you can see various type equity share capital, preference shares and debentures. In case of debentures you can see liability side a debenture sinking fund and at assets side debenture sinking fund investment for redemption of debentures.

Get a copy of prospectus of any recent public issue in which you can find what formalities companies have to fulfill before any public offering of equity, preference shares and debentures.

7.4 Term Loans

Term loans are another means of long term financing. It is provided by financial institutions (banks and others) on certain terms and conditions. Generally firm obtains term loans to finance its capital expenditure. For example, term loans can be used for setting up new projects or expansion of an existing project. The characteristics of term loans are as follows:

7.4.1Characteristics

Repayment of term loans is normally made over more than a year. The financial institution normally allows moratorium to firms. Moratorium means time period after taking a loan, during which the borrower is allowed not to make any repayment. After this period repayment schedule starts. Repayments are made in installments. Installments include both principal and interests. The companies are legally bound to pay the installments.

Term loans are secured against security provided by the companies in the form of charge over assets. Generally these securities are fixed assets. The fixed assets acquired by using funds from these term loans are called primary security. If any other current or future asset is also given as additional security for the loans, it is called secondary or collateral security. Charge over assets may be of two types. These two types are "fixed charge or "floating charge". For getting term loans, companies prepare a detailed project report for project and submit to the bank or financial institution. This detailed Project report contains brief profile of project, fund requirement, projected sales, projected profits, promoters' contribution, repayment schedule, projected cash flows etc.

Lenders normally impose some restrictions on borrowing companies. They may relate to maintenance of minimum assets, restrictions from taking additional loans, cash outflow for certain expenditures, appointment of nominee director on the board of directors.

7.5 Comparing Equity Financing & Debt Financing

We can compare debt and equity feature by feature to get a better understanding of similarities and differences between them.

EQUITY	DEBT
1. Equity shareholders are the owners of the company.	1. Debenture holders or lenders are creditors of the company.
2. Dividend to equity shareholders is not tax deductible.	2. Interest payment to these creditors is tax deductible.
3. Due to non tax deductibility of dividends cost of capital is more than debt financing.	3. Due to tax deductibility of interest cost of capital is less than equity or preference shares financing.
4. Dividend payment is not legal obligation for the company.	4. Company is legally bound to pay interest to creditors.
5. In case of profit too, it totally depends upon the companies discretion whether to pay dividend or not.	5. In case of loss too, companies have to pay interest. There is no choice.
6. Shares are not backed by any security.	6. These are secured by charge over assets in the form of fixed or floating charge.
7. Shares have voting rights.	7. Creditors are not having any voting rights.
8. Shareholders cannot impose any restrictions upon the company.	8. Creditors can impose certain restrictions the company.
9. Repayment is residual i.e. in case of liquidation or winding up after satisfying all the claims if any asset is left then these shareholders shall get their claim.	9. Repayment is contractual i.e. these creditors are having prior claim over shareholders.
10. Credit rating not required.	10. Credit rating is required

Managerial Tool Kit: Some Innovative Debt Financing Instruments

1. **Zero Coupon Bonds:** These are debt securities on which no explicit interest rate is offered by the issuer. These bonds are sold at a discount to their face value. So how does the investor of these bonds earn returns? The return to the investor is the difference between the face value and his purchase price.

2. **Deep Discount Bonds:** They are a type of zero coupon bonds. The only difference is that the purchase price is at a very high discount to the face value. For Example, IDBI in 1992, issued such bonds whose purchase price was kept at ₹ 2700 and the face value was ₹ 100000. The maturity period was 25 years. However, the investors had the option of redeeming their bonds every five years (such an option where the investor can redeem their investment before the maturity period is called **"put option"**. When the issuer has the option to redeem the bonds before the maturity period, it is called **"call option"**). In case of IDBI deep discount bonds, there was no call option.

3. **Secured Premium Notes:** They are secured debentures with attached warrants. A warrant is a right to purchase equity share at a specified price. The secured premium notes can be redeemed after 4-7 years. However, the investor has to exercise the warrant during a specified period.
4. **Floating Rate Bonds:** These are bonds where the coupon rate is not fixed. The coupon rate is quoted as a mark up over some benchmark rate. The benchmark rate can be T-bill rate, MIBOR etc. These market prices of these bonds have been found to remain stable. In an increasing interest rate scenario, these bonds protect the investor from the market risk.
5. **Equity Backed Bonds:** It has been a recent development. We know that issuers create charge over their fixed assets as a security for debenture holders. In case of equity backed bonds, a holding company- which is a unlisted shell company holding promoter's shares- sets aside a portion of promoter's shares as collateral while issuing bonds. These shares are held in a separate debenture trust or escrow account till the debt is repaid. Since, the real issuer is the holding company; it is the one who get the funds from investors. The promoter can use these funds when needed. Generally, this security cover is created to the tune of 200-300 % of value of debentures issued. In India, the companies that have issued such debentures are Crompton Greaves, Asian Paints, Kumar Developers etc.

Summary

- Financing means procurement of funds from various available sources. "Sources of finance" are the avenues from where a company may get funds for financing an activity or a project.
- Long Term Sources are those where repayment period is usually more than three years .
- Medium Term sources are those where repayment period is usually between one to three years.
- Short term sources are those where repayment period is usually less than one year.
- There are two long term sources of finance, first is share capital & second is loan fund. Share capital includes equity capital & preference capital. Loan funds include debentures & term loans.
- Equity capital is the permanent capital of the company. An equity share does not carry any preferential right.
- Equity shareholders are entitled to dividend and repayment of capital after the claims of preference shareholders are satisfied. Equity shareholders control the affairs of the company and have right to all the profits; left after the preference dividend has been paid.
- Preference shares are another kind of shares which are issued by the companies to raise capital. These shares have characteristics of equity shares and debt instrument both. This is because these shareholders get fixed rate of dividend as in case of a debt instrument. And also these shareholders are owners of the company and get dividend like equity shareholders.

- In case of liquidation; these shares have preferential right over the equity shareholders to the return of capital.
- Debentures are a long term debt instrument, issued by the companies for long term financing. Debenture holders are termed as creditors of the company to whom company pays interest. Unlike equity and preference shares debentures are a fixed income security.
- Debentures holders cannot vote because debenture holders are creditors of the company. In the event of winding up, debenture holders get priority over shareholders and some other creditors for distribution of assets. Debentures are redeemable after a certain period.
- Term loans are provided by financial institutions (banks and others) on certain terms and conditions. Generally terms loans are provided to finance capital expenditure of a firm. *Repayment* of term loans is normally made over more than a year.
- Term loans are secured against security provided by the companies in the form of charge over assets. Generally these securities are fixed assets. The fixed assets acquired by using funds from these term loans are called primary security. If any other current or future asset is also given as additional security for the loans, it is called secondary or collateral security.
- The provider of term loans impose some restrictions on borrowing companies. They may relate to maintenance of minimum assets, restrictions from taking additional loans, cash outflow for certain expenditures, appointment of nominee director on the board of directors.

Test Your Understanding

State whether the following statements are true (T) or False (F)

1. Equity Shareholders cannot participate in voting.
2. Equity Shareholders get fixed dividend every year.
3. Companies are legally bound to pay dividend to equity shareholders.
4. Company repays capital to equity shareholders after a certain period of time.
5. Equity shareholders get share in profit after payment of preference dividend.
6. Equity shareholders can transfer their shares to another person.
7. In case of equity shareholders dividends are tax deductible.
8. Preference shareholders get dividend at fix rate.
9. Cumulative preference shareholders get dividend after equity share holders.
10. Partly paid preference shares can also be redeemed.
11. Preference shareholders are having limited voting rights.
12. Debentures are redeemed by sinking fund.

13. Debenture holders are having charge over the assets of the company.
14. Loss making companies are also pay interest to the debentures holders.
15. Debentures interest affects financial leverage of the company.

Answers : 1. F, 2. F, 3. F, 4. F, 5. T, 6. T, 7. F, 8. T, 9. F, 10. F, 11. T, 12. T, 13. T, 14. T, 15. T

Multiple Choice Questions

Choose the correct alternative out of the given:

1. Equity shareholder's claim on profits & assets
   a) Fixed Claim b) Residual Claim
   c) No Claim d) First Claim
2. Equity shares can be matured
   a) After issue of one year b) After issue of five years
   c) As per terms & conditions d) None of the above
3. Dividend tax is paid by
   a) Company b) Equity shareholders
   c) Directors d) None of the above
4. Dividend is paid to the equity shareholders out of
   a) Pretax profit b) Profit before interest
   c) Profit before interest & depreciation d) Profit after tax
5. Preference shares carry characteristics of
   a) Debt b) Equity
   c) Debt & equity d) None of the above
6. Preference shareholders get priority in income & assets over
   a) Creditors b) Equity Shareholders
   c) Debenture holders d) Equity shareholders & debenture holders
7. Preference shareholders have
   a) Limited voting rights b) Unlimited voting rights
   c) No voting rights d) None of the above
8. Dividend to preference shareholders is taxable in the hands of
   a) Preference shareholders b) Equity shareholders
   c) No taxability d) Company
9. Debenture holders are the

a) Owners of the company b) Creditors of the company
c) Directors of the company d) None of the above

10. Interest to debenture holders is
    a) Tax deductible b) No tax benefit
    c) Tax benefit to debenture holders d) None of the above
11. In case of debentures credit rating is
    a) Mandatory b) Optional
    c) Not required d) None of the above
12. Debenture holders are having charge over
    a) Company's liability b) Cash
    c) Only debtors d) Assets
13. Term loans are provided by
    a) Financial institutions b) Government
    c) Stock exchange d) None of the above
14. Providers of term loan are having charge over company's assets in the form of
    a) Fixed charge b) Floating charge
    c) Foxed & floating charge d) None of the above
15. What goes with Debenture?
    a) A short term source of finance b) A medium term source of finance
    c) A long term source of finance d) None of the above

Answers: 1. b, 2. d, 3.a, 4. d, 5. c, 6. b, 7. a, 8. d, 9. b, 10. a, 11. a, 12. d, 13. a, 14. c, 15. c

Review Questions

Q1. List various methods of Long-term sources of finance. Explain any two of these. **(UPTU 2005, 2010)**

Q2. Distinguish between Long, Medium and short term sources of finance. What is the importance of Long term sources of finance, also give its various sources. **(UPTU 2009)**

Q2. Explain the merits & demerits of equity financing.

Q3. How equity financing is different from preference financing?

Q4. As an investor differentiate between equity and debt financing.

Q5. Explain the features of preference shares with its merits and demerits. **(UPTU 2007)**

Q6. Discuss the various types of debentures and its merits & demerits. **(UPTU 2007)**

Q7. What is term loans and how it is different from debentures?

Q8. Explain the characteristics of debentures and differentiate it with equity shares.

Q9. Preference shares carry characteristics equity and debt both. Substantiate.

References

1. Brealey, Richard A & Myres, Stewart C. (2007), Tata McGraw Hill, New Delhi
2. Damodaran, Aswath.(1994). Damodaran on Valuation, John Wiley & Sons, New York
3. Financial Management study material, The Institute of Chartered Accountants of India, New Delhi.
4. Khan, M Y & Jain (2007) P K, Financial Management, Tata McGraw Hill, New Delhi
5. Menon, Shailesh, (2010) "HNIs take a fancy to equity-backed corp bonds" The Economic Times", Lucknow.
6. Pandey, I M (2009). Financial Management, Vikas Publishing House, New Delhi
7. Work book on "Financial Management for Managers": The Institute of Chartered Financial Analysts of India, Hyderabad.

Capital Structure Decision

Learning Objectives:

By the end of this chapter and having completed the essential reading and activities, you should be able to:

- Understand the Concept of Capital Structure and its ingredients
- Have an understanding of how Capital Structure affects the value of the firm
- Differentiate between Relevance and Irrelevance Theories of Capital Structure
- Understand the relationship between Capital Structure and Value of the Firm
- Understand how Financial Leverage affects Value of the Firm and WACC

To start with...

Ace Bank Ltd. approached the directors of Growing Ltd. to finance their new power project. The directors of the company find the terms of the bank's offer attractive but before getting into any financing agreement with the bank they want to carefully evaluate effect of debt financing on the value of the firm.

Ram, a management trainee, is entrusted with task of preparing a report on effect of various financing options before the firm. Ram has been working furiously to finish the report on time. His report is almost ready. He included a thorough analysis, comparing capital structure before and after the above financing, its impact on WACC, value of the firm.

In financial management, debt financing plays a very important role because it impacts the firm in more ways than one, all at the same time .It is essential, therefore, to critically examine effects of any major debt financing decision.

For analysis of any such decision, you need to have clarity of concepts related to capital structure, factors affecting it, its theories etc. In this chapter, you will acquire necessary skills to carry out an analysis like Ram's. So Don't' Wait. Get Set Go!

8.0 Introduction

The term "Capital Structure" is made up of two words " capital " and "structure". The word capital means "the funds, contributed by owners as well as outsiders to start and run the business". Dictionary meaning of second word structure is that "the way in which something is organized, built or put together, a thing made of several parts put together in a particular way". Can we define the term "Capital Structure" now? Yes.

Capital Structure is "organization of capital or organization of various parts of capital like equity or debt capital". In other words Capital Structure is the combination of various long term sources of finance like equity shares, preference shares and debt capital.

We all know that every business has two principal sources of finance i.e. equity and debt. Every capital structure is made by combination of equity and debt capital.

We have discussed the effects of leverage in the previous chapters. We saw that as debt proportion increases i.e. increase in debt financing, financial leverage also increases. Financial leverage directly affects the shareholders' wealth. With every increase in financial leverage, firm's value also increases as well as financial risk.

Optimal capital structure is the one at which overall cost of capital is minimum and value of the firm maximum. It follows that capital structure affects value of the firm. However, amongst the researchers there hardly seems agreement on this.

Now the million dollar question is "what should be the capital structure of a business". Or in other words "what should be the proportion of debt and equity in the capital of a firm". This decision to hold a particular level of debt or equity is called "Capital Structure Decision".

There are many theories for capital structure decision. Some of them are called relevance theories because they conclude that capital structure directly affects value of the firm. Some other theories are called irrelevance theories because they state that capital structure does not affect value of the firm. Let us discuss each of them one by one.

8.1 Theories of Capital Structure

Before going into the capital structure theories, we should first understand the need of these theories. We all know that the objective of financial management is maximization of shareholders' wealth in the form of value of the firm. Value of the firm is derived by capitalizing the earnings at the rate of cost of capital. ("Capitalizing" means dividing earnings by cost of capital)

$$Value\ of\ the\ firm = \frac{Earnings}{Cost\ of\ capital\,(WACC)}$$

We can say that value of the firm depends upon two factors, first is earnings and second is cost of capital.

Earning is the subject matter of investment decision because investment decision decides level of earnings.

Cost of capital, or WACC, depends upon the proportion of individual sources in capital structure and their individual cost of capital. As we change proportion of different sources in capital structure, WACC also changes. Now we can say that with every change in capital structure, WACC also changes. And, due to change in WACC, value of the firm also changes. Now, the key issue that arises here is, "Is there any relationship between value of the firm and its capital structure"?

It is here that we need an understanding of relationship between value and capital structure of the firm. This understanding is provided by various theories of capital structure.

These theories are called capital structure theories.

There are two extreme and diametrically opposite viewpoints of capital structure theories. On one hand, there is the view of "relevance" which says that capital structure does affect the value of a firm. The other extreme is "Irrelevance" which says that capital structure does not affect the value of a firm. Now, we will discuss theories including and between these two extreme views. Capital structure theories include the following assumptions:

- There is no corporate tax.
- There are only two long term sources of finance i.e. equity and debt.
- All the earnings are distributed among shareholders.
- Capital markets are perfect. It means that investors are free to trade and credit risks are equal for individuals and firms i.e. investors can borrow funds at the same rate of interest as the firms.
- There is no change in the total assets of the firm.

8.2 Net Income Theory (Relevance Theory)

This theory describes the relationship between capital structure and value of the firm. It says that capital structure and value of the firm are related to each other. The theory describes relationship among cost of capital, leverage and value of a firm. The Net Income Theory says that if firm changes its capital structure, its WACC will change. Since WACC will change, the value of the firm will also change.

As previously discussed, value of the firm depends upon earning and cost of capital. This theory works on the assumption that K_d (cost of debt) is less than K_e (cost of equity). Now, If a firm starts increasing low cost debt financing, then return to shareholders will also increase due to leverage effect. The increase in return to the shareholders will result, increase in value of equity. Due to introduction of more low cost debt, WACC will also decrease and decrease in WACC means increase in value of the firm.

Now, If we reverse the above situation and a firm decreases its proportion of debt financing, then WACC will increase. Increase in WACC will result in decreased value of the firm.

According to Net Income Approach, value of the firm and value of equity are determined as follows:

Value of firm, V = E + B

Where, E = Value of equity, B = Value of Debt.

Where, Market value of equity; $E = \dfrac{Net\,Income}{K_e}$

Where, K_e = Equity Capitalization Rate OR Cost of Equity

This theory can be depicted graphically as follows:

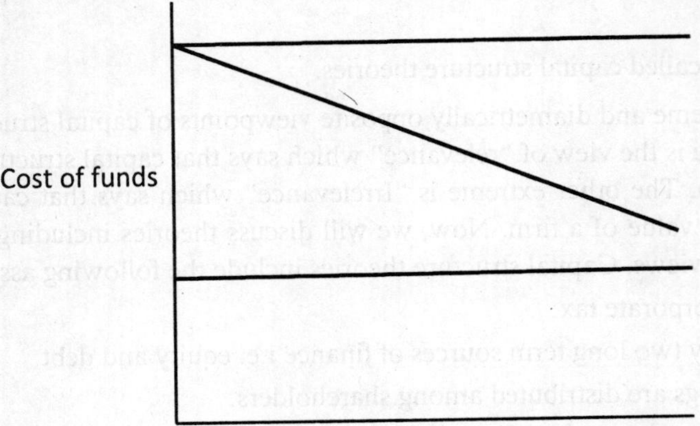

In the above graph, we can see that cost of equity is more than cost of debt for every degree of debt financing. As the debt financing increases (or financial leverage increases),

WACC decreases and goes nearer the cost of debt. It results in increase in value of the firm. The above graph also depicts that at the 100% levered firm WACC = cost of debt. However, this is not possible because a firm cannot be a 100% debt firm. Some amount of equity will certainly be there. But there can be a situation in which a firm may be an all equity firm or 0% levered firm. In that situation WACC = cost of equity.

Now as per NI approach we can conclude that at the point of minimum WACC, value of the firm will be maximum and capital structure at this point is termed as optimal capital structure.

Example 1

EBIT of a firm is ₹ 2,00,000 and cost of equity is 9%, cost of debt is 5% and debt is ₹ 500000. Calculate WACC and value of the firm.

Solution

EBIT	2,00,000
Less Interest	25,000
Net Profit	1,75,000
Cost of equity	9%
Value of equity	1,75,000/.09 = 19,44,444
Value of Debt	5,00,000

Total Value of the firm = 24,44,444

WACC = .05 (5,00,000/24,44,444) + .08 (19,44,444/24,44,444) = 8.2%

Now if the firm has increased its debt financing to ₹ 7,00,000 then

EBIT	2,00,000
Less Interest	35,000
Net Profit	1,65,000
Cost of equity	9%
Value OF Equity	1,65,000/.09 = 18,33,333
Value of debt	= 7,00,000

Total value of the firm = ₹ 25,33,333

WACC = 0.05(7,00,000/25,33,333) + .09(18,33,333/25,33,333) = 7.9%

Let us summarize above findings:

Debt	WACC	Value of firm
₹ 5,00,000	8.2%	₹ 24,44,444
₹ 7,00,000	7.9%	₹ 25,33,333

From the above example, it is clear that increased debt financing increases value of the firm and reduces WACC and the above example also shows that as per Net Income approach Capital Structure and Value of a firm are inter-related.

8.3 Traditional Approach (Relevance Theory)

Traditional approach is also a relevance theory. It says that capital structure and value of a firm are related to each other. According to this approach, a firm can achieve an optimal capital structure level by choosing a judicious mix of debt and equity i.e. a rational mix of debt and equity.

As per traditional approach, as the proportion of debt in the capital structure is increased, value of the firm also increases and there will be a point where WACC will be minimum and value of firm will be maximum. This is the point of optimal capital structure. At optimal capital structure, the overall cost of capital; WACC; will be minimized and the value of the firm will be maximized.

Now, as per traditional approach, after achieving optimal capital structure if firm introduces more debt then cost of debt will also start increasing along with cost of equity. WACC will also start increasing resulting in decrease in the value of the firm.

In summary, up to a certain limit, when financial leverage increases, value of the firm increases & WACC decreases. Beyond this limit, as financial leverage increases, WACC increases & value of the firm starts declining.

How does it happen? This theory works like this.

According to this approach, cost of debt is lower in comparison to equity. As the proportion of this low cost source of funds is increased, overall cost of capital goes down. However, as amount of debt in the capital structure increases, shareholders start considering the firm riskier. They start demanding higher returns owing to increased risk. So, the cost of equity starts increasing. However, overall cost of capital still decreases since the increase in cost of equity is still not high enough to neutralize the lower cost of debt.

Hence, WACC keeps decreasing despite increasing cost of equity. And the value of the firm keeps rising.

However, as more and more debt is taken, the lenders also begin to worry about increasing debt levels. This results in their demanding higher rates for *additional debt.* So, K_d starts moving up. Therefore, after a point, the cost of debt, as well as, cost of equity rises to an extent where WACC starts increasing. The point at which the WACC starts to increase is the point of optimal capital structure. The value of the firm is the maximum at this point.

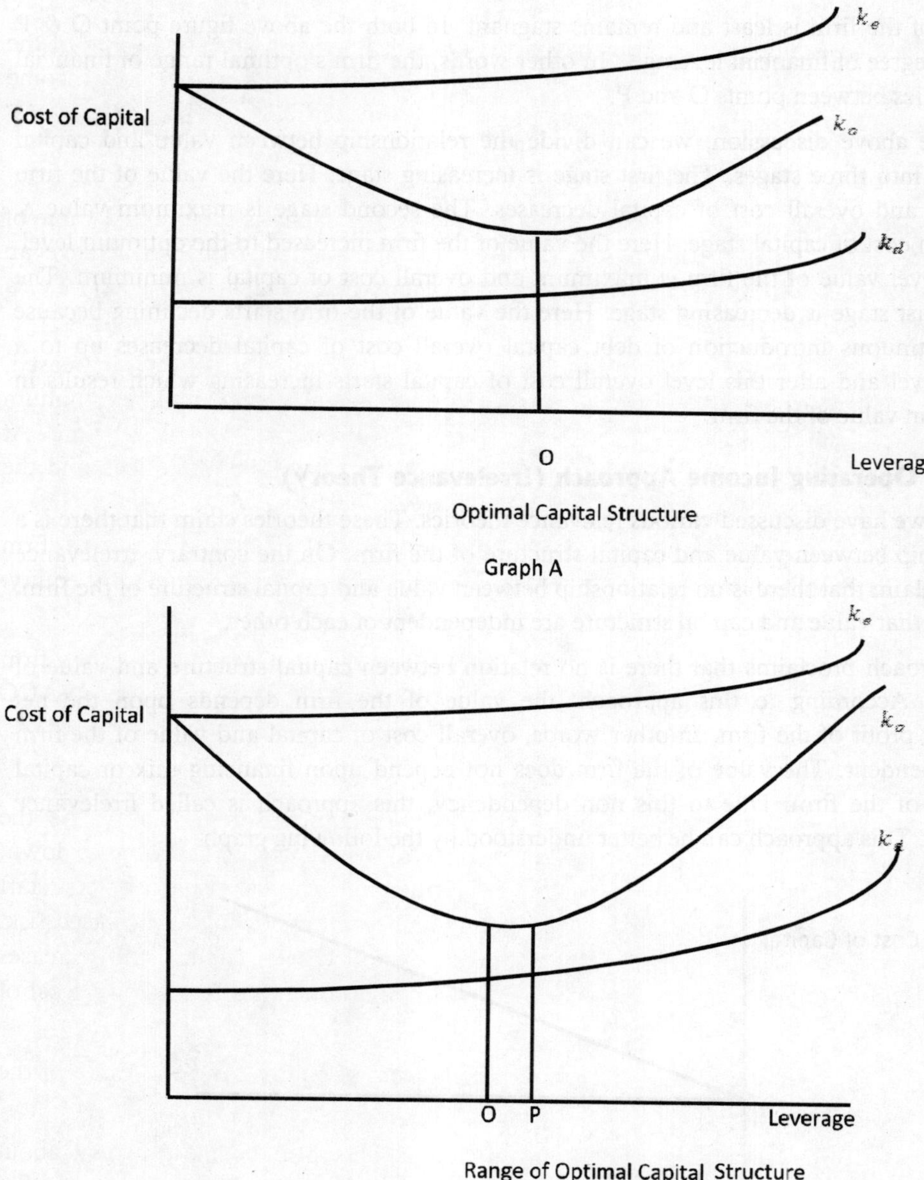

Optimal Capital Structure

Graph A

Range of Optimal Capital Structure

Graph B

We can understand this theory with the help of above two graphs. In the graph A, at the point O capital structure is optimal i.e. at this point WACC of the firm is minimum. In the graph B, there are two points O & P. The area between these two points shows the range of optimal capital structure. The range between these points O & P shows that between these points a firm's capital structure is optimal because between these point

WACC of the firm is least and remains stagnant. In both the above figure point O & P present degree of financial leverage. In other words, the firm's optimal range of financial leverage lies between points O and P.

From the above discussion, we can divide the relationship between value and capital structure into three stages. The first stage is increasing stage. Here the value of the firm increases and overall cost of capital decreases. The second stage is maximum value & minimum cost of capital stage. Here the value of the firm increased to the optimum level. At this level value of the firm is maximum and overall cost of capital is minimum. The third & last stage is decreasing stage. Here the value of the firm starts declining because with continuous introduction of debt capital overall cost of capital decreases up to a certain level and after this level overall cost of capital starts increasing which results in decrease in value of the firm.

8.4 Net Operating Income Approach (Irrelevance Theory)

Till now we have discussed various relevance theories. These theories claim that there is a relationship between value and capital structure of the firm. On the contrary, irrelevance theories claim that there is no relationship between value and capital structure of the firm. They say that value and capital structure are independent of each other.

This approach proclaims that there is no relation between capital structure and value of the firm. According to this approach; the value of the firm depends upon the net operating profit of the firm. In other words, overall cost of capital and value of the firm are independent. The value of the firm does not depend upon financing mix or capital structure of the firm. Due to this non dependency, this approach is called irrelevance approach. This approach can be better understood by the following graph-

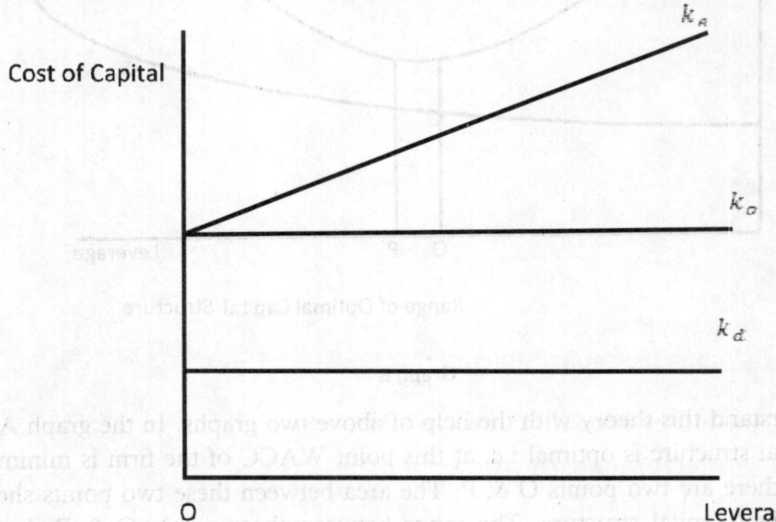

Leverage

This theory works on the assumption that cost of debt and overall cost of capital are constant. In the above graph we can see that k_d and k_o are constant. As the debt financing is increased or financial leverage increases, cost of equity also increases. The above figure shows that cost of debt and overall cost of capital remain unchanged irrespective of debt proportion in the capital structure. In case of all equity firm $k_e = k_o$ and when debt is introduced cost of equity increases but overall of cost of debt remains unchanged because increase in cost of equity is offset by benefit of low cost debt financing.

In this approach the value of the firm is $\frac{EBIT}{K_o}$

Here, EBIT = Net operating income, and K_o = overall cost of capital.

Also, value of equity E is given by:

E = V-B, where V = Value of the firm, and B = Value of Debt

Example 2

Prodigy Ltd. has an EBIT of 1400000 and overall cost of capital is 14%. Calculate overall cost of capital if 9% debt is introduced to the extent of 30%, 40% and 50% of the total capital fund of ₹ 1000000.

Solution

	30% Debt	**40% Debt**	**50% Debt**
EBIT	14,00,000	1,40,000	1,40,0000
Overall cost of capital	14%	14%	14%
Value of the firm	1,00,00,000	1,00,00,000	1,00,00,000
9% Debt	3000000	4000000	50,00,000
Value of equity	70,00,000	60,00,000	50,00,000
Interest on debt	2,70,000	3,60,000	4,50,000
Net Profit	11,30,000	10,40,000	9,50,000
Cost of equity	16.14%	17.33%	19%

From the above example we can conclude, based on NOI approach, that value of the firm does not depend upon the capital structure.

8.5 Modigliani-Miller Model (Irrelevance Theory)

Extension of The NOI Approach

In 1958, Franco Modigliani and Merton Miller gave this theory. According to the Modigliani-Miller, on the basis of some assumptions a firm's value does not depend upon its capital structure. In other words, there is no trade off between value and capital structure of a firm. The value of the firm depends upon the earnings and risk class of the firm, not on its financing mix. Modigliani-Miller gave two propositions in support of their theory.

Proposition 1 of this theory suggests that the value of the firm is obtained by capitalizing the operating profit of the firm. The capitalization rate will be a discount rate appropriate to the risk class to which firm belongs. Since here also operating income is being capitalized, this proposition is also known as *extension of net operating income approach*. The Modigliani – Miller also argue that value of levered firm is equal to the value of unlevered firm. To prove this proposition, they describe an arbitrage process that brings equilibrium in the market. In arbitrage, shares of high value firm are sold and that of low valued firm purchased.

Proposition 2 of this theory states that overall cost of capital will be equal in case of levered and unlevered firm. We know that in case of levered firm, as debt financing increases, earnings available to the equity shareholders increase, but financial risk also increases. The increment in earnings is set off by increased cost of equity due to increased financial risk. Thereby, the overall cost of equity remains the same.

8.5.1 Proposition 1

Modigliani-Miller's first proposition is based upon following assumptions:

- Capital markets are perfect. Securities are being traded in perfect capital market scenario. This means that investors are free to buy or sell securities, there is no transaction cost and information is freely available.
- There is 100% payout ratio i.e. firm distributes all its earnings to its shareholders.
- There are no corporate taxes.
- Firms belong to equivalent risk class based on their business risk.

According to proposition 1; if two firms are:

a) in the same risk class,

b) having same assets

c) working in same market segments and

d) have equal market share.

then the market value of these firms will be same irrespective of their capital structure. We may recall that in Net Operating Income Approach also; we found that there was no relationship between capital structure and value of the firm. Proposition 1 is similar to the net operating income approach. Proposition 1 states that value of unlevered firm is equal to the value of levered firm.

$$\textit{Value of the firm} = \frac{\textit{Net operating income}}{\textit{Firm's opportunity cost of capital}}$$

Let us understand it better with an example. Suppose two firms A & B are operating under same conditions as per assumptions above. Both the firms are all equity firms and have same assets and income which is ₹ 500 lakhs and opportunity cost of capital, 20%.The value of the firms is ₹ 2500 lakhs (=500 lakhs/20%) each.

Now let us change the capital structure of firms a little. Let us keep the Firm A as an all equity firm i.e. unlevered firm. Now let us say Firm B is 75% equity and 25% debt firm. Now a question arises. Will the difference in capital structure affect the value of the firms; given everything else remains the same?

The answer is "no". It is so; because as per MM, value of the firm does not depend upon capital structure of the firm. We have stated above that:

Value of a firm = market value of equity + market value of debt.

And

Value of levered firm = value of unlevered firm.

According to this approach, value of a firm can be found out by capitalizing firm's net operating income by its opportunity cost of capital. However, the opportunity cost of capital of an unlevered firm is equal to the opportunity cost of capital of a levered firm.

In other words, we can say that the value of the levered and unlevered firms, and the expected net operating income do not change with financial leverage. The WACC will not change with financial leverage i.e. WACC of the levered and unlevered firm is equal to their respective opportunity cost of capital. Modigliani-Miller have given an arbitrage process to prove their proposition 1.

Arbitrage Process

As discussed previously in NOI approach, the value of the two firms will be same if those firms are identical in all respects but their capital structures are different. Now, suppose that value of the above two firms is not the same and all the other conditions of this model are satisfied.

Now, let us see how the values of these two firms will equalize.

In this situation a process called **Arbitrage** will begin. What is meant by arbitrage? Arbitrage refers to the simultaneous act of buying an asset in a market where it is priced low and selling it in a market where it is priced higher. You may ask that how the same security commands two different prices in two markets? It happens due to temporary disequilibrium in these markets.

Now, it is the arbitrage which brings equilibrium to the market.

Going back to our two firms where we have assumed that they have different market values, let us see how arbitrage works. In this situation an investor will sell the securities of the firm having greater value and purchase the securities of the firm having lesser value by creating his personal leverage. As we know that market value of the levered firm is greater than unlevered firm, then an investor will sell his securities in levered firm and buy in unlevered firm. This concept can be better understood by considering the given example.

Suppose two companies NIPL & MSPL are similar in all respects except in their capital structure. NIPL is an all equity firm i.e. financed by equity alone whereas MSPL is a levered firm financed by equity and debt too i.e. levered firm. Particulars of the two firms are given below:

	NIPL (Unlevered)	**MSPL (Levered)**
Net Operating Income	1,30,000	1,30,000
Interest	--	40,000
Equity Earnings	1,30,000	90,000
Cost of Equity	0.100	0.12
Market value of equity	13,00,000	7,50,000
Cost of Debt	--	.05
Market value of Debt	--	8,00,000
Market value of the firm	13,00,000	15,50,000
WACC	0.100	0.094

Now, we can see that both the firms are having identical assets, same NOI but the value of MSPL is more than NIPL. The cheaper debt of MSPL has increased the value of MSPL by ₹ 2,50,000/-. Now as per MM this situation cannot exist for a long time and there will be equal value of both the firms. MM describe an arbitrage process that brings equality in the values of both the firms. Now we will see how arbitrage works in this situation?

Working of Arbitrage Process

Through arbitrage, an investor can earn same return at lesser investment. Or he may earn higher return on same investment.

Let us say an investor who has 10% equity shares of MSPL; a levered company. By holding 10% equity capital of MSPL the investor earns 10% of MSPL's equity earnings i.e. ₹ 9,000/-. Now this investor can sell his investment in MSPL at ₹ 75,000/-.He further takes a loan by creating his personal leverage equal to 10% of debt of MSPL i.e. ₹ 80,000/- at 5% interest. Now this investor has ₹ 1,55,000/- (75, 000 + 80,000) available for investment. He now purchases 10% equity shares of NIPL; an unlevered company for ₹ 1,30,000/-. The total earnings from NIPL investment is ₹ 13,000/- and investor's interest liability is ₹ 4,000/- (80,000*5%). The net earnings of that investor is ₹ 9,000/- (13,000 – 4,000). Now see that this amount of return is exactly equal to the return he was earning on his investments in MSPL.

In the above process it is clear that an investor can earn same return by adopting an alternate investment strategy. The above investor has surplus fund of ₹ 25,000/- (1,55,000 – 1,30,000) which he can invest in some other security and can increase his income. In the above process the risk of investor remains same and corporate leverage turns into personal leverage because the investor has taken personal loan of ₹ 80,000/-.

Now, as per MM Hypothesis; many other investors will adopt a similar arbitrage process. This will result in rise in sales of levered firm's shares i.e. MSPL and rise in purchase of unlevered firm's shares i.e. NIPL. The rise in sale of MSPL's shares will bring its share's price down. Also, rise in purchase of NIPL's shares will drive its price up. This process will continue until the market values of both the firms are equal. At this point, the cost of capital of both the firms will also equalize.

An investor can use arbitrage process in opposite direction too. Let us see how? Suppose that market value of levered firm is less than unlevered firm i.e. market value of MSPL is ₹ 8,00,000/- (Equity ₹ 400000 + Debt ₹ 4,00,000) and market value of NIPL is ₹ 13,00,000/-. Now the investor will sell its 10% investment in NIPL at ₹ 1,30,000/- and purchase 10% equity shares in MSPL at ₹ 40,000/-. Investor will now have ₹ 90,000/- still left (₹1,30,000 – ₹40,000). Out of this; he can invest ₹ 40,000/- (10% of ₹4,00,000/-) in 10% Govt. bonds. After investment in Govt. bonds he will still have ₹ 50,000/- (₹90,000 – ₹40,000) surplus fund. His total income from new investment will be ₹ 13,000 i.e. 9,000 (10% of MSPL's profits) and 4,000 from govt. bonds. By adopting this alternate strategy an investor can earn same level of return at lesser investment. In the above discussion you can see that investor is earning same return and having surplus fund of ₹ 50,000/- too.

8.5.2 Proposition 2

We saw in Unit 2 that financial leverage does not change firm's net operating income. However, leverage does affect a firm's earnings per share and return on equity. Also, a firm using financial leverage will have financial risk whereas an unlevered firm will not.

Financial risk refers to the risk of firm defaulting on its fixed financial commitments like interest, preference dividend etc. If the firm is not using leverage that means it does not have a fixed financial commitment. Therefore, we can say that as financial leverage increases financial risk also increases. No financial leverage would mean no financial risk as well. The financial risk arises from financial leverage and financial leverage arises from debt financing. Higher debt financing causes higher financial leverage and higher financial risk.

Now a question arises? Are the expectations of shareholders regarding their returns the same in both levered and in an unlevered firm? The answer is No. The reason is that shareholders' expectation of return increases with every increase in financial risk. For an unlevered firm opportunity cost of capital = cost of equity ($K_a = k_e$). But in case of levered firm, cost of equity is greater than opportunity cost of capital because in a levered firm an additional element pushes up cost of equity. This is called financial risk premium.

Financial risk premium is the additional return expected by the investors to compensate for increased financial risk. The relation between financial risk premium and financial risk is direct i.e. as the financial risk increases financial risk premium also increases. The difference between opportunity cost of capital and cost of equity in a levered firm is financial risk premium. Here one question also arises that why financial risk premium is added to the cost of equity? The answer is that as the financial risk increases, the shareholders require more return to compensate for their increased financial risk in that levered firm and that additional required return is called financial risk premium. The opportunity cost of capital for a levered firm is its WACC.

$$WACC(k_a) = k_e \times \frac{E}{E+D} + k_d \times \frac{D}{D+E}$$

$$k_e = k_a + (k_a - k_d)\frac{D}{E}$$

If the above formula is used for an unlevered firm then $K_e = k_a$ because for an unlevered firm D = 0. For a levered firm, as the debt portion increases (i.e. financial leverage increases) then risk premium i.e. $(k_a - k_d)\frac{D}{E}$ will also increase. This can be understood more clearly through the given example.

Example 3

MSPL has 5000 shares outstanding. The market value of these shares is ₹ 100000 i.e. @ ₹ 25/-. The expected NOI is ₹ 25000/- and EPS = ₹ 5/-. If MSPL is an unlevered firm then cost of equity is 25% i.e. 20,000/1,00,000. Now, suppose that MSPL takes a loan @ 10%. Its debt equity ratio becomes 1:1. The cost of equity will be as under-

$$k_e = k_a + (k_a - k_d)\frac{D}{E}$$

k_e = .25 + (0.25 - 0.10)1

k_e = 0.25 +0.15

k_e = 0.40

In the above example 0.15 is the risk premium to the equity shareholders for taking additional financial risk. Now, we can conclude on the basis of the above proposition 2, that in case of a levered firm the cost of equity will increase up to that level where additional financial risk will be compensated by increased cost of equity.

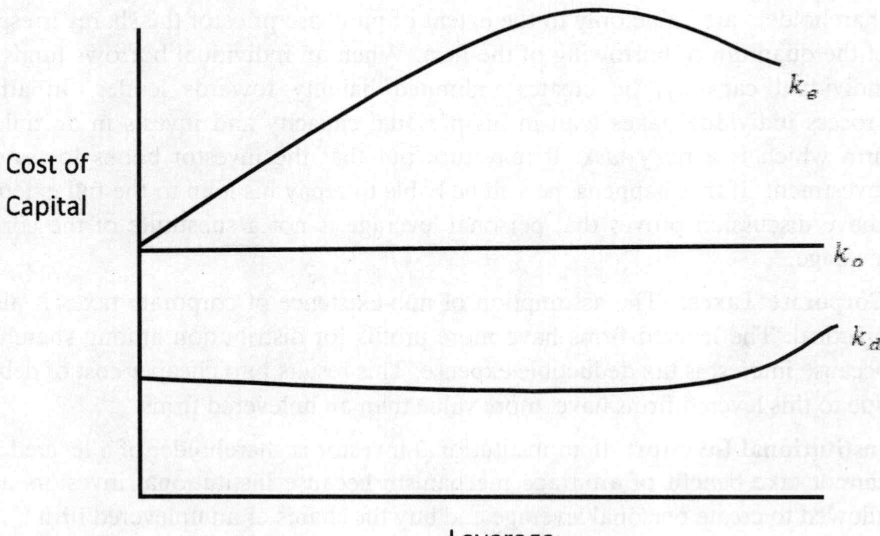

In the above figure it is shown that if debt level is low in a firm then it will not cause any financial risk. As per proposition 2 of MM Hypothesis opportunity cost of capital will not increase even if higher financial leverage. As the portion of debt capital increases; cost of equity also increases. However, after a certain level of debt capital is reached, rate of increase in cost of equity declines. This happens because beyond a certain level of debt, business risk shifts from shareholders to creditors.

8.5.3 Criticism of the MM Hypothesis

The propositions of MM work if underlying assumptions apply. However, most of these assumptions are not unrealistic and do not apply in real life. The arbitrage process may work only in the perfect capital market situation but in real life perfect capital market is never found! Also, arbitrage process will not work due to following reasons-

1. **Borrowing Rates:** The assumption that individual and firm can get funds at the same rate is not realistic. It is because borrowing rates for individual and firms are different. The firms hold higher credit worthiness as compared to individuals because firms have higher assets backing. Also, firms borrow huge amount of funds. Due to these reasons, firms may get funds at a rate lower than the rate charged to individuals. Due to difference in borrowing rates equilibrium process will fail.
2. **Transaction Cost:** Assumption of no transaction cost is also not realistic because any transfer of shares will involve transaction cost (brokerage etc.). Even if the transaction costs are low, the arbitrage process will be affected because arbitrage process assumes nil transaction costs.
3. **Non-Substitutability of Personal and Corporate Leverage:** Assumption of substitutability of personal and corporate leverage is also not practical. The liability of an individual and firms is different, because if a firm goes insolvent the

shareholders are liable only to the extent of purchase price of the shares irrespective of the quantum of borrowing of the firm. When an individual borrows funds in his individual capacity, he creates unlimited liability towards lender. In arbitrage process individual takes loan in his personal capacity and invests in an unlevered firm which is a risky task. It may turn out that the investor books losses on his investment. If that happens, he will be liable to repay his loan to the full extent. The above discussion proves that personal leverage is not a substitute of the corporate leverage.

4. **Corporate Taxes:** The assumption of non-existence of corporate taxes is also not practical. The levered firms have more profits for distribution among shareholders because interest is tax deductible expense. This results into cheaper cost of debts and due to this levered firms have more value than an unlevered firms.

5. **Institutional Investor:** If an institutional investor is shareholder of a levered firm it cannot take benefit of arbitrage mechanism because institutional investors are not allowed to create personal leverage and buy the shares of an unlevered firm.

8.5.4 Value of A Levered Firm As Per MM Approach

From the taxability point of view the main difference between levered firm & unlevered firm is that of levered firm getting tax shield for interest on debts. In other words, interest on debts is a tax-deductible expenditure for any levered firm. Consider the following example in which ABC Ltd. is an unlevered and XYZ Ltd. is a levered firm.

	ABC Ltd.	**XYZ Ltd.**
Net operating income	5,00,000	5,00,000
Less Interest on debts	1,00,000	
EBT	5,00,000	4,00,000
Less tax @ 50%	2,50,000	2,00,000
PAT	2,50,000	2,00,000
Total outflow	2,50,000	3,00,000
(Interest + dividend)		

Now, it is clear from the above example that total income available to security holders of XYZ Ltd. is more by ₹ 50000 than security holders of ABC Ltd. The only reason behind this increased income is that interest on debt is paid before taxes i.e. interest on debt is a tax deductible expense. The difference between income of levered firm & unlevered firm represents tax shield i.e. interest x tax rate => 1,00,000 x 50%. From the above discussion we can draw a conclusion that higher the leverage higher the income available to security holders.

Now we can get value of a levered firm by adding present value of tax shield (for perpetual debt) to the value of unlevered firm because the difference in income is of only tax shield as discussed above.

Present value of tax shield = $\frac{(i)(D)(i)}{(i)}$ = (D)(t)

Where i = interest on debt, D = value of debt, t =tax rate.

Now, value of levered firm = value of unlevered firm + (D)(t)

8.6 Capital Structure Decision

Now you are familiar with the concept of capital structure, relevance and irrelevance theories, trade off between capital structure and value of the firm. Now you also know that at optimal capital structure value of the firm is maximum and overall cost of capital is minimum.

It has also been discussed that in case of a levered firm the earnings available to equity shareholders are more than in case of an unlevered firm. Now a question arises that at which combination of debt and equity, capital structure will be optimal? Perhaps, our answer will disappoint you.

Like most of the life's questions, here also, there is no golden rule. There is no formula of deciding capital structure in which we put the value and get optimal capital structure. Therefore, a firm has to decide its capital structure on the basis of various factors like size of firm, nature of business and legal implications etc. Following are a few important factors to be considered while determining capital structure.

1. **Financial Distress**: Financial distress means a situation in which a firm faces difficulty in paying out its interest and principal towards repayment of debts. As we know that value of the levered firm is more than value of unlevered firm. But before going levered or increasing leverage, every firm should keep in mind that cost associated to debt should not be more than benefit from that debt. In case cost is more than benefit there will be a situation of financial distress. As the debt proportion increases in capital structure, financial risk also increases and chances of financial distress also increase. The firm should establish a trade off cost and benefit associated with debt financing. The financial distress bring down the value of the firm. Thus, the value of a levered firm = Value of an unlevered firm + PV of tax shield – PV of cost of financial distress.

2. **Agency Cost:** The claim of equity shareholders and debt holders does not in same position. Debt holders have primary claim over firm's assets and earnings. On the contrary, equity shareholders have residual claim over firm's assets and earnings. Due to variability of claim, there may be some confliction between debt holders and equity shareholders. The equity shareholders always want to increase their value and earnings. On the other hand, the debt holders want to secure themselves because equity shareholders manage and control the firm. To secure their interests, the debt holders may impose some restrictions upon the firm in the form of representative in the board, regular financial analysis, regular submission of report on financial position, maintenance of certain ratios etc. All these restrictions involve some indirect cost, these indirect costs are

called agency cost. Agency costs increase as the leverage increases i.e. increase in debt proportion. Agency cost may be direct also in the form of increased rate of interest and prices also.

3. **Product Life Cycle:** At the start up stage, the risks are high therefore, equity, being risk capital per se, is usually the primary source of finance. The start up firm cannot assume additional risks associated with financial leverage. During the growth stage, the risk of failure decreases and the emphasis shifts to financing growth. Rapid growth generally signals significant investment needs and requires huge sums of capital to fuel growth. This may entail large doses of debt and periodic induction of additional equity capital. As growth slows, seasonality and cyclicality become more apparent. As the business reaches maturity stage, leverage is likely to decline as cash flows accelerate.

4. **Control:** The equity shareholders control the affairs of the firm. The issue of new equity shares may dilute the control of present shareholders. The management may go for debt financing. The debt holders do not control the affairs of the firm. The preference shareholders also do not control over the firm. They cannot vote on every resolution. The preference shareholders can vote only on the issues which are going to affect their interests. The debt holders do not directly control the affairs of the firm but in some cases they impose a condition to appoint their representative in the board of directors.

5. **Flexibility:** Flexibility means that as and when required firm may raise funds. Sometimes firms need funds urgently, in that situation there should not be unwanted delays in raising funds. The capital structure should be flexible enough to adopt changing market situations like, if share market is favorable raising fund from issue of shares and in debt market is favorable raising fund from debts.

6. **Cash Flow:** While determining its capital structure a firm must consider its cash flow. There may be firms which generate high surplus funds due to less investment in working capital and other firms which generate low surplus funds due to high investments in working capital. The firms with high surplus funds should go for debt financing because due to surplus fund it can meet its obligation towards payment of interest and repayment of principals. The firms with low surplus funds should go for equity financing because in case of equity financing, it is not an obligation to pay dividend to the equity shareholders. The firms may defer the payment of equity dividend. Every firm which is going to raise funds should analyze its cash inflow and outflow.

7. **Legal Implications:** Every firm planning for raising funds should consider legal implications of every source of finance. There are certain guidelines and legal regulations for every source of finance. In case a firm fails to fulfill these regulatory requirements, it may face penalties from regulatory authorities.

8.7 Pecking Order Theory

The dictionary meaning of pecking order is ***"the order of importance amongst the members of a group in relation to each other".*** According to this theory, management raises finance in a particular order as name of this theory implies i.e. first, get finance from internally generated fund i.e. retained earnings. Second, if insufficient retained earnings or no retained earnings then from issue of debt. Third and last is from issue of equity shares.

This theory does not support the concept of optimal capital structure. Management raises fund as & when needed in a certain order. It depicts that cost associated with internal fund is minimum and cost associated with equity fund is maximum. In the order internal fund is placed on first and equity capital is on last position. According to this theory the management's reliance primarily on retained earnings is because management possess information about their internal resources and it does not want to bind itself in rules and regulation of capital market.

Illustrative Solved Examples

1. Vasuki Ltd. has a PAT of ₹ 600000, outstanding debentures of ₹ 2000000. The cost of equity & debentures is 15% & 10% respectively. Corporate tax rate is 40%.

Compute

a. Value of the firm by applying traditional approach.

b. Overall capitalization rate.

Solution

a. Value of equity = PAT/cost of equity

= 6,00,000/15% = 40,00,000.

Value of the firm 40,00,000 + 20,00,000 = ₹ 60,00,000.

b. Overall capitalization rate = EBIT/Total value of the firm.

Now, EBIT = $\frac{PAT}{(100 - Rate\ of\ tax)} + Intt.on\ debt$ = 6,00,000 x 100/60 + 2,00,000

EBIT = ₹ 12,00,000.

Overall capitalization rate = 12,00,000/60,00,000 = 20%.

Now, if in the above example Vasuki Ltd. wants to redeem its debentures by issuing fresh equity capital of ₹ 80,00,000 and it has been studied that cost of equity will be reduced by 3% & cost of debentures will remain same. Should Vasuki Ltd. go for this option.

EBIT as calculated above	12,00,000
Less : Intt. on debentures	1,20,000
Net Income	10,80,000
Less Tax	6,48,000

Now value of equity = 6,48,000/12% = 54,00,000

Overall value of the firm = 54,00,000 + 12,00,000 = ₹ 66,00,000.

Now, we can see that overall value of the firm is increased by ₹6,00,000. Vasuki Ltd. should go for the above option.

2. Cobra Ltd. has 1,00,000 shares outstanding. The market value of these shares is ₹ 25,00,000 i.e. @ ₹ 25/-. The expected NOI is ₹ 5,00,000/- and EPS = ₹ 5/-. Calculate Cobra Ltd.'s cost of equity. If Cobra Ltd. takes a loan resulting its debt equity ratio of 1.5 and cost of that loan is 10% then what will be the cost of equity of Cobra Ltd.

Solution

a. Cost of equity = NOI/Market value of equity

Cost of equity = 5,00,000/25,00,000 = 20%

b. $k_e = k_a + (k_a - k_d)\frac{D}{E}$

$k_e = .20 + (.20 - .10)1.5$

$k_e = .20 + .15$

$k_e = .35$

3. Calculate the value of ABC Ltd. & XYZ Ltd. on the basis of following data as per Net Operating Income Approach & Net Income Approach. Both the companies belong to same risk class. Corporate tax rate is 40%

	ABC Ltd.	**XYZ Ltd.**
10% Debentures interest	**nil**	**1,00,000**
Cost of equity	**15%**	**15%**
EBIT	**₹5,00,000**	**₹5,00,000**

Solution

Value as per NOI approach

	ABC Ltd.
EBIT	₹5,00,000
Less interest	nil
PBT	5,00,000
Less tax	2,00,000
PAT	3,00,000
Cost of equity	15%
Value of equity	20,00,000

Value of ABC Ltd. = ₹ 20,00,000.

Now as per MM approach, Value of levered firm = value of unlevered firm + debt(t)

Value of XYZ Ltd. = ₹20,00,000 + ₹10,00,000(.40) = ₹ 24,00,000.

Value as per NI approach

	ABC Ltd.	XYZ Ltd.
EBIT	5,00,000	5,00,000
Less interest	nil	1,00,000
PBT	5,00,000	4,00,000
Less tax	2,00,000	1,60,000
PAT	3,00,000	2,40,000
Cost of equity	15%	15%
Value of equity	20,00,000	16,00,000
Value of debentures	nil	10,00,000
Value of firm	20,00,000	26,00,000

4. **Calculate the value of Fortune Ltd. as per MM approach on the basis of following data:**

Net operating income	**10,00,000**
10% Debentures	**20,00,000**
Corporate tax rate	**50%**
Cost of equity	**15%**

Solution

Value of levered firm = Value of unlevered firm + debt(tax rate)

Value = 10,00,000 x .50/.15 + 20,00,000(.5)

Value = 33,33,333 + 10,00,000 = ₹ 43,33,333.

5. **The following information is of NOI Ltd. & BOI Ltd. The only difference between both the companies is that NOI Ltd. is a levered firm. NOI Ltd. has issued 25000 10% debentures @ ₹ 100 each.**

	NOI Ltd.	**BOI Ltd.**
EBIT	**10,00,000**	**10,00,000**
Less interest	**2,50,000**	**nil**
Profit for equityshareholders	**75,0000**	**10,00,000**
Cost of equity	**20%**	**25%**
Value of equity	**37,50,000**	**40,00,000**
Value of firm	**62,50,000**	**40,00,000**

Now, Atul an investor who holds 10% of NOI Ltd. Show how can Atul get benefit of arbitrage process & is there any limit for arbitrage.

Solution

Currently Atul is getting 10% of NOI Ltd.'s PAT ₹ 75000 i.e. 10% of ₹ 75000 and value of his investment is ₹ 375000 i.e. 10% of ₹ 37,50,000.

Now as per arbitrage process Atul will sell his investment in NOI Ltd. will borrow a sum of ₹ 2,50,000 which is equal to 10% NOI Ltd.'s debentures to create his personal leverage.

Now Atul has a sum of ₹ 6,25,000(3,75,000 + 2,50,000) which he will invest in 10% of BOI Ltd.'s equity.

After this arbitrage Atul will get as under

	NOI Ltd.	BOI Ltd.
Dividend Income	75,000	1,00,000
Less Interest	nil	25,000
Net Income	75,000	75,000

Atul is getting same return before and after arbitrage process but after this process Atul still has ₹ 2,25,000.

The arbitrage process ends in that situation when market value NOI Ltd. & BOI Ltd. will come to an equal level.

6. **Shoeb Ltd. has worked out following figures:**

Interest to debenture holders	**50,000**
Net operating income	**5,00,000**
Cost of equity	**15%**
Cost of debentures	**10%**

Compute

(i) WACC of Shoeb Ltd.

(ii) Shoeb Ltd. is planning to enter into a project which will require ₹ 15,00,000 more debt & increase in operating income of ₹ 2,00,000. Compute new WACC. Assume no corporate taxes.

Solution

(i) Value of debentures = 50,000/10% = 5,00,000

Value of equity = 5,00,000 – 50,000/15% = 30,00,000

$$\text{WACC} = 10 \times \frac{5,00,000}{35,00,000} + 15 \times \frac{30,00,000}{35,00,000} = 1.43 + 12.86 = 14.29\%$$

(ii) New net operating income = ₹5,00,000 + ₹2,00,000 = ₹ 7,00,000

Interest to debenture holders = ₹ 2,00,000

Profit for equity shareholders = ₹ 5,00,000.

Value of debentures = ₹ 20,00,000

Value of equity = 5,00,000/15% = ₹ 33,33,333.

$$\text{WACC} = 10 \times ₹\frac{20,00,000}{53,00,000} + 15 \times ₹\frac{33,00,000}{53,00,000} = 3.75 + 9.37 = 13.12\%$$

7. Balaji Ltd. has following figures

	₹
EBIT	**6,00,000**
8% Debentures	**12,00,000**
Cost of equity	**12%**

Compute

(a) Using traditional approach compute value of the firm & overall capitalization rate.

(b) Balaji Ltd. has to redeem 50% of its debentures but due to insufficient funds company is planning to issue new equity capital equal to its current redemption liability. It has been estimated that after redemption cost of debentures will remain same and cost of equity will reduce by 2% due to decrease in debentures. Give your advice.

Solution

(a) Value of the firm as per traditional approach

EBIT	6,00,000
Less Interest	96,000
Net Profit	5,04,000
Cost of equity	12%
Value of equity	42,00,000
Value of debentures	12,00,000
Total value of the firm	54,00,000

Overall capitalization rate = EBIT/Value of the firm

= 600000/5400000 = 11.11%

(b) EBIT	6,00,000
Less Interest	48,000
Net Profit	5,52,000
Cost of equity	10%
Value of equity	55,20,000
Value of debentures	6,00,000
Total value of the firm	61,20,000

Overall cost of capital = 6,00,000/61,20,000 = 9.80%

Balaji Ltd. should go for its redemption option because after redemption, value of the firm will increase by ₹ 7,20,000 and overall cost of capital will reduce by 1.31%.

Summary

- Capital Structure means the combination of various long term sources of finance like equity shares, preference shares and debt capital.
- Capital structure decision means the decision for an organized combination of debt & equity capital to maximize the value of the firm.
- Optimal capital structure is the one at which overall cost of capital is minimum and value of the firm maximum .
- There are two theories for capital structure decision. Some of them are called relevance theories because they conclude that capital structure directly affects value of the firm. Some other theories are called irrelevance theories because they state that capital structure does not affect value of the firm.
- Net income theory says that capital structure and value of the firm are related to each other. Change in capital structure will change its WACC and WACC will change firm's value. High debt high value.
- Traditional approach says that a rational mix of debt & equity maximizes the value of the firm because introduction of more & more debt will increase value of the firm only upto a certain level. After that level value of the firm starts decreasing.
- Net operating income approach says that there is no relationship between value and capital structure of the firm. The value of the firm is found out by capitalizing the net operating income at the rate of overall cost of capital.
- Modigliani-Miller also says that there is no relationship between firm's value and capital structure of the firm. Modigliani-Miller gave two prepositions. According to first preposition value of the firm can be found out by capitalizing the operating profit at the discount rate appropriate to the risk class to which firm belongs. In this preposition they also say that value of unlevered firm is equal to the value of a levered firm. To prove this they gave an arbitrage process. In arbitrage, shares of high value firm are sold and that of low valued firm purchased.
- According to the second preposition cost of capital will remain same in case of levered and unlevered firm.
- Pecking order theory says that there are three sources of finances i.e. internally generated funds, debt capital and equity capital. These sources should be utilized respectively.

Test Your Understanding

State whether following statements are true or false

1. Value of a firm does not depend upon earnings of the firm.

2. There is only one theory i.e. relevance theory.
3. As per NI approach there is a relationship between capital structure & value of the firm.
4. In NI approach if WACC increases value of the firm decreases.
5. As per NOI approach value of the firm depends upon the net operating profit of the firm.
6. In the analysis of different theories we always consider existence of taxes.
7. In NOI approach we assume that cost of debt is variable.
8. In traditional approach, as financial leverage increases value of the firm also increases but only up to a certain point.
9. At optimal capital structure, value of the firm is maximum and WACC is minimum.
10. MM theory assumes arbitrage works only it perfect capital market situation.
11. As per irrelevance theory cost of capital does not affect value of the firm.
12. MM theory is the extension of net operating income approach.
13. Arbitrage process maintains equilibrium in the market.
14. As debt financing increases financial leverage also increases.
15. There is no relationship between capital structure and value of the firm.

Answers : 1. F, 2. F, 3. T, 4. T, 5. T, 6. F, 7. T, 8. T, 9. T, 10. T, 11. F, 12. T, 13. T, 14. T, 15. F

Multiple Choice Questions

Choose the correct alternative out of the given

1. As financial leverage increases shareholders' wealth
   a) increases b) decreases
   c) no change d) none of the above
2. Capital structure is the mix of
   a) Preference shares & debt capital b) Long term debt & short term debt
   c) Debt capital & equity capital d) Equity, preference & debt capital
3. As per relevance theory, value of the firm is affected by
   a) Capital structure strategies b) Capital structure decision
   c) Capital structure d) None of the above
4. As per irrelevance theory, value of the firm is affected by
   a) Value of equity b) Capital structure does not affect value of the firm
   c) Value of debt capital d) Whole capital structure

5. In capital structure theories there are only

   a) One long term source of finance b) Two long term sources of finance

   c) Three long term sources of finance d) Four long term sources of finance

6. As per net income theory, with every change in capital structure

   a) WACC also changes b) WACC remains constant

   c) WACC always increases d) WACC always decreases

7. PBT of a firm is 100000, cost of equity 10%, value of debt 500000, value of firm will be

   a) 15,00,000 b) 10,00,000

   c) 20,00,000 d) 25,00,000

8. At optimal capital structure

   a. WACC is maximum & value is minimum

   b. Value is maximum & WACC is minimum

   c. Value & WACC both are minimum

   d. Value & WACC both are maximum

9. As per net operating income theory net operating profit affects

   a) Capital structure b) WACC

   c) Value of the firm d) None of the above

10. As per MM theory, value of levered firm is

    a. Less than the value of unlevered firm

    b. Equal to the value of unlevered firm

    c. More than the value of unlevered firm

    d. None of the above

11. Firm's net operating income is 150000 and opportunity cost is 15%, value of the firm will be

    a) 15,00,000 b) 20,00,000

    c) 1,00,00,000 d) 10,00,000

12. Arbitrage process maintains the

    a) market capitalization b) equilibrium in the market

    c) prices of securities d) capital structure

13. By going through arbitrage process, an investor can earn

    a) same return at more investment b) same return at less risk

    c) same return at lesser investment d) same return at equal investment

14. The expectation of shareholders increases with every increase in

a) risk b) sales

c) profit d) share capital

15. Financial risk premium is the risk premium for every increase in

a) share capital b) financial risk

c) non financial risk d) none of the above.

16. Which of the following factors does not matter in determining the choice of Debt Equity Mix? **(UPTU, 2009)**

a) Taxation b) Industry Norm

c) Variability of cash flows d) None of these

17. With which of the following names goes the Hypothesis of capital structure? **(UPTU, 2010)**

a) Modigliani and Miller b) J. E. Walter

c) M. J. Gordon d) None of the above

Answers : 1. a, 2. d, 3. c, 4. b, 5. b, 6. a, 7. a, 8. b, 9. c, 10. b, 11. d, 12. b, 13. c, 14. a, 15. b, 16. d, 17. d

Practical Problems

1. A company needs ₹ 31,25,000 for the construction of new plant. The following three plans are feasible :

(i) The company may issue 3,12,500 equity share at ₹ 10 per share.

(ii) The company may issue 1,56,250 equity shares at ₹ 10 each and 15,625 debentures of ₹ 100 each at 8% coupon rate.

(iii) The company may issue 1,56,250 equity shares at ₹ 10 each and 15625 preference shares of ₹ 100 each at 8% coupon rate.

(a) If the company's EBIT are ₹ 62,500, ₹ 1,25,000, ₹ 2,50,000, ₹ 3,75,000, ₹ 6,25,000, what are earnings per share under each of three financial plans. Assume a corporate tax rate is 40%.

(b) Which alternative would you recommend and why?

(c) Determine the EBIT-EPS indifference point by formulae between financial plan I and plan II & plan I and plan III. (CA, 2005).

Answer :

(i) EBIT	RS. 62,500	1,25,000	2,50,000	3,75,000	6,25,000
Plan 1 EPS	0.12	0.24	0.48	0.72	1.20
Plan 2 EPS	(0.24)	0	0.48	0.96	1.92

Plan 3 EPS	(0.56)	(0.32)	0.16	0.64	1.60

(ii) If company's sales are increasing, plan 2 is recommended.

(iii) Indifference point plan 1 & 2 ₹ 250000. Plan 1 & 3 ₹ 416666.67.

2. The Poker Ltd.'s operating income is ₹ 500000. The company has ₹ 800000 8% debentures & cost of equity is 12%. (i) Compute company's overall capitalization rate. (ii) Compute current value of the firm.

3. Calculate ABC Ltd.'s value as per MM theory on the basis of following information.
   (i) NOI ₹ 1000000
   (ii) 6% Debentures 1500000
   (iii) Equity capitalization rate 8%.
   (iv) Assume tax rate 40%.

4. The ABC Ltd. & XYZ Ltd. are identical in every respect. The only difference is ABC Ltd. has 6% ₹ 500000 debentures. As per net income approach valuation of both the companies is given below:

	ABC Ltd.	XYZ Ltd.
Net operating income	₹ 1,00,000	₹ 1,00,000
Cost of debt	NIL	30,000
Net income	1,00000	70000
Equity capitalization rate	8%	9%
Value of equity	12,50,000	7,77,778
Value of debt	NIL	5,00,000
Total value	12,50,000	1,277,778

If Ram has XYZ Ltd.'s shares of ₹ 5000. Show how Ram can earn same return in ABC Ltd. through arbitrage process.

5. The following data relates to Ram Ltd. & Shyam Ltd.

	Ram Ltd.	Shyam Ltd.
NOI	5,00,000	5,00,000
Cost of equity	8%	8%

The Ram Ltd. has ₹ 1500000 6% debentures outstanding. Assume no taxes. Calculate

(i) Market value of equity, debt of both the firms and market value of Ram Ltd. & Shyam Ltd.

(ii) Average cost of capital of both the firms.

6.	Ram Ltd.	Shyam Ltd.
6% Debentures	Nil	5,00,000
Return on investment	10%	10%

Total Assets	10,00,000	10,00,000

Corporate tax rate 40%

Equity Capitalization Rate 8%

Calculate

(i) WACC as per net operating income approach.

(ii) Value of the both firms as per net income & net operating income approach.

(iii) Mr. X holds 10% of Shyam Ltd. Can Mr. X earn same return from Ram Ltd. through arbitrage process. Show.

(iv) Which of the firm is having optimal capital structure.

7.

	XYZ Ltd.	ABC Ltd.
Debenture	10,00,000	Nil
Market value of equity	1500,000	20,00,000
Total Value	2,500,000	20,00,000
EBIT	2,50,000	2,50,000
Interest on debenture	1,00,000	nil
Net income	1,50,000	2,50,000

Calculate the value of both the firms using MM approach. Equilibrium value is 8% & there is no corporate taxes.

8. Parampara Ltd., EBIT is ₹ 20,00,000.Its equity capitalization rate is 15%. Corporate income tax is 50%. Parampara Ltd.'s payout is 100%. Calculate the value oi Parampara Ltd. as per MM approach in the following three situations.

(a) No debt

(b) 25,000, 10% debentures of ₹ 100 each.

(c) 15,000, 12% debentures of ₹ 100 each.

Review Questions

1. Explain the meaning of capital structure & and its importance in financial decision-making.
2. Discuss relevance & irrelevance theory. What are the main differences between both the theories?
3. What do you mean by net income approach? How does financial leverage and affects value of a firm?
4. What is optimal capital structure? Explain with the help of traditional theory.
5. What are the assumptions of net operating income theory?

6. Briefly discuss the net operating income theory of capital structure with the help of an example. **(UPTU 2005, 2007)**
7. What are the assumptions of MM theory? **(UPTU 2006, DU 2009)**
8. Explain the arbitrage process in MM theory.
9. How MM theory works & how this theory differs from relevance theories? **(UPTU 2010)**
10. Discuss the relationship between the cost of equity and financial leverage in accordance with MM theory. **(CA 2004)**
11. Give in brief main features of traditional approach to corporate financing system. Give its limitations also. **(UPTU 2007, 2009)**
12. What is net income approach in Capital Structure Planning? **(UPTU 2006, DU 2007)**
13. Explain why companies always prefer a debt equity mix in capital structure planning. **(UPTU 2006)**
14. Compare Traditional Approach and MM approach in capital structure planning? **(UPTU 2005, DU 2009)**
15. What is appropriate Capital Structure of a Company? Explain. **(DU)**
16. A company expects to have PE. ratio of 16.77, 15.00 & 13.82 in below given three cases of raising additional finances.

    a) issue of 4,00,000 equity shares @ 12.50 each
    b) issue os 11% preference shares of ₹ 50 lakhs
    c) issue of 10% debenture of ₹ 50 lakhs

    which of the above three alternatives of financing would you recommend? Expalin with reason **(DU)**

Case Study 1

Mr. Atul, CMD, Prodigy Ltd. is very happy because he got an offer from a multinational company to jointly establish a mega power project in India. Mr. Atul is very excited but worried too because acceptance of this offer will lead to an investment of ₹ 500 crore. Now Mr. Atul decided to call an emergency meeting to discuss the above offer.

It is estimated that the above project will generate an EBIT of ₹ 150 crore.

Mr. Atul said that this project is very profitable and acceptance of this offer will give international recognition to our company but the big issue is how to arrange this fund.

Mr. Arun, CFO said that we have a very good reputation in the market and we can arrange fund easily. We can finance this project by equity or equity & debt both.

Mr. Atul said to Mr. Arun that give me the detailed report on your every financing recommendations and future capital structure.

The current data is given below:

6% Preference Shares	1,500
8% Debentures	2,000
EBIT	900

Cost of equity is 12% & Corporate tax rate is 40%.

In future there are three financing options:

Option 1

Issue of 5crore equity shares of ₹ 100 each. Cost of equity will be 10%

Option 2

Issue of 5 crore 10% debentures of ₹ 100 each. Cost of equity will be 15%

Option 3

Issue of 2.5 crore equity shares of ₹ 100 each & 2.5 crore 10% debentures of ₹ 100 each. Cost of equity will be 13%.

Now all the options in every respect and advice Mr. Arun which of the financing option will be suitable for Prodigy Ltd.

Case Study 2 (DU 2006)

Two Companies are identical in all respects except that X Ltd., has debt of ₹ 5,00,000 borrowed at the rate of 12% whereas Y Ltd., has no debt in its capital structure. The total assets of both the companies anount to ₹ 15,00,000 on which the companies have earnings of 20%. You are required to do the following:

(i) Calculate value of companies and k_o using NI approach taking k_e as 18%.

(ii) Calculate value of companies and k_e using NOI approach taking k_o as 18%.

(iii) Compare the results and comment on the differences of the two approaches.

Case Study 3 (DU 2007)

5. The two companies U and L, belong to an equivalent risk class. These two firms are identical in every respect except that U Company is unlevered while Company L has 10% debentures of ₹ 30 lakhs. The other relevant information regarding their valuation and capitalization rates are as follows:

Particulars	Firm U	Firm L
	₹	₹
Net operating income (EBIT)	7,50,000	7,50,000
Interest on Debt (I)	--	3,00,000

Earnings to equity – holders (NI)	7,50,000	4,50,000
Equity capitalization rate (K_e)	0 .15	0.20
Market value of equity (S)	50,00,000	22,50,000
Market value of Debt (B)	--	30,00,000
Total value of firm (V)= (S+B)	50,00,000	52,50,000
Overall capitalization rate (ko)	0.15	0.143
Debt- equity ratio (B/S)	0	1.33

(i) An investor owns 10% equity shares of company L. Show the arbitrage process and the amount by which he could reduce his outlay through the use of leverage. of companies and k_o using NI approach taking k_e as 18%.

According to Modigliani and Miller, when will this arbitrage process come to an end?

References

1. Brealey, Richard A & Myres, Stewart C. (2007), Tata McGraw Hill, New Delhi
2. Damodaran, Aswath.(1994). Damodaran on Valuation, John Wiley & Sons, New York
3. Financial Management study material, The Institute of Chartered Accountants of India, New Delhi.
4. Khan, M Y & Jain (2007) P K, Financial Management, Tata McGraw Hill, New Delhi
5. Menon, Shailesh, (2010) "HNIs take a fancy to equity-backed corp bonds" The Economic Times", Lucknow.
6. Pandey, I M (2009). Financial Management, Vikas Publishing House, New Delhi
7. Work book on "Financial Management for Managers": The Institute of Chartered Financial Analysts of India, Hyderabad.

Cost of Capital

Learning Objectives:

By the end of this chapter and having completed the essential reading and activities, you should be able to:

- Understand the Concept of Cost of Capital
- Have an understanding of factors affecting Cost of Capital
- Calculate cost of various long term sources of finance
- Calculate weighted average Cost of Capital
- Use Cost of Capital in decision making

To start with...

ABC Ltd. is a well run , profit making and growing company. The company has good market reputation. The company's sources of funds consist of equity, preference share capital, debentures, and term loans from various financial institutions.

Rajeev a newly qualified chartered accountant got a promotion recently as Senior Manager (Finance) in this company. Based on his experience, he got his first assignment to arrive at the cost of funds being used by the company. He is supposed to do it for three years including current year. His senior Mr. Agarwal informed him that motive behind this exercise is that company felt its cost of capital is higher than other similar firms.. Rajeev is now planning to make a presentation on cost of capital and ways to reduce cost of capital.

Every company needs finance for running its business. In the previous chapter, we discussed various sources of finance. Every source of finance involves some cost, be it shares, debentures or any other.

In this chapter, we will discuss cost of various sources of finance, its calculation and its impact on financial decision making. Remember, calculating a cost is the first step towards saving it!

9.0 Introduction

In Unit II, we discussed investment decisions. We saw that firm is required to earn a minimum rate of return for accepting a project. For taking "accept" or "reject" decision we consider two things, first; cash flows arising out of that project and second; discount rate. The discount rate is the rate at which future cash inflows are discounted to get Present Value (PV) of future cash inflows. Moreover, if PV of future cash inflows is greater than PV of cash outflow then project is accepted; otherwise rejected. Now we can express the discount rate as **minimum required rate of return**. It is also termed as cost of capital because it is the minimum rate, which a project must generate. ***Now question arises. Is the minimum required rate of return equal to cost of capital?***

Consider an example to understand this. Let us say you are going to establish a project and for that you are in need of funds. For procurement of funds you decided to issue debentures having coupon rate of 9%, now 9% is the cost of debt for you because you will pay 9% over and above principal amount to debenture holders to satisfy their claim. How will this be possible? This will be possible only if your project generates at least 9% return after meeting other expenses. In case you earn less than 9%; project will be loss making .Therefore, this 9% is you minimum required rate of return from that project.

From this example, we may conclude that minimum required rate of return is cost of capital. We first calculate cost of capital as an output of financing decision and then use it as an input in investment decisions for evaluating a project. Remember Individual Rate of Return (IRR)? In IRR technique for evaluating a project, first we calculate IRR. And if IRR greater than cost of capital project is accepted otherwise rejected. It is very rare that IRR is exactly equal to the cost of capital. If it is, we should have a careful relook at our cash flow.

From the above discussion, it is clear that minimum required rate of return and cost of capital is same and we can let us try another way to understand it.

Suppose we want to establish a project. We can raise funds for this project through various sources, as discussed in earlier chapter on long term sources of finance. We saw that financing from these sources require some cost to firm like "interest" in case of debentures and term loan. And in case of equity financing; every shareholder expects a minimum rate of return from his investments. These expectations and interest payments are the cost of financing to the firm.

So what is the conclusion? It is that if a project fails to generate returns at a rate that satisfies the previously mentioned expectations; then it cannot be accepted. Now we can conclude that minimum required rate of return is the cost of capital. In other words, we can say that minimum required rate of return is the breakeven point for any capital investment. Minimum required rate of return is also known as **cutoff** rate and **hurdle rate**.

Managerial Tool Kit: Significance of Cost of Capital

Objective of financial management is to maximize wealth of shareholders. If cost of capital is less than rate of return earned by the firm on its assets, then the firm may use these excess returns in two ways. It may retain them in the firm for reinvestment. Alternatively, it may distribute them among the shareholders as dividends. In both the cases value of the firm will increase resulting maximization of wealth of the shareholders. Cost of capital plays very significant role in evaluating a project. In capital budgeting, we use cost of capital as discount rate in NPV or PI method. In addition, we use cost of capital as hurdle rate in IRR method. We accept the project only If IRR is greater than cost of capital. Otherwise, we reject it.

9.1 Factors Affecting Cost of Capital

Financial Policy: The overall cost of capital if significantly affected by financial policy of the firm. Financial policy means choice of sources of finance and the choice of proportion of debt and equity. The firms overall cost of capital will reflect the combined costs of all the sources of financing used by the firm. This overall cost of capital is termed as **Weighted Average Cost Of capital** (WACC). The weighted average cost of capital is the weighted average of after tax cost of each of the sources of capital used by a firm to finance a project. Here, the weights reflect the proportion of a particular source in total financing.

Risk: Risk and cost of capital are related directly to each other. To understand this, we will have to understand ***trade-off between*** risk and return, which is depicted through a chart. Trade off between two things means what happens to one thing if the other thing increases or decreases and vice versa.

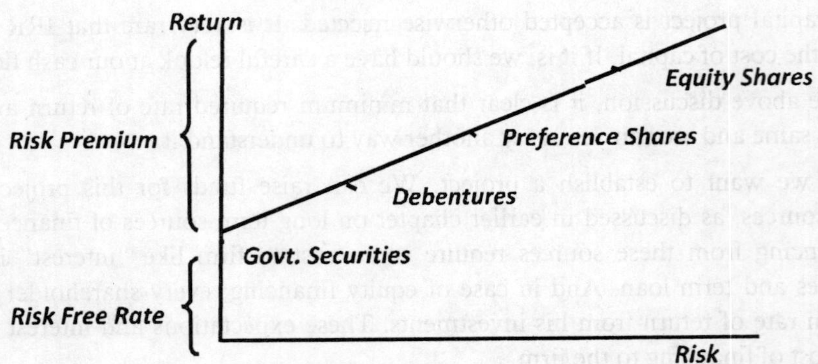

From the above chart it is clear that risk and return have a direct relationship. When risk increases, the expected return also increases. Let us take an example to understand this. We all know that Kisan Vikas Patra is an investment avenue where investment doubles in eight years seven months. Also, some finance companies in our country promise to double or sometimes triple the amount invested in six to seven years. Kisan Vikas Patra is a Govt. security with almost zero risk and but it gives lower rate of return than finance company schemes. Whereas, finance companies offer huge rate of return but involve heavy risk. The finance companies offer higher rate of return because higher rate of return compensates the higher risk inherent in them. If these companies offer rate of return equal to risk free rate i.e. rate of return on Govt. securities, no investor will be attracted to these companies. To attract investors companies offer higher rate of return on their securities.

You may ask that why do investors take high risk by investing in finance companies? Well, they do so in expectation of higher returns.

The same principal applies to cost of capital of other long term sources of finance. Debenture holders bear less risk than preference shares and therefore also accept lower returns than preference shares. Preference shares bear less risk than equity shares and hence have less cost of capital (meaning offer lower return) than equity shares. Equity shares bear maximum risk resulting maximum cost of capital. Every investor requires extra return for taking extra risk. The extra return over and above the risk free rate is called **risk premium** (Remember the chapter on risk and return? Now a question arises. What are various types of risks for which there exist a premium?

The different risks are described below:

1. ***Business Risk:*** This risk is associated with company's promise to pay claims of lenders and shareholders. It directly affects the profits of the company. If the company is involved in a more risky project than normal projects then investors require extra risk premium i.e. business risk premium for taking this extra risk.
2. ***Financial Risk:*** This type of risk is directly related to capital structure of the company. In case of high proportion of debt securities in the capital structure, companies will have high fixed financial commitments which results lower EPS.

The investors requires extra risk premium i.e. financial risk premium for taking this extra risk.

Simply put, the tradeoff between risk and return can be understood as "Higher the risk, higher the expected return and lower the risk; lower the expected return". You might have heard some people say ***"No risk no gain, more risk more gain."***

To calculate the required rate of return we add business risk premium and financial risk premium to risk free interest rate i.e. rate or return on Govt. securities.

9.2 Cost Of Debt

If a project is financed wholly by debt capital then minimum required rate of return from that project is cost of debt capital to the firm. For calculating cost of bonds/debentures, we need following information:

1) ***Net*** cash inflow at the time of issue of debentures. Net cash inflow is calculated by adding into the face value of debenture any premium if charged or by deducting any discount given. From this we further deduct flotation cost (flotation cost is expenses incurred in issue process of debentures) to get net cash inflow from issue of debentures. For example, a debenture with face value of ₹ 1,000 is issued at premium of 20% and flotation cost of issue is ₹ 100 per debentures then net cash inflow is ₹ 1,100(1,000+20% of 1,000-100).

2) ***Repayment: It is the amount payable*** at the time of maturity or net cash out flow at the time of redemption of debentures. The redemption may be at par, at premium or with interest for the final year.

3) ***Cash*** outflow in the form of interest. Interest payment may be annually, half yearly or quarterly. For calculating cost of capital it is assumed that interest payment is annually. While calculating interest amount, always remember to multiply interest rate to the Par Value of the debenture (excluding premiums or discounts).

After getting above values, we can calculate cost of debt by applying respective formulae. The students should note that they can calculate cost of any source of fund by applying a general principle and they don't have to really memorize different formula for different cases.

The underlying principle is that **"The cost of capital of any source of fund is the discount rate which equates the present value of all future outflows with the PV of all inflows".** Now let us see the application of this principle.

9.2.1 Cost of capital of redeemable debentures: Cost of redeemable debentures is calculated by applying following formula:

$$B_0 = \sum_{t=1}^{n} \frac{INT_t}{\left(1+k_d\right)^t} + \frac{B_n}{(1+k_d)^n}$$

Where B_0 = Net Cash inflows at the time of issue

INT = Annual Interest Payment

B_n = Cash outflow at the time of maturity.

k_d = Cost of debenture

Example 1

Mohit Surfactants Ltd. issues 15% debentures of face value of ₹ 100 each, redeemable at the end of 8 years at par. The debentures are issued at a discount of 6% and the flotation cost is estimated to be 2%. Calculate cost of capital of debentures if tax rate is 50%.

Solution:

$B_0 = 100 - 6\% - 2\% = ₹92$

INT = 100 * 15% = 15

Cost of capital according to above formula

$$92 = \sum_{t=1}^{8} \frac{15}{(1+k_d)^t} + \frac{100}{(1+k_d)^8}$$

$$92 = 15\left(PVFA_{8,k_d}\right) + 100\left(PVF_8, k_d\right)$$

By trial & error method we get $k_d = 16.90\%$

now after tax cost of debentures = $k_d = 1 - T$

cost of debenture = 16.9(1 – .50) = 8.45%

Sometimes principal too is amortized periodically. In that case principal is repaid periodically with interest then cash outflow includes interest and principal. Then formula for calculating cost of debentures is given below:

$$B_0 = \sum_{t=1}^{n} \frac{INT_t + B_t}{(1+k_d)}$$

Where INT_t and B_t are periodical payments of interest and principal.

9.2.2 Cost of Capital of Perpetual Debentures: Cost of perpetual debentures can be ascertained by applying following formula

$$k_d = \frac{I}{B_0}$$

Where k_d = cost of capital of perpetual debentures before tax, I = annual interest payment,

B_0 = net cash inflow at the time of issue.

The above cost is before tax and to get after tax cost we will have to adjust this with tax i.e.

After tax cost of capital of debentures = k_d (1 – T) where T is the tax rate.

9.3 Cost of Preference Share Capital

Cost of capital of preference share capital is calculated by applying following formula:

$$P_0 = \sum_{t=1}^{n} \frac{PD_t}{(1+k_p)^t} + \frac{P_n}{(1+k_p)^n}$$

Where P_o = Net Proceeds on issue of shares
PD = Annual preference dividend
P_n = Cash outflow at the time of redemption
k_p = Cost of preference shares
n = Years of redemption.

Example 2

Mohit Surfactants Ltd. issues 12% preference shares of the face value of ₹ 100 each at issue cost at ₹ 6 each. Calculate cost of capital of preference shares if redeemable after 10 years at a premium of ₹ 10each.

Solution

P_0 = 100 – 6 = 94
PD = 100 * 12% = 12
P = 100 + 10 = 110

$$94 = \sum_{t=1}^{10} \frac{12}{(1+k_p)^t} + \frac{110}{(1+k_p)^{10}}$$

94 = 12 x PVIA(10, k_p)+110 x PVIF (10, k_p)

by trial & error method we get k_p 13.68%

You can also get cost of capital of preference shares this formula :

$$k_p = \frac{PD + (P_n - P_0)/N}{(P_n + P_0)/2}$$

$$k_p = \frac{12 + (110 - 94)/10}{(110 - 94)/2}$$

$k_p = 13.57\%$

Important: We do not adjust tax in calculating cost of capital of preference shares because dividend payment to preference shareholders is not tax deductible.

9.4 Cost of Equity Share Capital

Before going into the calculation of cost of capital for equity shares we will first discuss that whether there is any cost involved with the equity shares or not. As we have discussed previously that the firm is not legally bound to pay the dividend to equity shares and equity shares are having residual claim over firm's profits and assets in case of liquidation.

Now it can be argued that if there is no fixed commitment like debentures and preference shareholders whether equity shares have a cost of capital. The answer is yes. Every investor has an expectation of required rate of return be it debenture holders, preference shareholders or equity shareholders and required rate of return depends upon the risk associated with respective investments.

To understand this let us take a real life example. If we are going to buy equity shares of a company, we do this in expectation of returns in the form of dividend or capital gain that we may get if we sell this share after some time. Now in case of equity shares we have to understand concept of opportunity cost for equity shares.

The opportunity cost is the return, which an investor forgoes by investing into alternate security. Any rational investor invests funds in expectation of dividend and capital appreciation. Alternatively, we can also say that any rational investor invests funds in expectation of a minimum rate of return. This required rate of return is the rate, which equates the current investment price with the present value of future dividend and future market price of share. This required rate of return is the cost of capital of equity shares.

Can you see now from this discussion that equity shares also involve costs to the company?

Measuring the cost of equity

The cost of capital of equity shares is the most difficult to measure because equity shares have some unique features. Unlike debentures and preference shares, the required rate of return of the equity-holders is not readily available. Payment of dividend and its rate is not fixed for equity shares. It totally depends upon discretion of board of directors. Equity shareholders have residual claim over profits and assets of the firm. After satisfying all the claims, profit left, if any, is distributed among equity shareholders. In case of winding up, after satisfying all claims, assets left, if any, are distributed among equity shareholders. Equity shares can be issued externally through sale of new shares to public or internally from retained earnings. Cost of equity shares from external sources is more than equity shares from internal sources because equity shares from internal sources do not involve any floatation costs. Now we will discuss various methods for calculating cost of capital of equity shares in detail.

9.4.1 Constant Growth Model: If dividend on equity shares is growing at a constant rate i.e. g then we cab calculate cost of equity shares under this model. As we all know that in case of equity shares if dividend is growing at a constant rate g then value of equity share is

$$P_o = \frac{D_1}{k_e - g}$$

where D_1 is expected dividend after year 1

then $D_1 = D_0(1+g)$

after solving above formula we get cost of capital of equity shares

$$k_e = \frac{D_1}{P_0} + g$$

Where k_e = cost of capital of equity shares, P_0 = present market value of shares, g = growth rate.

Example 3

Mohit Surfactants Ltd. has just declared and paid dividend at the rate 12% on the equity share of ₹ 100 each. The expected future growth rate in dividend is 10%. Calculate cost of capital of equity shares if present market value of shares is ₹ 150.

Solution

$P_0 = 150$, $g = .10$, $D_0 = 12$

$$k_e = \frac{D_0(1+g)}{P_0} + g$$

$$k_e = \frac{12(1+.10)}{150} + .10$$

$k_e = 0.188$ or 18.8%

Now if in the above example it is given that firm's retention ratio is 40% and return on equity is 24% in place of growth rate then we can get growth rate by applying this formula i.e. **g = b * r** where g is the growth rate, b is retention ratio and r is return on equity, g = .40 * .24 = .096 which is growth rate.

9.4.2 Zero Growth Dividend Model: Under this model it is assumed that dividend will remain stable at its current level for perpetuity in other words there will be no growth in dividends. Under this model we calculate cost of capital of equity shares by applying following formula

$$k_e = \frac{D_1}{P_0}$$

Where k_e = cost of equity share capital, D_e = expected dividend at the end of year1, P_0 = current market price of the share.

The logic behind the above formula is that in case of constant dividend growth model we take g as growth rate which is constant and if we put g = 0 because of growth rate is zero in the formula under constant dividend growth model we get formula under zero growth dividend model.

Example 4

Mohit Surfactants Ltd. is currently earning ₹ 1,00,000 and its shares' present market value is ₹ 175. The company has 10000 shares outstanding. The earning of the company is expected to remain stable and it has a payout ratio of 100%. Calculate cost of equity.

Solution:

$$D_1 = \frac{1,00,000}{10,000} = ₹\ 10,\ P_0 = ₹\ 175$$

$$= \frac{10}{175} = .0571 \text{ or } 5.71\%$$

9.4.3 Different Growth Rates in Dividend: Sometimes dividend grows at different pace in different phases like for year 1 to year 5 growth rate is 10% and 15% from year 6 to forever, it is called multiple stage growth. In this situation cost of capital of equity shares can be found out by applying formula:

$$p_0 = \sum_{t=1}^{n} \frac{DIV_0 (1+g_s)^t}{(1+k_e)^t} + \frac{DIV_{n+1}}{k_e - g_n} \times \frac{1}{(1+k_e)^n}$$

Where P_o = current market price, DIV_0 = current dividend, g_s = growth for n years, g_n = perpetual growth beginning from n + 1th year.

Important: We do not adjust tax in calculating cost of capital of equity shares because dividend payment to equity shareholders is not tax deductible.

9.4.4 Cost of Equity Capital through CAPM Model: Till now the methods discussed for calculation of cost of capital of equity capital involve use of dividends.

What can we do if dividend data is not available? In this case, we may use another method based upon risk and return trade off. As discussed earlier, risk and return are directly related. If an investor takes extra risk he wants risk premium for taking that extra risk to compensate for it. In other words, an investor will not take on additional risk unless she expects to be compensated with additional returns.

Capital Assets Pricing Model (CAPM) describes risk as diversifiable or unsystematic and non diversifiable or systematic risk. Diversifiable risk can be eliminated by diversification in portfolio but non diversifiable risk cannot be eliminated completely. Due to this non elimination, investor requires additional risk premium for taking additional risk. This model concerns with how expected return increases with every degree of increase in (non-diversifiable) risk.

$$k_e = r_f + \beta\left(r_m - r_f\right)$$

where k_e = Cost of capital of equity capital

r_f = Risk free interest rate

β = A measure of Non – diversifiable risk

r_m = Return from market.

Example 5

Mohit Surfactants Limited's β is 1.25. The market return is 10%. The risk free rate is 8%. Calculate cost of capital of equity capital.

Solution:

$k_e = r_f + \beta\left(r_m - r_f\right)$

= .08 + 1.25 (.10 - .08)

k_e = .105 or 10.5%

9.5 Cost of Retained Earnings

Retained earnings are that part of total earnings which is available for distribution to equity shareholders but not distributed among them. These earnings are retained in the business and are available for reinvestment by the company. How much earnings will be retained depends upon the dividend policy adopted by the company. We will discuss it in the next unit. Company can use retained earnings in two ways. First, retained earnings can be used in reinvestment. Second, they can be used to increase share capital in the form of new issue of equity shares through internal sources. Retained earnings are considered as shareholder's fund; however, the companies are not legally bound to pay any dividend on retained earnings. This is in spite of it being shareholders' fund. This is because these earnings are retained in the business in the form of Reserves & Surplus, and companies are not required to pay any dividend on it.

Due to the aforesaid reasons; it can be argued the retained earnings are free of any cost. This is not the case, however. There is some opportunity cost associated with retained earnings. How? It is because these retained earnings would have been invested by the equity shareholders, had these earnings been distributed among them. Since they have not been distributed (fully or partly), shareholders could not invest it into other securities on which they could get returns. These forgone returns are the opportunity cost of retained earnings.

The cost of equity capital, k_e, is also considered cost of retained earnings, k_r. It is because in case a company wants to get funds from external sources i.e. by issue of fresh capital or internal sources i.e. by retaining the earnings, it will have to consider rate of return at which shareholders are indifferent between distribution or reinvestment of these earnings. If the projects in which the firm has invested retained earnings is not earning returns expected by shareholders then shareholders will be disappointed. Thy will start selling their holdings. This will lower the market price, which will keep falling. Will this fall in the market price stop somewhere? Yes, it will stop at a price at which investment in this share will generate the required rate of return.

Hence, we can conclude that retained earnings are not free of cost.

9.6 Weighted Average Cost of Capital

Now we are able to calculate cost of capital of different sources of finance. However, it is not sufficient, because it does not provide us overall cost of capital of firm or minimum required rate of return of the firm ***as a whole.***

In this section, we will learn to obtain company's overall cost of capital. Overall cost of capital is also known as weighted average cost of capital (WACC).WACC plays most important role in financial decision-making; like evaluation of capital budgeting proposals, determination of minimum required rate of return etc. For calculation of WACC, we need two things. First; cost of individual sources of finance and second; proportion (or weights) of individual sources of finance in capital structure:

$$WACC = k_e w_e + k_p w_p + k_d w_d$$

Where WACC = weighted average cost of capital, k_e = cost of equity capital, w_e = proportion of equity capital, k_p = cost of preference shares, w_p = proportion of preference capital, k_d = cost of debt capital, w_d = proportion of debt capital.

Example 6

Mohit Surfactants Ltd. has the following capital structure that appears in the balance sheet

Capital	Amount (₹)	Weights (%)
Equity Share Capital	40,00,000	40
Preference Share Capital	30,00,000	30
Reserves & Surplus	10,00,000	10
Long Term Debt	20,00,000	20
Total	**10000000**	**100**

Solution

Cost of different sources is as under

Equity Share Capital = 14%, Reserves & Surplus = 14%, Preference Share Capital = 11%, Long Term Debt = 7%, Calculate WACC.

Solution

Weighted Average Cost of Capital = 0.40*0.14 +0.30*0.11+0.10*0.14+0.20*0.07

=0.117

=11.7%

9.6.1 Issues to be considered while calculating WACC

Followings are some issues that should be considered.

Weights: Weighted average cost of capital is calculated by assigning weights to individual sources of finance. These weights are nothing but proportion of a source in the total capital structure. However, weights may be calculated in three ways.

a) ***Historical Weights:*** They are calculated by dividing the book values of a particular source of finance by the book value of total capital. Book values are values that appear in the balance sheet. Historical weights system is based upon two assumptions. First, the firm will get additional funds in the same proportion as it has now. Second, the present capital structure is optimal and firm will continue with the same capital structure.

The problem with this system is that the firm is not able to get funds in the same proportion as they appear at present because of some constraints like market situation etc.

b) ***Marginal weights*** are calculated in proportion of new (or additional) long term financing.

For example, if a firm wants to invest in a project ₹ 10,00,000 and it will raise funds from equity 500000, from preference shares 3,00,000 and from debt 2,00,000 then we will assign weights for equity .5, preference shares .3 and debts .2 . As you can see, we have calculated these weights straight from the financing plan for the new project. We did not consider the existing capital structure ***before accepting the project,*** which appears in the balance sheet at present. This weighing system is based upon proportion of funds for new proposal from different sources.

c) Target weights are based upon the target capital structure of the firm. Target capital structure is the firm's optimal capital structure that the firm is supposed to reach somewhere in future. Weights are assigned to the different sources of finance based on this assumption that in the long run firm will reach optimal capital structure. If firm's present capital structure is considered optimal, the historical weights and target weights will be same.

Book Value Weight versus Market Values

The weights of different sources of finance; which are taken for the calculation of WACC can be based upon book value or market value. Book value is the rupee value of different items appearing in the balance sheet.

Whereas, market value is rupee value at which an item can be traded in the market. In practice, we take book value weights for calculating WACC. However, it is advisable to take market value weights to calculate WACC. The book value weights are easy to calculate and do not fluctuate. However, the limitation of book value weights is that they do not fully reflect economic values.

The market value weights are based upon proportion of each source at their market value. The advantages of market value weights are that they provide current required rate of return of investor and reflect the economic values. The limitation behind market value weights is that market values are volatile and fluctuate very frequently. WACC calculated on the basis of market value weights will be more than WACC calculated on the basis of book value weights if market values are more than book values because weights will be higher; cost of different sources remaining the same.

Eg. Firm having capital structure as follows:

Source of Finance	**Amount**	**After Tax Cost (%)**
Debt of finance	40,00,000	4 %
Preference shares	15,00,000	8.5 %
Capital equity shares	20,00,000	11.5 %
Capital retained Earnings	25,00,000	10.00 %
	100,00,000	

Sol. Complete Cost Capital

Debt	**Weight**	**Specific Cost**	**Weighted Cost (weight x Sp. Cost)**
Debt	40	4	1.6
Preference shares	15	8.5	8.5 x .15
Equity share	20	11.5	20 x 11.5
Retained Earning	25	10.00	25 x 10

$$\text{Debt weight} = \frac{\textit{Debt Capital}}{\textit{Total Capital}} = \frac{40,00,000}{100,00,000} = 40$$

9.7 Weighted Marginal Cost of Capital (WMCC)

Weighted marginal cost of capital means cost of capital related to additional financing. In WACC, we calculate overall cost of capital of a firm having different sources of financing. In WMCC we calculate on cost of capital of additional financing e.g. If a firm intends to establish a project having capital investment of ₹ 10,00,000 and it wants to finance it from different sources of finance then cost of capital of ₹ 10,00,000 from different sources is called WMCC. In other words, WMCC is WACC of new or incremental cost of new capital issued by the firm.

Activity

Download financial statements of any two similar reputed public limited companies. However, before downloading, ensure that the companies have all types of capital like equity, preference and debt capital. Now get the information about redemption of preference shares and debentures. After compilation of all the data, calculate cost of capital as discussed above. Now compare the cost of capital in all respects including companies' capital structure.

After this activity, you will find yourself more confident in the above concepts.

Illustrative Solved Examples

1. Arihant Ltd. has following capital structure:

Particulars	Amount	Weight	Cost of Capital
Equity Share Capital	10,00,000	.4	9%
6% Preference Share Capital	7,00,000	.28	6%
8% Debentures	8,00,000	.32	4%

Calculate WACC of Arihant Ltd.

Solution: WACC of Arihant Ltd. will be as follows:

Particulars	Amount	Weight	Cost	Weighted Cost of Capital
Equity Share Capital	10,00,000	.4	9%	.036
6% Preference Share Capital	7,00,000	.28	6%	.0168
8% Debentures	8,00,000	.32	4%	.0128
25,00,000		1.00	.0656	

WACC of Arihant Ltd. is 6.56%.

2. Based on following data calculate WACC based on market value of Jupiter Ltd.

Equity Share Capital (₹ 10 each)	15,00,000
6% Debentures (₹ 100 each)	9,00,000

Jupiter Ltd. has paid dividend of ₹ 3 per share, its growth rate is 10%, Its shares & debentures are being traded at ₹ 20 & ₹ 90 respectively.

Solution: WACC of Jupiter Ltd. will be as follows

$$k_e = \frac{D_1}{P_0} + g$$

$$= \frac{3 \times 1.1}{2_0} + 10 = 26.5\%$$

$$k_d = \frac{I}{B_0}$$

$$= \frac{6}{60} = 6.67\%$$

now market value of equity share is 1,50,000 * 20 = 3,00,0000

now market value of debentures is 9,000 *90 = 8,10,000

total market value = 30,00,000 + 8,10,000 = 38,10,000

weights = equity 30,00,000/38,10,000 + debentures 8,10,000/30,00,000

WACC = .79 * .265 + .21 * .067 = .224 = 22.4%

3. Calculate cost of capital of Angel Ltd. in the following cases.

   (i) Five year 9% preference shares issued at ₹ 100 & redeemable at a premium of ₹ 10.

   (ii) 9% irredeemable debentures issued at par.

   (iii) Dividend paid at 20% on equity shares of ₹ 10 each, growth rate is 10% and CMP is 25.

Consider tax rate at 35%

Solution : (i) $$P_0 = \sum_{t=1}^{n} \frac{PD_t}{(1+k_p)^t} + \frac{P_n}{(1+k_p)^n}$$

$$100 = \sum_{t=1}^{5} \frac{9}{(1+k_p)^t} + \frac{110}{(1+k_p)^5}$$

After trial & error cost of preference shares is 10.06%

(ii) $k_d = \dfrac{I}{B_0}$

$$k_d = \frac{9}{100} = .09$$

After tax cost = .09(1-.35) = 5.85%

$(iii)\, k_e = \dfrac{D_1}{P_0} + g = \dfrac{2(1.1)}{25} + .1 = .088 + .1 = .188 = 18.8\%$

4. **Pilot Ltd. issues 12% preference shares with a face value of ₹ 100 & flotation cost of 3%. Calculate the cost of preference shares if (a) preference shares are irredeemable and (b) if the preference shares are redeemable after 8 years at a premium of 10%**

Solution : (i) Cost of irredeemable preference shares = 12/97 = 12.37%

(ii) $P_0 = \sum_{t=1}^{n} \dfrac{PD_t}{(1+k_p)^t} + \dfrac{P_n}{(1+k_p)^n}$

$$97 = \sum_{t=1}^{8} \frac{12}{(1+k_p)^t} + \frac{110}{(1+k_p)^8}$$

After trial & error method we get cost of preference share = 13.42%

5. **Compute Prodigy Ltd.' s WACC based on following information.**

   (a) **10%, 15 years debentures (face value ₹ 500 each) of ₹ 5,00,000 issued at 2% flotation cost, redeemable at 10% premium.**

   (b) **12% preference shares (face value ₹ 100 each) of ₹ 10,00,000 issued at 5% discount .**

   (c) **Equity shares of ₹ 10,00,000, CMP ₹ 50.**

   Assume tax rate is 45%, growth rate is 5% and expected dividend is ₹ 8.

Solution: (a)

$$B_0 = \sum_{t=1}^{n} \frac{INT_t}{(1+k_d)^t} + \frac{B_n}{(1+k_d)^n}$$

$$490 = \sum_{t=1}^{15} \frac{50}{(1+k_d)^t}$$

After trial & error we get cost of debentures 10.58%

After tax cost of debentures is 10.58(1-.45) = 5.819

(b) k_p = = 12.63%

(c) $k_e = \frac{D_1}{P_0} + g$

$k_e = \frac{8}{50} + 5\% = 21$

Weight = debenture (5,00,000/25,00,000), preference shares (10,00,000/25,00,000), equity shares (10,00,000/25,00,000)

WACC = .2*5.819 + .4*12.63 + .4*21

WACC = 14.62%

6. Angel Ltd. wishes to raise additional finance of ₹ 15 lakhs. The company has ₹ 500000 in the form of retained earnings available for investment purpose. The following are the further details:

(a) Debt equity ratio 20 : 80

(b) Cost of debt at the rate of 8% before tax upto ₹ 2,50,000 and beyond that 12% before tax.

(c) Earning per share ₹ 12

(d) Dividend payout 25% of earnings

(e) Expected growth rate in dividend 10%

(f) Current market price per share, ₹ 40.

(g) Tax rate 50%

Required

(i) Calculate the post tax average cost of additional debt.

(ii) Calculate of cost of retained earnings & cost of equity

(iii) Calculate overall WACC after tax of additional finance.

Solution : (i) Angel Ltd. will raise additional ₹ 15 lakhs In the ratio of 20 : 80 to maintain its debt equity ratio i.e. debt ₹ 3,00,000 & equity ₹ 12,00,000. Now debt up to ₹ 2,50,000 will cost to the Angel Ltd. ₹ 10,000 @4% after tax & up to ₹ 50,000, ₹ 3,000 @6% after tax.

Now post tax cost of additional debt = $\frac{10,000 + 3,000}{2,50,000 + 50,000} = 4.33\%$

(ii) Dividend = 25% of ₹12 = ₹ 3, g = 10% i.e. future dividend = 3.30.

$$k_e = \frac{D_1}{P_0} + g = \frac{3.30}{40} + 10\% = 18.25\%$$

Now we know that cost of retained earnings = cost of equity then cost of retained earnings will also be 18.25%.

(iii) Angel Ltd. will raise equity capital of ₹ 7,00,000 because out of additional investment of ₹ 15 lakhs it invest ₹ 3 lakhs from debt, ₹ 5 lakhs from retained earnings and rest ₹ 7 lakhs from equity capital.

WACC = debenture (30,000/15,00,000).043 + retained earnings (5,00,000/15,00,000).1,825 + equity capital (7,00,000/15,00,000).1825 = 23.2%

7. Natural Group's balance sheet reveals the following information.

Equity Shares Capital (₹ 10 each)	₹ 6,00,000
10% Debentures	8,00,000
12% Term Loan	1,00,0000
	24,00,000

(i) Compute the WACC. The company is paying dividends at a consistent rate of 40% per annum.

(ii) What will be the difference if the current price of equity share is ₹ 40.

(iii) Determine the effect of Income Tax on the cost of capital in each situation. Assume tax rate is 50%.

Solution : (i) WACC = equity (6,00,000/24,00,000) * .15 + debentures (8,00,000/24,00,000) * .1 + term loan (10,00,000/24,00,000) * .12 = 12.05%

(ii) Cost of equity capital = 4/40 = 10%

WACC = equity (6,00,000/24,00,000) * .10 + debentures (8,00,000/24,00,000) * .1 + term loan (10,00,000/24,00,000) * .12 = 10.80%

(iii) After tax cost, debentures = 10(1-50%) = 5%, term loan = 12(1-50%) = 6%

WACC = equity (600000/2400000) * .15 + debentures (8,00,000/24,00,000) * .05 + term loan (10,00,000/24,00,000) * .06 = 7.95%

WACC = equity (6,00,000/24,00,000) * .10 + debentures (8,00000/24,00,000) * .05 + term loan (10,00,000/24,00,000) * .06 = 6.7%

Summary

- The discount rate is the rate at which future cash inflows are discounted to get PV of future cash inflows. It is also termed as cost of capital because it is the minimum rate, which a project must generate.
- Financial policy means choice of sources of finance and the choice of proportion of debt and equity.

- Risk and cost of capital are related directly to each other. High risk goes with high return and low risk goes with low return.
- Cost of capital of redeemable debenture is the discount rate which equates the present value of all future outflows with the PV of all inflows.
- Cost of perpetual debenture is found out by dividing annual interest payment by net cash inflows at the time of issue.
- Cost of capital of redeemable debenture is the discount rate which equates the present value of all future outflows including annual preference dividend and cash outflow at the time of redemption with the PV of all inflows.
- Dividend growth model calculates cost of equity in case of dividend on equity shares is growing at a constant rate.
- In case of zero growth in dividend cost of equity will be calculated as per zero growth dividend model.
- In case of different growth rates in dividend cost of equity is present value of all future dividends.
- CAPM model says that every investor requires additional risk premium for taking additional risk. Excess of market risk over risk free rate is extra risk taken by an investor.
- Cost of retained earnings is the opportunity cost of equity shareholders because these retained earnings would have been invested by the equity shareholders, had these earnings been distributed among them.
- WACC is the overall cost of capital of all the sources. A weight is assigned to the cost of capital of individual sources and total of all the weighted cost of individual sources is WACC
- WMCC is the weighted marginal cost of additional financing.

Test Your Understanding

State whether following statements are true or false

1. The minimum required rate of return is equal to the cost of capital.
2. The minimum required rate of return is necessary for getting investment from an investor.
3. Risk & return both are having inverse relationship.
4. Rate of return on Govt. securities is risk free rate.
5. Investors require same rate of return for every degree of risk.
6. For calculating cost of debentures, we need cash inflow form issue of debentures and cash outflow at the time of redemption.

7. The only difference between cost of preference shares and redeemable debentures is the tax effect.
8. Equity shares are free of cost.
9. CAPM describes risk as systematic & unsystematic.
10. Cost of retained earnings is equal to the cost of equity share capital.

Answers : 1. T, 2. T, 3. F, 4. T, 5. T, 6. F, 7. T, 8. F, 9. T, 10. T

Multiple Choice Questions

Choose the correct alternative out of the given:

1. Retention ratio is 40% & return on equity is 10%, compute growth rate.
   a) 5% b) 3%
   c) 4% d) 4.25%
2. Risk free interest rate is the rate
   a) On Govt. securities b) On FD₹
   c) On debentures by private companies d) On preference shares by private companies
3. Discount rate is known as
   a) Risk free rate b) Rate if income tax
   c) Cost of capital d) None of the above
4. Required rate of return of investors increases as
   a) Risk increases b) Risk decreases
   c) Cost of capital increases d) None of the above
5. Pre tax cost of debt is 7% & tax rate is 35%, after tax cost of debt is
   a) 4.65% b) 4.75%
   c) 7% d) 4.55%
6. In formula $k_d = \frac{I}{B_o}$, B_o denotes
   a) Net cash inflow at the time of issue
   b) Net cash outflow at the time of redemption
   c) Market price of debenture
   d) Face value of debenture
7. In calculation of WACC weight shows
   a. Proportion of assets

b. Proportion of different sources of finance

c. Proportion of liability

d. Proportion of equity capital

8. In CAPM beta denotes

a) Non-diversifiable risk
b) Diversifiable risk
c) Average risk
d) None of the above

9. Cost of retained earnings is equal to

a) Cost of debts
b) Coat of preference shares
c) WACC
d) Cost of equity shares

10. Calculate cost of equity if, risk free rate is 8%, beta is 2.2, return from market is 12%

a) 16.9%
b) 16.8%
c) 17%
d) 17.8%

11. Calculate WACC if, weight of equity capital, preference capital & debenture is .2, .5 & .3 and cost of capital is 12%, 10% & 7% respectively. Tax rate is 50%.

a) 8.95%
b) 8.55%
c) 8.45%
d) 8.5%

12. Calculate cost of equity if, CMP is ₹ 50, growth rate is 10%, company will pay dividend of ₹ 8 at the end of current year. Tax rate is 50%.

a) 26%
b) 28%
c) 26.5%
d) 25%

13. Weighted marginal cost of capital is

a. Weighted average cost of capital

b. WACC of new financing

c. Average cost of equity & preference shares

d. Average cost of preference shares & debentures.

14. Calculate cost perpetual debentures if, coupon rate is 9.5%, debentures of ₹ 100 each issued at a discount of 4% & floatation cost is 1%. Tax rate is 35%

a) 6.5%
b) 7.5%
c) 8.5%
d) 5.5%

15. The cost of capital is not similar to one of the following: **(UPTU 2009)**

a) Cut off rate
b) Target Rate
c) Hurdle Rate
d) Internal Rate of Return

16. The Weighted Average Cost of Capital (WACC) is not similar to: **(UPTU 2009)**

a) Overall cost of capital b) Risk adjusted Returns

c) Required Rate of Return d) Minimum Rate of Return

17. ABC limited issues 12% perpetual debentures of ₹ 100 each. The tax rate is 50%. Find the debenture cost: **(UPTU 2010)**

a) 12% and 6% b) 6% and 12%

c) 12% and 12% d) 6% and 6%

Answers: 1. c, 2. a, 3. c, 4. a, 5. d, 6. a, 7. b, 8. a, 9. d, 10. b, 11. c, 12. a, 13. b, 14. a, 15. d, 16. b, 17. d

Practical Problems

1. A company issues ₹ 10,00,000, 12% debentures of ₹ 100 each. The debentures are redeemable after the expiry of fixed period of 7 years. The company is in 35% tax bracket. Required:

   (i) Calculate the cost of debt after tax, if debentures are issued at

   (a) Par (b) 10% discount (c) 10% premium

   (ii) If brokerage is paid at 2%, what will be the cost of debentures, if issue is at par. (IPCC, 2006)

Answer: (i) (a) 7.8% (b) 9.71% (c) 6.07%; (ii) 8.17%

2. JKL Ltd. has the following book-value capital structure as on march 31, 2003.

Equity Share Capital (200000 shares)	₹ 40,00,000
11.5% Preference Shares	10,00,000
10% Debentures	30,00,000
	80,00,000

The equity shares of the company sells for ₹ 20. It is expected that the company will pay next year a dividend of ₹ 2 per equity share, which is expected to grow at 5% p.a. forever. Assume a 35% corporate tax rate.

Required:

(i) Compute WACC of the company based on existing capital structure.

(ii) Compute the new WACC, if the company raises an additional ₹ 20 lakhs debt by issuing 12% debentures. This would result in increasing the expected equity dividend to ₹ 2.40 and leave the growth rate unchanged, but the price of equity share will fall to ₹ 16 per share.

Comment on the use of weight in the computation of WACC .(CA, 2003)

Answer : (i) 11.375% (ii) 12.66%

3. ABC Ltd. wishes to raise additional finance of ₹ 20 lakhs for meeting its investment plans. The company has ₹ 4,00,000 in the form of retained earnings available for investment purpose. The following are the further details:

(h) Debt equity ratio 25 : 75

(i) Cost of debt at the rate of 10% before tax upto ₹ 2,00,000 and beyond that 13% before tax.

(j) Earning per share ₹ 12

(k) Dividend payout 50% of earnings

(l) Expected growth rate in dividend 10%

(m) Current market price per share, ₹ 60.

(n) Tax rate 30% and shareholders' personal tax rate is 20%

Required

(i) Calculate the post tax average cost of additional debt.

(ii) Calculate of cost of retained earnings & cost of equity

(iii) Calculate overall WACC after tax of additional finance. (CA, 2008)

Answer : (i) 8.26% (ii) Cost of retained earnings is equal to cost of equity i.e. 21% (iii) 17.815%

4. AY Ltd.'s balance sheet reveals following figures:

Equity share capital of ₹ 10 each	₹ 5,00,000
8% Preference shares	7,00,000
9% Debentures	10,00,000
	22,00,000

CMP of equity shares is ₹ 18. Company will pay dividend of ₹ 3 and growth rate is 10% per annum.

Required:

(i) WACC of current capital structure.

(ii) WACC If company wants to raise an additional ₹ 15,00,000 debt by issuing 8% debentures. After this issue the dividend will increase to ₹ 5 and growth rate will 12% per annum & market price will be ₹ 15. Assume tax rate is 50%.

Answer (i) 10.64% (ii) 10.4%

5. Moonlight Ltd.'s cost of debt is 10%, current debt equity ratio is 0.7:1, return on Govt. securities is 7.5%, premium for risk is 5% WACC is 9%. Calculate Moonlight Ltd.'s non-diversifiable risk. Ignore taxation.

6. A firm has a bond outstanding ₹ 3,00,00,000. The bond has 12 years remaining until maturity, has a 12.5% coupon and is callable at ₹ 1,050 per bond, it had flotation

cost of ₹ 4,20,000 which are being amortized at ₹ 30,000 annually. The flotation cost for a new issue will be ₹ 9,00,000 and the current interest rate will be 10%. The after tax cost of debt is 6%. Should the firm refund the outstanding debt? Show detailed workings. Consider corporate income tax rate at 50%. (CA 2010)

Answer : The firm should refund the outstanding debt.

7. XYZ Ltd. has the following book value capital structure :

Equity Share Capital (₹ 10 each fully paid up)	15,00,00,000
11% Preference Share Capital (₹ 100 each fully paid up)	1,00,00,000
Retained Earnings	20,00,00,000
13.5% Debentures (₹ 100 each)	10,00,00,000
15% Term Loan	

The next expected dividend on equity shares per share is ₹ 3.60. The growth rate is 7% & CMP is ₹ 40. Preference shares are redeemable after 10 years & CMP is ₹ 75. Debentures redeemable after 6 years, are selling at ₹ 80 per debentures. Income tax rate is 40%.

(i) Calculate WACC using book value proportion & market value proportion.

(ii) Calculate WMCC if it raises ₹ 10,00,00,000 next year, given the following information:

(a) The amount will be raised by equity and debt in equal proportion,

(b) The company expects to retain ₹ 1,50,00,000 earnings next year.

(c) The additional issue of equity shares will result in the net price per share being fixed at ₹ 32.

(d) The debt capital raised by way of term loans will cost 15% for the first ₹ 2,50,00,000 & 16% for the next ₹ 2,50,00,000. (CA 2000)

Answer : (ii) (b) 12.5% (c) 13.625% (d) 13.925%

8. Peacock Ltd. expecting its growth rate of 10% per annum in next two years. The growth rate is likely to be 9% and after that 7% per annum. If the last dividend paid was ₹ 2 per share & the required rate of return is 18%. Calculate the current value of equity shares.

9. A company issues ₹ 8,00,000, 15% debentures of ₹ 100 each. The debentures are redeemable eight years.

Calculate the cost of debt in following situations :

(a) issued at 8% discount

(b) issued at par

(c) issued at 5% premium.

(d) issued at 10% premium & flotation cost 4%.

Review Questions

Q1. "Debt is the cheapest source of finance" Discuss. **(UPTU 2009)**

Q2. What is cost of capital? Explain its role in financial decision-making. **(UPTU 2005, 2010)**

Q3. What is the significance of determining the overall cost of capital? **(UPTU 2006)**

Q4. Explain the problems faced for determining the cost of capital? **(UPTU 2006)**

Q5. What is the meaning of significance of cost of capital & what are the factors affecting cost of capital.

Q6. What is the difference between cost of redeemable and perpetual debentures? Explain with the help an example.

Q7. How the cost of debt is measured? **(UPTU 2005, DU 2009)**

Q8. What is weighted average cost of capital? Is there any difference between weighted average cost of capital and weighted marginal cost of capital?

Q9. Equity shares also include costs. Explain this sentence. What are various models of calculating cost of equity shares?

Q10. Explain the method of calculating cost of preference shares. How it is different from cost of equity shares.

Q11. Explain the concept of cost of retained earnings and explain how its calculated. **(UPTU 2005)**

Q12. Calculate the cost of issued capital in each of the following cases **(DU)**

(i) A company issues 10% debentures of Rs 10,00,000 (a) at par (b) at 10% discount (c) at 20% premium assuming tax rate to be 28%.

(ii) A company has 11% debentures of Rs. 5,00,000 standing in its balance sheet as an 31-3-2002 maturing after 5 yrs. Assume the same debentures could be issue now only at a discount of the same debentures could be issue now only at a discount of 20%.

Case Study 1*

To Use or Not to Use-That is the question

That evening Prabodh K Agashe could not join his family for dinner. He had a crucial meeting with his VP finance Sekhar, which went on and on. Being a CEO has its own costs, Prabodh wondered. The meeting that was keeping these gentlemen in their offices was to decide the fate of the new investment proposal that Prabodh and his team had been working upon for last few weeks. This project could prove to be a very profitable one. And this was the first major investment decision Prabodh was going to take.

---

* Published in "Cases in Management", MJP Publishers, Chennai. Reprinted with permission.

His company, Tristar Ltd was a professionally managed company having interests in areas of pigments, dyes and colors. The company was operating in 6 countries with 8 manufacturing facilities and a marketing presence in around 10 countries. Its International operations were generating around 43% of its revenues.

The company which started off in 1985 with a modest turnover of ₹ 1.27 lakhs had crossed several milestones over the years. The total revenues of the company for the year ended 2004-05 were ₹ 461 crores and it earned a net profit of ₹ 48 crores.The operations of the company were divided into three major groups.

Pigments Group: This group mainly operated in India, Srilanka, and Indonesia. It had manufacturing facilities in all the three countries. This group also produced generic products to cater to demands of institutional buyers. Its main clientele included textile manufacturers, paint manufacturers and the food industry.

Dyes Group: Operating mainly from India this group has been facing rough weather of late. This group has its major manufacturing facilities in India and it exports products to its subsidiaries in Bahrain, Malaysia and Srilanka.This marketing arrangement has worked well for the company over the years.

Colors Division: Producing colors for domestic uses, this group had manufacturing facilities in all the countries where Tristar had a presence. Contributing maximum to the total revenues of the company, this division produced liquid and cement based colors for use in buildings and homes.

The company was planning to set up a new industrial pigments division in Bangladesh. The project involved substantial outlay of funds and Mr. Sekhar A., the finance head of the company, was doing the number crunching. Prabodh had recently taken charge of the company and came from an engineering background. He had recently attended an MDP on finance for non-finance executives and was increasingly able to make sense of reports from Sekhar's desk.

That evening the duo was supposed to make their minds up on the Bangladesh project. But somehow Prabodh was not entirely convinced about the discount rate Sekhar was using for financial evaluation of the project. The fourth floor corner office of PSA Towers was filled with animated discussion between them.

Prabodh: But why can't you use the discount rate that we used for our Gurgaon project only 15 days back. Why do you need to calculate a special rate for Bangla Project?

Sekhar: We possibly can not do it. Bangla project is riskier than the Gurgaon one and this has got to be reflected in our discount rate.

Prabodh: Ok Ok....but what I understand is that our company falls into a particular risk category and anything belonging to our investment portfolio will carry the same risk as the company's. Why not use what you finance types call weighted average cost of capital of Tristar Ltd?

Sekhar: Using Tristar's overall cost of capital as the acceptance criterion for Bangla project is not advisable. We could do that if the Bangla project was being financed by a corpus looking exactly the same as Tristar's capital structure. Viewed in isolation, the Bangla project has a very different risk profile than Tristar's.

Prabodh: It would save you lot of bother if you used Tristar's and I don't see any problems there.

Sekhar: I agree that using Tristar's cost of capital as the discount rate will be very simple and convenient. However, it might result into some very good projects getting screened out and the bad one's qualifying.

Prabodh: That is the problem with you finance types…the more you speak, the less I understand.Ok lets have another cup of coffee and you give me a lowdown on this cost of capital thing.

Sekhar: It's like this…The overall cost of capital of Tristar is a proportionate average of the costs of the various components of the firm's financing. The most difficult to measure is the cost of equity capital.

Prabodh: Yeah…you remind me of my MDP.I guess there are these four models called Dividend Discount Model Approach, Capital Asset Pricing Model Approach and Pre-Tax cost of Debt plus Risk Premium Approach.

Sekhar: I am impressed……..here we can use the dividend discount model and Capital asset pricing model approach.

Prabodh: Wait a minute...For dividend discount model you need to calculate the growth rate of our company…isn't it?

Sekhar: We do….and that could be done using internal growth model, arithmetic average or geometric growth models.

Prabodh: Ok….then you will find the averages of these and arrive at the growth rate. And I am sure you are aware of the limitations of using these models.

Sekhar: You can count on me….after this we can calculate the cost of equity using dividend growth model…

Prabodh: That is fine…what about CAPM…I suppose you require risk free rate of return and betas for that….

Sekhar: Yeah….and we can choose amongst a set of government securities for risk free rate of return…since our project is a long-term one, I propose to take-up rate of return of long dated securities. Beta part is easy…after all we have sensex data available and we can do some number crunching with our stock's rate of return.

Prabodh: And I suppose then you propose to burp out the cost of our debt capital. But what do you do about our current liabilities and sundry creditors?. Do you propose to impute some cost to them also?

Sekhar: I assume that providers of such capital are smart enough. They already build the cost of funds into the pricing of their products.

Prabodh: That was smart…..and what is the cost of long term and short-term debt you propose to take?

Sekhar: My reports tell me I could take up short-term debt at around 14 pc and long term debt at around 12 pc. With this after-tax cost of debt can be found out.

Prabodh: Right…we are only one step short of calculating our overall cost of capital and we probably can use both market value weights and book value weights. I leave the choice to your discretion. But coming back to the Bangla Project, why do you have reservations against using this cost for evaluating it?

Sekhar: Well I have precisely two reasons for this-one; the new project is into a new line of activity and does not have the same risk as our firm has on average. Two, the new project is going to alter the capital structure of our firm and we are in for an increased leverage after this project.

Prabodh: Are you scaring me Sekhar….I am aware that Bangla is new but it is promising also. Anyway what do you propose then….what do you think should be the discount rate for evaluating Bangla?

Sekhar: See, this project is a kind of expansion-cum-diversification project, and such projects offer medium to high risk. On overall basis we can call it a medium risk project. That riskiness should be reflected in the discount rate we are using. And for that I propose that we adjust the overall cost of capital of Tristar Ltd upwards. I propose a risk-premium be added to the company's overall cost of capital. This premium can be decided by us and I hope we can do a good job at that.

Prabodh: Our cost of capital is already high…I don't want to lose Bangla simply because your numbers can't justify it. Let me think it over….ok we meet tomorrow again.

Exhibit 1

Capital Structure of TriStar Ltd

(₹ Crore)

Sources of Capital	**Book Value**	**Market Value**
Short-term Debt	547.23	547.23
Long-term Debt	246.77	246.77
Total Debt	794.00	794.00
Net Worth	1,732.42	3,844.49
Total	**2,526.42**	**4,638.49**

Exhibit 2

10 year financial data of Tristar Ltd.

Year	EPS	DPS	Average Share Price	Book Value Per Share	Dividend Payout Ratio	Dividen d Yield	Earnings Yield	Return on Equity
2001-02	6.1	2	177	48.55	0.234	0.0,110	0.034	0.13
2002-03	5.4	2	128	49.32	0.234	0.0,160	0.042	0.11
2003-04	6.2	2	100	52.22 6	0.234	0.0,200	0.062	0.12
2004-05	4.2	3	101	6.30	0.351	0.0,300	0.042	0.06
2005-06	10.5	3	198	49.56	0.351	0.0,150	0.053	0.21
2006-07	5.5	3	254	54.55	0.351	0.0,120	0.022	0.10
2007-08	6.6	3	123	78.22	0.316	0.0,240	0.054	0.08
2008-09	4.8	3.5	260	54.33	0.368	0.0,130	0.018	0.09
2009-10	12	4	204	55.21	0.421	0.0,200	0.059	0.22
2010-11	4.3	4	202	62.32	0.421	0.0,200	0.021	0.07

Exhibit 3

Betas for the companies similar to Tristar Ltd.

1	SKF Paints and Pigments Ltd	0.30
2	Pigments India Ltd	0.25
3	Rainbow Paints Ltd	0.80
4	Color-Chem Indusries Ltd	0.42
5	Streaks Industries Ltd	0.21

Answer the following questions :(See Exhibits Also)

1. What are different components of cost of capital of a firm? How the average cost of capital of a firm is computed?
2. What is the difference between a firm's overall cost of capital and the discount rate it should use for evaluating new projects?

3. Is Prabodh right when he contends that firm's overall cost of capital can be used as a proxy for the discount rate for evaluating Bangla project? Comment on Sekhar's objection to it?
4. Calculate the cost of capital of Tristar Ltd. Make suitable assumptions.
5. What discount rate should Tristar use for evaluating Bangla Project? Why?
6. In the last paragraph above; comment on Prabodh saying "I don't want to lose Bangla simply because your numbers can't justify it".

Case Study 2 (DU 2007)

Determine the weighted average cost of capital using book value weights based on the following data:

Book value structure

14% Debentures (₹ 100 per debenture)	₹ 8,00,000
15% Preference shares (₹ 100 per share)	₹ 2,00,000
Equity shares (₹ 10 per share)	₹10,00,000
	₹ 20,00,000

Recent market price of all these securities are:

Debentures : ₹ 110 per debenture; Preference shares: ₹ 120 per share; Equity shares : ₹ 22. per share.

Dividend expected on equity shares at the end of the year is ₹ 2 per share; anticipated growth rate in dividends is 7%. The company pays all its earnings in the form of dividends. Corporate tax rate is 40%.

Case Study 3 (DU 2008)

The following is the capital structure of ABC Ltd.	₹
Equity Share Capital (Face Value ₹ 10 each)	5,00,000
12% Preference Shares Capital (Face Value ₹ 100)	4,00,000
8% Debentures (Face Value ₹100)	6,00,000
	15,00,000

Equity shares are currently selling at ₹ 15 each. The company paid a dividend of ₹2 per share for the last year. The dividends are expected to increase at 5% p.a. The preference shares and debentures are being traded at 90% and 80%. Tax rate applicable to company is 40%.

Find out the Weighted Average Cost of Capital of the firm using:

(i) Book value weights, and

(ii) Market value weights.

State under what situation the WACC calculated on BV and MV bases would be same.

References

1. Brealey, Richard A & Myres, Stewart C. (2007), Tata McGraw Hill, New Delhi
2. ICAI study Material on Financial Management, The Institute of Chartered Accountants of India, New Delhi.
3. Khan, M Y & Jain (2007) P K, Financial Management, Tata McGraw Hill, New Delhi
4. Pandey, I M (2009). Financial Management, Vikas Publishing House, New Delhi
5. Van Horne, James C. (2007), Pearson Prentice Hall, New Delhi
6. Work book on "Financial Management for Managers": The Institute of Chartered Financial Analysts of India, Hyderabad.

Unit-4

Dividend Decision

CHAPTER 10 The Dividend Decision

Learning Objectives:

By the end of this chapter and having completed the essential reading and activities, you should be able to:

- Understand the Concept of Dividend & Retained Earnings
- Have an understanding of various approaches of dividend decision
- Debate whether dividend is relevant or irrelevant
- Understand the factors affecting dividend decision
- Explain the tradeoff between corporate dividend policy and market price of the shares
- Understand the various alternative forms of dividend

To start with...

Vasko Ltd.'s shares are listed in Bombay Stock Exchange. The daily trading volume of company's share is not satisfactory. The share price of the company varies only upto 0.5% of the issue price. It indicates that the share is not attracting a lot of investor interest.

Vasko Ltd. is manufacturer of wind mill converters. Due to some internal problem company could not utilize its 100% capacity. Now company has got a huge order from a multinational company for supply of 10000 wind mill converter in next 2 years. To meet the above order company has to increase its capacity which will require a capital expenditure of ` 100 crores.

The company is willing to arrange the required fund by issue of new equity shares. Due to previous response of investors, company is planning to declare dividend before new issue so that new issue may be fully subscribed.

Board of directors entrusted this task to company's CFO Mr. Shoeb to present a report on how much dividend to declare, its impact on value of the company, factors to be considered while its declaration and any other alternative to cash dividend available to the company.

Declaration of dividend is an inescapable decision for every public limited company. In case the company opts for declaring the dividend, it is a tricky decision to figure out the amount of dividend.

In this chapter, we will discuss concept of dividend, various dividend model, dividend policy & factors affecting dividend.

10.0 Introduction

As and when we hear the term "dividend" the first thing which strikes our mind is that it relates to a company. To be precise, a public limited company. Now we all know that there are mainly three types of business ownership structures. First is proprietorship, second is partnership firm and the third is company. In all these cases, business owner gets its share of profit from its business.

In the first case, the proprietor gets 100% of profit because he is the sole (only) owner of its business. In second case of partnership firms, profit is shared between all the partners. Partners get profit in a certain percentage as defined in partnership deed (agreement). In the third case of a company, profit is shared between all the shareholders. Shareholders get their share of profit from the company. This share of profits received by the shareholders is called dividend. In all the three cases the one thing is common i.e. share of profit.

Therefore, we can conclude that profit, which a company distributes to its shareholders, is called dividend.

As per the Companies Act, 1956, it is not obligatory for the company to declare dividends. In other words, companies may or may not declare dividends. Dividends are share in the profits of the company which a company distributes to its shareholders. Why? It is because shareholders are the owners of the company. Dividends can be distributed out of present or past profits. It is an inescapable decision for a company.

Companies face two decisions regarding dividends. First is whether to pay or not to pay. Second decision is how much to pay or how much to retain in business. The undistributed profit of the company is called retained earnings. Retained earnings play very important role in financing decision because retained earnings are also a source of financing. Payment of dividends to shareholders is also very important because every shareholder invests his money in expectation of returns from the company.

Managerial Tool Kit-1

Dividends and The Companies Act, 1956

- Payment of dividend is not mandatory for companies. The companies may or may not declare dividends.
- Dividends can be paid only out of profit. This profit may be current year's profit after providing depreciation or undistributed previous year's after providing depreciation.
- Dividends can be paid out of reserves. These reserves must be free reserves and not capital reserves. The free reserves are reserves created out of profits and not those that are created for any specific purpose.
- In case companies are going to declare dividend over 10%, companies are required to transfer some percentage of profit to "general reserve" before declaring dividend.
- Interim dividend is the dividend, which is paid during the year. It is paid usually in the middle of the year. Board of directors can declare interim dividend.
- Final dividend is for the whole year & it is declared in annual general meeting
- Dividend can be paid only by cash, cheque or by dividend warrant.
- After declaration of dividend, whether interim or final, the companies are required to transfer the amount of dividend to a separate bank account. This transfer must be in 5 working days. This bank account can be used only for payment of dividend. After transfer the dividend must be paid to the shareholders within 30 days.
- In case dividend in not claimed by shareholders within 30 days of declaration, companies are required to transfer unclaimed dividend to a separate account called Unclaimed Dividend Account of ......Company Limited/Company (Private) limited. In case dividend is not claimed within seven years from the date of dividend becoming due, every company is required to transfer the unclaimed amount to Government in Investor Education and Protection Fund along with interest.

Managerial Tool Kit -2

Dividends and The Income Tax Act, 1961

- As per Income Tax Act, 1961 dividend whether interim or final paid by the company is tax free in the hands of shareholders.
- Every company-declaring dividend is required to pay Dividend Distribution Tax. This tax is paid @ 16.995% including surcharge, education cess & higher education cess. The dividend distribution tax is calculated on the quantum of dividend. This tax must be deposited with in 14 days from the date of declaration or payment of dividend, whichever is earlier.

Managerial Tool Kit-3

Dividends-Practical Issues

- Dividend declaration date is the date on which dividend is declared by the board of directors.
- Record date is the date on which share transfer book is closed for determining the investor who will receive the declared dividend.
- Ex-dividend date is the date from which investor can buy shares ex-dividend. After buying ex-dividend shares, the investor get himself registered in shares transfer book before record date for being eligible to receive dividend.
- Payment date is the date on which dividend warrants are dispatched to the shareholders.
- Dividend Rate is the percentage of dividend to the Face Value.

  Dividend Rate = (Dividend Per Share/Face Value of share) X 100
- Dividend Yield is the percentage of dividend to the Market Value

  Dividend Yield = (Dividend Per Share/Market Value of share)X 100
- Dividend Payout or Dividend Payout ratio is the percentage of dividend to the Earning per Share. It is usually represented by "1-b" (1 – retention ratio).

  Dividend Payout Ratio (1-b) = (Dividend Per Share/Earning Per Share) X 100
- Retention Ratio is the ratio of (undistributed profits per share/Earnings Per share) x 100. It can also be calculated as b (1- dividend payout ratio)

10.1 Dividend Models

There are a number of theories on dividends. These theories are also known as dividend models. Let us first get some familiarity with these models. This will answer "what" and "why" of these models.

First question that arises is whether these theories tell us whether to pay dividend or not? The answer is "No". All the models only describe the relationship between the dividend policy adopted by the company and market price of the shares.

There are two approaches to dividend models. First is called "relevance approach" and second is called "irrelevance approach".

Relevance approach says that dividend policy does affect market price of shares. Irrelevance approach says that dividend policy does not affect market price of the shares.

Now we will discuss various models under these two approaches.

10.1.1 Walter's Model (Relevance Approach)

According to James E Walter, dividend policy of a company affects value of the company (Market price of shares). In other words, there exists a relationship between dividend policy and value of the firm. Walter's model works on the following assumptions:

1. The firm distributes all of its earnings among shareholders (100% dividend) or does not distribute it at all (0% dividend).
2. Firm is an all equity firm. There is no debt financing.

3. Firm uses only retained earnings to finance its investments.
4. Earnings and dividends remain constant.
5. Firm has an infinite life.
6. Cost of capital and rate of return on investments remain constant.
7. $$P_0 = \frac{D}{k_e} + \frac{\frac{r}{k_e}(E-D)}{k_e}$$

Where P_0 = **Current Market Price,**

D = Dividend per Share,

E = Earnings per Share,

r = Rate of Return,

k_e = **Cost of Equity.**

As per Walter's Model market price of a share is the sum of present value of all future dividend and present value of capital gain on this share. D is constant dividend for perpetuity and $\frac{D}{k_e}$ is present value of all future dividends. The firm is retaining an amount equal to (E – D) for perpetuity. The firm invests it every year at rate of return r. Therefore, the present value of perpetual return earned is $\frac{r(E-D)}{k_e}$. Now this present value is also perpetual in nature, therefore present value of this perpetual return is $\frac{\frac{r}{k_e}(E-D)}{k_e}$.

The Walter's Model is an "all or nothing approach". Three types of firms adopt this kind of approach. First is Growth Firm. For a growth firm, the rate of return is more than cost of equity. Hence, this type of firm will not declare any dividend and reinvest all of its earnings at a rate of return "r". Second is Declining Firm. For such firms, the cost of equity is more than rate of return. Hence, this type of firm will distribute all of its earnings among its shareholders. Third is Normal Firm. In this type, cost of capital is equal to rate of return and this type of firm is indifferent between dividend distribution and retention. It may retain all of its earnings or alternatively, distribute these entire earnings among shareholders.

Example 1

The earnings per share of Mohit Surfactants Ltd. is ₹ 10 and cost of equity is 10%. The company is evaluating dividend payout ratio and is considering there options: (a) 50% (b) 25% (c) 100%. Compute the share price as per Walter's model. Company can earn a return of (a) 15% (b) 10% (c) 6% on its retaining earnings for each of the three alternative payout choices.

Solution

Case 1: r = 15%, k_e = 10%

Pay out ratio Price

(a) 50%

DPS = 10 * 50% = 5 , Price = $\frac{5}{1} + \frac{\left(\frac{.15}{.1}\right)(10-5)}{.1} + \frac{\left(\frac{.15}{.1}\right)(10-5)}{.1}$

125.00

(b) 25%

DPS = 10 * 25% =2.5 Price= $\frac{2.5}{1} + \frac{(.15)(10-25)}{.1}$

137.50

(c) 100%

DPS = 10 *100% = 10 Price = $\frac{10}{1} + \frac{\left(\frac{.15}{.1}\right)(10-10)}{.1}$ 100.00

Conclusion

Market price is highest when dividend is lowest because r > k_e

Case 2: r = 10%, k_e = 10%

Pay out ratio	*Price*

(a) 50%

DPS = 10 * 50% = 5 $\frac{5}{.1} + \frac{\left(\frac{.10}{.1}\right)(10-5)}{.1}$ 100

(b) 25%

DPS = 10 * 25% =2. 5 $\quad \dfrac{2.5}{1} + \dfrac{\left(\dfrac{.10}{1}\right)(10-2.5)}{.1} \quad + \quad 100$

(c) 100%

DPS = 10 *100% = 10 $\quad \dfrac{.10}{.1} + \dfrac{\left(\dfrac{.10}{.1}\right)(10-10)}{.1} \quad 100$

Conclusion

Market price is constant irrespective of dividends since $r = k_e$

Case 3: r = 6%, k_e = 10%

Pay out ratio	***Price***
(a) 50%	

DPS = 10 * 50% = 5 $\quad \dfrac{5}{1} + \dfrac{\left(\dfrac{.15}{.1}\right)(10-5)}{.1} \quad 80$

(b) 25%

DPS = 10 * 25% =2. 5 $\quad \dfrac{2.5}{.1} + \dfrac{\left(\dfrac{.06}{.1}\right)(10-2.5)}{.1} \quad 70$

(c) 100%

DPS = 10 *100% = 10 $\quad \dfrac{10}{.1} + \dfrac{\left(\dfrac{.06}{.1}\right)(10-10)}{.1} \quad + \quad 100$

Conclusion

Market price is highest when dividend payout is highest because $r < k_e$

From the above example, we can conclude that in case of growth firm, when payout ratio is minimum value of the firm is maximum. In case of normal firm, payout ratio does not affect value of the firm. In case of declining firm, when payout ratio is maximum value of the firm is maximum.

10.1.2 Gordon's Model (Relevance Approach)

According to Myron Gordon, the dividend policy of the firm affects the value of the firm. Gordon's model works on the following assumptions:

1. The firm either distributes 100% of its earnings among shareholders or retains internally.
2. Firm is an all equity firm. There is no debt financing i.e it has no debt.
3. Firm uses only retained earnings to finance its investments i.e. no external financing available.
4. Earnings and dividends remain constant.
5. Firm has an infinite life.
6. Cost of capital and rate of return on investments remain constant.
7. There are no taxes.
8. Firm's retention ratio is constant.
9. Cost of equity is greater than firm's growth rate where growth rate = retention ratio x return on equity i.e. **g = b x r.**

$$P_0 = \frac{D_1}{k_e - g}$$

Where P_o = Current Market Price, D_1 = Dividend per Share of next year, k_e = Cost of Equity, g = Growth rate in dividend.

Like Walter's model, Gordon also suggests that there is a relationship between dividend policy of the firm and value of the firm. According to Gordon, market price of the share is present value of infinite stream of all future dividends. The all future dividends are capitalized by cost of equity as reduced by growth rate. This model is also called **Dividend Capitalization Model.** This model also works on all or nothing approach i.e. either firm distributes all its earnings as dividend or retains all.

Example 2

The earnings per share of Mohit Surfactants Ltd. is ₹ 10 and cost of equity is 10%. The company is evaluating dividend payout ratio and is considering a 50% payout. Compute the share price as per Gordon's model. Company can earn a return of 15%.

Solution

r = 15%, k_e = 10%

Pay out ratio		***Price***
50%		
DPS = 10 * 50% = 5	$\frac{5}{.1-.5*.15}$	200

10.1.3 Traditional Model (Relevance Approach)

Graham & Dodd gave this model. According to them, investors prefer current dividend more than retained earnings or capital gains. We can understand this more clearly by an example. Suppose two companies A Ltd. & B Ltd. are similar in all respects except payment of dividend. A Ltd.'s payout ratio is less than B Ltd.'s payout ratio. B Ltd.'s shares are traded at much higher price than of A Ltd.. The reason behind B Ltd.'s higher price is payment of higher dividend. Investors prefer current dividend and because of their preference for current dividend, they show their interest in B Ltd.'s share.

Therefore, this model is an example of the proverb ***"A bird in hand is worth more than two in the bush."*** For investors current dividend is like a bird in hand and capital gain is like two in bush. This conclusion is based on the assumption that investors always prefer current dividend.

Investors discount capital gains i.e. distant dividend at much higher rate than discount rate of current dividend because level of certainty attached to the current dividend is more than distant dividend.

$$P = m \times \left(D + \frac{E}{3} \right)$$

P = market price of the share, m = a multiplier, D = dividend per share, E = earnings per share

In this model weight given to the dividend is equal to the four times of weight given to the earnings. This can be understood by replacing E by D + R, where D is dividend per share and R is retained earnings per share.

$$P = m x \left(D + \frac{D+R}{(3)} \right)$$

$$P = m \times \left(\frac{3D + D + R}{3} \right)$$

$$P = m \times \left(\frac{4D + R}{3} \right)$$

In this model, the weights provided by Graham & Doss are based on their subjective judgment. These weights are not based on any empirical analysis.

10.1.4 Radical Approach (Relevance Approach)

Radical approach is based on tax rates. According to this approach, dividend and capital gains are taxed at different rates. In case dividend tax is more than tax on capital gains,those companies' shares will perform better which provide capital gains because shareholders will pay less tax on capital gains . In case dividend tax is less than tax on capital gains then those companies' shares will perform better which provide dividends because shareholders get less return in the form of capital gain and less capital gains means less tax liability.

10.1.5 Modigliani and Miller Model (Irrelevance Approach)

This model comes in the category of irrelevance theories. These theories argue that declaration of dividend does not affect the market value. In other words, there is no relationship between declaration of dividend and market value of a firm.

Modigliani and Miller gave this model. They argue that dividend decision i.e. declaration of dividend by a firm, does not affect its value. Modigliani and Miller argued that value of a firm depends on its earnings. It is irrelevant from the firm's value point of view whether and how profits are bifurcated between dividend and retained earnings. This model works upon following assumptions:

1. Capital markets are perfect. It means investors behave rationally, information is freely available, large number of buyers and sellers are present and single investor's act cannot alter market price. In addition, no transaction and floatation cost exist.
2. There is no tax and if any tax exists then rate of that tax is same for both dividend and capital gain.
3. The firm has fixed investment policy.
4. Investors can predict future market price and future dividend and there is only one discount rate for whole period.
5. Investment and dividend both are independent decisions.

A firm working in perfect capital market may face the following three situations regarding payment of dividends:

1. **Firm has sufficient cash to pay dividend.** In this situation shareholders get dividend in the form of cash. When the firm pays cash dividend its assets reduces by the cash payment. The shareholders get cash but also lose their claim in the firm's assets by the cash received. The net gain or loss is nil and value of the firm remain unaffected.
2. **The firm does not have enough cash to pay dividend.** In this situation, there may be right issue to existing shareholders or new issue to new shareholders for getting cash to pay dividend to its existing shareholders. In case of right issue, the existing shareholders give cash and get back cash in the form of dividend. The firm's value will remain same because; on one hand existing shareholders receive shares against cash and on the other hand; they receive cash back in the form of dividends. In case of new issue is public issue, the new shareholders pay cash and get new shares of the firm and the existing shareholders transfer a portion of their claim to the new shareholders in the form of new shares in exchange of cash. There will not be any gain or loss & firm's value will remain same.

3. **In this third and last situation, the firm does not pay any dividend and shareholder creates its homemade dividend by selling its shares in the market for getting cash**. Now the shareholder will have reduced number of shares by number of shares sold. Shareholder has exchanged a part of his claim in the firm to a new shareholder for cash. The net effect i.e. value of the will remain same.

As per the MM's dividend hypothesis, it is not necessary for a shareholder to depend entirely on dividends for getting cash. He can get cash by selling shares in the market. In the absence of taxes, floatation cost and difficulties in selling, he can get cash from market without reducing his wealth, by creating homemade dividend.

To prove their model MM has given following derivation:

Suppose,

P_0 = current market price,

n = present number of shares,

m = additional shares issued at year end at year end market price to finance capital expenditure,

P_1 = year end market price,

I_1 = investment made at year end with money being raised at year end market price,

X_1 = earnings in year 1,

k_e = cost of equity.

$$P_0 = \frac{D_1 + P_1}{1 + k_e}$$

Now multiplying both sides by n, we get:

$$nP_0 = \frac{n(D_1 + P_1)}{1 + k_e}$$

Now, from numerator, adding and subtracting mP_1, we get

$$nP_0 = \frac{n(D_1 + P_1) + mP_1 - mP_2}{1 + k_e}$$

now mP_1 is the total issue in t_1 is equal to total invesstment in t_1 less retained earnings i.e.

$$mP_1 = I_1 - (X_1 - nD_1) = I_1 - X_1 + nD_1$$

Therefore

$$nP_0 = \frac{nD_1 + P_1(n+m) - \{I_1 - (X - nD_1)\}}{1 + k_e}$$

$$nP_0 = \frac{(n+m)P_1 - I_1 + X_1}{1+k_e}$$

Example 3

XYZ Ltd. has 100000 equity shares outstanding at the beginning of the year. The current market price is ₹ 100 and the directors have declared a dividend of ₹ 5 per share. Equity shareholders except a return of ₹ 15%.

1. Applying MM model calculate the market price of the share when the recommended dividend is (i) declared and (ii) not declared.
2. If the proposed investment is ₹ 100 lacs and the estimated future profits are ₹ 50 lacs compute how many new shares have to be issued in both the situation i.e. if dividends are declared and dividends are not declared.
3. Show that the declaration or non-declaration of dividend does not change the market price.

Solution

1. Dividend = ₹ 5

$P_1 = P_0(1+k_e) - D_0$

= 100(1 + .15) – 5

= 115 – 5 = **₹ 110**

Retained Earnings = PAT – dividend

$X_1 - nD_1$

= 50,00,000 – (1,00,000*5)

Retained Earnings = ₹ 45,00,000

Money required through issue of equity share capital

= $I_1(X_1 1 - nD_1)$

= 100L – 45L = 55L

New shares to be issued = 55,00,000/110 = 5,0000.

Value of the firm

$$nP_0 = \frac{(n+m)P_1 - I_1 + X_1}{1+k_e}$$

1,00,000*100 = (1,00,000+50,000)110-1,00,00,000+50,00,000/1.15

1,00,00,000 = 1,00,00,000.

2. Dividend = 0

$\mathbf{P_1 = P_0\,(1 + k_e) - D_0}$

= 100(1 + .15) – 0

= 115 – 0 = **₹ 115**

Retained Earnings = PAT – dividend

X_1 -nD_1

= 50,00,000 – (1,00,000*0)

Retained Earnings = ₹ 50,00,000

Money required through issue of equity share capital

= I_1($X_1$1-nD_1)

= 100L – 50L = 50L

New shares to be issued = 50,00,000/115 = 43479.

Value of the firm

$$nP_0 = \frac{(n+m)P_1 - I_1 + X_1}{1+k_e}$$

1,00,000*100 = (1,00,000+43,479)115-1,00,00,000+50,00,000/1.15

1,00,00,000 = 1,00,00,000.

Conclusion

Now we can see in both the above cases market value of the firm remain same. It proves that declaration and non-declaration of dividend affect market price of the shares but it does not affect value of the firm.

Criticism of MM approach: we have discussed the MM approach. It is clear from the above discussion that MM theory works on certain assumptions. However, these assumptions seem to be unrealistic as discussed below:

- The investor will be indifferent between dividend and capital gains if rate of tax is same for both the incomes. However, in reality dividend and capital gains are taxed at different rates.
- The assumption of no floatation costs seems to be unrealistic because in realty external financing involves some issue cost like brokerage, underwriter's fees, printing of offer document etc.
- If there is an uncertainty about the firm's future then shareholders may prefer current dividend. Shareholders may attach higher value to the firms that pay high dividend.
- According to MM theory, investment and financing decisions are independent. They argued that firm invests upto the point where rate of return is equal to the cost of capital. However, in reality, the position is different. For some firms it becomes very difficult to arrange finance for investment projects because of investment

unwillingness of investors. At this point of time, dividend policy becomes important. Firms, which find it difficult to arrange external funds, may opt for low payout.

- As per MM, firms can issue new equity shares at current market price. However, in reality, firms sell equity at a discount to attract investors to invest in the firm's security. In such a case, policy of dividend becomes important because due to low issue price of new equity, firms rely more on retained earnings.

10.1.6 Linter's Model

John Linter gave this theory in 1950. This model does not explain any relationship between dividend and value of the firm. This model explains the behavior of corporate dividends. It attempts to predict what will be the next year's dividend & factor on which dividends depend. The current year's dividend depends upon the current year's earnings and last year's dividend. Based on a number of surveys and many corporate interviews, Linter given the following conclusions:

(1) Firms set their long-term dividend payout ratio. This payout ratio varies from firm to firm. Some firms may set a high payout ratio and some set low payout ratio. However, in long run firms maintain their ratio.

(2) Managers are less concerned about quantum of dividend as compared to changes in dividend. For example, if last year's dividend was ₹ 15 and if current year's is also ₹ 15 then it is OK. However, if current year's dividend is ₹ 20 then managers will be highly concerned about this increase in dividend.

(3) Change in earnings is followed by change in dividend but managers set a smooth path for that change. Not every change in earnings has reflection in dividend. For example, if earnings increase by 25% then it is not necessary that dividend is also increased by 25%. Dividends may be increased only by 5%.

(4) The dividend is increased only up to that level which a firm can sustain in future also. Managers are reluctant to effect changes that may have to be reversed.

As per this model, future dividend may be calculated by:

$$D_1 = D_0 + \{(EPS * r) - D_0\} * c$$

Where,

D_1 = Dividend in year 1

D_0 = Dividend in current year

EPS = Earnings per share
r = target payout ratio
c = adjustment factor

10.2 Dividend Policy

Corporate dividend policy means that a policy that decides whether and how much dividend is to be paid. You can understand now that this policy can also be called the policy that decides how much profits should be ploughed (invested) back in the business.

It also means that if firm decides to pay dividend, then what will be the quantum of that dividend or what will be the payout ratio. A firm should keep in mind following points while deciding its dividend policy:

- The payment of dividend shows that how much management is confident about the future prospects of the firm.
- External financing is costlier than internal financing i.e. financing through retained earnings.
- Management's control over the firm may get diluted because of external financing.
- Objective of financial management is maximization of wealth of shareholders and every capital budgeting decision affects the value of the firm.

The followings are some approaches towards dividend policy of a firm:

(i) **Residual Approach:** under this approach, firms make first provision for their capital expenditures out of total earnings and after making provision residual earning is distributed as dividend. In this approach firms have two options. In **option one,** Capital expenditures are financed entirely by internal sources. After financing, residual earnings are distributed as dividend. This option affects the capital structure of the firm because capital expenditure is wholly financed by internal sources and not in the proportion of capital structure. In **option two,** capital structure of the firm remains unaffected because in this option capital expenditure is bifurcated into firm's debt equity ratio. The equity proportion of capital expenditure is financed by internal sources. Out of total earnings, firms make provision upto the equity proportion of capital expenditure and residual earnings are distributed as dividend.

(ii) **Constant Approach:** Under this approach, firms fix a dividend rate. Dividends are declared at this fix rate and this rate is applicable to each year. The level of earnings is not important under this approach. The firms may increase this rate of dividend. In case, if a firm wants to increase this rate then first it will ensure itself that this level of earnings will be maintained in future years also. Only after this it will increase its rate of dividend. In case the firm is not sure that increased earnings will be maintained in future year also, then firm may split dividend in two portions. First portion is regular dividend and second portion is special dividend. The motive behind this spit is to convey a message to the shareholders that this special dividend may not continue in next year. This special dividend is only because of current year's increased earnings.

(iii) **Constant Payout Ratio Approach:** Under this approach, firms fix a dividend payout ratio. In this approach payout ratio remains same for future years but quantum of dividend changes every year. The quantum of dividend depends upon the level of earnings i.e. the more the earnings; the more the dividends and the less the earnings; the less the dividends.

Considerations in dividend policy

The followings are some reasons for payment of dividends:

- **Clientele Effect:** If an investor invests in shares of a company, he has his own preferences in mind. Different investors may have different preferences. For example; some investors prefer cash dividend and some other investors prefer capital gains. Investors invest in companies as per their preferences. Companies with high payout ratio have those investors whose preference is cash dividend. Companies with low payout ratio have those investors whose preference is capital gains. This is called clientele effect. Due to this clientele effect, it will be difficult for a firm to change its dividend policy.
- **Signal Effect:** The payout of dividend give signal about the company. Management of a firm has better knowledge about the companies' future prospects than investors have. Investors get signal about the companies' future prospects based on dividend payout. High dividend payout means that company is in good condition and it is likely to maintain high dividend payout in future also. Low dividend payout gives negative signal about the company i.e. the future prospect about the company is not very good. This negative signal affects the stock price adversely.
- **Agency Costs:** The shareholders do not have access to all the information about the company. The management also does not share all information with the shareholders. Shareholders think that management does not always act with the objective of shareholder's wealth maximization. To keep an eye on the actions of management, shareholders may establish a mechanism and cost associated to this mechanism is called agency costs. Here the payment of dividend plays an important role. High and regular payment of dividend reduces agency costs.
- **Uncertainty:** When shareholders are uncertain, they prefer current dividend than capital gains. Due to their preference for current dividend, they discount capital gains at higher rate than discount rate for current dividend. In this situation, firms paying high dividend enjoy high value and firms paying low dividend bear low value.
- **Tax differentials:** Tax rates plays very important role in dividend policy. There are two type of taxes first is corporate taxes and second is personal taxes. In case personal tax is more than corporate tax then firms will keep low payout. In case personal tax is less than corporate tax then firms will keep high payout.
- **Homemade Dividend:** Prices of shares tend to fluctuate very sharply. In these fluctuating markets, investors expecting high or low payout will not sell or buy their shares respectively. In this fluctuating situation, investors' choices may be very different from each other. Investors preferring low dividend would go for low payout in place of buying new stocks in such a market. Investors preferring high dividend would go for high payout in place of selling their shares. This situation makes it difficult for an investor to create homemade dividend.
- **Behavioral Aspect:** If dividends and capital gains are same in all respect then which income, an individual will prefer? Individuals prefer dividend rather than selling

their shares to get capital gain. This is a behavioral aspect of individuals that they prefer current income in the form of dividend and still like to keep their investments intact. They do not want their capital to get reduced. This tendency of protecting capital encourages investors to prefer dividends.

10.3 Factors Affecting Dividend Division

The following factors affect dividend decision of a firm-

- **Liquidity:** Liquidity plays an important role in dividend decision. A company will have to pay dividend within 14 days from the date of declaration. A firm, having high liquidity despite low profitability, prefers high payout and a firm, having low liquidity, despite high profitability prefers low payout.
- **Requirement of Funds:** The firms preferring to finance its capital expenditure out of its internal resources it will go for low payout ratio.
- **Cost:** Financing from external equity is costlier than financing from retained earnings because fresh issues are made at a discount. This leads to under pricing of IPOs.
- **Control:** Financing from external equity causes loss in control except in case of right issue. This is so because in case of fresh issue, existing shareholders share their control with new shareholders, but in case of financing from internal sources shareholding is not affected.
- **Expectation:** Shareholders expectations also play a very important role in determining dividend payout ratio. In case shareholders show their interest in current dividend, the companies pay higher dividend. However, in case shareholders are more interested in capital gains, firm may declare lower payout.
- **Taxes:** Dividend from any domestic company is exempt in the hands of recipient. However, the company paying dividends has to pay a distribution tax on its distributed profit @ 16.995%. The long-term capital gain arising on transfer of these shares is also exempt in the hands of transferor.
- **Access to external financing:** If a firm has easily accessible external financing resources then that firm may declare higher payout. However, in case of a firm not having access to external financing, lower payout is declared. It is because these types of firms mainly depend upon their internal sources.
- **Inflation:** During the period of inflation, generally, companies declare lower payout or no dividend. It is because companies may find their depreciation provision not enough to replace its assets. The depreciation provisions are made based on original cost of assets.

10.4 Alternate Forms of Dividend

There are some other unconventional ways by which firms reward their shareholders:

10.4.1 Bonus Shares: Bonus shares are issued out of firm's reserves & surplus. In other words through bonus issue, firms capitalizes their reserves. ***Recently Reliance Industries Ltd. announced huge bonus of one share for every share held by its shareholders.*** After issue of bonus shares proportionate holding of a shareholder remains the same. However, EPS, market price and value per share declines. A firm can issue bonus shares only out of its reserves created from profits and share premium collected in cash only. There are certain regulations on issue of bonus shares. Like, a firm can issue bonus only if its article of association authorizes it to do so. In addition, bonus cannot be given to partly paid shares and it cannot be issue in lieu of dividend. There are certain benefits of bonus shares. For example, higher dividend income to the shareholders in future that is exempt in the hands of shareholders. After bonus issue, no. of shares outstanding in the market is increased in the market. This promotes more trading in the firm's shares.

Price after bonus issue = (No. of shares before bonus issue *current market price)/No. of shares after bonus issue.

10.4.2 Stock Split: Stock split means reduction in the par value of shares. For example, par value of a share is ₹ 100 and there is 4:1 split. In this case, the every shareholder will get four shares with a par value of ₹ 25 in lieu of every share with a par value of ₹ 100. In the share split, firm's reserves remain intact because there is no capitalization of reserves as in the case of bonus shares. The book value, EPS and market price reduces as in case of bonus issue due to increase in no. of shares. After splitting the shares the shareholder's fund remain same as before share split.

Price after stock split = (No. of shares before stock split *current market price)/No. of shares after stock split.

10.4.3 Reverse Split: It is the opposite of stock split. In stock split, par value is reduced but in case of reverse split, par value is merged. For example, if a company's share's par value is ₹ 10 each and there is 1: 4 reverse split. The par value of shares will increase to ₹ 40 per share because four shares with par value of ₹ 10 each will be merged into a single share with par value ₹ 40.

Price after reverses split = (No. of shares before reverses split *current market price)/No. of shares after reverses split.

10.4.4 Buy Back:- Buy back of share means purchasing of its own shares by the company from its shareholders. Buy back can be done by two methods. First is Tender method in which the company offers buy its shares back, directly from shareholders, at a specified price in a specified period, which is usually one month. Second method is open market purchase method in which the company buys back its shares from the secondary market. The buyback causes reduction in capital of the company and increase in EPS. Generally companies buyback its shares when a) it has surplus cash b) it wants to increase its market price and c) wants to maintain its capital structure in the current form. There are certain advantages like increase in future dividends and strong cash flow position in future.

Price after buy back = No. of shares before buy back *current market price/No. of shares after buy back.

Illustrative Solved Examples

1. **ABC Ltd. earns return on investment at the rate of 20%, earnings per share is ₹ 15, payout ratio is 50%, cost of equity is 12%. Compute its market price per share as per Walter's model and classify ABC Ltd.**

Solution: As per Walter's model $P_0 = \frac{D}{k_e} + \frac{\frac{r}{k_e}(E-D)}{k_e}$

D = 15 * 50% = 7.5, r = .2, k_e = .12, E = 15

$$P_0 = \frac{7.5}{.15-.05} = ₹\ 166.67$$

The price of ABC Ltd.'s share is ₹ 166.67. As per Walter's model ABC Ltd. belongs to growth firm because its rate of return is more than its cost of equity.

2. **XYZ Ltd. has a book value of ₹ 150. Its return on equity is 10%. It retains 50% of its earnings and opportunity cost of capital is 15%. Calculate XYZ Ltd.'s current share price.**

Solution: Earnings = 150*10% = ₹ 15

Dividends = 15*50% = ₹ 7.5

g = b * r i.e. 0.50 * 0.10 = 0.05 i.e. 5%

$$P_0 = \frac{D_1}{k_e - g}$$

$$P_0 = \frac{7.5}{.15-.05} = ₹\ 75$$

In the above example it is assumed that earnings and dividend will take place a year later. If above earnings are of today then year later dividend will be 15*1.05*50% = ₹ 7.875.

3. **Bhola Ltd. & Chola Ltd. are similar in all respect except in return to shareholders. Bhola Ltd.'s dividend policy is not to pay any dividend. It provides only capital appreciation at the of 20% per year. Chola Ltd. provides only dividend at the rate of 18% per year.**

Required

(a) **If both the shares are being traded at ₹ 125, dividend tax and capital gains tax is same i.e. 25%, compute after tax return from both the companies.**

(b) If dividend tax is 20% and capital gains tax is 30%, compute after tax return from both the companies.

Solution: (a) Bhola Ltd., price at the end of one year = 125 + 20% = 150

Gain = 150 – 125 = 25

Less Tax = 6.25

Net Gain = 18.75

Return = 18.75%

Chola Ltd., Dividend = 125 * 18% = 22.5

Less Tax = 5.625

Net Gain = 16.875

Return = 13.5%

(b)	Bhola Ltd.	Chola Ltd.
Market Price	125	125
Dividend	22.5	
Capital Gain	25	
Tax	7.5	4.5
Net Gain	17.5	18
Return	14%	14.4%

4. Angel Ltd.'s issued capital includes 50000 equity shares of ₹ 10 each. It has a credit balance in capital reserve is ₹ 25 lacs. If current market price is ₹ 50, show the effect of following three situations.

(1) 2 : 3 bonus issue

(2) 5 : 4 stock split

(3) 2 : 4 reverse split

Solution

(1) Company is issuing 3 shares for every 2 shares held.

No. of shares after issue of bonus shares = 50000 * 3/2 = 75000

Bonus shares = 75,000 – 50,000 = 25,000.

Capital Reserve to be capitalized = 25,000 * 10 = 2,50,000. ₹ 2,50,000 will be transferred from capital reserve to equity share capital & capital will increase to ₹ 7,50,000.

Price after bonus issue = No. of shares before bonus issue *current market price/No. of shares after bonus issue.

= 50,000*50/75,000 = ₹ 33.33

(2) Company is issuing 5 shares for every 4 shares held.

New par value of shares = 10*4/5 = ₹ 8

No. of shares after stock split = 50000*5/4 = 62500.

Price after stock split = No. of shares before stock split *current market price/No. of shares after stock split.

= 50000*50/62500 = ₹ 40.

In this case total capital will remain same except no. of shares which will increase to 62500 and par value which will reduce to ₹ 8 per shares.

(3) Company is issuing 2 shares for every 4 shares held

New par value of shares = 4*10/2 = ₹ 20

No. of shares after reverse split = 50,000*2/4 = 25,000.

Price after reverse split = No. of shares before reverse split *current market price/No. of shares after reverse split.

= 50,000*50/25,000 = 100.

In this case total capital will remain same except no. of shares which will reduce to 25,000 and par value which will increase to ₹ 20 per shares.

5. **Rajiv Corporation has EPS of ₹ 10, equity capitalization rate is 12%, rate of return is 15%. If payout ratio is 40% calculate market price of the share and optimum payout ratio as per Walter.**

Solution : $P_0 = \frac{D}{k_e} + \frac{\frac{r}{k_e}(E-D)}{k_e}$

D = 10 * 40% = 4, E = 10, k_e = 12%, r = 15%

$$\text{Price} = \frac{4}{.12} + \frac{\frac{.15}{.12}(10-4)}{.12} = 33.33 + 62.5 = ₹\,95.83$$

We can see that rate of return is more than cost of equity i.e. 15%>12%. It means Rajiv Corporation is a growth company & we have discussed that in case of growth company payout ratio should be nil

6. **Meenaxi Ltd. earned a profit of ₹ 500000 this year. It maintains its debt equity ratio at 2 : 1. Meenaxi Ltd. follows residual dividend policy and going to spend ₹ 450000 on a new project. Calculate amount of dividend if company does not want to maintain its debt equity ratio & it wants to maintain its debt equity ratio.**

Solution: In case Meenaxi Ltd. does not want to maintain its debt equity ration then dividend will be residue profit after meeting its capital expenditure i.e. ₹ 50,000 (₹ 5,00,000 – ₹ 4,50,000).

In case Meenaxi Ltd. wants to maintain its debt equity ratio, it will divide its capital expenditure in to the ratio of debt & equity i.e. ₹ 4,50,000*2/3 & ₹ 4,50,000/3

The proportion to be financed by debt is ₹ 3,00,000 & to be financed by equity is ₹ 1,50,000.

Amount of dividend = ₹ 500000 – 150000 = ₹ 3,50,000.

7. **(a) Atul has 5000 shares of A Ltd. A Ltd. just reduced dividend by 5 ₹ as compared to previous year's ₹ 15. Market price of A Ltd.'s shares is ₹ 500. What will Atul do if he does not want to reduce his inflows.**

(b) If in the above situation A Ltd. just increased dividend by ₹ 5 as compared to previous year's ₹ 15. What does Atul do if he does not want to spend extra inflows.

Solution :(a) Dividend = 5,000*(15 - 5) = ₹ 50,000

Reduced Dividend = 50,000 – (5,000*15) = 25,000.

Now Atul will sell some shares to maintain his inflows.

No. of shares to be sold = 25,000/500 = 50.

(b) Dividend = 5,000*(15 + 5) = ₹ 1,00,000

Increased Dividend = 1,00,000 – (5,000*15) = 25,000.

Now if Atul does not want to spend his extra inflows he will purchase shares from increased inflows.

No. of shares to be purchased = 25,000/500 = 50

8. On the basis of following information calculate dividend per share for next year.

Dividend per share for current year	**₹ 10**
Earnings for net year	**₹ 20**
Target payout ratio	**0 .8**
Adjustment rate	**0 .7**

Solution: $D_1 = D_0 + \{ (EPS * \text{Target Payout}) - D_0 \} * \text{Adjustment Factor}$

$$= 10 + \{(20*.8)-10\}*.7 = 10 + \{6\}*.7 = 14.2$$

The dividend for next year will be ₹ 14.2

Summary

- Companies face two decisions regarding dividends. First is whether to pay or not to pay. Second decision is how much to pay or how much to retain in business. The undistributed profit of the company is called retained earnings.
- There are various theories related to dividends called dividend theories. They are also known as dividend models. These models describe the relationship between the dividend policy adopted by the company and market price of the shares.
- There are two approaches to dividend models. First, is "relevance approach" and second "irrelevance approach". Relevance approach says that dividend policy does affect market price of shares. Irrelevance approach says that dividend policy does not affect market price of the shares.
- According to James E Walter, dividend policy of a company affects value of the company (Market price of shares). In other words, there exists a relationship between dividend policy and value of the firm. Walter's model is based on relevance approach. The Walter's Model is an "all or nothing approach".
- Another dividend model on relevance approach is given by Myron Gordon. This model states that the dividend policy of the firm affects the value of the firm. Like Walter's model, Gordon also suggests that there is a relationship between dividend policy of the firm and value of the firm. According to Gordon, market price of the share is present value of infinite stream of all future dividends. The all-future dividends are capitalized by cost of equity as reduced by growth rate. This model is also called **Dividend Capitalization Model.** This model also works on all or nothing approach i.e. either firm distributes all its earnings as dividend or retains all.
- Traditional approach given by Graham & Dodd is yet another dividend model. According to them, investors prefer current dividend more than retained earnings or capital gains. This model is an example of the proverb ***"A bird in hand is worth more than two in the bush."*** Investors discount capital gains i.e. distant dividend at much higher rate than discount rate of current dividend because level of certainty attached to the current dividend is more than distant dividend.
- Radical approach is based on tax rates. According to this approach, dividend and capital gains are taxed at different rates. In case dividend tax is more than tax on capital gains, those companies' shares will perform better which provide capital gains because shareholders will pay less tax on capital gains. In case dividend tax is less than tax on capital gains then those companies' shares will perform better which provide dividends because shareholders get less return in the form of capital gain and less capital gains means less tax liability.
- Modigliani and Miller gave a dividend model based on irrelevance approach. They argue that dividend decision i.e. declaration of dividend by a firm, does not affect its value. Modigliani and Miller argued that value of a firm depends on its earnings. It

is irrelevant from the firm's value point of view whether and how profits are bifurcated between dividend and retained earnings.

- As per the MM's dividend hypothesis, it is not necessary for a shareholder to depend entirely on dividends for getting cash. He can get cash by selling shares in the market. In the absence of taxes, floatation cost and difficulties in selling, he can get cash from market without reducing his wealth, by creating homemade dividend.
- John Linter gave another theory in 1950. This model does not explain any relationship between dividend and value of the firm. This model explains the behavior of corporate dividends. It attempts to predict what will be the next year's dividend & factors on which dividends depend. The current year's dividend depends upon the current year's earnings and last year's dividend.
- Corporate dividend policy means that a policy that decides whether and how much dividend is to be paid. It is also the policy that decides how much profits should be ploughed (invested) back in the business.
- There are many approaches to corporate dividend policy.
- In Residual Approach firms make first provision for their capital expenditures out of total earnings and after making provision residual earning is distributed as dividend. In another approach, called Constant Approach, firms fix a dividend rate. Dividends are declared at this fix rate and this rate is applicable to each year. The level of earnings is not important under this approach. The third approach is called Constant Payout Ratio Approach. Under this approach, firms fix a dividend payout ratio. In this approach payout ratio remains same for future years but quantum of dividend changes every year. The quantum of dividend depends upon the level of earnings i.e. the more the earnings; the more the dividends and the less the earnings; the less the dividends.
- There are many reasons why firms pay dividend. a) Clientele Effect: Investors invest in companies as per their preferences for cash or capital gain. Companies with high payout ratio have those investors whose preference is cash dividend. Companies with low payout ratio have those investors whose preference is capital gains. b) Signal Effect: The payout of dividend give signal about the company. Management of a firm has better knowledge about the companies' future prospects than investors have. Investors get signal about the companies' future prospects based on dividend payout. c) Agency Costs: To keep an eye on the actions of management, shareholders may establish a mechanism and cost associated to this mechanism is called agency costs. Here the payment of dividend plays an important role. High and regular payment of dividend reduces agency costs. D) Uncertainty: When shareholders are uncertain, they prefer current dividend than capital gains. Due to their preference for current dividend, they discount capital gains at higher rate than discount rate for current dividend. In this situation, firms paying high dividend

enjoy high value and firms paying low dividend bear low value. Some other reasons why companies pay dividend are tax differentials and homemade dividend.

- Amongst the factors that affect dividend decision of the firm are Liquidity, Requirement of Funds, Cost, Control, Expectation, Taxes, Access to external financing, Inflation
- **Some of the alternate forms of dividend are** Bonus shares, Stock split, Reverse Split, Buy back.

Test Your Understanding

State whether following statements are true or false

1. As per Walter declaration of dividend does not affect market price of the stocks.
2. Dividend payout is the percentage to the EPS.
3. Walter assumes that firms do not follow going concern approach.
4. Gordon assumes that all firms are levered.
5. Gordon says that market price depends upon the declaration of dividend.
6. Companies cannot buy their shares.
7. MM approach assume that situation of perfect capital market cannot be achieved.
8. In case of growth companies optimum pay out ration will be zero.
9. Companies are bound to declare dividend.
10. Interim dividends are declared during the year.
11. In stock split face value of shares are reduced.
12. Shareholders pay current market price for every bonus issued.
13. On declaration date dividend is announced.
14. As per MM approach value of the firm will remain same whether dividends are declared are not.
15. In case of normal companies, companies may or may not pay dividend.

Answer : 1. F, 2. T, 3. F, 4. F, 5. T, 6. F, 7. F, 8. T, 9. F, 10. T, 11. T, 12. F, 13. T, 14. T, 15. T

Multiple Choice Questions

Choose the correct alternative out of the given

1. Dividend yield is expressed as a percentage of

   a) market price b) issue price

   c) market price – dividend declared d) none of the above

2. The date on which register of member is closed for payment of dividend called

   a) Declaration date b) Payment date

c) Record date d) None of the above

3. Dividend per share = 3, Earning per share = 12, Payout ratio = ?

   a) 25% b) 40%

   c) 20% d) 60%

4. On payment date

   a) Dividend is declared b) Dividend is announced

   c) Board approves dividend d) Dividend is actually paid

5. The approach in which companies either distribute entire profits or distribute no profit, is called

   a) Professional approach b) Moderate approach

   c) Long term approach d) All or nothing approach

6. According to various dividend models companies should

   a) Pay no dividend b) Distribute all their earnings as dividend

   c) Not issue shares d) None of the above

7. ABC Ltd. retains 40% of its earnings, rate of return = 12%, growth rate = ?

   a) 8.4% b) 4.8%

   c) 3.33% d) Incomplete information

8. Bajrang Ltd.' s current year's dividend = 8, cost of equity = 10%, growth rate = 5%, share price of Bajrang Ltd. = ?

   a) 160 b) 190

   c) 120 d) 60

9. Corporate dividend tax is paid by

   a) Equity shareholders b) Preference shareholders

   c) Companies d) Govt. to companies

10. As per Walter's model, sum of pv of dividends and pv of capital gains is equal to

    a) Future earnings b) Value of share

    c) Current profit d) None of the above

11. As per MM approach value will be more, in case of payment of dividend, than in case of

    a) non payment of dividend

    b) payment of all earnings as dividend

    c) payment of 50% of earnings as dividend

d) value will be unaffected in either case.

12. When bonus shares are issued, companies capitalize its

a) reserves b) short term liabilities

c) long term liabilities d) none of the above

13. Pawan Putra Ltd. reduced its face value of shares, it is called

a) reduction in share capital b) enhancement in number of shares

c) stock split d) buy back

14. EPS = 10, DPS = 3, retention ratio = ?

a) 30% b) 50%

c) 65% d) 70%

15. Required rate of return = 15%, Earnings = 800000, No. of shares = 80000, growth rate = 7%, Market price = ?

a) 135 b) 125

c) 150 d) 133.33

16. Which of the following is a bonus share?

a) Issue of more shares to shareholders

b) Issue of bonds

c) Cash payment to shareholders

d) None of the above

Answers : 1. a, 2. c, 3. a, 4. d, 5. d, 6. d, 7. b, 8. a, 9. c, 10. b, 11. d, 12. a, 13. c, 14. d, 15. b, 16. d

Practical Problems

1. A company has a book value per share of ₹ 137.80. Its return on equity is 15% and it follows a policy of retaining 60% of its earnings. If the opportunity cost of capital is 18%, what is the price of the share today?
2. Sahu & company earns ₹ 6 per share having capitalization rate of 10% and has a return on investment at the rate of 20%. According to Walter's model, what should be the price per share at 30% dividend payout ratio? Is this the optimum payout ratio as per the Walter? (CA, 2002)
3. Bala Ji Ltd. has 60000 outstanding shares. The current market price per share is ₹ 150 each. It is expected that current year's income will be ₹ 600000. The company's board is considering a dividend of ₹ 8 per share at the end of current financial year. The company needs to raise ₹ 1500000 for its expenditure. The capitalization rate for Bala Ji Ltd. is 10%. Find out the effect on value of the firm if dividend is paid or not paid as per MM approach.

4. The following figures are collected from the annual report of XYZ Ltd:

Net Profit	₹ 30,00,000
Outstanding 12% preference shares	₹ 1,00,00,000
No. of equity shares	3,00,000
Return on investment	30%

What should be the approximate dividend payout ratio so as to keep the share price at ₹ 42 by using Walter model?

5. Salasar Ltd.'s following information is given:

Dividend Policy	Retention Ratio	Growth Rate	Cost of equity
A	0	0	10
B	15	8	12
C	25	12	18

The company's current year's earnings are ₹ 1500000 and expected to remain same in future years. Compute the market value of Salasar Ltd. under above three dividend policy.

6. Pawanputra Ltd.'s following information is given

Net profit	10,00,000
Retention Ratio	70%
No. of shares	2,50,000
Rate of return	20%
Equity capitalization rate	12%

Compute:

(i) Market value applying Walter's model.

(ii) Optimum payout ratio & value at that ratio.

7. Takshak Ltd. has a paid up capital of ₹ 5000000 which includes 500000 equity shares of ₹ 10 each. Current market price is ₹ 40. Equity capitalization rate is 15% and dividend declared is ₹ 5 per share.

Required:

(i) Calculate the market value (a) in above case (b) if no dividend is declared.

(ii) No. of new shares to be issued if after paying dividend company retains ₹ 2500000, proposed investment of ₹ 1500000.

(iii) No. of shares to be issued if no dividend is declared.

8. The following information relates to Vidyarthi Ltd.

Year	Capex	Net Profit
1	6,00,000	10,00,000
2	8,00,000	15,00,000
3	12,00,000	18,00,000
4	16,00,000	14,00,000

Share capital of Vidyarthi Ltd. is 50,000 shares of ₹ 10 each & current dividend is ₹ 5 per share.

Required

(i) What will be dividend per share as per residual dividend policy?

(ii) Calculate dividend per share if company follows a constant dividend policy of 75%. Whether it will require any external financing, if yes, how much every year?

(iii) If company increases dividend by 5% every year calculate quantum of external financing required every year.

Review Questions

1. What is dividend? Explain the position of dividend under Companies Act,1956.
2. Explain the walter's model with the help of an example. What are its shortcomings if any? **(UPTU 2009)**
3. How Gordon's model works? Explain along with assumptions. **(UPTU 2007)**
4. Why MM theory called irrelevant theory? Explain with the help of an example.
5. What do you mean by alternatives to dividend? Explain any two alternatives.
6. What do you mean by growth firm, declining firm and normal firm?
7. What factors to be kept in mind while declaring dividends by a finance manager? **(UPTU 2005,2006, 2007)**
8. Differentiate among stock split, buy back and bonus shares.
9. Write a note on Walter's dividend model and compare it with Gordon's model. **(UPTU 2010)**
10. Explain various dividend models. **(UPTU 2006)**
11. Bonus shares may be a boon or bane for a company. Explain. **(UPTU 2007)**
12. Shareholders sometimes resist ploughing back of profits. Comment. **(UPTU 2007)**
13. What is property Dividend? **(DU)**
14. Distinguish between Scrip dividend and Bond dividend **(DU)**
15. Explain briefly main determinants of dividend policy of a firm. **(DU 2006, 2007 2009)**

Case Study 1 (UPTU, 2009)

The following information is available for Awadh Corporation:

Earnings Per Share	₹ 4.00
Rate of Return on Investments	18 percent
Rate of Return Required by Shareholders	15 percent

What will be the price per share as per Walter Model if payout ratio is 40 percent? 50 percent? 60 percent?

Case Study 2 (DU 2007)

5. Explain briefly the main determinants of dividend policy of a firm.

(b) Using the data given below:

EPS	7
P/E	10
k_e	12%
No. of outstanding shares	75,000
Expected Dividend	5
Expected Net Income	5,00,000
New Investment	8,00,000

Show, using MM hypothesis, the payment of dividend does not affect value of the firm.

Case Study 3 (DU 2008)

ABC Ltd. has a capital of ₹ 10,00,000 in equity shares of ₹ 100 each. The shares are currently quoted at par. The Company proposes to declare a dividend of ₹ 10 per share at the end of the current financial year. The capitalization rate for the risk class to which the company belongs is 12%.

What will be the market price of the share at the end of the year, if :

- A dividend is not declared?
- A dividend is declared?
- Assuming that the company pays the dividend and has net profit of ₹ 5,00,000 and makes new investments of ₹ 10,00,000 during the period, how many new shares must be issued?

  Use the MM model.

References

1. Brealey, Richard A & Myres, Stewart C. (2007), Tata McGraw Hill, New Delhi
2. Damodaran, Aswath. (1994). Damodaran on Valuation, John Wiley & Sons, New York
3. ICAI study Material on Financial Management, The Institute of Chartered Accountants of India, New Delhi.

4. Khan, M Y & Jain (2007) P K, Financial Management, Tata McGraw Hill, New Delhi
5. Kishore, Ravi. M (2009), Financial Management, Taxmann Publications, New Delhi
6. Pandey, I M (2009). Financial Management, Vikas Publishing House, New Delhi
7. Van Horne, James C. (2007),Financial Management & Policy, Pearson Prentice Hall, New Delhi
8. Work book on "Financial Management for Managers": The Institute of Chartered Financial Analysts of India, Hyderabad.

CHAPTER 11 Working Capital Management: An Overview

Learning Objectives:

By the end of this chapter and having completed the essential reading and activities, you should be able to:

- Have an overview of Working Capital Decision
- Explain the Concept and components of working capital
- Identify the factors affecting working capital requirement
- Understand the objective of working Capital Management

To start with...

Imagine you are buying a car. Of course the first thing you need is money to purchase it. But once purchased, do you still need money to run the car? Yes , you do. You need money to pay for the fuel. And if you want a driver, then you need money to pay his salary. The money you spent to buy the car can be termed as fixed capital. And the money you spend in fuel and salary can be understood as working capital.

This situation is very similar to a business isn't it? In business also, you need fixed capital to buy fixed assets like plant and machinery. But afterwards, you need money to meet day to day expenses like raw material, labor, electricity etc. The money spent on these expenses is called working capital.

In this chapter we will gain a deeper understanding of working capital and its importance.

11.0 Introduction

By now we are familiar with the concept of capital. In the simplest form the word capital represents funds contributed by the owners of business. These and other funds received from the creditors are utilized for purchasing assets. Business purchases these assets to earn return by using them. The assets are divided broadly into two categories; Long Term (Fixed Assets) and Short Term (Current Assets). Current assets like cash, stocks etc. are necessary for meeting day to day expenses of business. Funds required for meeting day to day expenses of the business are referred to as working capital.

11.1 Defining Working Capital

We can define working capital in two different ways. One is called Gross Working capital and other is called Net working Capital.

Gross working capital is nothing but sum total of current assets of a firm.

The net working capital of the firm is defined as the difference between its current assets and current liabilities. We are already familiar with current assets and current liabilities. The current assets of a firm are those that are either in the form of cash or are expected to be converted into cash in the short term (generally less than a year).

Perhaps you also remember what current liabilities are. These are the obligations of the business which are to be repaid in the short term (again usually less than a year).

Let us have a closer look at current assets and current liabilities.

11.1.1 Current Assets

1. Cash and marketable securities: These are the most liquid assets a firm has; marketable securities are those investments e.g. government securities, that can generally be converted into cash quickly, at low cost, and with little or no loss of value.

2. Inventory: It includes raw materials, work in process and finished goods. Out of these, the finished goods and raw material inventory are more liquid than the work in process inventory. Some times another item called *Consumable stores and spares* also forms a small part of total inventory.

3. Accounts receivable: Accounts receivable represents the credit sales of the firm. They are also known as Sundry Debtors or Book Debts. When the debtors make payment of their dues to the firm the account receivables convert into cash. Sometimes you may see Bills Receivables in balance sheets? What are bills receivables? They represent the credit sales in which the seller has written a bill that has been duly accepted by the buyer.

4. Prepaid Expenses: These are those expenses, which have been paid for goods and services whose benefits have not been received yet.

5. Loan and Advances: They are loans and advances given by the firm to other firms for a short period of time.

11.1.2 Current Liabilities

The current liabilities are those obligations of firm that are expected to become due within the year. This means they are required to be repaid within one year. They generally include the following:

1. **Accounts payable:** This represents credit purchases. It is also known as Sundry Creditors, or supplier's credit. Some times you may see Bills Payable in balance sheets. Bills payable means those credit purchases on which the buyer has accepted the obligation by signing on a bill written by the seller.
2. **Accrued expenses:** In the normal course of doing business, firms accrue wages and salaries to their employees and taxes to the government. They can further be classified as "Due and Unpaid" and "Accrued but Not Due (therefore not paid)".
3. **Current portion of long-term debt:** Any long-term debt (bonds, bank debt) that is expected to come due within the year is classified as a current liability; it differs qualitatively from accounts payable because it is usually refinanced with new long term debt.
4. **Bank Overdrafts:** These include withdrawals in excess of credit balance standing in the firm's current accounts with banks.
5. **Short-term Loans:** Short-terms borrowings by the firm from banks and others form part of current liabilities as short-term loans.
6. **Provisions:** These include provisions for taxation, proposed dividends and contingencies.

11.2 Difference Between the Concepts of Gross Working Capital (GWC) & Net Working Capital (NWC)

What are the differences between these two concepts? The focus of Gross Working Capital concept is on the *level* of current assets. The finance manager is interested in optimization of investment in current assets. His concern is that the investments in current assets should neither be too high nor too low. Also, GWC concept draws attention to the sources of finance for the current assets. The finance manager should be ready to arrange funds whenever need for more current assets is felt.

On the other hand the concept of Net working Capital is a qualitative concept. It actually represents the use of long term funds made to finance the working capital requirements. It also represents the buffer available to the firm to repay maturing current liabilities. If current assets are sufficiently in excess of current liabilities then the firm is more comfortable repaying its current liabilities as and when they arise. Therefore, NWC is essentially a measure of liquidity and extent to which long term funds are being used to finance current assets.

Perhaps you are feeling slightly confused that if you hear "Working Capital", should you think of Gross Working Capital or Net Working Capital? Right?

Do not worry. Here is the answer. Whenever you hear or read "Working Capital" you should think about Gross Working Capital (Sum total of Current Assets). You should think about Net Working Capital ONLY when you are specifically asked to do so.

11.3 The Working Capital Decision: The Liquidity-Profitability Trade Off

Like most corporate finance decisions, the decisions on how much working capital to hold involve a trade-off. What is the meaning of trade-off? Trade-off between two things means that both can not be increased or decreased simultaneously. If one is increasing, the other will decrease and vice versa.

Now, the question is what kind of trade-off exists in working capital? In Working capital, this trade off is between the liquidity and profitability of the firm.

You are already aware that liquidity of a firm means its ability to meet its short term liabilities as they become due. If the firm is not able to repay its current liabilities on time, this situation is known as **technical insolvency**.

Profitability means the return generated on assets of the firm.

If the firm has a large net working capital (i.e., current assets that significantly exceed current liabilities), it may reduce the liquidity risk (risk of technical insolvency) faced by the firm. But it can have a negative impact on cash flows and thereby the profits.

Similarly, if NWC is small, profitability will be higher but liquidity will go down.

What should we do then? We should find out the net effect on value to determine the optimal amount of working capital.

This is why the working capital decision is also said to be the decision of finding right balance between the liquidity and profitability. Sometimes it is also said that "managing the working capital is like managing a double edge sword".

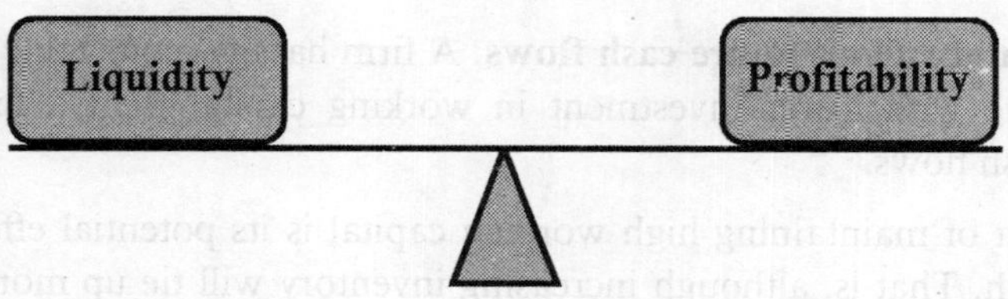

11.4 Effect of Working Capital Changes on Cash Flows

Whenever there is an increase in working capital that means more funds are locked up there and this reduces the cash flows. The opposite happens whenever working capital is increased.

However the effect of changes in working capital on cash flows depends on many factors.

11.4.1 Magnitude of working capital investment needed for operations: The effects of working capital changes on cash flows are likely to be larger with respect to overall cash flows and value, for firms that have to maintain large investments in working capital relative to operating cash flows and sales. For example, a manufacturer of heavy machinery is likely to experience much larger changes in cash flows as a consequence of increases or decreases in his or her inventory than will a service business, such as a temp agency, which has lower working capital requirements.

11.4.2 Composition of working capital: Different items of working capital have different effect on cash flows. Increases in marketable securities, for instance, have a less negative impact on cash flows because they earn a positive return (interest or dividends on these securities) while they are held.

Whereas, increase in inventory shall affect cash flow more strongly since on the one hand inventory held does not earn any return; and on the other hand, the inventory holding involves various administrative and carrying costs.

11.4.3 The liquidity effect and operating effect

As per the traditional view of working capital, increasing working capital will generally reduce the liquidity risk faced by the firm, whereas decreasing working capital will generally increase the liquidity risk. The effects of working capital changes on liquidity risk depend on a number of factors:

11.4.3.1 Access to financing: Generally large firms have easy access to sources of finance like commercial paper than smaller firms. Therefore firms with larger requirements of working capital experience less effect on cash flows owing to changes in working capital than smaller firms.

11.4.3.2 State of the economy: It has been observed that during economic downturn firms face higher liquidity risk than during boom or normal economic conditions.

11.4.3.3 Uncertainty about future cash flows: A firm having predictable and stable cash flows can survive with lower investment in working capital than a firm with highly unpredictable cash flows.

A second benefit of maintaining high working capital is its potential effect on revenues and future growth. That is, although increasing inventory will tie up more cash, it might also enable the firm to increase sales or at least avoid lost sales as a consequence of not having the desired item in stock when a customer wants it. A similar argument can be made about accounts receivable: though offering more generous credit increases investment in accounts receivable, which impacts cash flow negatively, it might also increase sales and operating profits.

An alternative view of liquidity-profitability trade-off: The cost trade-off

We can understand the liquidity-profitability trade off in a different manner also. In liquidity-profitability trade-off we compare benefits of high working capital and low working capital. Alternatively, we can also compare the costs of having high working capital (current assets) with that of having low working capital.

What are these costs? There are two types of costs: **a) Cost of Liquidity and b) Cost of Illiquidity.**

Cost of Liquidity:

This is the cost arising due to high level of working capital. It means that high current assets will increase liquidity. But this liquidity will not be free. Firm has to bear some cost for this increased liquidity. The cost is in the form of having low return on idle cash, inventory and debtors. If the investment in these assets is higher, then opportunity cost of funds tied up in them is also higher. This is called "cost of liquidity".

Cost of Illiquidity:

This is the cost arising due to low level of working capital. Low working capital means low investment in current assets or low liquidity. Low liquidity will bring some disadvantages. The examples of these costs are: inability to repay current liabilities on time, lost sales due to lower stock, low sales due to strict credit policy, expensive borrowings to meet current obligations etc. Taken together, these costs are called "cost of illiquidity".

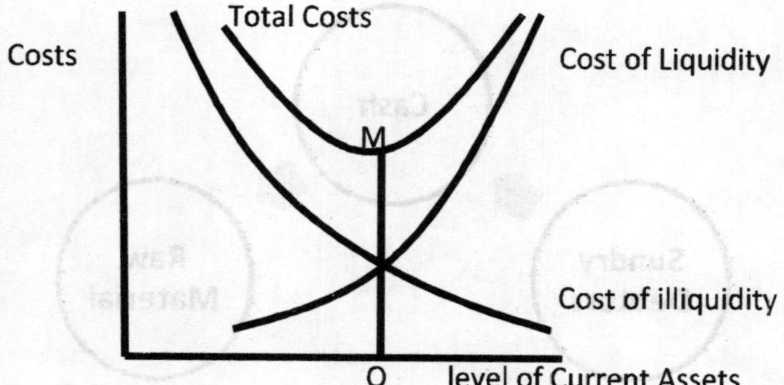

Again we have a dilemma. High liquidity would have high costs of liquidity and low cost of illiquidity (see figure). Low liquidity will have high cost of illiquidity but low cost of liquidity. What should be done in such a scenario? The wise thing to do will be to have a level of working capital (current assets) where the sum total of cost of liquidity and cost of illiquidity is minimum. In the graph above, the point of minimum total costs (cost of liquidity + cost of illiquidity) is M. At this point, the level of current assets is at O, which is the optimum level of current assets.

11.5 Optimal Level of Working Capital

Let us come back to our question: "What should be the optimum amount of working capital that the firm should hold"? We have already seen that there is a trade off involved. Increasing the working capital means the liquidity risk will be low and the firm should be able to capitalize on opportunities of making higher sales by meeting supply commitments; but at a higher level of working capital investment the cash flows shall be negatively affected and this will impact the profitability of the firm.

Ideally then, the optimum working capital shall at a level where the benefits of having larger working capital exceed its associated costs.

11.6 The Concept of Operating Cycle

The concept of operating cycle is based on the fact that it takes time in converting raw materials into finished goods, being able to sell finished goods and finally getting payment for the credit sales. Cash leaves the firm when payment for raw materials is made. It comes back only when the payment from debtors after credit sales have been received. However, this cash comes back with profit added to it. Time taken in this process is known as Operating Cycle. This can be represented by the following diagram:

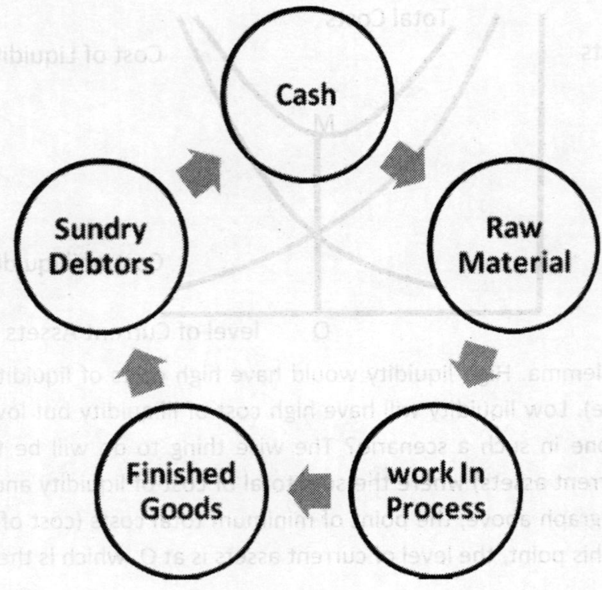

The operating cycle therefore can be defined as the time duration required to convert sales, after the conversion of resources into inventories, into cash. The operating cycle of a manufacturing company involves three phases:

1. Acquisition of resources: such as raw material, labor, power and fuel etc.
2. Manufacture of Product: This includes conversion of raw material into work-in-progress into finished goods.
3. Sale of Product: either for cash or on credit. Credit sales create account receivable for collection.

The cash inflows in the above cycle are less certain and happen after cash outflows generally. This is the reason cash is required to maintain liquidity to purchase raw materials and pay expenses such as wages and salaries, other manufacturing, administrative and selling expenses and taxes. This is so because the cash inflows and outflows do not occur simultaneously. Also to guard against future contingencies, cash, stock of raw materials and finished goods, work in progress are held.

The length of operating cycle of any firm can be calculated as follows:

Gross Operating Cycle = Inventory Conversion Period (ICP) + Average Collection Period (ACP) Equation 1

Inventory Conversion Period = Raw Material Conversion Period (RMCP) + work in process Conversion Period (WIPCP) + Finished goods Conversion Period (FGCP)

The equation 1 represents the Gross Operating Cycle. There is another concept of Net Operating Cycle.

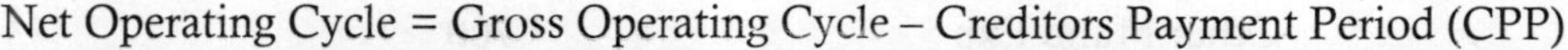
Net Operating Cycle = Gross Operating Cycle – Creditors Payment Period (CPP)

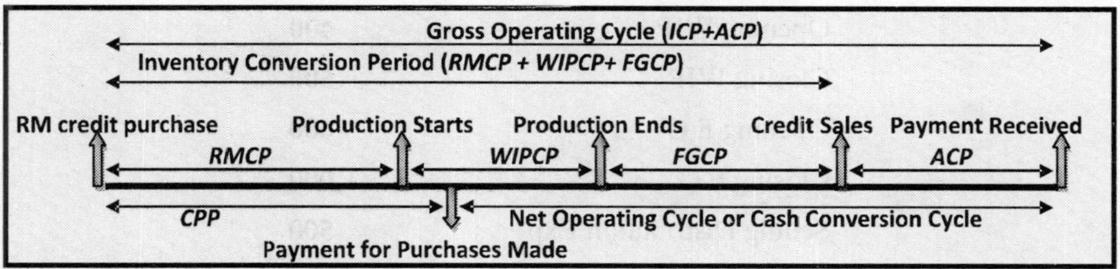

Payment for Purchases Made

The net operating cycle is also known as ***Cash Conversion Cycle***. The logic of net operating cycle is simple. If the firm is getting its raw material on credit then its cash is not going out for the period equal to the period allowed by creditors for repayment. Therefore the Creditors payment period is deducted from Gross operating cycle to obtain the net time period for which the cash remains invested in the day to day operations of the firm.

While calculating cash conversion cycle, the amount of depreciation and non cash charges should be deducted from the expenses.

The formulae for calculating various components of operating cycle are as follows:

$$RMCP = \frac{Average\ Raw\ Material}{Annual\ raw\ Material\ Consumption / 360}$$

$$WIPCP = \frac{Average\ WIP\ Inventory}{Annual\ Cost\ of\ Production / 360}$$

$$FGCP = \frac{Average\ finished\ goods\ Invntory}{Annual\ Cost\ of\ Good\ Sold / 360}$$

$$ACP = \frac{Average\ Debtors}{Annual\ Credit\ Sales / 360}$$

$$CCP = \frac{Averg\ Creditors}{Annual\ Crdit\ Purchase / 360}$$

Example 1: **From the following data calculate the Gross Operating Cycle and Net Operating Cycle:**

Purchase of RM	**7,000**
Opening R M	**900**
Closing R M	**1,000**
Direct Labor	**500**

Other Manu Exp	**700**
Opening WIP	**400**
Closing WIP	**500**
Opening F G	**600**
Closing F G	**1,000**
Selling Distribution Exp	**500**
Opening Debtors	**800**
Closing Debtors	**1,100**
Opening Creditors	**500**
Closing Creditors	**700**
Sales (Credit)	**9,000**

Solution

Average Stock of RM	=(Opening_RM+Closing_RM)/2	950
Annual Cons. Of RM	=Opening_RM+RM_Purchase-Closing_RM	6,900
RMCP	=(Average_Stock_RM/Annual_Consmpn_RM)*360	49.56 days
Average WIP	=(Opening_WIP+Closing_WIP)/2	450
Annual Manu Cost	=Annual_Consmpn_RM+Opening_WIP+Direct_Labor+Other_Manu_Exp-Closing_WIP	8,000
WIPCP	=Average_WIP/Annual_Manu._Cost*360	20.25 days
Average Stock of FG	=(Opening_FG+Closing_FG)/2	800
Annual Cost of Goods Sold	=Opening_FG+Annual_Manu._Cost-Closing_FG	7,600
FGCP	=Average_FG/Annual_COGS*360	37.89 days
Average Stock of Debtors	=(Opening_Debtors+Closing_Debtors)/2	950
ACP	=Average_Debtors/Credit_Sales*360	38 days
Average Stock of Creditors	=(Opening_Creditors+Closing_Creditors)/2	600
CPP	=Average_Creditors/RM_Purchase*360	30.85 days
GOC	=RMCP+WIPCP+FGCP+ACP	145.7 days
NOC	**=GOC-CCP**	114.8 days

11.7 Permanent and Temporary Working Capital

If we look at the concept of operating cycle above we might conclude that the amount of working capital invested in a firm becomes zero at the end of operating cycle. However, this is not true. In any firm there exists a continuous need for working capital. There is always some amount that stays invested in current assets ***permanently.*** This minimum amount of working capital investment is known as Permanent working Capital or Fixed Working Capital or Core Current Assets.

However, the need for working capital actually keeps fluctuating in line with the changes in production, sales and seasonal changes. This changing component, over and above, the permanent component is known as Temporary or Fluctuating or Variable working capital.

In the figure the fixed and permanent components are shown separately:

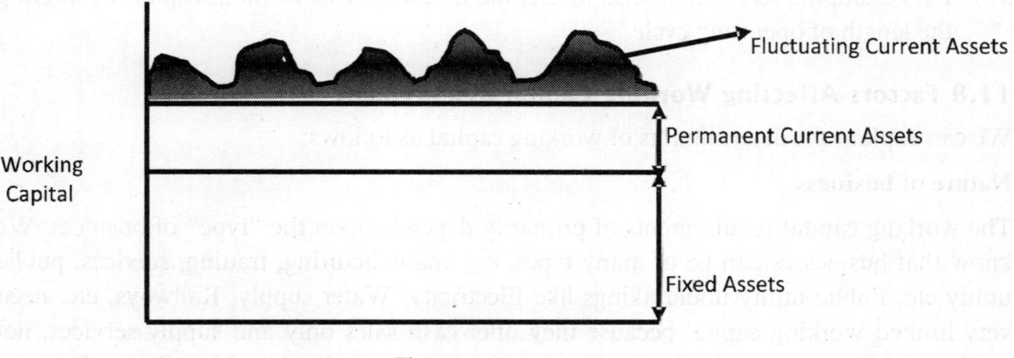

As we can the temporary working capital keeps fluctuating where as the permanent component remains fixed. However it is not necessary that the permanent component remains fixed. For a growing firm the permanent portion will also keep increasing with time.

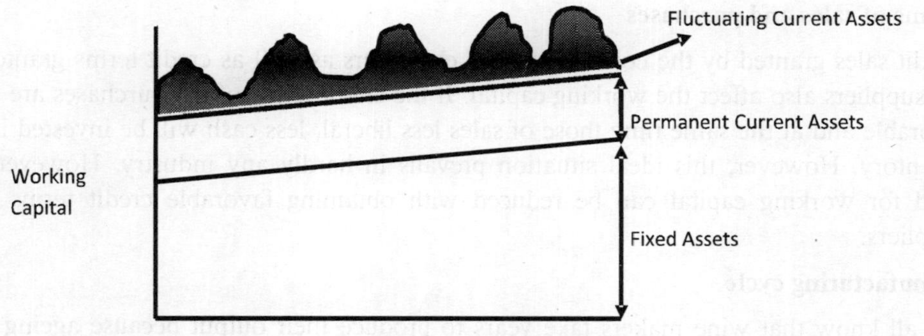

Here we can see that permanent portion of working capital is increasing with time owing to growth in firm.

There are many reasons why changes in working capital take place. Some of the important reasons are as follows:

1. Foremost reason is the trend in sales and operating expenses. These trends are of three types seasonal, cyclical or long term. In all these cases the need for working capital will change from time to time. For example if there is long term trend of increasing price of a key raw material then there will be a necessity of holding raw material inventory to guard against rising prices.
2. The attitude or policy of management on keeping current assets in proportion to revenue also affects the investment in working capital. For Example if the management adopts a conservative working capital policy then it may maintain a very high amount of current assets in relation to sales.
3. Ever-changing technology also affects the investment in working capital by altering the length of operating cycle.

11.8 Factors Affecting Working Capital Requirement

We can explain the determinants of working capital as follows:

Nature of business

The working capital requirements of primarily depends upon the "type" of business. We know that businesses can be of many types, e.g. manufacturing, trading, services, public utility etc. Public utility undertakings like Electricity, Water supply, Railways, etc. need very limited working capital because they offer cash sales only and supply services, not products and as such no funds are ties up in inventories and receivables. But at the same time have to invest fewer amounts in fixed assets. In case of trading concerns the need for inventories is the maximum. These two types form the extremes of the working capital requirement continuum. In between lie the manufacturing concerns, which have sizable working capital along with fixed investments, as they have to build up the inventories.

Terms of sales and purchases

Credit sales granted by the concerns too its customers as well as credit terms granted by the suppliers also affect the working capital. If the credit terms of the purchases are more favorable and at the same time those of sales less liberal, less cash will be invested in the inventory. However, this ideal situation prevails in hardly any industry. However, the need for working capital can be reduced with obtaining favorable credit terms from suppliers.

Manufacturing cycle

We all know that wine makers take years to produce their output because ageing is so essential to wine making process. Imagine how much stock (or working capital) must be tied up in case of firms in winemaking business? The length of manufacturing cycle influences the quantum of working capital needed. Manufacturing process always involves a time lag between the time when raw materials are fed into the production line and finished goods are finally turned out by it. The length of the period of manufacture in turn depends on the nature of product as well as production technology used by a concern. The longer the manufacturing cycle, the higher will be requirement of working capital.

Inventory turnover

High inventory turnover means low requirement of working capital. With a better inventory control, a firm is able to reduce its working capital requirements. When a firm has to carry on a large slow moving stock, it needs a larger working capital as against another whose turnover is rapid. A firm should determine the minimum level of stock, which it will have to maintain throughout the period of its operation.

Business cycle

Business cycles of boom and bust affect the requirement of working capital by firms. However this relationship is not authentically established. Generally, in a period of boom i.e., when the business is prosperous, there is need of larger amount of working capital due to increases in sales, rise in price etc. Generally, the higher requirement of working capital precedes booms and not follows them. In times of recession, the working capital requirement goes down by the same logic.

Technological Changes

Changes in technology may lead to improvements in processing of raw materials, savings in wastage, greater productivity, and more speedy production. It may also reduce the length of manufacturing cycle. These improvements may enable the firm to reduce investments in inventory and there by working capital.

Nature and supply of raw materials

Some times raw material may be of special type and have to be imported or transported great distances. In this case the firm is bound to maintain a huge stock. Also, the inventory of raw materials, spares and stores depends on the condition of supply. Promptness in supplies of the raw material reduce the working capital investment. However if the supplies are unpredictable then in order to maintain continuity of production process, the firm may have to increase the investment in working capital.

Market conditions

In a competitive market, firms are forced to offer liberal credit terms to their customers. This results in increase in sundry debtors and a thereby increase in investment in working capital. It has another effect also. When competition is keen, a larger inventory of finished goods is required to promptly serve customers who may not be inclined to wait because other manufacturers are ready to meet their needs.

Seasonality of operation

Firms, which have marked seasonality in their operations usually, have highly fluctuating working requirements. Let us take an example to illustrate this point. Consider a firm manufacturing woolen blankets. The sale of blankets reaches a peak during the winter months and drops sharply during the summer period. The working capital need of such a firm is likely to increase considerably in winter months and decrease significantly during summer season.

Dividend policy

It has a significant influence on the working capital position of a firm. If the firm is following a conservative dividend policy, the need for working capital can be met with retained earnings. However if the firm is aggressive then it would require a large cash outgo at the time of payment of dividend and therefore would require additional investment in working capital.

Working capital cycle

Larger the working capital cycle, more is the requirement of working capital.

11.9 Working Capital Policies

Working capital policy relates to the decision about the amount of current assets that the firm wants to keep in relation to sales or fixed assets. There are three broad strategies firms follow. They are: 1) Conservative Approach 2) Aggressive Approach and 3) Moderate Approach. These approaches can be depicted by the following diagram:

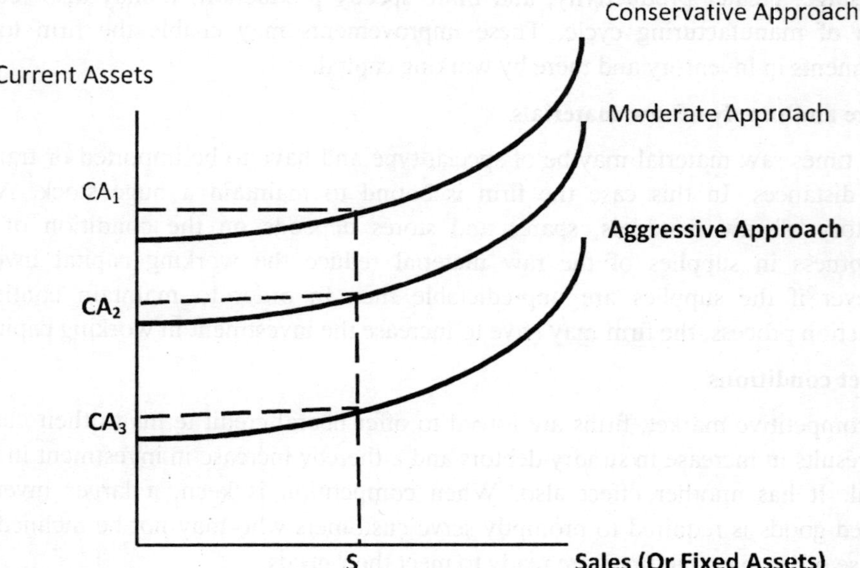

Conservative Approach: As the name suggests, this approach is a low risk approach. In this approach, the level of current assets in relation to sales is kept at a higher level. Since current assets are higher, the firm has low liquidity risk. Also, the firm has a buffer or cushion to meet contingencies, seasonal fluctuations etc. But as you know, lower risk means lower returns also. Why are returns lower in this policy? It is because current assets offer lower rate of return. Since in this policy we are making higher investment in low-return current assets, overall returns go down.

Aggressive Approach: In this approach, the investment in current assets is kept at a lower level. Due to this the liquidity risk of the firm increases. Also, the firm's ability to meet sudden changes in demand, contingencies decreases. Then what is the fun of such a policy? This policy results in higher returns. This is so because here investment in low return current assets is low.

Moderate Approach: In this policy, the investment in current assets is neither too high nor too low. As we can see in the diagram above, in moderate approach, current assets **CA_2 is** between **CA_3 and** CA_1. This policy results in moderate risk and moderate returns.

Computation of Working Capital Needs

Mainly there are three methods of estimating working capital needs.

1. Percentage of sales method
2. Regression analysis method
3. Operating cycle method

Out of these, operating cycle method is most popular. In this method various items of current assets and current liabilities are estimated. Then desired cash balance is added to the current assets. From this current liabilities are subtracted. This gives the value of net working capital required.

Various items of current assets and current liabilities are computed as follows:

1. Raw Material Stock:

$$Raw\ Material\ Stock = \frac{Budgeted\ Production\ Units\ x\ Material\ Cost\ Per\ Units}{360/52/12}\ x\ RMCP$$

2. Work in Process Stock

$$WIP\ Stock = \frac{Budgeted\ production\ in\ Units\ x\ Unit\ WIP\ Costs}{360/52/12}\ x\ WIPCP$$

3. Finished Goods Stock

$$FG\ Stock = \frac{Budgetd\ \Pr oduction\ in\ Units\ x\ Unit\ \cos ts\ of\ \Pr oductioin}{360/52/12}\ x\ FGCP$$

4. Debtors

$$Debtors = \frac{Budgeted\ Creditors\ Sales\ In\ Units}{360/52/12} x\ ACP$$

5. Creditors

$$Creditors = \frac{Budgeted Credit\ Sales\ in\ Units}{360/52/12} x\ CPP$$

6. Outstanding Expenses

$$Outstanding\ Expenses = \frac{Budgeted\ Production\ in\ units\ x\ per\ unit\ expenses}{360/52/12} x\ Lag\ in\ payment\ of\ expenses$$

Here, RMCP = Raw Material Conversion Period

WIPCP = Work in Process Conversion Period

FGCP = Finished Goods Conversion Period

ACP = Average Collection Period

CPP = Creditors Payment Period

Note: In all the above formulas the denominator contains the term 360/52/12 You may be wondering which of these values is actually used in the formula? This will be determined by the periods multiplied. For example, if in formula for debtors, ACP is given in months, then we will take thee value of 12 in denominator. If ACP is in days, then we will take the value of 360 in the denominator.

Illustrative Solved Example

Pawan Tanay Limited has approached you for estimation of the working capital for the coming year. They have supplied the following data:

Raw material cost per unit	₹ 45
Direct Labor cost per unit	₹ 20
Production Overheads per unit	₹ 42
Profits per unit	₹ 23
Selling price per unit	₹ 140

Other information is: Raw material/Finished goods are in stock for 1.5 months. Work in process is usually held for 1 month. Suppliers allow a credit period of 1.25 months. Average collection period is 2 months. Payment of wages and overhead is delayed by 15 days (half a month). 80% sales are on credit. The firm desires to have a cash balance of ₹ 100000. It is expected that the firm will produce 80000 units of the product this year.

Solution

$$Raw\ Material\ Stock = \frac{Budgeted\ Production\ in\ Units}{360/52/12} x RMCP$$

$$\frac{80,000\,x\,45}{360}x45$$

= 4,50,000

$$\text{WIP Stock}=\frac{\text{Budgeted Production in Units x Units WIP Costs}}{360/52/12}$$

$$\frac{80,000\times(45+50\%\text{ of }20+50\%\text{ of }42)}{360/52/12}\times 30$$

= 5,06,667

$$\text{FG Stock}=\frac{\text{Budget Production in Unit x Units Costs of Production}}{360/52/12}\times \text{FGCP}$$

$$\frac{80,000\times 107}{360}\times 45$$

=1,07,000

$$Debtors=\frac{budgeted\ Credit\ Sales\ in\ Units\ x\ Unit\ Cost\ of\ Sales}{360/52/12}x\ ACP$$

$$\frac{80,000\times 80\%\times 107}{360}\times 60$$

= 11,41333

$$\text{Creditors}=\frac{80,000\times 45}{360}\times 37.5$$

= 3,75,000

$$\text{Otustanding Wages}=\frac{\text{Budgeted Production in Units x Per Unit Wages}}{360/52/12}\times \text{Log in Payment Of Wages}$$

$$\frac{80,000\times 20}{360}\times 15$$

= 66,667

$$\text{Outstanding Overhead}=\frac{\text{Budgeted production in Units x Per units Overheads}}{360/52/12}\times \text{Log in Payment 0}$$

$$\frac{80,000\,x\,42}{360}x15$$

=1,40,000

From the above data, we can calculate the working capital as follows:

	Desired Cash		1,20,000
	RM stock		4,50,000
	WIP Stock		5,06,667
	FG Stock		1,07,000
	Debtors		11,41,333
A	Total Current Assets		***23,25,000***
	Less Creditors	3,75000	
	Outstanding Wages	66,667	
	Outstanding overheads	1,40,000	
B	Total current Liabilities		***5,81,667***
C=A-B	Net working Capital		**17,43,333**

Summary

- Current assets like cash, stocks etc. are necessary for meeting day to day expenses of business. Funds required for meeting day to day expenses of the business are referred to as working capital.
- We can define working capital in two different ways. One is called Gross Working Capital and other is called Net Working Capital. Gross Working Capital is nothing but sum total of current assets of a firm. The Net Working Capital of the firm is defined as the difference between its current assets and current liabilities.
- The current assets of a firm are those that are either in the form of cash or are expected to be converted into cash in the short term (generally less than a year). The main types of current assets are Cash and Marketable securities, Inventory, Receivables, Prepaid Expenses and short-term loans and advances.
- The current liabilities are those obligations of firm that are expected to become due within the year. This means they are required to be repaid within one year. They generally include Accounts payable, accrued expenses, bank overdraft, short term loans and provisions.
- Gross working Capital and Net working capital are two distinct concepts. The focus of Gross Working Capital concept is on the ***level*** of current assets. The concept of Net working Capital is a qualitative concept. It actually represents the use of long term funds made to finance the working capital requirements. It also represents the buffer available to the firm to repay maturing current liabilities.

- Like most corporate finance decisions, the decisions on how much working capital to hold involve a trade-off. In Working capital, this trade off is between the liquidity and profitability of the firm.
- Liquidity of a firm means its ability to meet its short term liabilities as they become due. If the firm is not able to repay its current liabilities on time, this situation is known as **technical insolvency**. Profitability means the return generated on assets of the firm.
- Working capital decision is also said to be the decision of finding right balance between the liquidity and profitability. Sometimes it is also said that "managing the working capital is like managing a double edge sword".
- Whenever there is an increase in working capital that means more funds are locked up there and this reduces the cash flows. The opposite happens whenever working capital is increased.
- The effect of changes in working capital on cash flows depends on many factors viz. Magnitude of working capital investment needed for operation, Composition of working capital, The liquidity effect and operating effect, Access to financing, State of the economy, Uncertainty about future cash flows.
- The optimum working capital shall at a level where the benefits of having larger working capital exceed its associated costs.
- The operating cycle therefore can be defined as the time duration required to convert sales, after the conversion of resources into inventories, into cash. The operating cycle of a manufacturing company involves three phases, viz. Acquisition of resources, Manufacture of Product, Sale of Product.
- This minimum amount of working capital investment needed permanently in the firm is known as Permanent Working Capital or Fixed Working Capital or Core Current Assets.
- The need for working capital actually keeps fluctuating in line with the changes in production, sales and seasonal changes. This changing component, over and above, the permanent component is known as **Temporary** or **Fluctuating or Variable Working Capital**.
- There are various factors that affect the requirement of working capital. They are **Nature of business, Terms of sales and purchases, Manufacturing cycle, Inventory turnover, Business cycle, Technological Changes, Nature and supply of raw materials, Market conditions, Seasonality of operation, Dividend policy and Working capital cycle.**
- Working capital policy relates to the decision about the amount of current assets that the firm wants to keep in relation to sales or fixed assets. There are three broad strategies firms follow. They are: 1) Conservative Approach 2) Aggressive Approach and 3) Moderate Approach.

- Mainly there are three methods of estimating working capital needs viz. Percentage of sales method, Regression analysis method, Operating cycle method.

Test Your Understanding

State whether the following statements are true/false

1. Higher the liquidity, higher will be the profitability.
2. Gross working capital means Current assets – Current liabilities.
3. Higher the net working capital, higher is the liquidity.
4. Aggressive working capital policy means lower proportion of current assets.
5. Higher the length of operating cycle, higher is the WC requirement.
6. A manufacturing firm would have a higher working capital requirement than a power utility.
7. Production policy does not affect the WC requirement.
8. The need for working capital arises due to non synchronization of cash inflows and outflows.
9. Cash conversion cycle is also known as Net Operating cycle.
10. Gross Operating cycle is sum of inventory conversion period and debtors collection period.

Answers : 1.F 2.F 3.F 4. T 5.T 6. T 7.F 8.T 9.T 10.T

Multiple Choice Questions

1. Which of the following is not a technique of calculating working capital? **(UPTU 2009)**

   a) Cash forecasting method b) Regression Method

   c) Operating Cycle Method d) None of these

2. The excess of current assets over current liabilities is known as: **(UPTU 2009)**

   a) Net Current Assets b) Net Working capital

   c) Working Capital d) All of above

3. Is Gross working capital equal to:

   a) Total Current Assets b) Total Current Assets minus liabilities

   c) Total Current Liability Minus asset d) None of the above

4. Accounts Receivables are known as:(UTPU, 2010)

   a) Sundry Creditors b) Sundry Debtors

   c) B/R d) B/P

5. If the average collection period of a company is higher than the credit period extended by it, the firm is supposed to have a

   a) Satisfactory liquidity position. b) Liquidity crunch

   c) High Liquidity d) Either (a) or (c) above

6. Which of the following is a determinant of working capital of a firm?

   a) Depreciation policy b) Nature of business

   c) Production policy d) All of the above

7. In which of the following firms the ratio of current assets to total assets is highest?

   a) Power utility firm b) Hotels

   c) Laundry d) Construction and real estate firms

8. Technical insolvency refers to

   a) Bankruptcy of the firm

   b) Inability to pay debts by a firm for the purchase of machinery.

   c) Inability to pay debts by a firm for debenture redemption.

   d) Inability to honor its current liabilities

9. If the current assets and current liabilities are ₹, 2,000 lakh and ₹ 1,000 lakh respectively. How much amount can be borrowed on a short-term basis without reducing current ratio below 1.5?

   a) ₹ 400 lakh. b) ₹ 500 lakh.

   c) ₹ 600 lakh. d) ₹ 800 lakh.

10. Working capital margin is

    a) The difference between current assets and current liabilities

    b) Gross Current Assets

    c) Cash Credit Limit

    d) The portion of working capital which will be financed through long-term sources

11. What is the Net Operating Cycle for a firm with ACP 40 days, CPP of 50 days and an ICP of 60 days?

    a) 70 days. b) 50 days

    c) 60 days d) 90 days

12. What are the properties of current assets?

    a) Quick conversion in other assets b) Short life

    c) Low turnover d) a) and b) above

13. The minimum level of current assets required by the firm to maintain continuity of its operations is known as:

    a) Core current assets b) Working Capital

    c) Gross Working Capital d) None of these

14. Which of the following will not increase the length of the operating cycle?

    a) having unused cash in bank b) Poor collection of receivables

    c) Long production process d) None of these

15. Which of the following is not a current liability?

    a) Sundry Creditors b) Bills Payables

    c) Expenses Outstanding d) None of these

Answers : 1. d 2.b 3.A 4.b 5.B 6.d 7.d 8.d 9.a 10.d 11.b 12. D 13.a 14.a 15.d

Review Questions

1. Discuss different types of working capital. Explain in brief various factors which determine its need.
2. Explain cost of liquidity and cost of illiquidity in determining the optimum level of current assets. **(UPTU 2006)**
3. "Managing working capital is to manage a double edge sword". Comment. **(UPTU 2005)**
4. Write down the various concepts of working capital. **(UPTU 2005,2007)**
5. What is the concept of operating cycle? What is its significance in working capital management? Illustrate.
6. What does negative working capital signify? Explain.
7. Discuss the various approaches to working capital management?
8. Write short notes on:

    a) Gross and Net working capital

    b) Permanent and temporary working capital

9. What is meant by profitability-liquidity trade off in working capital management? Explain.
10. Explain the factors having a bearing on working capital needs. **(DU 2007, 2009)**

Case Study 1 (DU 2010)

10. The data of ABC Ltd. is as under:

Production for the year	69,000 units
Finished gods inventory	3 months
Raw materials inventory	2 months consumption
Production process	1 month
Credit allowed by creditors	2 months
Credit given to debtors	3 months
Selling price per unit	50 each
Raw material	50% of selling price
Direct wages	10% of selling price
Overheads	20% of selling price

There is a regular production and sales cycle, and wages and overheads accrue evenly. Wages are paid in the next month of accrual. Material is introduced in the beginning of production cycle. Work-in-process involves use of full unit of raw materials in the beginning of manufacturing process and other conversion costs equivalent to 50%.

You are required to find out working capital requirement of the ABC Ltd.

Case Study 2 (DU 2010)

The relevant information of XYZ Ltd. For the year ended 2009 is given below:

Sales	₹ 80,000	
Cost of goods sold	₹ 56,000	
	Opening ( )	Closing ( )
Inventory	9,000	12,000
Accounts Receivable	12,000	16,000
Accounts Payable	7,000	10,000

What is the length of net operating cycle? Assume 365 days in a year.

References

1. Brealey, Richard A & Myres, Stewart C. (2007), Tata McGraw Hill, New Delhi
2. Damodaran, Aswath. (1994). Damodaran on Valuation, John Wiley & Sons, New York

3. Khan, M Y & Jain (2007) P K, Financial Management, Tata McGraw Hill, New Delhi
4. Kishore, Ravi. M (2009), Financial Management, Taxmann Publications, New Delhi
5. Pandey, I M (2009). Financial Management, Vikas Publishing House, New Delhi
6. Van Horne, James C. (2007),Financial Management & Policy, Pearson Prentice Hall, New Delhi
7. Work book on "Financial Management for Managers": The Institute of Chartered Financial Analysts of India, Hyderabad.

CHAPTER 12 Management of Cash

Learning Objectives:

By the end of this chapter and having completed the essential reading and activities, you should be able to:

- Define cash in its various interpretations
- Know the motive behind holding cash
- Identify the factors affecting cash needs
- Understand the Objectives of Cash Management
- Use various cash management models
- Prepare cash budgets

12.0 Introduction

Cash, by definition, is the most liquid asset of all. It is also called the lifeblood of business. Its efficient management is crucial to the solvency of the business. It is so because cash is the focal point of the funds flows in a business.

Cash is the common denominator of all the current assets. As we know that by definition current assets are those that can be converted into cash within a year. So eventually all the current assets can be converted into cash. This shows how important management of cash is.

How is cash defined? Cash can be defined in two ways. The narrow definition of cash suggests that cash is currency, checks, drafts and demand deposits of bank. The broad view of cash includes near-cash or cash equivalents as well. What are cash-equivalents? They are marketable securities, time deposits of banks etc. We know that marketable securities are those short term money market instruments or government securities which can easily be sold in the market.

However, cash is a type of asset which if left idle, does not produce any return. Still we find that in all business there is some amount of cash in hand or bank. Why do firms hold cash when it does not produce any return?

12.1 Motives for Holding Cash

12.1.1. The transaction motive

Cash inflows and cash outflows in the normal routine of business do not happen at the same time. Due to this sometime the firm will have surplus cash and at other times it will be in deficit. But firm will be required to pay off its routine expenses irrespective of whether it is in surplus cash situation or otherwise. Due to this the firm will be required to hold some cash balance. This is known as keeping cash with transaction motive. It refers to the holding of cash to meet anticipated obligations whose timings are not perfectly synchronized with the receipt of cash.

12.1.2. The precautionary motive

In business many events may be unforeseen. They can not be anticipated or planned in advance. Examples are floods, strikes, a debtor turning bad etc. Due to this uncertainty the firm keeps some cash for unanticipated payment obligations. Holding cash as a precaution serves as an emergency fund for a firm. The precautionary cash balances serve as a cushion to meet unexpected contingencies.

12.1.3. Compensating motive

Banks provide a variety of services to business firms, such as clearance of check, supply of credit and so on. For some of these services the bank charges a commission or fee; for other services there is an indirect compensation. This indirect compensation is often a minimum balance of cash. This amount is required to be kept with the bank. This balance compensates banks for services rendered because it represents cost free funds for them. Banks can use this cash for lending and earn a return.

12.1.4. The speculative motive

The speculative motive refers to the desire of the firm to take advantage of opportunities which present themselves at unexpected moments and which are typically outside the normal course of business. Economists have described this reason for holding cash as creating the ability for a firm to take advantage of special opportunities that if acted upon quickly will favor the firm. An example of this would be purchasing extra raw materials at a discount on payment of immediate cash.

Out of these four motives of cash management described above the most important ones are transaction motive and compensation motive. It has not been observed that firms deliberately keep balances for speculation. Also, for unforeseen contingencies (precautionary motive) firms rely on bank overdrafts etc.

12.2 Factors Determining Cash Needs

12.2.1 Synchronization of Cash flows

In a firm there are regular cash inflows and outflows. But do they always happen together or simultaneously? No, often, they do not occur simultaneously. This leads to need of the firm to hold some cash to make necessary payments. The more is the gap between inflows and outflows, the more will be the need to hold cash. How can we find out the extent to which our cash inflows and outflows are not occurring simultaneously (non-synchronization)? One very important tool is cash budget. We can prepare cash budget for a desired period, say one year. Then we can forecast month-wise cash inflows and outflows for this one year. Through this, we can estimate the months in which there will be cash surplus and months in which there will be a deficit.

12.2.2 Costs of Cash Shortage

It is entirely possible that despite good planning and budgeting, some times cash shortage happens. Whenever it happens, the firm incurs some extra expenses. These costs are called costs of cash shortage. Some authors call them **Short Costs** also. These costs include costs of conversion of marketable securities into cash, cost of bank borrowings to meet shortfall, loss of un-availed cash discounts due to shortage, loss of goodwill due to non-payment of obligations because of shortage and excess interest rates charge by lenders in the situation of emergency borrowing.

12.2.3 Costs of Excess Cash Balances

So shortage of cash has costs. But does excess cash also has some costs? The answer is yes. When excess cash balances are being maintained, they lie unused. If we were not keeping them with the firm, then we could have invested them somewhere (marketable securities) and earned some return. But since we are keeping the cash with the firm, and not investing, we are losing the return we could have earned on marketable securities. This is an opportunity cost to the firm for keeping excess balances.

12.2.4 Administrative costs of cash management

They are the costs of having staff and offices for the purpose of cash management. They include salary, storage and handling, stationary etc.

12.2.5 Costs related to Uncertainty

Cash forecasts and budgets may not always prove accurate. It may happen that receipts are taking more time than expected and there are some defaults as well. Also, payments are happening earlier and of higher amount. Such uncertainties can not be fully eliminated but they can be certainly reduced. We can reduce it by 1) more sophisticated forecasting and budgeting 2) keeping precautionary balances 3) having good overdraft arrangements with banks.

12.3 Cash Management Objectives: the risk return Trade-Off

Before discussing the strategies of cash management, it is important to have a clear understanding of goals of cash management. Following are two goals of cash management:

- To have sufficient cash balances so that current obligations are met, and
- To reduce the unused cash holding in the firm.

Look carefully. What do you find? Aren't these two goals conflicting with each other? The financial manager has to balance these twin objectives. Cash management should result in neither too much cash nor too little. Both the situations will have a different risk-return character.

If cash is kept at a high level, then the chances of firm defaulting on its obligations (risk) will be low. But at the same time, since the idle cash balances will not produce any income, returns will also be low.

On the other hand, what happens if cash balance is kept at a low level? Here, the returns will be high since cash is not kept unused and is invested in marketable securities. But at the same time, the chances of defaulting on obligations of the firm (risk) shall also be high.

This is the key concept of risk-return trade-off in cash management. With this understanding, let us see what should finance manager try to achieve in cash management.

12.3.1 Meeting the cash outflows

The primary objective of cash management is to ensure that cash is available as and when required. Enough cash must be on hand to meet the disbursal needs that arise in the normal course of business. The firm should be able to make the payments at different point of time without any liquidity problem. It means that the firm should have sufficient cash to meet the payment schedules and disbursement needs. It will help the firm in (a) avoiding the chance of default in meeting financial obligations, otherwise the goodwill of the firm is adversely affected, (b) availing the opportunities of getting cash discounts by making early or prompt payments, and (c) meeting unexpected cash outflows without much problem.

12.3.2 Minimizing the Cash Balance

Investment in idle cash balance must be reduced to a minimum. This objective of cash management is based on the idea that unused asset earns no income for the firm. The funds locked up in cash balance are a dead investment and has no earning. Therefore, whatever cash balance is maintained, the firm is foregoing interest income on that balance. The objective of the cash management therefore, should be to keep minimum cash balance.

However, the objective of cash management i.e., maintaining the minimum cash balance must be looked into together with the other objectives i.e., maintaining the payment schedule etc., which require that a firm must have sufficient liquidity (even at the cost of-reducing profitability). But the objective of minimum cash balance results in reduced liquidity and increased profitability.

These objectives appear opposite in nature. The financial manager has to achieve a trade-off between them. He has to ensure that the minimum cash balance being maintained by the firm is not affecting the payment schedule and all disbursement needs. The cash management strategies are needed to reconcile these two goals wherever possible.

What to do when the manager has to chose between one of these? The answer is; meeting payment commitments takes higher priority than minimizing the cash balance.

12.4 Determining the Optimum Cash Balance

12.4.1 Optimum cash balance under certainty: Baumol's Model

This model considers cash management similar to an inventory management problem.

Assumptions of Baumol's model

1. The firm is able to forecast it cash need with certainty
2. The firms cash payments occur uniformly over a period of time
3. The opportunity cost of holding cash is known and it does not change over a period of time

4. The firm will incur the same transaction cost whenever it converts its securities to cash.

Let's assume that the firm sells securities and starts with a cash balance of C rupees. As the firm spends cash, its cash balance decreases steadily and reaches to zero. The firm at this point sells enough marketable securities so that cash balance becomes C again. This process keeps repeating over time. The average cash balance at any point in time will be C/2.

This can be graphically represented as:

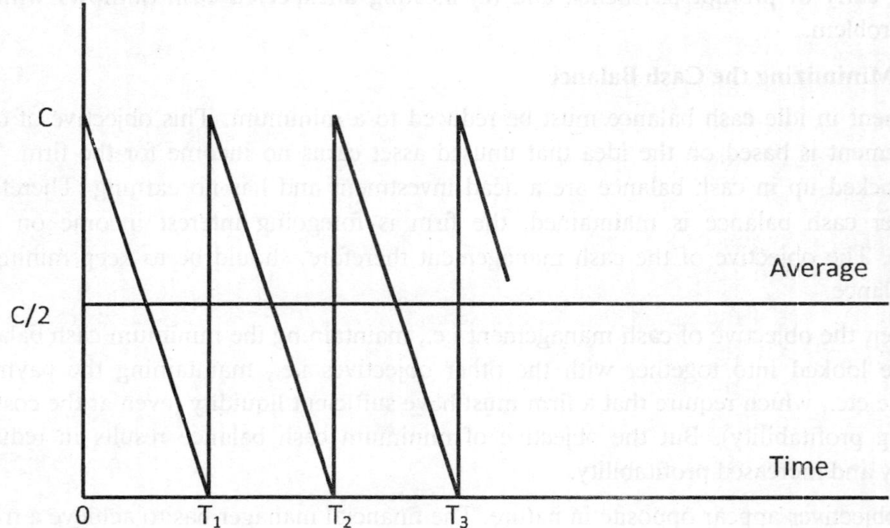

In Baumol's model there are two types of costs connected with cash management. One is called holding cost or opportunity cost of holding idle cash. If opportunity cost is k, then holding cost will be k*C/2.

The other cost is known as transaction cost or cost of converting marketable securities into cash. If each time the firm spends "b" rupees to convert marketable securities into cash then the transaction cost can be found out by b*T/C.

Baumol model says that optimum cash balance C* is the one at which the total cost of cash management will be minimum. The total cost is nothing but sum of holding cost and transaction cost as described above.

$$Total\cos t = k\,x\frac{C}{2} + bx\frac{T}{C}$$

The optimum cash balance, at which total cost is minimized, can be given by the following formula:

$$C = \sqrt{\frac{2bT}{k}}$$

Where C* is the optimum cash balance, b is the conversion cost per transaction, T is the total cash needed during the year and k is the opportunity cost of holding cash balance. The optimum cash balance will increase with the increase in conversion cost "b" and total funds required and decrease with the opportunity cost.

Limitations of Baumol's model

The biggest limitation of Baumol model is that it assumes that the cash flows are certain and known in advance. It does not allow the cash flows to fluctuate. Also, it assumes uniform spending of cash. Firms in practice do not use their cash balance uniformly nor are they able to predict daily cash inflows and outflows.

12.4.2 Optimum Cash Balance under uncertainty: the Miller-Orr Model

The Miller-Orr Model overcomes the shortcomings present in the Baumol's model. It assumes that net cash flows are not certain and not known in advance. In fact, cash flows follow normal distribution with a zero mean & standard deviation.

The MO model talks about a ceiling and a floor within which cash flows are assumed to fluctuate. They are called control limits. These two control limits are known as upper control limit & the lower control limit. There is a return point as well.

What happens if the firm's cash flow reaches the upper limit? Here, firm buys sufficient marketable securities so that its cash balance reduces and comes down to return point. Similarly, when the firm's cash flows go down and reach the lower limit, it sells marketable securities to the extent that its cash balance goes up to return point.

Graphically the Miller Orr model can be depicted as follows:

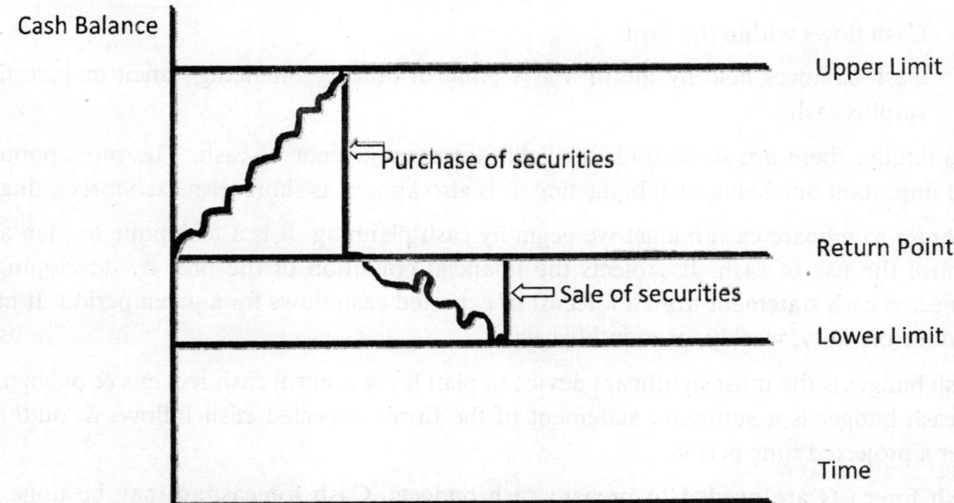

The formula for optimum cash balance, called "Z" in M-O model is as follows

$$Z = \sqrt[3]{\frac{3b\sigma}{4i}}$$

Where, b = fixed cost of conversion per transaction

σ = variance of daily cash balances

i = opportunity cost of carrying cash per day

Here, Lower limit is decided by the management.

Upper Limit = Lower Limit + 3Z

Return Point = Lower Limit + Z

Average Cash Balance = Lower Limit + 4/3 Z

The assumptions of this model are more realistic. It allows for random fluctuations in cash balances within a preset limit. The manager can find out the variance of daily cash balances from the past data of the firm. As mentioned previously, the lower limit is decided by the management based on liquidity position.

12.5 Cash Budgeting

We already know the goal of cash management. It is to reduce the amount of cash being used within the firm so as to increase profitability, but without reducing business activities or exposing the firm to undue risk in its financial obligations.

In cash management, the finance manager has to worry about:

1. Cash flows into & out of the firm,
2. Cash flows within the firm
3. Cash balances held by the firm at a point of time by financing deficit or investing surplus cash.

Thankfully, there are some tools available for management of cash. The most popular and important one being cash budgeting. It is also known as short term cash forecasting.

In order to prepare cash budget we begin by cash planning. It is a technique to plan and control the use of cash. It protects the financial condition of the firm by developing a projected cash statement from a forecast of expected cash flows for a given period. It may be done on daily, weekly, or monthly basis.

Cash budget is the most significant device to plan for & control cash receipts & payments. A cash budget is a summary statement of the firm's expected cash inflows & outflows over a projected time period.

Cash forecasts are needed to prepare cash budgets. Cash forecasting may be done on short or long term basis.

12.5.1 Utility of Cash Budget

Following are the benefits of preparing cash budgets:

1. It helps in identifying in advance the periods when cash is likely to be in surplus or in deficit.
2. It helps the firm to take advantage of cash discounts, plan capital expenditure and make payments for its liabilities on due date.
3. It prevents a situation when the firm is forced to make emergency borrowing at high costs.
4. It prevents excess accumulation of cash since finance manager can plan investment much before the months of surplus cash.
5. Depending on the uncertainty associated with business, the finance manager can change the time horizon of cash budget and may even get daily budgets prepared.

12.5.2 Short-term forecasting methods (covering periods of one year)

There are two important methods of short term cash forecasting.

a) The receipts & disbursement method
b) The adjusted net income method

12.5.2.1 The receipts & disbursement method

In this method the first important task is to decide on a planning horizon. Generally the planning horizon should not be too short or too long. If it is too short then some of the important events of the future may not be reflected in the budget. If the period is too long then the assumptions and forecasts might go wrong because inherent uncertainty about future. Also the planning horizon differs from firm to firm. The planning horizon can be a year subdivided into four quarters. It may be a quarter subdivided into months, or months divided into weeks. The choice of planning horizon depends on the liquidity position of the firm. Under tight liquidity conditions, the firm may prepare cash budget for shorter durations.

In receipt and payments method we take into account all expected receipts and payments that might occur during the chosen planning horizon. They are included in the cash budget irrespective of their accounting treatment. The basis on which they are estimated is as follows:

Cash sales are estimated by projected sales and past trends of credit and cash sales. This basis is also used for estimating collection of accounts receivables. Disposal of fixed assets can be estimated from capital expenditure budget. Other inflows may relate to interest on investments and due to raising loans etc. these figures may come from investment and financing budget.

In case of outflows, the purchases can be divided into two components; cash and credit; based on past trends and current/expected terms of credit offered by suppliers. Payment of other manufacturing expenses including wages and salaries come from production plan and payroll structure.

Repayment of loans can be estimated again from financing plan. Capital expenditure budget shall provide inputs for any projected capital expenditure. Other general, administration and selling expenses can be obtained sales promotion schemes and incentive plans.

Following Mini case shall clarify the concept of cash budget clearly:

Mini-case: ***(Adapted from ICWA Inter Dec 2006)***

Prepare the cash budget of fashion fabrics for the months April, 2006 to July, 2006 (four months) from the details given below:

a) Estimated sales during 2006

February	March	April	May	June	July	August
12,00,000	12,00,000	16,00,000	20,00,000	18,00,000	16,00,000	14,00,000

b) On an average 20% of sales are cash. The credit sales are realized in the third month (January sales in March)

c) Purchases amount to 60% of sales. Purchases made in a month are generally sold in the third month and payment for purchases is also made in the third month.

d) Variable expenses (other than sales commission) constitute 10% of sales and there is a time lag of half a month in these payments.

e) Commission on sales is paid at 5% of sales value and payment is made in the third month.

f) Fixed expenses per month amount to ₹ 75000 approximately.

g) Other items anticipated:

Interest payable on deposits (Due April, 06)	₹ 1,60,000
Sales of old assets (Due May 06)	₹ 12500
Payment of Taxes (Due June 06)	₹ 80000
Purchase of fixed assets (Due July 06)	₹ 650000

Opening cash Balance is ₹ 150000.

Solution

Cash Budget for Fashion fabrics for April, May, June and July 2006:

		April	***May***	***June***	***July***
Opening balance	A	1,50,000	35,000	5,000	1,40,000
Receipts					
Cash Sales		3,20,000	4,00,000	3,60,000	3,20,000
Collection from Debtors		9,60,000	9,60,000	12,80,000	16,00,000
Sale of Old Assets		--	125000	--	--

Total Receipts	B	12,80,000	14,85,000	16,40,000	19,20,000
Payments					
Payment for purchases		9,60,000	12,00,000	10,8,000	9,60,000
Variable Expenses		60,000	80,000	1,00,000	90,000
Variable expenses		80,000	1,0,000	90,000	80,000
Commission on sales		60,000	60,000	80,000	1,00,000
Fixed Expenses		75,000	75,000	75,000	75,000
Other Expenses					
Interest on Deposits		1,60,000	--	--	--
Tax		--	--	80,000	--
Purchase of Fixed Assets		--	--	--	6,50,000
Total Payments	C	12,95,000	15,15,000	15,05,000	19,55,000
	A+B-C	35,000	5,000	1,40,000	1,05,000

Caveat

Cash budget is an extremely appealing but not so precise tool. We must not forget that these numbers are just estimates and the actual figures may be different from estimates. How different can they be? Well the answer lies in the future but we may say that the deviation depends on the extent of volatility in business.

In view of the inherent uncertainty, the finance manager should prepare multiple budgets under different assumptions. For example the budgets may be prepared under three scenarios: pessimistic, optimistic and normal. This would give the firm a better basis for decision making rather than just a single estimate.

12.5.2.2 The adjusted net income method

In this method we trace the flows of working capital. It is also called sources & uses method. One of the objectives of this approach is to project the company's need for cash at a future date, generally for more than one year and normally for two to seven years. Another objective of this approach is to find out whether the company can generate the required funds internally. If it can not then what amount will have to be raised from external sources?

In this approach, the data usually comes from other budgets of the firm like sales budget, capital expenditure budget, financing plan etc. Generally the format contains sources of cash, uses of cash and adjusted net balances.

What is the use of this method? The benefits are as follows:

1. It indicates company's future cash needs.
2. It helps to evaluate proposed capital projects

3. It helps to improve corporate planning.

12.6 Cash Management Strategies

Firms can manage cash in virtually all areas of operations that involve the use of cash. The goal is to receive cash as soon as possible while at the same time waiting to pay out cash as long as possible. The two objectives in managing cash flows are:

- Accelerate cash collections as soon as possible
- To decelerate or to delay cash disbursements as soon as possible

12.6.1 Accelerating cash collections

The amounts of check sent by customer, which are not yet collected, are called collection or deposit float. In other words, it is the difference between bank balance of the firm shown by firm's books and bank's books.

The delay between customers's sending the check and it getting credited in firm's account arises from many factors. The delay has three components viz. Mailing Time, Lethargy and Processing Time. First, it is caused by the mailing time i.e. the time taken by the check in reaching the firm after the customer has dispatched it. Second, the delay is caused by lethargy. Lethargy is defined as the time taken by the seller in depositing the check in its bank after it has been received from the customer. Finally, delay due to processing time, i.e., the time taken by the firm in processing the check for internal accounting purposes.

This float also depends on the processing time taken by the banks. After the check has been deposited in the bank, delay is caused due to the inter bank system to get credit in the desired account.

The greater the firms' deposit float, the longer the time it takes in converting check into usable funds. Attempt should be made to reduce the firm's deposit float by reducing the mailing time, lethargy and processing & collection time.

What are the ways of accelerating cash collections? Let us have a look at some.

How to accelerate cash collections

Some of the ways in which cash collections can be improved are as follows:

- **Early conversion of payment into cash:** There are two ways in which the payments by customers can be converted into cash. One is decentralized collections and the other is concentration banking. However, both are quite inter-linked. In **decentralized collections,** the firm attempts to open many collection centers for receiving the payments from customers. If the firm instructs its customers to pay only to its head office or a single centre, chances are high that mailing time shall be higher for some customers who are situated far off. As an example, you may think of Bill Payment points of various mobile operators. Perhaps within your city itself you might have come across more than one bill payment point for your mobile bill.

Further, in **concentration banking**, the payments are processed by branches of firm's bank situated in the cities where collection centers have been established. Now this arrangement reduces mailing time, lethargy as well as processing time. The processing time is reduced because in concentration banking arrangement, the checks deposited by the customers are sent for local clearing only.

- **Lock-box system**- This system is not prevalent in India. In this system, the firm ties up with postal department and its bankers. In this system, customers can deposit their checks in the post office in a post office box or lock box. The key to this lock box is given to the firm's banker in that city. On regular intervals an official of the bank collects all the checks dropped in the lock box and puts them into processing.
- **Prompt billing to Customers:** The customers can pay only when they have been sent a correct bill for their transactions. The firm should attempt to generate error-free bills as fast as possible and arrange to make them reach the customers on time.

Managerial Tool Kit

Technological Up-gradation in Banking and Cash Management[8]

The methods described above actually belong to a bygone era. Now-a-days, due to advancement in banking technology, firms can convert the payments of customers into cash pretty fast. We present here are some of the recent developments in banking technology. Following two systems offer a cost effective way of funds transfer.

RTGS (Real Time Gross Settlement): RTGS system is a funds transfer mechanism where transfer of money takes place from one bank to another on a 'real time' and on 'gross' basis. This is the fastest possible money transfer system through the banking channel. Settlement in 'real time' means payment transaction is not subjected to any waiting period. The transactions are settled as soon as they are processed. 'Gross settlement' means the transaction is settled on one to one basis without bunching with any other transaction. Considering that money transfer takes place in the books of the Reserve Bank of India, the payment is taken as final and irrevocable. RTGS is applicable only on transactions exceeding ₹ 100000.

National Electronic Fund Transfer (NEFT) is an online system for transferring funds of Indian financial institution (especially banks). This facility is used mainly to transfer funds below ₹ 1,00,000. The Reserve Bank of India has instructed banks that they should not use RTGS for amounts below ₹ 1 lakh (100 thousand). The new rule came into effect on 1 January 2007. For small transactions, RBI has asked banks to offer National Electronic Fund Transfer (NEFT) which provided T+0 and T+1 settlement system (depending on the time a customer gives instruction to the bank for transferring the fund).

12.6.2 How to control disbursements

1. There is no advantage in paying sooner than agreed. By delaying payments much as possible, the firm makes maximum use of trade credit as a source of funds- a source which is interest free. However, the firm should take care that it does not exceed the credit period allowed by suppliers. Regular breach of credit period may jeopardize the image and goodwill of the firm among suppliers.
2. **Disbursement or payment float:** is defined as the difference between the book balance and the bank balance of an account. For example, assume that your firm

opens a current account with ₹ 5,000 at SBI. You receive no interest on the ₹ 5,000 and pay no fee to have the account. Now assume that you receive your telephone bill in the mail and that it is for ₹ 1,000. You write a check for ₹ 1,000 and mail it to the telephone company. At the time you write the ₹ 1,000 check you also record the payment in your bank register. Your bank register reflects the book value of the current account.

Suppose you are sending the check by mail. The check will literally be "in the mail" for a few days before it is received by the telephone company. It may take several more days before the telephone company cashes the check. The time between the moment you write the check and the time the bank cashes the check there will be a difference in your book balance and the balance the bank statement (or passbook) for your current account. This difference is float. This float can be managed. If you know that the bank will not learn about your check for five days, you could take the ₹ 1,000 and invest it or use it for the five days and then place it back into your current account "just in time" to cover the ₹ 1,000 check.

12.7 Types of Short-Term Investment Opportunities

Idle cash balances will not generate any return by itself. In fact, if cash is lying idle, then it would have an opportunity cost. This opportunity cost will be the return foregone by keeping the cash idle and not investing it in business or in some other avenue.

Therefore, after keeping a minimum cash balance in the current account of the firm, any extra cash can be profitably invested in securities that are considered liquid and safe. This will enable the firm to earn some extra money without compromising the liquidity. The finance manager should, however, carefully select securities for such short term investments because here liquidity and safety of funds are more important objectives than the returns.

Some of the avenues of investment for short term cash management are as follows:

Treasury bills: These are short-term government securities. Usually, they are sold at a discount and redeemed at par. The difference is the return on security. They can be bought & sold any time; thus they have liquidity. Also, they do not have the default risk since they are issued by the government.

Commercial papers: are short-term, unsecured securities issued by highly creditworthy large companies. They are issued with a maturity of three months to one year.

Certificates of deposits: These are negotiable certificates issued by banks as a proof of deposit for a fixed duration at an agreed interest rate. They are negotiable instruments that make them marketable securities.

Bank deposits: A firm can deposit its temporary cash in a bank for a fixed period of time. The interest rate depends on the maturity period.

Summary

- Cash is the lifeblood of business. Cash can be defined in two ways. The narrow definition of cash suggests that cash is currency, checks, drafts and demand deposits of bank. The broad view of cash includes near-cash or cash equivalents as well. Cash equivalents are marketable securities, time deposits of banks etc.
- However, cash is a type of asset which if left idle, does not produce any return. Cash is held for **The transaction motive, The precautionary motive, Compensating motive and The speculative motive.**
- The important Factors Determining Cash Needs are Synchronization of Cash flows, Costs of Cash Shortage, Costs of Excess Cash Balances, Administrative costs of cash management, Costs related to Uncertainty.
- The goals of cash management are To have sufficient cash balances so that current obligations are met, and To reduce the unused cash holding in the firm. These two objectives are at variance with each other. The finance manager has to strike a balance between these two objectives. This is the key concept of risk-return trade-off in cash management.
- A major portion of time devoted in cash management goes in Meeting the cash outflows, **Minimizing** the Cash Balance. Whenever there is a conflict between these two objectives, the finance manager prefers meeting payment commitments over minimizing the cash balance.
- There are two prominent models to obtain the minimum or optimum cash balance to hold. First is Baumol's Model. It is called a deterministic model since it assumes predictable cash flows. Second is Miller and Orr's model which assumes cash flows are probabilistic.
- The most popular and important tool for cash management is cash budgeting. It is also known as short term cash forecasting.
- A cash budget is a summary statement of the firm's expected cash inflows & outflows over a projected time period. Cash forecasts are needed to prepare cash budgets. Cash forecasting may be done on short or long term basis.
- The benefits of preparing cash budgets include, identification of cash surplus and shortage, enabling the firm to take advantage of cash discounts, plan capital expenditure and make payments for its liabilities on due date, It prevents a situation when the firm is forced to make emergency borrowing at high costs, preventing excess accumulation of cash,
- There are two important methods of preparing cash budgets, viz.,The receipts & disbursement method and The adjusted net income method
- Major cash management strategies include Accelerating cash collections as soon as possible and decelerating or delay cash disbursements as soon as possible

- In accelerating the cash collections, the focus is on reducing the float. Float is the difference between bank balance of the firm shown by firm's books and bank's books. Other strategies include, **Early conversion of payment into cash, decentralized collections concentration banking, Lock-box system, Prompt billing to customers.**

  For controlling disbursement, the focus is on increasing the payment float. Payment float is defined as the difference between the book balance and the bank balance of an account.

  The cash not needed for short durations can be invested in liquid securities to earn some returns. The instruments in which cash can be invested are Treasury bills, Commercial papers, Certificates of deposits and Bank deposits.

Test Your Understanding

State whether the following statements are true/false

1. Cash in firms may be broadly defined to include near cash also, e.g. marketable securities.
2. Brokerage paid on sale of marketable securities is a short cost.
3. Ability to deal with uncertainty in cash management does not depend on firm's overdraft arrangements
4. Higher the cash balances, higher will be profitability and lower the liquidity.
5. There are three motives for holding cash balances.
6. Baumol model can be applied when the cash flows can not be predicted with certainty.
7. There are no costs associated with excess cash balances.
8. Firms generally keep large cash balance for speculative motive.
9. Cash budget is based on operating cash flows.
10. The opportunity cost of idle cash balances is the rate of return on marketable securities.

Answers : 1.T 2.T 3.F 4.F 5.T 6.T 7.T 8.F 9. F 10.T

Multiple Choice Questions

1. What is cash budget?

   a) An account of surplus cash b) An account of expected cash receipt

   c) An account of cash payment d) None of these

2. While investing surplus cash, which factor is considered most important by finance manager?

   a) Liquidity b) Safety

c) Returns d) None of these

3. The broad definition of cash includes:
   a) Notes, coins and bank balances b) Bank Drafts
   c) Marketable securities d) All the above.
4. Cash management does not include:
   a) Stretching accounts payables
   b) Shortening accounts receivables
   c) Shortening inventory conversion period
   d) None of these
5. "Float" is defined as:
   a) Difference between firms books and bank's books
   b) Surplus cash
   c) Liquidity
   d) None of these
6. Baumol Model of cash management assumes:
   a) Certainty in cash flows b) Uncertainty in cash flows
   c) Equal cash flows d) None of these
7. Float arises due to:
   a) Mailing time b) Lethargy
   c) Processing time d) All the above
8. Which of the following is not a motive for cash holding?
   a) Transaction Motive b) Profit Maximization Motive
   c) Speculative Motive d) Precautionary Motive
9. Which of the following is a method of accelerating cash collections:
   a) Lockbox system b) Concentration Banking
   c) Decentralized collection d) None of these
10. RTGS stands for:
   a) Real Time Gross Settlement
   b) Random Technique Gross Settlement
   c) Real Transaction Gross Settlement
   d) None of these

Answers : 1. d, 2. b, 3.d, 4. d, 5. a, 6.a, 7.d, 8. b, 9. d, 10. d

Review Questions

1. What are various motives for holding cash? **(UPTU 2005)**
2. What do you understand by cash budget? Explain. **(UPTU 2010)**
3. Explain the concept of Deposit Float and Payment Float.
4. Discuss the utility of cash budget as an effective tool of cash management.
5. What are the factors that determine the cash needs of the firm.
6. Describe the Baumol model of obtaining optimum cash balances. **(DU 2007, 2008)**
7. What is cash budget? **(DU)**
8. What do you mean by lock box system?
9. Explain, in brief, the 'non- synchronization of cash flows' and 'short costs' as factors in determining the cash needs of a firm. **(DU 2010)**

Case Study (DU 2007)

Prepare the cash budget for July-December from the following information:

(i) The estimated sales, expenses, etc. are as follows:

(₹ Lakhs)

	June	*July*	*Aug.*	*Sep.*	*Oct.*	*Nov.*	*Dec.*
Sales	35	40	40	50	50	60	65
Purchases	14	16	17	20	20	25	28
Wages and Salaries	12	14	14	18	18	20	22
Misc. Expenses	5	6	6	6	7	7	7
Interest Received	2	-	-	2	-	-	2
Sale of shares	-	-	20	-	-	-	-

(ii) 20 per cent of the sales are on cash and the balance on credit.

(iii) 2 per cent debts are uncollectible; 50 per cent of the total accounts receivable are collected in the month of the sales and the rest during next month.

(iv) The time- lag in payment of misc. expenses and purchase is one month. Wages and salaries are paid fortnightly with a time- lag of 15 days

References

1. Brealey, Richard A & Myres, Stewart C. (2007), Tata McGraw Hill, New Delhi
2. ICAI study Material on Financial Management, The Institute of Chartered Accountants of India, New Delhi.

3. Khan, M Y & Jain (2007) P K, Financial Management, Tata McGraw Hill, New Delhi
4. Kishore, Ravi. M (2009), Financial Management, Taxmann Publications, New Delhi
5. Pandey, I M (2009). Financial Management, Vikas Publishing House, New Delhi
6. Van Horne, James C. (2007),Financial Management & Policy, Pearson Prentice Hall, New Delhi
7. Work book on "Financial Management for Managers": The Institute of Chartered Financial Analysts of India, Hyderabad.
8. www.wikipedea.org

CHAPTER 13 Management of Inventory

Learning Objectives:

By the end of this chapter and having completed the essential reading and activities, you should be able to:

- Understand different kinds of inventories and why they are held
- Identify various costs associated with inventories
- Know various inventory management models
- Describe various inventory control techniques
- Prepare cash budgets

To start with...

Another important component of working capital is stock of materials. Almost all firms in manufacturing and trading have to necessarily have some amount of stocks. Why do firms keep stocks? When should they order for new stocks? Are there ways by which stocks can be classified and managed to yield optimal return on investment in stocks?

This chapter seeks to answer some of these questions. Let us begin first by clearly identifying what "stocks" constitutes.

13.0 Introduction

The word "inventory" is another name given to the stock of material that a firm holds. Almost all the firm involved in manufacturing and trading keep some amount of stocks or inventory. This is the layman's definition of inventory. The Institute of Chartered Accountants of India has defined inventory as ***"tangible property held a) for sale in the ordinary course of business or 2) in the process of production for sale or c) for consumption in the production of goods or service for sale, including maintenance supplies and consumables other than machinery spares"***. Inventory is shown under current assets of a business. In the balance sheet, the details of inventory are shown as under:

Schedule-7 INVENTORIES (As taken, valued and certified by the management) (₹ Cr.)

A. Stores and Spares (at cost)	2.16
B. Loose Tools (at cost)	2.85
C. Finished Goods (At lower of cost or net realizable value)	14.39
D. Raw Material (at cost)	13.38
E. Work in Process (at estimated cost)	4.55
F. Scrap (At estimated realizable value)	2.50
Total	

Inventory can be divided into four types:

1) Raw Material: This is the rupee value of all the unprocessed direct material purchased by the firm for further processing. For example, a firm engaged in manufacturing sugar will need stock of cane for manufacturing sugar. The stock of cane will be its raw material inventory.

2) Work- in – Process: This represents the stock of those raw materials which have been taken to factory and have been entered in the manufacturing process. Though they have entered the manufacturing process, they are not yet ready for sale. They are also known as "Work-in- Progress" or "Semi-finished" stocks. Sometimes they are simply referred to as "WIP".

For example, on any given day in a sugar factory, there will be some cane juice, some cane juice being boiled etc. It is also important to remember that on any given day, the WIP inventory will have goods at different stages of manufacturing process.

3) Finished Goods: These are the final product of a manufacturing process, ready to be sold and distributed. For example sugar stock produced by a sugar mill.

4) Stores & Spares: This is also known as "consumable spares". It covers sundry supplies, maintenance stores, fabricated parts, components, tools, jigs, fixtures and other equipments. Some times it is also referred to as "Loose Tools" or simply "Spares".

13.1 Motives for Holding Inventory

Like cash, there are three principal motives for holding inventory:

a) **Transaction Motive**: Facilitates uninterrupted production & delivery of order at a given right time. This motive means holding of inventory for satisfying sales and production requirements. Normally, every production process takes some time. When the customers come for purchase, the firm needs ready goods so that it can deliver them to customers on time. If the firm does not have ready finished goods, and the customer needs goods immediately, the firm would not be able to supply on time. Therefore some amount of finished goods must be kept ready so that sales are not lost. Similarly, in production process, the factory may demand raw materials continuously. If the firm does not have ready stock of raw material, then it will order for purchase. Till the raw materials arrive, it may have to stop its production process. Therefore, in order to keep the production process uninterrupted, raw materials stock has to be kept. The same logic can be applied on WIP inventory at different stages of production process.

b) **Precautionary Motive**: Is for unexpected changes in demand and supply factors. Inventory kept with precautionary motive is kept to act as a buffer if the actual level of activity (sales or production) exceeds the planned or anticipated levels. Again, this motive is applicable to all types of inventory viz. raw material, work in process and finished goods. For example, a restaurant keeping extra supplies to meet extra demand on Saturday and Sundays.

c) **Speculative Motive**: This motive means keeping large stocks in anticipation of change in prices that would enable the firm to take advantage of changes in prices and getting quantity discounts. This motive also works when the firm is anticipating a change in the product.

13.1.1 Inventory Holding- Practical Considerations- These motives are the theoretical explanations for holding stock. But in reality, inventory serves the "decoupling" purpose. What is decoupling? It means making two processes independent of each other. For example, holding raw material inventory will decouple production and purchase functions. If we do not hold any raw material inventory, what will happen? Then every time there is a requirement of raw material in the factory (production process), immediate purchase will be needed. The production process will ***"depend"*** on the purchase to run smoothly. But by keeping raw material stock, we decouple production and purchase process. The production runs smoothly even if purchase of materials is taking time. Need a policy for balanced investment in inventory include excessive (dangers), inadequate (dangers).

Similarly, WIP inventory acts to decouple various stages of production process. One stage of production process becomes independent of previous stage if some WIP inventory is kept from the previous stage.

Likewise, the Finished goods inventory decouples selling & distribution from production. If finished goods are readily available in stock, the marketing team does not need to consult the production department before committing supply of an order.

13.2 Costs Associated with Inventory

Inventory has the following costs associated with it:

13.2.1 Ordering Costs: These are the costs arising in placing an order for supply of goods. In placing an order the following costs arise:

1) Stationary and order preparation costs
2) Costs of follow up of order including travel etc.
3) Transportation
4) Costs of inspection of supplies upon arrival
5) Salary and Wages of purchase department staff
6) Costs of setting up production run, if materials are produced internally

Here it may be pointed out that a large proportion of ordering costs are fixed in nature. They do not vary with number of orders. The finance manager should try to figure out the variable component of ordering cost. This is more relevant for decision making.

Ordering costs are expressed as Rupees per order. Total ordering costs can be calculated by multiplying ordering costs per order and number of orders.

13.2.2 Carrying Costs

These are the cost of holding inventories. They are expressed as rupees per unit per time period or percentage of inventory value per period. They include:

a) Handling and storage including costs of warehouse space, depreciation, heating etc.
b) Cost of funds invested in inventories (opportunity cost of funds)
c) Obsolescence and deterioration costs
d) Insurance and Taxes (personal property tax or business tax)
e) Damage due to Theft, Fire, Natural Disaster

13.2.3 Stock-Out Costs

What does Stock-out mean? It means a situation when no inventory is left. What are stock-out costs? These are costs arising out of not being able to satisfy demand for inventory because no inventory is left anymore. They arise when actual demand is higher than available supply. Stock-out costs can arise in all three types of inventory, i.e., Raw Materials, Work-in-Process and Finished Goods. In case of raw material inventory, stock-out costs include higher prices paid for emergency orders. In case of WIP, the stock-out costs include costs of speeding up production or cost of stoppage in production. In case of finished goods, the stock-out costs include profits and goodwill sacrificed on lost sales. Also, it includes profits and goodwill sacrificed on future lost sales.

13.4 Techniques of Inventory Control: The EOQ Model

After taking a look at the various costs associated with the inventory, we are ready to learn management of inventory. The objective of inventory management is to arrive at a level of inventory where total costs associated with it are minimized. Need a policy for balanced invested in inventory include excessive (dangers), inadequate (dangers).

There are various inventory control models available. One of the simplest models of inventory control is Economic Order Quantity (EOQ) model. This model attempts to find out the quantity of a material that should be ordered (in both cases, either external purchase or internal production) so that the total costs associated with inventory of that material is minimized. Here the total costs would include Ordering Costs and Carrying Costs as described above. Why do we not include Stock-out Costs? We do not include stock-out costs because they are difficult to quantify objectively. Different people may place different values on lost sales due to stock-out.

Assumptions of EOQ Model:

1) Demand or usage of material is known with certainty.
2) The demand for material remains constant.
3) The Lead Time for replenishment of inventory is nil. (What is Lead Time? Lead Time is time it takes between placing an order and receiving the goods.) This assumption actually means that new supply of an item arrives the moment its last unit is consumed.
4) Price of inventory remains constant, whatever be the order size.
5) Ordering and carrying costs remain constant.

Graphically, the inventory consumption looks like a saw tooth EOQ model.

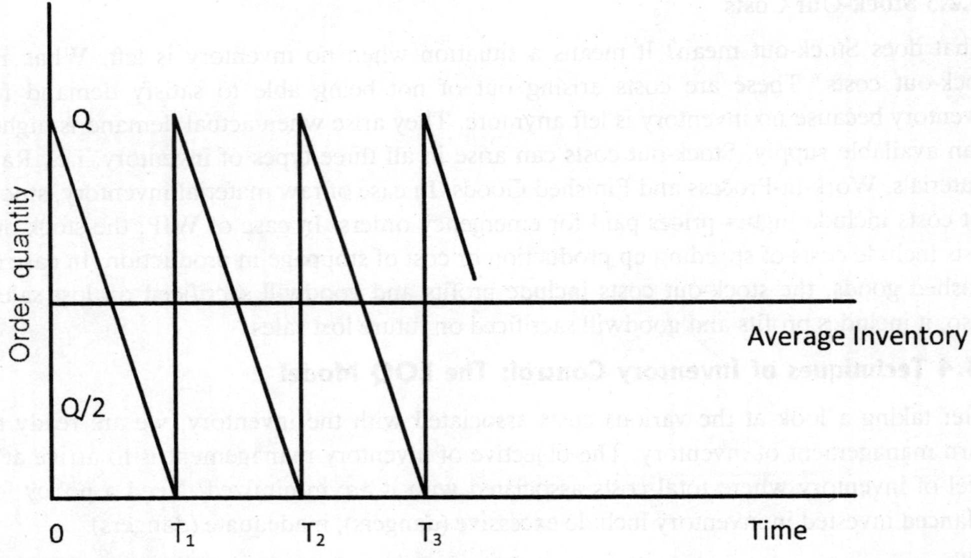

Now let us define the variables of EOQ model.

Let, A = annual consumption of inventory

S = cost of placing an order or setup costs

C = annual carrying costs per unit

Q = Order Quantity

Q^*= Economic Order Quantity

Now, by definition, Economic Order Quantity is the order quantity at which total costs will be minimized.

Total Costs = Carrying Costs + Ordering Costs

= Average Inventory x Annual carrying cost per unit + No. of orders in a year x ordering cost per order

= Q/2 x C + A/Q x S

By differentiation, the order quantity at which total cost is minimized, comes to be:

$$Q^* = \sqrt{\frac{2AS}{C}}$$

This is economic order quantity. Graphically we can show it as follows:

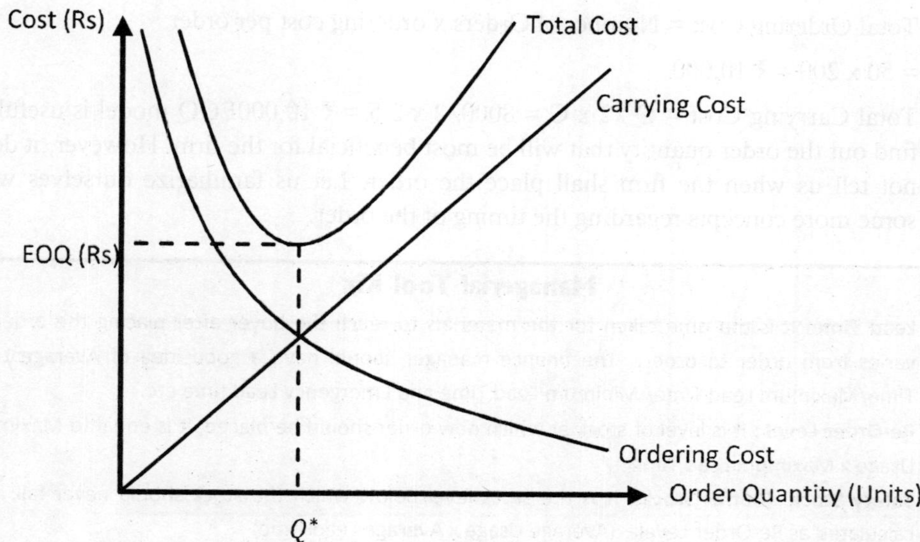

As we can see in the above diagram, total ordering cost declines as order quantity is increased. Total carrying cost increases as order quantity is increased. The total cost first declines and then increases. The economic order quantity is found on X axis at the point where total cost is minimized.

Example 1: The annual consumption of an item X is 400000 units. The unit cost of this item is ₹ 10. The ordering cost per order is ₹ 200 and carrying cost is 25% per annum. Calculate: 1) Economic Order Quantity 2) Number of orders per year 3) Total Cost 4) Total Ordering Cost 5) Total Carrying Cost

Solution

1) Economic Order Quantity = $\sqrt{\frac{2AS}{C}}$

Given A = 40000 units, S = ₹ 200 and Carrying cost = 25% per annum. Now we can find out carrying cost per unit by multiplying unit cost of item with per annum cost. We get, 25% x 10 = ₹ 2.50 as per unit carrying cost. Now putting these values in the formula we get,

$$\frac{2x400000\,x\,200}{2.5}$$

= 8,000 units.

2) Number of orders per year = Annual Consumption / Economic Order Quantity

= 4,00,000/8,000

= 50 orders

3) Total Cost = A/Q* x S + Q*/2 x C = 40,000/8,000 x 200 + 8,000/2 x 2.5 = ₹ 20,000

4) Total Ordering Cost = Number of Orders x ordering cost per order

= 50 x 200 = ₹ 10,000

5) Total Carrying Cost = $Q^*/2$ x C = 8000/2 x 2.5 = ₹ 10,000EOQ model is useful to find out the order quantity that will be most beneficial for the firm. However, it does not tell us when the firm shall place the order. Let us familiarize ourselves with some more concepts regarding the timing of the order.

Managerial Tool Kit

- **Lead Time:** It is the time taken for the materials to reach the buyer after placing the order. It varies from order to order. The finance manager should have a good idea of Average Lead Time/Maximum Lead Time/ Minimum Lead Time and Emergency Lead time etc.
- **Re-Order Level :** It is level of stock at which new order should be placed. It is equal to Maximum Usage x Maximum Lead Time
- **Safety Stock (Buffer Stock):** It is the stock level below which the stock should never fall. It is calculated as Re-Order Level – (Average Usage x Average Lead Time)
- **Maximum Stock Level:** It is calculated as Re-Order Level + Economic Order Quantity – (Minimum Usage x Minimum Lead Time)
- **Average Stock Level** :(Maximum Stock Level + Safety Stock Level)/2
- **Danger Level:** it is equal to Average Usage x Emergency Lead Time.

13.5 ABC Analysis

Within the inventory of a firm, different items have different values. Some are high value items and some others are moderate to low value. It makes sense to manage higher value items more carefully. This is because, the potential for savings is higher in a high value item than in a lower value item. Also, generally, higher value items have lower safety stock owing to their higher value. Whereas, the safety stock in case of lower value stocks is higher.

ABC approach seeks to classify items of inventory in three classes A, B and C as per their value in rupee terms. In "A" category, the highest value items are listed. Typically, A category will include say, 15% of items representing about 80% of value of total inventory. IN "B" category, the next 15-20% items are kept representing about 15-20% of total inventory value. Finally in "C" category, about 60-70% items are kept that represent only 15-20 % of value of total inventory.

Graphically, we can represent ABC classification as follows:

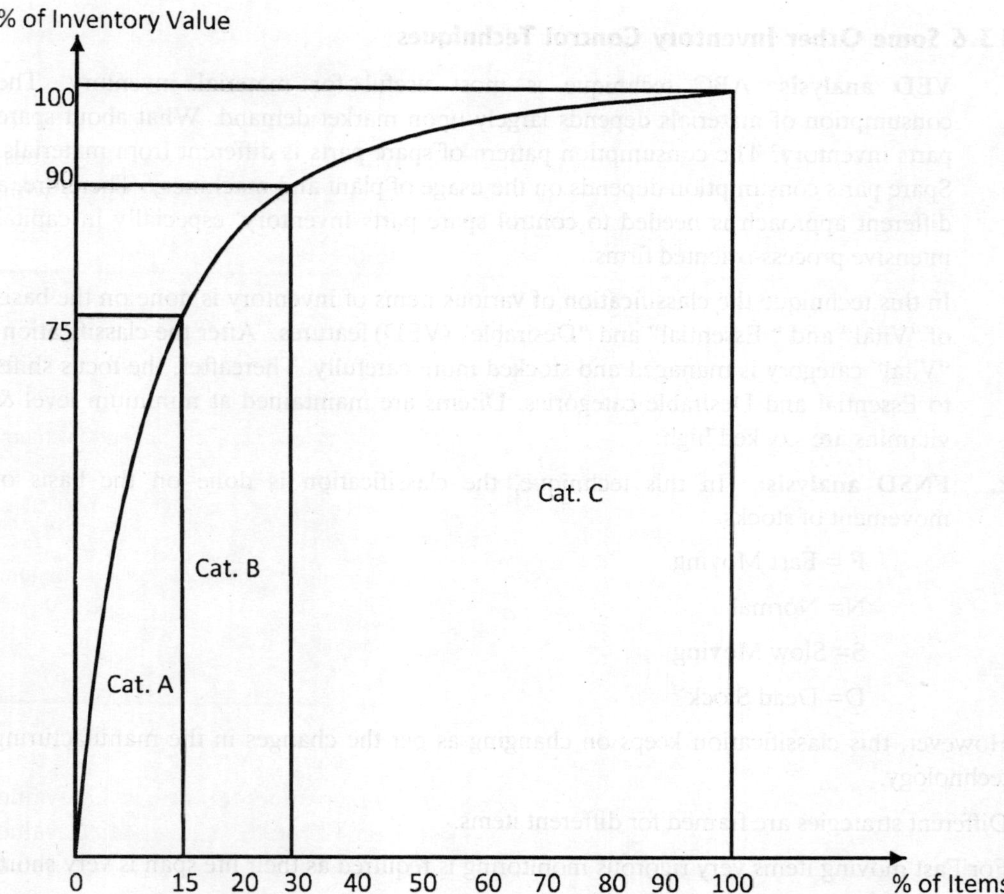

Once these items are classified in A, B and C categories, appropriate control strategies are developed separately for each class.

"A" items are controlled by using price control techniques. In "A" items safety stocks are generally lower and therefore they call for strict control. They require maximum follow up and should be handled by expert managers. Their order quantity and re-order level should also be very carefully determined.

"B" items require moderate follow up and control. In case of "B" items moderate amount of safety stock can be maintained. The management responsibility of such items can be given to middle management.

In case of "C" items, the control can be exercised by general control techniques. They do not require rigorous follow up and review. The safety stock can also be maintained at a higher level. Normally, expert managers are not required to control "C" category items.

ABC technique basically accords priority to various items of inventory based on their contribution to total inventory value. It can be applied easily to all kinds of inventory e.g. spare parts, materials etc.

13.6 Some Other Inventory Control Techniques

1. **VED analysis**: ABC technique is most useful for material inventory. The consumption of materials depends largely upon market demand. What about spare parts inventory? The consumption pattern of spare parts is different from materials. Spare parts consumption depends on the usage of plant and machinery. Therefore, a different approach is needed to control spare parts inventory, especially in capital intensive process-oriented firms.

   In this technique the classification of various items of inventory is done on the basis of "Vital" and " Essential" and "Desirable" (VED) features. After the classification, "Vital" category is managed and stocked more carefully. Thereafter, the focus shifts to Essential and Desirable categories. Ditems are maintained at minimum level & vitamins are stocked high.

2. **FNSD analysis:** In this technique, the classification is done on the basis of movement of stocks.

   F = Fast Moving

   N= Normal

   S= Slow Moving

   D= Dead Stock

However, this classification keeps on changing as per the changes in the manufacturing technology.

Different strategies are framed for different items.

For Fast moving items very rigorous monitoring is required as their life span is very short. Otherwise, frequent stock-out situation may arise.

In case of Normal items, generally the life span may stretch up-to one year. The projection of purchase of such items is governed by future demand of end product.

Slow moving items last for longer time, even in excess of two years. The inventory manager must have strong justification for ordering new purchase of such items.

Dead items represent the ones that have been lying in the inventory for a very long time and there seems to be no imminent demand for them. Now these items impose carrying cost on the system. If there appears no possible use of them in future, then they must be sold as scrap as soon as possible.

Illustrative Solved Example

Mini Case

Multigrain Limited is interested in creating a scientific inventory management system. It has hired you as its consultant. It has compiled the following information for your reference.

Annual Consumption of Material	100000 units
Ordering Cost per order	₹ 50
Average carrying cost per unit	₹ 10
Maximum Usage Rate	400 units per day
Average Usage Rate	270 units per day
Average Lead Time	9 days
Maximum Lead Time	15 days
Minimum Lead Time	3 days
Emergency Lead Time	2 days

You are required to compute:

a) EOQ

b) Maximum Stock Level

c) Safety Stock

d) Danger Stock Level

e) Re Order Level

Solution:

a) EOQ = $\sqrt{\frac{2AS}{C}}$

$= \sqrt{\frac{2x100000x50}{10}}$

= 1000 units.

b) Re Order Level = Maximum usage per period x Maximum Lead time

= 400 x 15

= 6,000 units

c) Maximum stock level = Reorder level + Economic order Quantity – Minimum Usage X Minimum lead time

= 6,000 + 1,000 – Minimum Usage x 3

In order to calculate Minimum usage, we can use the formula:

Average usage = (Maximum Usage + Minimum Usage)/2

We get:

270 = (400 + Minimum usage)/2

It gives, minimum usage = 140 units. Putting this value in above equation of maximum stock level ; we get:

Maximum stock level = 6,000 + 1,000 – 140 x 3 = 6580 units

d) Safety stock level = Reorder level – Average Stock Level x Average Lead Time

= 6,000-270 x 9

= 3,570 units

e) Danger Level = Average Usage x Emergency Lead Time

= 270 x 2

= 540 units.

Summary

- Inventory or stock is defined as (ICAI) ***"tangible property held a) for sale in the ordinary course of business or 2) in the process of production for sale or c) for consumption in the production of goods or service for sale, including maintenance supplies and consumables other than machinery spares"***. Inventory is shown under current assets of a business.
- Inventory can be divided into four types, viz. Raw material, work in process, finished goods and stores & spares.
- Generally the Motives for Holding Inventory are a)Transaction Motive b)Precautionary Motive and c) Speculative Motive.
- Practically, inventory is held for decoupling various stages of business. Raw material inventory will decouple production and purchase functions. WIP inventory acts to decouple various stages of production process. Finished goods inventory decouples selling & distribution from production.
- Inventory has the various costs associated with it. They are Ordering Costs, Carrying Costs and Stock-Out Costs.
- The objective of inventory management is to arrive at a level of inventory where total costs associated with it are minimized.
- There are various inventory control models available. One of the simplest models of inventory control is Economic Order Quantity (EOQ) model. This model attempts to find out the quantity of a material that should be ordered so that the total costs (Ordering Costs and Carrying Costs) associated with inventory of that material is minimized.
- EOQ model assumes a) Demand or usage of material is known with certainty b) The demand for material remains constant. C) The Lead Time for replenishment of inventory is nil. D) Price of inventory remains constant, whatever be the order size. E) Ordering and carrying costs remain constant.

- At the EOQ level of order quantity, total inventory cost is at the minimum and also, the ordering cost is equal to carrying cost at this level.
- ABC analysis is an important technique of inventory monitoring and control. ABC approach seeks to classify items of inventory in three classes A, B and C as per their value in rupee terms. In "A" category, the highest value items are listed. Typically, A category will include say, 15% of items representing about 80% of value of total inventory. IN "B" category, the next 15-20% items are kept representing about 15-20% of total inventory value. Finally in "C" category, about 60-70% items are kept that represent only 15-20 % of value of total inventory. Once these items are classified in A, B and C categories, appropriate control strategies are developed separately for each class.
- Other inventory control techniques include VED (Vital , Essential and Desirable) analysis, and FNSD (Fast ,Normal, Slow and Dead) analysis.

Test Your Understanding

State whether the following statements are true/false

1. Inventory includes cash and marketable securities.
2. Inventory is usually held with speculative motive.
3. In EOQ model, the consumption pattern is assumed to be varying.
4. EOQ model does not consider carrying costs since they can not be objectively computed.
5. In EOQ model, the optimum order quantity is the one at which total cost is minimized.
6. In ABC analysis, items are classified as per their contribution to total inventory value.
7. Lead time is time taken in converting raw materials into finished goods.
8. Safety stock is also known as minimum stock or buffer stock.
9. VED analysis is more useful in spare parts inventory.
10. In ABC analysis, the items in A category require least efforts to manage.

Answers : 1. F 2.F 3.F 4.F 5.T 6.T 7.F 8.T 9.T 10.F

Multiple Choice Questions

1. The general motive of holding inventories is: **(UPTU 2010)**

   a) Transaction Motive b) Precautionary Motive

   c) Speculative Motive d) All the above

2. ABC analysis is a method of controlling: **(UPTU 2010)**

a) Cash b) Credit
c) Inventory d) None of above

3. In ABC analysis, "C" items must be monitored:
a) Closely b) Loosely
c) Moderately d) None of these

4. The term "inventory" includes:
a) Raw Materials b) Work in Process
c) Finished Goods d) All the above

5. The economic order quantity is the optimum order size at which total costs are:
a) Maximum b) Minimum
c) Moderate d) None of these

6. The annual consumption of an item is 3,000 units. The cost of ordering per order is ₹ 30 and the carrying cost per unit is ₹ 20. The EOQ will be:
a) 400 units b) 300 units
c) 100 units d) None of these

7. In the question no. 6 above, how many orders per year will be placed?
a) 15 b) 10
c) 5 d) None of the above

8. In the question 6 above, what will be average gap between two orders?
a) 30 days b) 36 days
c) 46 days d) None of these

9. Which of the following is not an inventory classification technique:
a) ABC analysis b) VED analysis
c) FNSD d) JIT

10. In EOQ model, the average inventory is calculated as:
a) EOQ/2 b) EOQ/3
c) EOQ d) None of these

Answers : 1. d 2. c 3.b 4. d 5.b 6.b 7.b 8.b 9. d 10. a

Review Questions

1. Explain the techniques for inventory control. **(UPTU2005)**
2. Explain ABC classification technique of inventory control. **(UPTU 2007)**
3. What is inventory management **(DU)**

4. Explain various risks involved in holding inventories? **(DU)**
5. How is re-orderd point determined. Illustrate with an example. **(DU)**
6. What are the assumptions of EOQ model? Explain. **(DU 2007)**
7. Write short notes on a) VED analysis b) ABC analysis.
8. Why ordering costs and Carrying cost are equal at EOQ level? **(DU 2007 Adapted)**
9. Explain in detail the EOQ model of inventory management.
10. Write short notes on:
    a) Reorder Point
    b) Danger Level
    c) Safety stock

Case Study (DU 2010)

A company manufactures a product from a raw material, which is purchased at ₹ 60 per kg. The company incurs a handling cost of ₹ 360 plus freight of ₹ 390 per order. The incremental carrying cost of inventory of raw material is ₹ 0.50 per kg per month. In addition, the cost of working capital finance on the investment in inventory of raw material is ₹ 9 per kg. per annum. The annual production of the product is 1,00,000 units and 2.5 units are obtained from 1 kg of raw material.

(i) Calculate the economic order quantity of raw material.

(ii) Advice, how frequently should orders for procurement of raw material be placed, assuming 360 days in a year.

(iii) If the company proposes to rationalize placement of orders on quarterly basis, what percentage of discount in the price of raw material should be negotiated.

References

1. Brealey, Richard A & Myres, Stewart C. (2007), Tata McGraw Hill, New Delhi
2. Khan, M Y & Jain (2007) P K, Financial Management, Tata McGraw Hill, New Delhi
3. Kishore, Ravi. M (2009), Financial Management, Taxmann Publications, New Delhi
4. Pandey, I M (2009). Financial Management, Vikas Publishing House, New Delhi
5. Van Horne, James C. (2007),Financial Management & Policy, Pearson Prentice Hall, New Delhi
6. Work book on "Financial Management for Managers": The Institute of Chartered Financial Analysts of India, Hyderabad.

CHAPTER 14 Management of Receivables

Learning Objectives:

By the end of this chapter and having completed the essential reading and activities, you should be able to:

- Understand the Concept of receivables and its management
- Have an understanding of various variables of receivable management
- Understand the factoring mechanics

To start with...

Akash just completed his MBA and decided to join his family business. His father Abhishek deals in FMCG products. He started his business as a private limited company and now he has a turnover of hundred crores. Pawan is very happy because his son is going to join his business.

In FMCG business you can not survive without making credit sales. After joining Akash, observed that there was a continuous increase in the figure of receivables and bad debts since last four years.

Akash decided to take steps to correct this situation. He felt that control of receivables and bad debts was possible applying receivables management strategies and to establishing a credit policy for his business.

Receivables are found in every business. These are the assets of the firm. If receivables are not managed properly, they may become bad debts. But if we manage them well, we can control receivables and bad debts both.

In this chapter, we will discuss how to manage receivables, concept of credit policy, credit evaluation and factoring.

Happy Learning!!

14.0 Introduction

We can sell our products and services in two ways. First, we provide the goods and services and get the payment immediately. This is known as cash sales. Second, we provide our goods and services now and get the payments later. This is known as credit sales. In case of cash sales, seller realizes payments at the time of sales i.e. sales and payments are synchronous. In case of credit sales, seller does not realize payments at the time of sales i.e. sales and payments are not synchronous. In credit sales, payments are deferred i.e. seller realizes payments some time after making sales. The total amount yet to be received from customers of credit sales is termed as **"receivables"** of the business. They are also known as "debtors" or "sundry debtors". These receivables are assets for a firm. They are shown under current assets in the balance sheet.

In today's scenario, receivables can be found in every business. Practically every firm has to make some sales on credit. The decision to sell on credit is made with the objective of increasing sales of the firm. Some customers, who cannot purchase goods on cash, will want to purchase on credit. If firm's policy is to sell goods only on cash or permit credit very selectively, then many customers seeking credit purchase will buy goods from somewhere else. In this case firm will incur two losses. First will be loss of current sales to a customer. Second, the firm may lose the customer forever. This is the loss of future sales.

But when a firm sells goods on credit, receivables increase. Since receivables are assets, total assets of the firm increase. However, risk of bad debts also increases with the increase in receivables.

Here a need of management of receivables arises.

To keep receivables at a justified level and bad debts at low level, every business has to manage its receivables in a prudent manner.

In your financial accounting curse in the previous semester, you must have come across the word"bad debts". It represents those receivabels where the buyer has defaulted and there is little change of recovery in future.

But we come to know of our recievables turning into bad debts long after the sales has taken place. So, bad debts arising out of sales of one period will actually affect the projects of the preriod in which we recognize their occurence.

This is in contravention of the "matching concept" of accounting which says that in order to arise at the correct profit, all the expences of losses of a period must be subtracted from sales of that period only. But since we do not know how much of this periods sales will become bad debts in future, how do we arrive at the correct profit as per matching concept?

We do it by creating an "estimate" of bad debts that might happen in future. Our estimates is baed on our past expences. This estimates is called "Provisions of Bad debts". How do we treat "Provision for bad debts" in accounting? We create this provision out of current years profits. Now by doing this we have followed the matching concept to the maximum extent possible. In future, it may turn out that actual bad debts are "more" or "less" than the provision made. But, as of now, we have done our best by creating a provision for bad debts.

14.1 Objectives of Receivable Management

- To keep bad debts at low level.
- To set up firm's credit policy.
- To evaluate credit worthiness of customers.
- To smoothing the collection from debtors.
- To get the benefits of factoring.

14.2 Benefits & Costs of Receivable Management

Benefits

- In this competitive market, a firm cannot ignore the credit sales. A good credit policy not only boosts sale of the firm but also brings new customers. The customers are likely to favor firms, which provide them goods on liberal credit.

- More sales mean more profit. So long as cost of credit sales is less than gains from these credit sales, the credit sales will boost profit of the firm also.

Costs

- Firms procure funds on interest. In case of credit sales, payments from debtors are deferred. From the time of credit sales till the payments are made by the customer, the funds of the firm gets blocked in the receivables. Due to blocking of funds firm bears the interest cost in the form of cost of receivables.
- In case, if customers are delaying payments (not paying on due date), firm (seller) bears another cost called delinquency cost. This cost is the cost incurred on reminders, letters and telephone calls made to customers to collect dues. Additionally, delinquency costs include opportunity cost of the funds blocked in receivables beyond due date.
- Cost of bad debts. In cases of credit sales, there is always exists a possibility of default by customers. If a customer defaults, the firm bears a cost in the form of bad debts.
- Firms incur some cost on evaluation of creditworthiness of customers, collection from them and maintenance of record of customers. This is called administrative cost.

In receivables management we try and keep our receivables at a level where the benefits from having them is higher than the costs. Management of receivables means timely collection from debtors, minimization of bad debts, formulation of credit policy, evaluation of credit worthiness of customers and control of receivables. The following are the three aspects of receivables management:

(1) Credit Policy

(2) Credit Evaluation

(3) Control of receivables

14.3 Credit Policy

In some businesses, credit sales are very high. In some others, credit sales are low. However, the common factor in both the cases is that some amount of credit sales is there. Quite often, businesses cannot avoid credit sales totally. While credit sales can not be avoided, they can certainly be controlled. In fact, we saw earlier that credit sales have benefits as well as costs. Therefore, it makes sense to exercise control over receivables.

To control the receivables, a need arises to establish a credit policy."**Credit policy can be termed as a set of guidelines enabling a firm to take decisions of granting or not granting credit to customers"**. In practice, some firms may follow strict credit policy and some follow liberal credit policy. To establish an effective credit policy a firm has to determine the following variables:

(a) Credit Standards

(b) Credit Terms

(c) Collection of receivables

14.3.1 Credit Standards: Credit standards mean criteria that should be fulfilled by a customer before firm makes any credit sales to him. While establishing a credit policy, setting credit standards is often very challenging. Whether the standards should be too high or too low? Broadly, firm may adopt two approaches to credit standards. One, strict credit standards and other, liberal credit standards. Both the approaches have their pros and cons.

In case firm sets strict credit standards, it will result it low collection cost, low quantum of receivables and low bad debts. However, strict credit standards may also reduce the growth rate of sales.

In case of liberal credit standards, the sales growth may increase. However, the firm may also face increased possibility of default by customers resulting in heavy bad debts, increased quantum of receivables and higher cost debtors collection.

This discussion shows that firm should be very careful while establishing a new credit policy or altering its present credit policy. However, the credit policy may not be uniform for all the customers. It may vary from customer to customer. Generally, firms adopt liberal credit standards for its old customers with good payment record & creditworthiness and strict credit policy for its new customers.

14.3.2 Credit Terms: Credit terms means payment terms and conditions under which firms grant credit to its customers. Credit terms are usually depicted in the format "X/Y Net Z", where

(i) X=Cash Discount

(ii) Y=Discount Period

(iii) Z=Credit Period

14.3.2.1 Credit Period: Credit period means the time lag between sales and payment. In other words, credit period means length of time over which customers are required to pay for their purchases. The credit period may vary anywhere between 10 days to 60 days. However, it differs from industry to industry. Credit period plays very important role in credit policy. Long credit period can boost sales figure by attracting new customers. However, it may also result in high amount of receivables, thereby increasing possibility of increased bad debts.

Similarly short credit period has its own flaws and benefits. Short credit period can reduce the possibility of bad debts by lowering the receivables. However, it also reduces the sales growth.

Thus, the every firm should fix its credit period after considering the effect of the long as well as short credit period.

14.3.2.2 Cash Discount/Discount Period: Cash discount can be termed as incentive given to the customers for early and prompt payment. Discount period is the time period within which, if, customer makes payment, then he will get a discount. For example, ABC Ltd. gives credit to its customers at 3/15 net 45, it means 3% discount if payment is made within 15 days otherwise full payment is to be made within 45 days. In the example, 15 days is discount period because customer can get discount only if he makes payment within 15 days. The discount rate is 3%.

The cash discount directly affects the average collection period. If customers start making payment early to get the benefit of cash discount, naturally the average collection period shall go down.

A reduction in discount rate can be brought about in two ways. It may be done either through lower discount rate for the same period or by offering same discount rate for shorter period. Similarly, an increase in discount rate can be brought about by offering higher discount rate for same period or same discount rate for longer period. The increase as well as decrease in discount rates affects the collection from debtors. Higher discount rate may increase the sales and lower discount rate may decrease the sales.

Any decrease in discount period means early collection from debtors and results in reduced receivables. Increase in discount period means longer time taken in collection from debtors and increase in amount involved in receivables.

The decision to change any of the parameters of credit terms affects cost and benefits from receivables. The firm should do cost and benefit analysis before making any change in discount rate or credit period. Sometimes firms have to liberalize their credit terms to bring parity with other firms and to meet the competition. Liberalization in credit terms means increased discount rate for the same credit discount period or equal discount rate for long credit period. The liberal credit terms will result in increased sales and higher profit but it also increases risk of bad debts. The bad debts risk increases because quantum of receivables increases due to liberal credit terms.

14.3.2.3 Collection of Receivables: Collection refers to follow up with the debtors to expedite payments. Every firm should have a collection policy. The objective of collection policy should be to expedite the payment from slow paying customers and to decrease the risk of bad debts. In a strong collection procedure, every customer should be intimated in advance that the due date of payment is approaching. This intimation may be through letters emails or phone calls. After the due date, firm should dispatch letters, make telephone calls or arrange personal visits of officers to the customers. There should also be a threat of legal action to the customers not making payments despite all the efforts. However, legal action should be taken only after exhausting all other options. Also, the financial position of the customer must be taken into account before initiating legal action. It may so happen that a few customers are willing to pay but due to financial crunch they are unable to make payments.

The collection policy should be neither very strict nor very liberal. A strict collection policy may repel some customers or affect the growth in sales. In case of a liberal credit policy, customers may delay the payments. They may take it for granted. So there should be a balanced collection policy which ensures timely payments and reduces the risk of bad debts.

14.4 Credit Evaluation

Credit evaluation means the assessment of credit worthiness of customer. Why do firms assess credit worthiness of customers? The answer is, if a firm sells goods on credit with no credit policy, credit standards, control of receivables, the risk of default by customers will be very high. To protect itself from bad debts and delays in payment from customers, every firm needs to evaluate the credit worthiness of its customers. An effective credit evaluation saves the firms from the cost of bad debts, cost of collection from customers and cost of delayed payments. In the evaluation process, firms decide that whether credit is to be given to a particular customer or not. If yes, then how much and on what terms. Evaluation of credit worthiness involves some cost also. It may be in the form of

In credit evaluation, firms judge following 3 Cs of a customer:

1) **Capacity:** Capacity means the customer's ability to meet his obligation. It refers to assessing the financial position of the customer.

2) **Character:** Character means the willingness of the customer to meet his obligation.

3) **Collateral:** Collateral means the security offered by customer for taking credit.

In the assessment of previously mentioned 3 Cs, firms take following two steps, (1) Collection of credit information (2) Analysis of credit information.

Collection & analysis of credit information: In the process of credit evaluation of a customer firms collect information from the various sources. The following are the sources of information about a customer:

- **Financial Statements:** A firm can get information about the customer's credit worthiness and his paying capacity through his financial statements. By going through the profit & loss account and balance sheet of the customer, firms get information about the customer's wealth, profitability and his liabilities. Financial statements provide very useful information about the customer. Firms may analyze the credit worthiness on the basis of various ratios calculated with the help of financial statements. Based on these ratios firms may assess the credit worthiness of a prospective customer.

- **Bank Reference:** Bank where the customer maintains his account can also be a very useful source of information. Based on information given by bank the credit worthiness of a customer can be judged very easily. Generally, banks do not provide information about their customers. In such a case, firm may approach its bank to contact customer's bank. The customer's bank may provide necessary information to another bank.

- **Credit Scoring:** Credit scoring is a numerical tool to assess the credit worthiness of a customer. In credit scoring, credit analysts rank each customer. The ranking is given to various factors of a customer. These ranking then multiplied by the pre assigned weights to each factor. Based on these scores, credit worthiness of a customer's is assessed.
- **Credit Rating Agency:** Credit rating agencies are also a source of information about the customer. These agencies give the ratings to the various customers. These ratings are given on the basis of information gathered by these agencies. Based on these ratings a firm may take decision about the credit worthiness of a customer. In India such ratings are not very popular. However, some agencies have started these ratings e.g., ONICRA.

14.5 Control of Receivables

After credit standards and credit evaluation, control of receivables is another important aspect of receivables management. Without control of receivables all the efforts made to set credit standards and credit evaluation will not give any fruitful result. In control process, every firm needs to keep close watch on all the receivables. The firms should regularly monitor its receivables. There are four tools for monitoring and control of receivables, which are given below:

1. Average Collection Period
2. Ageing Schedule
3. Line of credit
4. Collection Matrix

1. **Average Collection Period:** Average collection period provides number of days of sales outstanding. Average collection period is calculated by the following formula:

$$\textbf{\textit{Average Collection Period}} = \frac{\textit{Average Receivables}}{\textit{Average Daily Credit Sales}}$$

   The average collection period should be calculated on regular intervals like every 30 days or 45 days. e.g. if average collection period of a firm is 25 days and this firm's credit period is 20 days ,it means that firm should review its collection procedure. The receivables will be in control if average collection period is less than or equal to the credit period.

2. **Ageing Schedule:** In this method, a schedule (table) is prepared consisting of age brackets in days and % of total receivables falling in that age brackets. "Age" here is nothing but no. of days for which the particular receivable has remained unpaid. This schedule can be prepared at any given point of time. At that point, different receivables are classified into different ages. The ageing schedule provides information about the slow paying debtors. This schedule is compared with the

previous ageing schedule which provides the résult of action taken on the basis of previous ageing schedule. An illustrative ageing schedule is given below:

Age (days)	%age of total receivables
00 – 30	55
31 – 45	15
46 – 60	12
61 – 75	10
76 and above	8

3. **Line of credit:** Line of credit is another important tool of control of receivables. Line of credit means the maximum outstanding amount permissible for a particular customer at any point of time. Line of credit varies from customer to customer. It should be reviewed from time to time. If customers' outstanding balances are within line of credit, then it may be concluded that receivables are under control. If a particular customer's outstanding balance is below the line of credit and its next billing will take outstanding balance beyond the line of credit then the line of credit may be temporarily increased. After periodic review line of credit may be increased or decreased. Sometimes based on past experiences line of credit for a particular customer can be reduced to nil.
4. **Collection Matrix:** We have discussed various methods of control of receivables but these methods have their limitations. Average collection period and ageing schedule are based on credit sales and collection from debtors. If credit sales and collection from debtors for a period is different as compared to the previous period, average collection period and ageing schedule will be different. Due to this difference comparison of data will be problematic. Another limitation of both the method is that you cannot correlate credit sales and receivables of same period.

To overcome the above limitations we prepare a matrix called collection matrix. This matrix is prepared form the percentage of collection of a month's credit sales. In the following matrix collection schedule of credit sales of April, May, June are given. 25% of credit sales of April month are collected in the same month, 28% in May, 40% in June, and 5% in July. The pattern is seen in the next two months also.

Month of Sales	**April**	**May**	**June**	**July**
Month of collection				
April	25			
May	28	30		
June	41	18	40	
July	8	40	36	5
Aug	-	12	20	18
Sep	-	-	22	

Through collection matrix, receivables can be controlled very effectively. Collection matrix provides outstanding receivables of credit sales made in each period. Based on the collection matrix, firms may take additional steps to collect from slow paying or non-paying customers.

14.6 Factoring

In this chapter, we have discussed about the management of receivables. The management of receivables involves mainly three activities i.e. (1) Credit Policy (2) Credit Evaluation (3) Credit Control. The firms perform these three activities itself. These activities involve very valuable time of management and other costs. If size of firm is small, the firm can bear this cost of managing receivables. But as the size of firm increases, the management of receivables becomes more & more tedious job for the firm. Some firm establishes a separate credit department for management of receivables.

However, it is also possible to get the services of specialized agencies for receivables management for fee. The entire receivables management function can be outsourced to an external agency. Once this is done, the firm can concentrate more on its core business rather than on managing its debtors.

These specialized agencies are called factors. Factors are specialized organizations having specialties in credit management. The services related to receivables management that they provide are called factoring services.

In factoring, the factor (firm offering factoring services) manages the receivables of the client firm availing services of the factor. The process of factoring starts with an agreement between the firm and factor. Factor assesses the credit worthiness of customer and terms of credit for the respective customers. The information of agreement between the firm and factor is given to the customers. The customers make payment directly to the factor instead of seller as per terms of agreement. After receiving payments from debtors, the factor transfers it to the seller. Sometimes the factor purchases the receivables and makes payment at the time of purchase. After this type of agreement at the time of collection from debtors, factor keeps that collection. Based on the terms of agreement the factor provides following services to the firm:

- Purchasing the receivables.
- Management of receivables.
- Protection against default by the debtors.
- Advancing cash against the receivables.

Costs & Benefits of factoring

Costs: Followings are the costs, which a firm, going for factoring, may bear:

1. Factors charge fees & commission for their services. Sometimes this fees & commission are very substantial. Normally fees & commission are the percentage of amount involved.

2. Factors provide advance against the security of receivables. The rates of interest are higher than normal interest rate of banks.
3. Sometimes the customers may not feel comfortable while dealing with factors.

Benefits: Followings are the benefits, which a firm, going for factoring, may get:

1. Factoring saves time & effort of management and management can pay more time to the business.
2. Factoring improves the cash position of the firm. Firm coverts its receivables into cash in less time.
3. Factors are specialized in debtors' management. It improves the working capital management of the firm.
4. Factoring reduces the risk of bad debts. Once the factors evaluate the credit worthiness of the customer then firm extends credit to that customer.

Types of factoring

Following are some important types of factoring.

- Non – recourse factoring
- Pure factoring
- Non – notification factoring

- **Non – recourse factoring:** In this type of factoring factor takes full management of debtors. He evaluates the credit worthiness of debtors, collections from debtors and also bears the risk of bad debts. In this type of factoring receivables are sold out to the factors. Factor makes payment to the client firm immediately after purchasing the receivables or after collection from debtors. Customers make payments directly to the factor. Factor prepares and keeps complete report on debtors including their ledgers.
- **Pure factoring:** In this type of factoring, factors are responsible for collecting the receivables. They do not bear the risk of bad debts. If any of the debtors becomes bad then firm will have to bear the losses. In case factor gives advance against the debtors and any of debtors becomes bad then the firm refunds the amount received against those debtors.
- **Non – notification factoring:** In this type of factoring, customers have no idea about the factoring agreement between the factor and selling firm. Factor keeps the ledger of the customer in his books. Factor deal with customer pretending that he has no agreement with the selling firm.

Before going for factoring every firm should analyze various costs and befits of factoring. Then the firm may accordingly decide about opting for factoring services.

Summary

- In credit sales, payments to be obtained by seller from the buyer are deferred. The total amount yet to be received from customers of credit sales is termed as "receivables" of the business. They are also known as "debtors" or "sundry debtors". These receivables are assets for a firm. They are shown under current assets in the balance sheet.
- Decision to sell on credit results in increased sales. No credit sales may mean loss of current as well as future sales.
- Increased receivables due to credit sales also mean increased chances of bad debts. To keep receivables at a justified level and bad debts at low level, every business has to manage its receivables in a prudent manner.
- The objectives of receivables management are a) To keep bad debts at low level. B)To set firm's credit policy. C) To evaluate credit worthiness of customers. D) To smoothing the collection from debtors. E) To get the benefits of factoring.
- There are some Costs associated with receivables. They include costs of funds locked up in receivables, Cost of bad debts, cost on evaluation of creditworthiness of customers, costs of collection from them and maintenance of record of customers.
- In receivables management we try and keep our receivables at a level where the benefits from having them is higher than the costs. Management of receivables means timely collection from debtors, minimization of bad debts, formulation of credit policy, evaluation of credit worthiness of customers and control of receivables.
- Three important aspects of receivables management are 1) Credit Policy, 2) Credit Evaluation and 3) Control of receivables.
- Credit policy can be termed as a set of guidelines enabling a firm to take decisions of granting or not granting credit to customers. Credit policy can be strict as well as liberal.
- The variables of credit policy are (a) Credit Standards (b) Credit Terms and (c) Collection of receivables
- Credit standards mean criteria that should be fulfilled by a customer before firm makes any credit sales to him. If credit standards are strict then collection cost, quantum of receivables and bad debts are low but growth in sales will also be low. It will be vice versa with strict credit standards.
- Credit terms means payment terms and conditions under which firms grant credit to its customers. Credit terms are usually depicted in the format "X/Y Net Z" where X=Cash Discount, Y=Discount Period and Z=Credit Period. Liberal credit terms would result in increased sales, increased average collection period, increased

discount, increased bad debts and increased costs of collection. These will be vice versa with strict credit standards.

- Collection refers to follow up with the debtors to expedite payments. Every firm should have a collection policy. The objective of collection policy should be to expedite the payment from slow paying customers and to decrease the risk of bad debts. The collection policy should be neither very strict nor very liberal.
- Credit evaluation means the assessment of credit worthiness of customer. In credit evaluation, firms judge 3 Cs of a customer: Capacity, Character and Collateral. Firms take following two steps to assess 3 Cs, viz. (1) Collection of credit information (2) Analysis of credit information.
- Collection & analysis of credit information can be done with the help of Financial Statements, Bank Reference, Credit Scoring and taking help of Credit Rating Agency.
- After credit standards and credit evaluation, control of receivables is another important aspect of receivables management. 1. Average Collection Period, 2. Ageing Schedule, 3. Line of credit, 4. Collection Matrix
- The specialized agencies undertaking the task of receivables management on behalf of the firm are called factors. Factors are specialized organizations having specialties in credit management. The services related to receivables management that they provide are called factoring services.
- The factor provides following services to the firm viz. Purchasing the receivables, Management of receivables, Protection against default by the debtors, Advancing cash against the receivables.
- The costs of factoring include factoring commission and interest on advances against receivables.
- Factoring has many benefits including saving of time and effort and improving cash position of the firm, amongst others.
- Factoring has many types, mainly recourse and non-recourse, pure and non-notification factoring.

Test Your Understanding

State whether following statements are true or false

1. Receivables management means early recovery of dues.
2. Receivables management includes payables also.
3. Management of receivables involves some cost also.
4. Credit terms means rate of discount given to the customers.
5. Credit standards means conditions to be satisfied by the customer.

6. 60 days credit period means payment to be made within 60 days.
7. In credit evaluation, credit worthiness of customers is assessed.
8. Collection of Information completes the process of credit evaluation.
9. Receivables cannot be controlled.
10. Factoring is a service of management of receivables.
11. Factors charge commission against their services.
12. Factoring improves liquidity position of firms.
13. Credit scoring is based on questionnaire given to the customer.
14. Credit rating means rating provided by selling firm.
15. Delinquency costs are opportunity costs.

Answers : 1. F, 2. F, 3. T, 4. F, 5. T, 6. T, 7. T, 8. F, 9. F, 10. T, 11. T, 12. T, 13. T, 14. F, 15. T

Multiple Choice Questions

Choose the correct alternative out of the given:

1. Receivables relate to
   a) Credit Sales b) Credit Purchase
   c) Loans d) none of the above
2. Delinquency costs are costs incurred on
   a) Bank Loans b) Unsecured Loans
   c) Receivables d) None of the above
3. Credit Period means
   a) Repayment should be after this period
   b) Repayment should be before this period
   c) Repayment should be by the end of this period
   d) Payment to the creditors should be after this period
4. ABC Ltd.'s average receivables is Rs. 200000, average daily credit sales is 10000, average collection period is
   a) 15 days b) 10 days
   c) 25 days d) 20 days
5. Factors are specialized organizations in
   a) Receivables management b) Credit evaluation
   c) Credit control d) Collection of receivables

6. Increasing the discount rate also means
   a) Same discount rate for short period
   b) Same discount rate for longer period
   c) More discount rate for a specific customer
   d) None of the above
7. 2/10 means
   a) 2% discount if payment is within 10 days
   b) 10% discount if payment is within 2 days
   c) 2% discount if payment is after 10 days
   d) 10% discount if payment is after 2 days
8. Credit evaluation means
   a) Our creditworthiness is judged
   b) Creditworthiness of suppliers is judged
   c) Customers' creditworthiness is judged
   d) None of the above
9. Line of credit refers to the maximum amount
   a) Of sales to a customer
   b) Of credit sales to a customer
   c) Of payment from a customer
   d) Outstanding of a customer at any point of time
10. In non recourse factoring, factor
   a) Only collects from debtors
   b) Fully manages the receivables
   c) Only evaluates the credit worthiness of customers
   d) None of the above
11. Credit rating agency
   a) Takes the guarantee of credit worthiness of a customer
   b) Provides the payment schedule of a customer
   c) Gives recommendations to grant credit to a customer
   d) Provides information about the creditworthiness of a customer
12. Receivables are
   a) Debtors and bills receivables
   b) Only debtors
   c) Only bills receivables
   d. none of the above

Answers : 1. a, 2. c, 3. c, 4. d, 5. a, 6. b, 7. a, 8. c, 9. d, 10. b, 11. d, 12. a

Review Questions

1. What do you mean by receivables and what are the various costs & benefits of receivables?
2. Briefly describe credit policy and its elements.
3. What is factoring and what are the costs & benefits from factoring?
4. Can receivables be controlled, if yes, how?
5. How will you evaluate a customer's credit worthiness?
6. Write short notes on
   (i) Credit Policy
   (ii) Types of Factoring
7. Write a short note about 'Concentration Banking' and 'Lock-Box system to speed-up recovery form debtors. **(DU 2006)**
8. Discuss the consequences of lengthening and shortening of the 'credit period' by the firm. **(DU 2010)**

Case Study (DU 2007)

A Ltd. has current sales of ₹ 6,00,000 per annum. To push up sales, A is considering a more liberal credit policy as one of the strategies. The current average collection period of the company is 30 days. Proposed increases in collection period and their impact on sales and default rate (on total sales) are given below:

Credit Policy	*Increase in Collection period*	*Increase in Sales* ₹	*Default rate*
I	15 days	25,000	0.5%
II	30 days	60,000	1.0%
III	40 days	70,000	2.0%

A Ltd. is selling its product at ₹ 10 each. Average cost per unit at the current level is ₹ 8 and variable cost per unit is ₹ 6.

If A Ltd. Requires a rate of return of 20 per cent on its investment which credit policy do you recommend and why? Assume 360 days a year.

References

1. ICAI study Material on Financial Management, The Institute of Chartered Accountants of India, New Delhi.
2. Khan, M Y & Jain (2007) P K, Financial Management, Tata McGraw Hill, New Delhi

3. Kishore, Ravi. M (2009), Financial Management, Taxmann Publications, New Delhi
4. Pandey, I M (2009). Financial Management, Vikas Publishing House, New Delhi
5. Van Horne, James C. (2007),Financial Management & Policy, Pearson Prentice Hall, New Delhi
6. Work book on "Financial Management for Managers": The Institute of Chartered Financial Analysts of India, Hyderabad.

CHAPTER 15 Introduction to Working Capital Financing

Learning Objectives:

By the end of this chapter and having completed the essential reading and activities, you should be able to:

- Understand various sources of financing working capital
- Differentiate between internal and external sources of working capital finance
- Understand the role ofcommercial banks in working capital financing
- Discuss the Pros and Cons of various sources of working capital finance

To start with...

Having determined working capital requirement of a firm, the next question is how to finance it. Working capital is represented by current assets, and like all assets, it is a use of funds. Now use of funds is possible when funds are available and funds can be available when there is source of funds!!

This chapter intends to introduce the reader to possible sources of working capital finance .Needless to repeat, like all decisions in finance, the choice and combination of sources of funds for working capital, is also governed by the objective of shareholder's wealth maximization.

15.0 Introduction

We have already learnt that working capital is nothing but sum total of current assets of a firm. These assets are raw materials, work in process stock, finished goods stock and receivables etc. These assets keep getting converted into cash. But this conversion takes place after some time lag. Till the time (cash cycle) these assets get reconverted into cash, the funds of the firm remain blocked in them. The firm has to decide wherefrom it shall arrange funds to invest in current assets. The sources from where funds are raised to invest in current assets are known as **"sources of working capital finance".**

Let us have a look at the diagram below. It is a simplified schematic representation of a balance sheet.

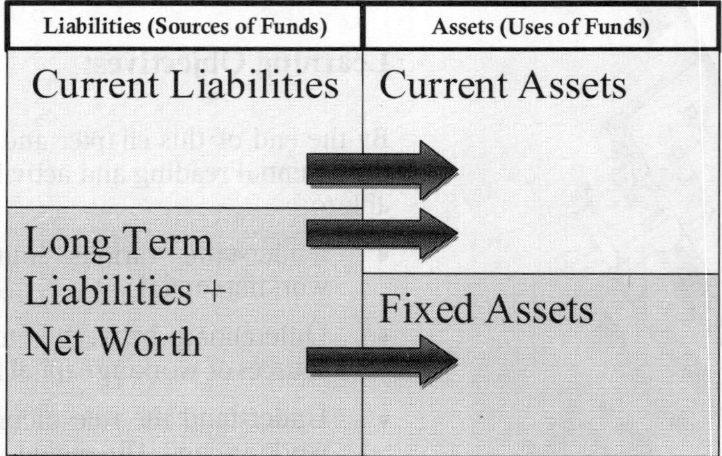

What do the arrows represent? They represent the flow of funds from sources to uses. Liabilities are the sources and assets are uses of funds.

Generally, the working capital (current assets) is financed by a mix of long as well as short term sources. However, we have already discussed the long term sources of finance.

In this chapter, we will concentrate on short term sources of finance, i.e., current liabilities.

15.1 Kinds of Sources of Working Capital Finance

As already stated, the sources of working capital finance can both be short term as well as long term. This classification is based on the maturity. There is another classification based on degree of formality associated with arrangement of funds from these sources.

1) **Spontaneous Sources:** They are also known as informal sources or spontaneous current liabilities. These are the sources of funds which automatically arise during the course of business. The firm does not have to make exclusive efforts or enter into formal agreements to get funds from such sources. The examples of these sources are, Trade Creditors, Accrued Expenses etc.

   Another notable feature of spontaneous sources is that they do not have an ***explicit cost.*** It does not mean that they are cost free. What it means is that there is a cost associated but not apparent. We will discuss this issue at length shortly.

2) **Formal Sources:** They are also known as negotiated sources. These sources do not arise automatically and have an explicit cost associated with them. They have to be negotiated with banks, financial institutions and general public. They are governed strictly by terms of contract between the firm and providers of funds. Examples of such sources are bank financing, commercial paper, bill financing, factoring, public deposits etc.

15.1.1 Spontaneous Sources of Finance

a) **Trade Credit:** Trade credit means the supplier of goods allows the buyer to make payment for goods purchased, after an agreed period of time. This time period is known as credit period. Since the firm (buyer) is not making payments immediately, the credit purchase made by it is a source of funds.

The trade credit can be obtained in two ways. The first is called Open account system. In this system, the buyer has an informal obligation to make payment on due date. The supplier, after dispatching the goods, sends invoice to the buyer. The acceptance of receipt of goods on invoice is considered an automatic promise to make payment on due date. The supplier does not insist on a legal document from the buyer for his obligation to pay. This system works when buyer and seller have a long association and supplier is very confident about the credit worthiness of buyer. In the balance sheet of the buyer, such credit purchases are shown as "Accounts Payable".

Another manner in which trade credit is given is through bills/notes. Here, the supplier insists on a legal document from buyer to evidence his obligation to make payment for purchases on due date. This happens when the supplier is unsure of the creditworthiness of the buyer. This legal document may be a "Bill of Exchange" or a Promissory Note. The amount of credit sales made against these documents is shown in the balance sheet of supplier as "Bills Receivable" (In case of Bill of Exchange) or "Notes Receivable" (In case of Promissory Notes). This system is a formal system as against open accounts system described above. Trade credit is also shown in the balance sheet as "Sundry Creditors".

Suppliers usually offer cash discount to encourage the buyer to make early payments. For example, a supplier may offer credit terms of "2/10 Net 30". What it means is that the supplier shall give 2% (known as "% discount") discount on total amount if payment is made in 10 days (known as "discount period"). However, if payment is made beyond 10 days then no discount will be given and maximum period allowed will be 30 days (known as "Credit Period").

Now the question is, since trade credit is a source of funds, does it have some costs also? The answer is that though trade credit appears to be free, it actually does involve some costs both to the buyer and the seller.

For the supplier, by giving credit, his funds are blocked till the buyer makes the payment. Therefore, he incurs an opportunity cost on these blocked funds. In addition, if the buyer pays within the discount period, there will be the loss to the supplier due to cash discount.

For the buyer, there is no explicit cost of trade credit. However, if the buyer is not able to pay within discount period, then he incurs a loss of cash discount. This becomes his cost. This cost of trade credit can be computed by the following formula:

$$\text{Cost of Trade Credit} = \frac{\%\,\text{discount}}{1\text{-}\%\,\text{discount}} \times \frac{365}{\text{Credit Period - Discount Period}}$$

For example, if the credit terms of a supplier are 2/10 Net 30, the cost of trade credit will work out to be 37.2 %.

So the buyer should compare the cost of trade credit with his alternative sources of financing and then decide whether to avail it or not.

So, if you are planning to use trade credit in future as buyer, what should you remember? You should always remember that if you make your payments regularly on due dates, then you will generate goodwill among suppliers and will start getting more favorable credit terms. However, if you frequently delay the payments beyond the due dates, your credit worthiness will suffer. The supplier may not offer you good credit terms. Even if he does, he might not quote you good prices since he would know that you will not make payment on time. Therefore, he will try to recover their cost of fund due to delay through higher prices.

Accruals

Accruals represent expenses incurred by the firm but not yet paid by the firm. That means the firm has availed itself of the benefit or service represented by these expenses, but the payment has not yet taken place. Consider your land line phone. You keep using the phone for the entire month but you get the bill only at the end of the month. On any given day during the month, say on 17th of a month, you call up the telephone company to find out how much bill from 1st of the month till date is. Say it is Rs 1000. This amount is your accrued bill. You have already utilized the telephone services worth Rs 1000 but you have not yet paid for them. This is what the concept of accruals is.

For a firm, examples of accruals are wages and salary, income tax etc. Till such time these are paid when due, they are shown in the balance sheet as accrued expenses.

Accruals are also termed as "spontaneous sources of finance". They fulfill both the preconditions. First, they automatically arise during the course of business and second, they do not have an explicit cost. However, they are not entirely cost free. For example, income tax rate applicable may be higher if payments are being made at longer intervals. Rate applicable in quarterly payments may be lower than that applicable in case of half yearly payments.

As students of finance, we must be a cautious in using accruals as reliable source of short term funds. This is so because it is difficult to predict what will be actual level of accruals. Since their prediction is difficult, they can not be relied upon during working capital planning.

Also generally the period and payment of accruals is beyond the control of management and governed by labor and other laws.

15.1.2 Non Spontaneous Sources of Financing Working Capital

The main non spontaneous sources of working capital finance are:

a) Bank Finance
b) Factoring
c) Commercial Paper

Now let us discuss each source in detail.

a) **Bank Finance:** Commercial banks are the most important sources of working capital funds. The banks provide finance in the following forms:

   1) **Overdraft:** In an overdraft facility, the customer is allowed to withdraw more than credit balance in his current account. It is a running account facility. Within a stipulated limit and time period, the customer can withdraw and deposit any number of times. Generally, banks provide two kinds of overdrafts. First, Clean Overdraft in which the bank does not ask for any security and grants overdraft against personal or third party guarantee. Second is Secured overdraft. In this, bank asks for securities like NSC, Term Deposit Receipts, LIC policies etc.

   2) **Cash Credit:** This is also a running account facility similar to overdraft. In this facility also the borrower is allowed to withdraw up to a pre-specified limit as many times as he likes. This facility is granted for one year. After one year it is reviewed and can be renewed for another year. The main difference between cash credit and overdraft is the security. In cash credit, the security is usually stocks and book debts (receivables).

3) **Bills discounting/purchase:** Bills discounting/purchase is a facility in which bank advances money against a credit sale backed by a genuine bill of exchange. We know that bills can be of two types 1) Demand Bills and 2) Time Bills or Usance Bills. When the bank provides advance against demand bills, it usually advances 100% of the bill amount. This is known as purchase of bills. However, when the bank provides advance against time bills, it does not provide 100% financing. Instead, only 70-80% advance is made. This is known as discounting of bills.

   Bills finance is a self-liquidating arrangement. When the due date of bill comes, the customer pays to the bank and bank, in turn, deducts its commission and interest for the period of the advance. Thereafter, bank credits the remainder amount into the borrower's account.

4) **Letter of Credit:** Generally buyers wish to make payment for goods only after satisfying themselves about the quality and quantity. Whereas, the sellers want to receive payments before the supply of goods. Here the needs of buyers and sellers have a conflict.

   Banks, by mechanism of Letter of Credit (LC) come to the aid of both buyers and sellers in such cases.

   A letter of credit is a written document issued by buyer's bank, at the request of buyer, in favor of seller. Buyer's bank gives an undertaking that if seller presents a bill of exchange to the seller's bank with all other necessary documents, buyer's bank will make full payment of the bill amount to the seller's bank.

   LC is usually prepared in quadruplicate by the buyer's bank. Original LC is sent directly to the seller's bank. One copy each is sent to both buyer and seller and one copy is kept as office copy by the buyer's bank.

   Now, once the seller has got an LC from buyer's bank, he is assured of his payments once he dispatches the goods. Similarly, the buyer is relieved of having to pay in advance and is assured of his quantity and quality.

   LC is a bridge constructed by banks on which both buyer and seller meet and deal with each other successfully.

5) **Working Capital Demand Loan:** We saw earlier that cash credit and overdrafts are running account facility in which borrower is allowed to keep on depositing and withdrawing any number of times within a year, and within the limit. This is not so in working capital demand loan. Here the loan amount is either given in a lump sum or in installments. However, any repayments do not entitle the borrower to withdraw again. Any amount deposited by the borrower reduces the outstanding against his name permanently and he can not reuse that amount. WCDL is given for a minimum period of one day to a

maximum of six months. Further, on request of borrower, it may be "rolled-over" (extended) for maximum six months. It may be noted that the amount of working capital demand loan given can not exceed the drawing power of the borrower (Maximum Permissible Bank Finance).

Mode of Security in Bank Finance

When banks provide finance to a borrower, they need some cushion to fall back on, in case of default by the borrower. This cushion is provided by the borrower to the banks in the form of certain rights in various kinds of assets/property of the borrower. This is known as security for a loan. Security for bank financing can be created by the following modes by the borrower:

1) **Mortgage:** Mortgage is transfer of legal or equitable interest in a specific immovable property for the purpose of creating security for a debt. Mortgage is of two types broadly i) Equitable Mortgage and ii) Registered Mortgage. In mortgage, the possession of the property being mortgaged remains with the borrower. However, the bank gets the full legal title. The borrower who is mortgaging his property is called mortgager and the bank is called mortgagee.

2) **Pledge:** As per Sec 172 of the Indian Contracts Act, pledge is a bailment of goods, as a security for payment of a debt, or performance of a promise against some advance. In pledge the possession of the property is transferred. The person pledging the goods (borrower) is known as bailor (pledger) and the bank is known as bailee (pledge). However, the bailee (bank) is supposed to take reasonable care of goods in his possession. The bank has the right to sell the pledged property if the borrower fails to repay the debt. If the borrower fully repays his debt with interest, the pledged goods are returned to him. In pledge, the borrower signs a document also stating that he is handing over the specified property to the bank with the motive of pledge against specified debt.

3) **Lien:** Lien means the right of a party to retain the goods of some other party till repayment of debt to him. Lien is of two types i) Particular Lien and ii) General Lien. In particular lien, the right of retaining goods applies on the debt associated with these goods is repaid. Whereas, in general lien, the right is applied till all dues of the lender are repaid. Bankers have the right to general lien. That means, a banker can retain all deposits of the borrower who has not repaid his loan.

4) **Hypothecation:** hypothecation is creating a security of movable property in favor of a lender (bank). For example, if a firm may hypothecate its stock, cars, machinery etc. In hypothecation, the possession remains with the borrower. However, the bank has the right to take possession of and sell the hypothecated property in the event of default. It may be noted

here that pledge is a ***fixed charge*** (security) on a specific asset. However, hypothecation is a kind of ***floating charge***. For example, if stocks of a firm have been hypothecated, thereafter, the firm does not stop using these goods. It will keep on selling these goods and manufacturing new goods just like it did before hypothecation. The goods going out after sales will be automatically released from hypothecation and the new goods coming in get automatically hypothecated to the bank. This is why hypothecation is called a floating charge.

b) **Factoring:** For a detailed discussion on factoring please see page 372 in chapter 14, Management of Receivables.

c) **Commercial Paper (CP)**

Commercial paper is an unsecured promissory note issued by firms to raise short term funds. Commercial papers were introduced in India in 1990 on the recommendation of Vagul committee. Commercial papers can be issued only by the firms that are financially very sound and have high credit rating.

Investment in commercial paper market can be done by Banks, Financial Institutions, Mutual Funds, Insurance Firms and corporate.

The eligibility for issuing commercial papers is as follows:

1) The tangible net worth of the issuing company should not be less than Rs 4 crore.
2) The issuing company should have a sanctioned working capital limit of not less than Rs 25 crore from banks and/or financial institutions.
3) The borrowing account of the issuing company should be classified as Standard Asset by its Bank or Financial Institution.
4) The minimum credit rating of the issue should be P-2 from CRISIL and equivalent grade from CARE, ICRA or any other agency identified by Reserve Bank of India.
5) CP can be issued for maturity ranging from 15 days to 1 year.
6) Minimum investment in CP should be Rs 5 lakhs per investor. CPs can be issued for a minimum amount of Rs 1 crore.
7) CPs can be issued in physical as well as dematerialized form.

The CP is sold at a discount to face value. Unlike other debt instruments, It does not carry explicit coupon rates. Investors return is equal to the discount, i.e., difference between Redemption Price (Face Value) and the issue price. Interest yield on CP can be calculated using the formula:

$$\text{Interest Yield on CP} = \frac{\text{Redemption Price - Issue Price}}{\text{Issue price}} \times \frac{360}{\text{Days of Maturity}}$$

However, the cost of CP to the issuing company will be different from interest yield to the investor because interest is a tax deductible expense. Therefore, if the effective tax rate is T, then effective cost of CP to the issuer will be equal to Interest Yield x (1-T).

Also, in addition to the discount, issuing company also has to pay rating charges, stamp duty and issuing and payment charges.

Merits

1) CP is cheaper than working capital finance from banks.
2) CPs is useful in tight monetary conditions when bank lending freezes up.
3) For an investor, CPs represents highly liquid and safe investment option.
4) Issuing company does not have to be bound by limitation of end use of funds.
5) Issuing company does not have to create any security against issue of CP.

Demerits

1) CPs can not be redeemed before maturity. Firm does not have a call option.
2) Only highly rated companies can issue Commercial papers.
3) If issuing company is unable to pay the investors at maturity there is no option for postponement of repayment.

Summary

- The sources from where funds are raised to invest in current assets are known as **"sources of working capital finance".** Generally, the working capital (current assets) is financed by a mix of long as well as short term sources. However, we have already discussed the long term sources of finance. In this chapter, we will concentrate on short term sources of finance, i.e., current liabilities.

- **Spontaneous Sources** are also known as informal sources or spontaneous current liabilities. These are the sources of funds which automatically arise during the course of business and do not have explicit cost. **Formal Sources are another category.** They are also known as Negotiated sources. These sources do not arise automatically and have an explicit cost associated with them.

- **Trade Credit, accrued expenses and provisions are examples of spontaneous sources of working capital finance. Though they do not have an explicit cost, however they are not entirely cost free.**

- The main non-spontaneous sources of working capital finance are a)Bank Finance b) Factoring and c) Commercial Paper.

- Bank finance is provided in the form of Overdraft, Cash Credit, Bills Discounting/Purchase, Letter of credit and working capital demand loan.

- **Banks usually require some security against financing provided. These securities are created by many methods viz. Mortgage, Pledge, Lien and Hypothecation. Factoring: **
- Commercial paper is an unsecured promissory note issued by firms to raise short term funds. Commercial papers were introduced in India in 1990 on the recommendation of Vagul committee. Commercial papers can be issued only by the firms that are financially very sound and have high credit rating. Commercial papers are sold at a discount to the face value.

Test Your Understanding

State whether the following statements are true/false

1. Accruals are a non-spontaneous source of finance.
2. Trade credit is a cost free source of finance.
3. Hypothecation is a fixed charge where as pledge can be fixed as well as floating.
4. Commercial Papers are issued by commercial banks.
5. Any profitable company can issue commercial papers.
6. Working Capital Demand Loan is granted for six months initially.
7. Mortgage is done for immovable property.
8. Working capital is financed by short term funds only.
9. Cash credit and overdraft are both running account facilities.
10. Bankers enjoy the right of general lien.

Answers : 1. F 2.F 3.F 4.F 5.F 6.T 7.T 8.F 9.T 10.T

Multiple Choice Questions

1. Which of the following is known as commercial paper? **(UPTU 2009)**

a) Short term securities b) Long term securities

c) Long term unsecured securities d) None of the above

2. What is L.C.? **(UPTU 2010)**

a) Letter of Credit b) Letter of control

c) Letter of cost d) None of these

3. The major difference between pledge and hypothecation is:

a) In hypothecation the possession of goods is transferred to lender

b) In Pledge the possession of goods is transferred to lender

c) In both pledge and hypothecation, possession remains with lender.

d) None of these

4. Which of the following are spontaneous liabilities?

   a) Sundry Creditors b) Salary accrued but not due

   c) Provision for payment of bonus d) All of these

5. The difference between Cash Credit and Overdraft facilities is:

   a) Cash credit is granted against security of inventory where as overdraft is against financial assets

   b) Overdraft is granted against security of inventory where as cash credit is against financial assets

   c) Cash credit is a running account whereas overdraft is not.

   d) None of these.

6. The minimum investment in commercial papers is:

   a) Rs 10 lakh b) Rs 5 lakh

   c) Rs 15 lakh d) Rs 20 lakh

7. Mortgage is of two types. These types are:

   a) Equitable Mortgage and Registered Mortgage

   b) Simple Mortgage and complicated mortgage

   c) Equitable Mortgage and Listed Mortgage

   d) None of these

8. What will be the approximate cost of trade credit if credit terms are 2/10 Net 45?

   a) 30% b) 21%

   c) 37% d) None of these

9. Clean overdraft means:

   a) Overdraft without security

   b) Overdraft that has been repaid

   c) Overdraft to a borrower wit excellent credit standing

   d) None of these

10. Commercial paper are issued:

   a) At a discount to face value b) At a fixed coupon rate

   c) Only in dematerialized form d) None of these

Answers : 1. a 2.a 3.b 4.d 5.a 6.b 7.a 8.b 9.a 10.a

Review Questions

1. Write down the role of commercial banks in providing working capital to small scale industrial sectors?

2. Throw light on role of commercial banks in working capital management. **(UPTU, 2007)**
3. What is meant by spontaneous sources of working capital? Discuss in detail.
4. Discuss briefly commercial papers as a source of working capital finance. How is the cost of commercial papers computed?
5. What are different methods by which a bank creates security for its loans? Describe.
6. Write short notes on:
   a) Letter of Credit
   b) Working Capital Demand Loan
   c) Hypothecation and Pledge

References

1. Bhalla, V K, (2009), Working Capital Management, Text and Cases, Anmol Publications Pvt. Ltd. New Delhi
2. Damodaran, Aswath. (1994). Damodaran on Valuation, John Wiley & Sons, New York
3. Khan, M Y & Jain (2007) P K, Financial Management, Tata McGraw Hill, New Delhi
4. Kishore, Ravi. M (2009), Financial Management, Taxmann Publications, New Delhi
5. Pandey, I M (2009). Financial Management, Vikas Publishing House, New Delhi
6. Van Horne, James C. (2007),Financial Management & Policy, Pearson Prentice Hall, New Delhi
7. Work book on "Financial Management for Managers": The Institute of Chartered Financial Analysts of India, Hyderabad.

Table 1: Future Value of a single flow of Re 1 (FVIF table)

	Interest Rate													
Year	***1%***	***2%***	***3%***	***4%***	***5%***	***6%***	***7%***	***8%***	***9%***	***10%***	***11%***	***12%***	***13%***	***14%***
1	1.010	1.020	1.030	1.040	1.050	1.060	1.070	1.080	1.090	1.100	1.110	1.120	1.130	1.140
2	1.020	1.040	1.061	1.082	1.103	1.124	1.145	1.166	1.188	1.210	1.232	1.254	1.277	1.300
3	1.030	1.061	1.093	1.125	1.158	1.191	1.225	1.260	1.295	1.331	1.368	1.405	1.443	1.482
4	1.041	1.082	1.126	1.170	1.216	1.262	1.311	1.360	1.412	1.464	1.518	1.574	1.630	1.689
5	1.051	1.104	1.159	1.217	1.276	1.338	1.403	1.469	1.539	1.611	1.685	1.762	1.842	1.925
6	1.062	1.126	1.194	1.265	1.340	1.419	1.501	1.587	1.677	1.772	1.870	1.974	2.082	2.195
7	1.072	1.149	1.230	1.316	1.407	1.504	1.606	1.714	1.828	1.949	2.076	2.211	2.353	2.502
8	1.083	1.172	1.267	1.369	1.477	1.594	1.718	1.851	1.993	2.144	2.305	2.476	2.658	2.853
9	1.094	1.195	1.305	1.423	1.551	1.689	1.838	1.999	2.172	2.358	2.558	2.773	3.004	3.252
10	1.105	1.219	1.344	1.480	1.629	1.791	1.967	2.159	2.367	2.594	2.839	3.106	3.395	3.707
11	1.116	1.243	1.384	1.539	1.710	1.898	2.105	2.332	2.580	2.853	3.152	3.479	3.836	4.226
12	1.127	1.268	1.426	1.601	1.796	2.012	2.252	2.518	2.813	3.138	3.498	3.896	4.335	4.818
13	1.138	1.294	1.469	1.665	1.886	2.133	2.410	2.720	3.066	3.452	3.883	4.363	4.898	5.492
14	1.149	1.319	1.513	1.732	1.980	2.261	2.579	2.937	3.342	3.797	4.310	4.887	5.535	6.261
15	1.161	1.346	1.558	1.801	2.079	2.397	2.759	3.172	3.642	4.177	4.785	5.474	6.254	7.138
16	1.173	1.373	1.605	1.873	2.183	2.540	2.952	3.426	3.970	4.595	5.311	6.130	7.067	8.137
17	1.184	1.400	1.653	1.948	2.292	2.693	3.159	3.700	4.328	5.054	5.895	6.866	7.986	9.276
18	1.196	1.428	1.702	2.026	2.407	2.854	3.380	3.996	4.717	5.560	6.544	7.690	9.024	10.575
19	1.208	1.457	1.754	2.107	2.527	3.026	3.617	4.316	5.142	6.116	7.263	8.613	10.197	12.056
20	1.220	1.486	1.806	2.191	2.653	3.207	3.870	4.661	5.604	6.727	8.062	9.646	11.523	13.743
25	1.282	1.641	2.094	2.666	3.386	4.292	5.427	6.848	8.623	10.835	13.585	17.000	21.231	26.462
30	1.348	1.811	2.427	3.243	4.322	5.743	7.612	10.063	13.268	17.449	22.892	29.960	39.116	50.950
40	1.489	2.208	3.262	4.801	7.040	10.286	14.974	21.725	31.409	45.259	65.001	93.051	132.782	188.884
50	1.645	2.692	4.384	7.107	11.467	18.420	29.457	46.902	74.358	117.391	184.565	289.002	450.736	700.233

Table 1 Continued:

Year	*Interest rate*												
	15%	*16%*	*17%*	*18%*	*19%*	*20%*	*21%*	*22%*	*23%*	*24%*	*25%*	*30%*	*40%*
1	1.150	1.160	1.170	1.180	1.190	1.200	1.210	1.220	1.230	1.240	1.250	1.300	1.400
2	1.323	1.346	1.369	1.392	1.416	1.440	1.464	1.488	1.513	1.538	1.563	1.690	1.960
3	1.521	1.561	1.602	1.643	1.685	1.728	1.772	1.816	1.861	1.907	1.953	2.197	2.744
4	1.749	1.811	1.874	1.939	2.005	2.074	2.144	2.215	2.289	2.364	2.441	2.856	3.842
5	2.011	2.100	2.192	2.288	2.386	2.488	2.594	2.703	2.815	2.932	3.052	3.713	5.378
6	2.313	2.436	2.565	2.700	2.840	2.986	3.138	3.297	3.463	3.635	3.815	4.827	7.530
7	2.660	2.826	3.001	3.185	3.379	3.583	3.797	4.023	4.259	4.508	4.768	6.275	10.541
8	3.059	3.278	3.511	3.759	4.021	4.300	4.595	4.908	5.239	5.590	5.960	8.157	14.758
9	3.518	3.803	4.108	4.435	4.785	5.160	5.560	5.987	6.444	6.931	7.451	10.604	20.661
10	4.046	4.411	4.807	5.234	5.695	6.192	6.727	7.305	7.926	8.594	9.313	13.786	28.925
11	4.652	5.117	5.624	6.176	6.777	7.430	8.140	8.912	9.749	10.657	11.642	17.922	40.496
12	5.350	5.936	6.580	7.288	8.064	8.916	9.850	10.872	11.991	13.215	14.552	23.298	56.694
13	6.153	6.886	7.699	8.599	9.596	10.699	11.918	13.264	14.749	16.386	18.190	30.288	79.371
14	7.076	7.988	9.007	10.147	11.420	12.839	14.421	16.182	18.141	20.319	22.737	39.374	111.120
15	8.137	9.266	10.539	11.974	13.590	15.407	17.449	19.742	22.314	25.196	28.422	51.186	155.568
16	9.358	10.748	12.330	14.129	16.172	18.488	21.114	24.086	27.446	31.243	35.527	66.542	217.795
17	10.761	12.468	14.426	16.672	19.244	22.186	25.548	29.384	33.759	38.741	44.409	86.504	304.913
18	12.375	14.463	16.879	19.673	22.901	26.623	30.913	35.849	41.523	48.039	55.511	112.455	426.879
19	14.232	16.777	19.748	23.214	27.252	31.948	37.404	43.736	51.074	59.568	69.389	146.192	597.630
20	16.367	19.461	23.106	27.393	32.429	38.338	45.259	53.358	62.821	73.864	86.736	190.050	836.683
25	32.919	40.874	50.658	62.669	77.388	95.396	117.391	144.210	176.859	216.542	264.698	705.641	4499.880
30	66.212	85.850	111.065	143.371	184.675	237.376	304.482	389.758	497.913	634.820	807.794	2619.996	24201.432
40	267.864	378.721	533.869	750.378	1051.668	1469.772	2048.400	2847.038	3946.430	5455.913	7523.164	36118.865	700037.697
50	1083.657	1670.704	2566.215	3927.357	5988.914	9100.438	13780.612	20796.561	31279.195	46890.435	70064.923	497929.223	20248916.240

Table 2: Future Value of an annuity of Re 1 (FVIA table)

	Interest Rate													
Year	*1%*	*2%*	*3%*	*4%*	*5%*	*6%*	*7%*	*8%*	*9%*	*10%*	*11%*	*12%*	*13%*	*14%*
1	1.000	1.000	1.000	1.000	1.000	1.000	1.000	1.000	1.000	1.000	1.000	1.000	1.000	1.000
2	2.010	2.020	2.030	2.040	2.050	2.060	2.070	2.080	2.090	2.100	2.110	2.120	2.130	2.140
3	3.030	3.060	3.091	3.122	3.153	3.184	3.215	3.246	3.278	3.310	3.342	3.374	3.407	3.440
4	4.060	4.122	4.184	4.246	4.310	4.375	4.440	4.506	4.573	4.641	4.710	4.779	4.850	4.921
5	5.101	5.204	5.309	5.416	5.526	5.637	5.751	5.867	5.985	6.105	6.228	6.353	6.480	6.610
6	6.152	6.308	6.468	6.633	6.802	6.975	7.153	7.336	7.523	7.716	7.913	8.115	8.323	8.536
7	7.214	7.434	7.662	7.898	8.142	8.394	8.654	8.923	9.200	9.487	9.783	10.089	10.405	10.730
8	8.286	8.583	8.892	9.214	9.549	9.897	10.260	10.637	11.028	11.436	11.859	12.300	12.757	13.233
9	9.369	9.755	10.159	10.583	11.027	11.491	11.978	12.488	13.021	13.579	14.164	14.776	15.416	16.085
10	10.462	10.950	11.464	12.006	12.578	13.181	13.816	14.487	15.193	15.937	16.722	17.549	18.420	19.337
11	11.567	12.169	12.808	13.486	14.207	14.972	15.784	16.645	17.560	18.531	19.561	20.655	21.814	23.045
12	12.683	13.412	14.192	15.026	15.917	16.870	17.888	18.977	20.141	21.384	22.713	24.133	25.650	27.271
13	13.809	14.680	15.618	16.627	17.713	18.882	20.141	21.495	22.953	24.523	26.212	28.029	29.985	32.089
14	14.947	15.974	17.086	18.292	19.599	21.015	22.550	24.215	26.019	27.975	30.095	32.393	34.883	37.581
15	16.097	17.293	18.599	20.024	21.579	23.276	25.129	27.152	29.361	31.772	34.405	37.280	40.417	43.842
16	17.258	18.639	20.157	21.825	23.657	25.673	27.888	30.324	33.003	35.950	39.190	42.753	46.672	50.980
17	18.430	20.012	21.762	23.698	25.840	28.213	30.840	33.750	36.974	40.545	44.501	48.884	53.739	59.118
18	19.615	21.412	23.414	25.645	28.132	30.906	33.999	37.450	41.301	45.599	50.396	55.750	61.725	68.394
19	20.811	22.841	25.117	27.671	30.539	33.760	37.379	41.446	46.018	51.159	56.939	63.440	70.749	78.969
20	22.019	24.297	26.870	29.778	33.066	36.786	40.995	45.762	51.160	57.275	64.203	72.052	80.947	91.025
25	28.243	32.030	36.459	41.646	47.727	54.865	63.249	73.106	84.701	98.347	114.413	133.334	155.620	181.871
30	34.785	40.568	47.575	56.085	66.439	79.058	94.461	113.283	136.308	164.494	199.021	241.333	293.199	356.787
40	48.886	60.402	75.401	95.026	120.800	154.762	199.635	259.057	337.882	442.593	581.826	767.091	1013.704	1342.025
50	64.463	84.579	112.797	152.667	209.348	290.336	406.529	573.770	815.084	1163.909	1668.771	2400.018	3459.507	4994.521

Table 2 Continued:

Year	Interest Rate 15%	16%	17%	18%	19%	20%	21%	22%	23%	24%	25%	30%	40%
1	1.000	1.000	1.000	1.000	1.000	1.000	1.000	1.000	1.000	1.000	1.000	1.000	1.000
2	2.150	2.160	2.170	2.180	2.190	2.200	2.210	2.220	2.230	2.240	2.250	2.300	2.400
3	3.473	3.506	3.539	3.572	3.606	3.640	3.674	3.708	3.743	3.778	3.813	3.990	4.360
4	4.993	5.066	5.141	5.215	5.291	5.368	5.446	5.524	5.604	5.684	5.766	6.187	7.104
5	6.742	6.877	7.014	7.154	7.297	7.442	7.589	7.740	7.893	8.048	8.207	9.043	10.946
6	8.754	8.977	9.207	9.442	9.683	9.930	10.183	10.442	10.708	10.980	11.259	12.756	16.324
7	11.067	11.414	11.772	12.142	12.523	12.916	13.321	13.740	14.171	14.615	15.073	17.583	23.853
8	13.727	14.240	14.773	15.327	15.902	16.499	17.119	17.762	18.430	19.123	19.842	23.858	34.395
9	16.786	17.519	18.285	19.086	19.923	20.799	21.714	22.670	23.669	24.712	25.802	32.015	49.153
10	20.304	21.321	22.393	23.521	24.709	25.959	27.274	28.657	30.113	31.643	33.253	42.619	69.814
11	24.349	25.733	27.200	28.755	30.404	32.150	34.001	35.962	38.039	40.238	42.566	56.405	98.739
12	29.002	30.850	32.824	34.931	37.180	39.581	42.142	44.874	47.788	50.895	54.208	74.327	139.235
13	34.352	36.786	39.404	42.219	45.244	48.497	51.991	55.746	59.779	64.110	68.760	97.625	195.929
14	40.505	43.672	47.103	50.818	54.841	59.196	63.909	69.010	74.528	80.496	86.949	127.913	275.300
15	47.580	51.660	56.110	60.965	66.261	72.035	78.330	85.192	92.669	100.815	109.687	167.286	386.420
16	55.717	60.925	66.649	72.939	79.850	87.442	95.780	104.935	114.983	126.011	138.109	218.472	541.988
17	65.075	71.673	78.979	87.068	96.022	105.931	116.894	129.020	142.430	157.253	173.636	285.014	759.784
18	75.836	84.141	93.406	103.740	115.266	128.117	142.441	158.405	176.188	195.994	218.045	371.518	1064.697
19	88.212	98.603	110.285	123.414	138.166	154.740	173.354	194.254	217.712	244.033	273.556	483.973	1491.576
20	102.444	115.380	130.033	146.628	165.418	186.688	210.758	237.989	268.785	303.601	342.945	630.165	2089.206
25	212.793	249.214	292.105	342.603	402.042	471.981	554.242	650.955	764.605	898.092	1054.791	2348.803	11247.199
30	434.745	530.312	647.439	790.948	966.712	1181.882	1445.151	1767.081	2160.491	2640.916	3227.174	8729.985	60501.081
40	1779.090	2360.757	3134.522	4163.213	5529.829	7343.858	9749.525	12936.535	17154.046	22728.803	30088.655	120392.883	1750091.741
50	7217.716	10435.649	15089.502	21813.094	31515.336	45497.191	65617.202	94525.279	135992.154	195372.644	280255.693	1659760.743	50622288.099

Table 3: Present Value of a Single Flow of Re 1 (PVIF table)

	Interest Rate													
Year	***1%***	***2%***	***3%***	***4%***	***5%***	***6%***	***7%***	***8%***	***9%***	***10%***	***11%***	***12%***	***13%***	***14%***
1	0.990	0.980	0.971	0.962	0.952	0.943	0.935	0.926	0.917	0.909	0.901	0.893	0.885	0.877
2	0.980	0.961	0.943	0.925	0.907	0.890	0.873	0.857	0.842	0.826	0.812	0.797	0.783	0.769
3	0.971	0.942	0.915	0.889	0.864	0.840	0.816	0.794	0.772	0.751	0.731	0.712	0.693	0.675
4	0.961	0.924	0.888	0.855	0.823	0.792	0.763	0.735	0.708	0.683	0.659	0.636	0.613	0.592
5	0.951	0.906	0.863	0.822	0.784	0.747	0.713	0.681	0.650	0.621	0.593	0.567	0.543	0.519
6	0.942	0.888	0.837	0.790	0.746	0.705	0.666	0.630	0.596	0.564	0.535	0.507	0.480	0.456
7	0.933	0.871	0.813	0.760	0.711	0.665	0.623	0.583	0.547	0.513	0.482	0.452	0.425	0.400
8	0.923	0.853	0.789	0.731	0.677	0.627	0.582	0.540	0.502	0.467	0.434	0.404	0.376	0.351
9	0.914	0.837	0.766	0.703	0.645	0.592	0.544	0.500	0.460	0.424	0.391	0.361	0.333	0.308
10	0.905	0.820	0.744	0.676	0.614	0.558	0.508	0.463	0.422	0.386	0.352	0.322	0.295	0.270
11	0.896	0.804	0.722	0.650	0.585	0.527	0.475	0.429	0.388	0.350	0.317	0.287	0.261	0.237
12	0.887	0.788	0.701	0.625	0.557	0.497	0.444	0.397	0.356	0.319	0.286	0.257	0.231	0.208
13	0.879	0.773	0.681	0.601	0.530	0.469	0.415	0.368	0.326	0.290	0.258	0.229	0.204	0.182
14	0.870	0.758	0.661	0.577	0.505	0.442	0.388	0.340	0.299	0.263	0.232	0.205	0.181	0.160
15	0.861	0.743	0.642	0.555	0.481	0.417	0.362	0.315	0.275	0.239	0.209	0.183	0.160	0.140
16	0.853	0.728	0.623	0.534	0.458	0.394	0.339	0.292	0.252	0.218	0.188	0.163	0.141	0.123
17	0.844	0.714	0.605	0.513	0.436	0.371	0.317	0.270	0.231	0.198	0.170	0.146	0.125	0.108
18	0.836	0.700	0.587	0.494	0.416	0.350	0.296	0.250	0.212	0.180	0.153	0.130	0.111	0.095
19	0.828	0.686	0.570	0.475	0.396	0.331	0.277	0.232	0.194	0.164	0.138	0.116	0.098	0.083
20	0.820	0.673	0.554	0.456	0.377	0.312	0.258	0.215	0.178	0.149	0.124	0.104	0.087	0.073
25	0.780	0.610	0.478	0.375	0.295	0.233	0.184	0.146	0.116	0.092	0.074	0.059	0.047	0.038
30	0.742	0.552	0.412	0.308	0.231	0.174	0.131	0.099	0.075	0.057	0.044	0.033	0.026	0.020
40	0.672	0.453	0.307	0.208	0.142	0.097	0.067	0.046	0.032	0.022	0.015	0.011	0.008	0.005
50	0.608	0.372	0.228	0.141	0.087	0.054	0.034	0.021	0.013	0.009	0.005	0.003	0.002	0.001

Table 3 Continued:

	Interest Rate												
Year	*15%*	*16%*	*17%*	*18%*	*19%*	*20%*	*21%*	*22%*	*23%*	*24%*	*25%*	*30%*	*40%*
1	0.870	0.862	0.855	0.847	0.840	0.833	0.826	0.820	0.813	0.806	0.800	0.769	0.714
2	0.756	0.743	0.731	0.718	0.706	0.694	0.683	0.672	0.661	0.650	0.640	0.592	0.510
3	0.658	0.641	0.624	0.609	0.593	0.579	0.564	0.551	0.537	0.524	0.512	0.455	0.364
4	0.572	0.552	0.534	0.516	0.499	0.482	0.467	0.451	0.437	0.423	0.410	0.350	0.260
5	0.497	0.476	0.456	0.437	0.419	0.402	0.386	0.370	0.355	0.341	0.328	0.269	0.186
6	0.432	0.410	0.390	0.370	0.352	0.335	0.319	0.303	0.289	0.275	0.262	0.207	0.133
7	0.376	0.354	0.333	0.314	0.296	0.279	0.263	0.249	0.235	0.222	0.210	0.159	0.095
8	0.327	0.305	0.285	0.266	0.249	0.233	0.218	0.204	0.191	0.179	0.168	0.123	0.068
9	0.284	0.263	0.243	0.225	0.209	0.194	0.180	0.167	0.155	0.144	0.134	0.094	0.048
10	0.247	0.227	0.208	0.191	0.176	0.162	0.149	0.137	0.126	0.116	0.107	0.073	0.035
11	0.215	0.195	0.178	0.162	0.148	0.135	0.123	0.112	0.103	0.094	0.086	0.056	0.025
12	0.187	0.168	0.152	0.137	0.124	0.112	0.102	0.092	0.083	0.076	0.069	0.043	0.018
13	0.163	0.145	0.130	0.116	0.104	0.093	0.084	0.075	0.068	0.061	0.055	0.033	0.013
14	0.141	0.125	0.111	0.099	0.088	0.078	0.069	0.062	0.055	0.049	0.044	0.025	0.009
15	0.123	0.108	0.095	0.084	0.074	0.065	0.057	0.051	0.045	0.040	0.035	0.020	0.006
16	0.107	0.093	0.081	0.071	0.062	0.054	0.047	0.042	0.036	0.032	0.028	0.015	0.005
17	0.093	0.080	0.069	0.060	0.052	0.045	0.039	0.034	0.030	0.026	0.023	0.012	0.003
18	0.081	0.069	0.059	0.051	0.044	0.038	0.032	0.028	0.024	0.021	0.018	0.009	0.002
19	0.070	0.060	0.051	0.043	0.037	0.031	0.027	0.023	0.020	0.017	0.014	0.007	0.002
20	0.061	0.051	0.043	0.037	0.031	0.026	0.022	0.019	0.016	0.014	0.012	0.005	0.001
25	0.030	0.024	0.020	0.016	0.013	0.010	0.009	0.007	0.006	0.005	0.004	0.001	0.000
30	0.015	0.012	0.009	0.007	0.005	0.004	0.003	0.003	0.002	0.002	0.001	0.000	0.000
40	0.004	0.003	0.002	0.001	0.001	0.001	0.000	0.000	0.000	0.000	0.000	0.000	0.000
50	0.001	0.001	0.000	0.000	0.000	0.000	0.000	0.000	0.000	0.000	0.000	0.000	0.000

Table 4: Present Value of an Annuity of Re 1 (PVIA table)

Year	Interest Rate 1%	2%	3%	4%	5%	6%	7%	8%	9%	10%	11%	12%	13%	14%
1	0.9901	0.9804	0.9709	0.9615	0.9524	0.9434	0.9346	0.9259	0.9174	0.9091	0.9009	0.8929	0.8850	0.8772
2	1.9704	1.9416	1.9135	1.8861	1.8594	1.8334	1.8080	1.7833	1.7591	1.7355	1.7125	1.6901	1.6681	1.6467
3	2.9410	2.8839	2.8286	2.7751	2.7232	2.6730	2.6243	2.5771	2.5313	2.4869	2.4437	2.4018	2.3612	2.3216
4	3.9020	3.8077	3.7171	3.6299	3.5460	3.4651	3.3872	3.3121	3.2397	3.1699	3.1024	3.0373	2.9745	2.9137
5	4.8534	4.7135	4.5797	4.4518	4.3295	4.2124	4.1002	3.9927	3.8897	3.7908	3.6959	3.6048	3.5172	3.4331
6	5.7955	5.6014	5.4172	5.2421	5.0757	4.9173	4.7665	4.6229	4.4859	4.3553	4.2305	4.1114	3.9975	3.8887
7	6.7282	6.4720	6.2303	6.0021	5.7864	5.5824	5.3893	5.2064	5.0330	4.8684	4.7122	4.5638	4.4226	4.2883
8	7.6517	7.3255	7.0197	6.7327	6.4632	6.2098	5.9713	5.7466	5.5348	5.3349	5.1461	4.9676	4.7988	4.6389
9	8.5660	8.1622	7.7861	7.4353	7.1078	6.8017	6.5152	6.2469	5.9952	5.7590	5.5370	5.3282	5.1317	4.9464
10	9.4713	8.9826	8.5302	8.1109	7.7217	7.3601	7.0236	6.7101	6.4177	6.1446	5.8892	5.6502	5.4262	5.2161
11	10.3676	9.7868	9.2526	8.7605	8.3064	7.8869	7.4987	7.1390	6.8052	6.4951	6.2065	5.9377	5.6869	5.4527
12	11.2551	10.5753	9.9540	9.3851	8.8633	8.3838	7.9427	7.5361	7.1607	6.8137	6.4924	6.1944	5.9176	5.6603
13	12.1337	11.3484	10.6350	9.9856	9.3936	8.8527	8.3577	7.9038	7.4869	7.1034	6.7499	6.4235	6.1218	5.8424
14	13.0037	12.1062	11.2961	10.5631	9.8986	9.2950	8.7455	8.2442	7.7862	7.3667	6.9819	6.6282	6.3025	6.0021
15	13.8651	12.8493	11.9379	11.1184	10.3797	9.7122	9.1079	8.5595	8.0607	7.6061	7.1909	6.8109	6.4624	6.1422
16	14.7179	13.5777	12.5611	11.6523	10.8378	10.1059	9.4466	8.8514	8.3126	7.8237	7.3792	6.9740	6.6039	6.2651
17	15.5623	14.2919	13.1661	12.1657	11.2741	10.4773	9.7632	9.1216	8.5436	8.0216	7.5488	7.1196	6.7291	6.3729
18	16.3983	14.9920	13.7535	12.6593	11.6896	10.8276	10.0591	9.3719	8.7556	8.2014	7.7016	7.2497	6.8399	6.4674
19	17.2260	15.6785	14.3238	13.1339	12.0853	11.1581	10.3356	9.6036	8.9501	8.3649	7.8393	7.3658	6.9380	6.5504
20	18.0456	16.3514	14.8775	13.5903	12.4622	11.4699	10.5940	9.8181	9.1285	8.5136	7.9633	7.4694	7.0248	6.6231
25	22.0232	19.5235	17.4131	15.6221	14.0939	12.7834	11.6536	10.6748	9.8226	9.0770	8.4217	7.8431	7.3300	6.8729
30	25.8077	22.3965	19.6004	17.2920	15.3725	13.7648	12.4090	11.2578	10.2737	9.4269	8.6938	8.0552	7.4957	7.0027
40	32.8347	27.3555	23.1148	19.7928	17.1591	15.0463	13.3317	11.9246	10.7574	9.7791	8.9511	8.2438	7.6344	7.1050
50	39.1961	31.4236	25.7298	21.4822	18.2559	15.7619	13.8007	12.2335	10.9617	9.9148	9.0417	8.3045	7.6752	7.1327

Table 4 Continued:

	Interest Rate												
Year	*15%*	*16%*	*17%*	*18%*	*19%*	*20%*	*21%*	*22%*	*23%*	*24%*	*25%*	*30%*	*40%*
1	0.8696	0.8621	0.8547	0.8475	0.8403	0.8333	0.8264	0.8197	0.8130	0.8065	0.8000	0.7692	0.7143
2	1.6257	1.6052	1.5852	1.5656	1.5465	1.5278	1.5095	1.4915	1.4740	1.4568	1.4400	1.3609	1.2245
3	2.2832	2.2459	2.2096	2.1743	2.1399	2.1065	2.0739	2.0422	2.0114	1.9813	1.9520	1.8161	1.5889
4	2.8550	2.7982	2.7432	2.6901	2.6386	2.5887	2.5404	2.4936	2.4483	2.4043	2.3616	2.1662	1.8492
5	3.3522	3.2743	3.1993	3.1272	3.0576	2.9906	2.9260	2.8636	2.8035	2.7454	2.6893	2.4356	2.0352
6	3.7845	3.6847	3.5892	3.4976	3.4098	3.3255	3.2446	3.1669	3.0923	3.0205	2.9514	2.6427	2.1680
7	4.1604	4.0386	3.9224	3.8115	3.7057	3.6046	3.5079	3.4155	3.3270	3.2423	3.1611	2.8021	2.2628
8	4.4873	4.3436	4.2072	4.0776	3.9544	3.8372	3.7256	3.6193	3.5179	3.4212	3.3289	2.9247	2.3306
9	4.7716	4.6065	4.4506	4.3030	4.1633	4.0310	3.9054	3.7863	3.6731	3.5655	3.4631	3.0190	2.3790
10	5.0188	4.8332	4.6586	4.4941	4.3389	4.1925	4.0541	3.9232	3.7993	3.6819	3.5705	3.0915	2.4136
11	5.2337	5.0286	4.8364	4.6560	4.4865	4.3271	4.1769	4.0354	3.9018	3.7757	3.6564	3.1473	2.4383
12	5.4206	5.1971	4.9884	4.7932	4.6105	4.4392	4.2784	4.1274	3.9852	3.8514	3.7251	3.1903	2.4559
13	5.5831	5.3423	5.1183	4.9095	4.7147	4.5327	4.3624	4.2028	4.0530	3.9124	3.7801	3.2233	2.4685
14	5.7245	5.4675	5.2293	5.0081	4.8023	4.6106	4.4317	4.2646	4.1082	3.9616	3.8241	3.2487	2.4775
15	5.8474	5.5755	5.3242	5.0916	4.8759	4.6755	4.4890	4.3152	4.1530	4.0013	3.8593	3.2682	2.4839
16	5.9542	5.6685	5.4053	5.1624	4.9377	4.7296	4.5364	4.3567	4.1894	4.0333	3.8874	3.2832	2.4885
17	6.0472	5.7487	5.4746	5.2223	4.9897	4.7746	4.5755	4.3908	4.2190	4.0591	3.9099	3.2948	2.4918
18	6.1280	5.8178	5.5339	5.2732	5.0333	4.8122	4.6079	4.4187	4.2431	4.0799	3.9279	3.3037	2.4941
19	6.1982	5.8775	5.5845	5.3162	5.0700	4.8435	4.6346	4.4415	4.2627	4.0967	3.9424	3.3105	2.4958
20	6.2593	5.9288	5.6278	5.3527	5.1009	4.8696	4.6567	4.4603	4.2786	4.1103	3.9539	3.3158	2.4970
25	6.4641	6.0971	5.7662	5.4669	5.1951	4.9476	4.7213	4.5139	4.3232	4.1474	3.9849	3.3286	2.4994
30	6.5660	6.1772	5.8294	5.5168	5.2347	4.9789	4.7463	4.5338	4.3391	4.1601	3.9950	3.3321	2.4999
40	6.6418	6.2335	5.8713	5.5482	5.2582	4.9966	4.7596	4.5439	4.3467	4.1659	3.9995	3.3332	2.5000
50	6.6605	6.2463	5.8801	5.5541	5.2623	4.9995	4.7616	4.5452	4.3477	4.1666	3.9999	3.3333	2.5000

Subject Index